STUDIES OF THE AMERICAS

edited by

James Dunkerley

Institute for the Study of the Americas
University of London
School of Advanced Study

Titles in this series are multi-disciplinary studies of aspects of the societies of the hemisphere, particularly in the areas of politics, economics, history, anthropology, sociology and the environment. The series covers a comparative perspective across the Americas, including Canada and the Caribbean as well as the USA and Latin America.

Titles in this series published by Palgrave Macmillan:

Cuba's Military 1990-2005: Revolutionary Soldiers during Counter-Revolutionary Times
By Hal Klepak

The Judicialization of Politics in Latin America
Edited by Rachel Sieder, Line Schjolden, and Alan Angell

Latin America: A New Interpretation
By Laurence Whitehead

Appropriation as Practice: Art and Identity in Argentina
By Arnd Schneider

America and Enlightenment Constitutionalism
Edited by Gary L. McDowell and Johnathan O'Neill

Vargas and Brazil: New Perspectives
Edited by Jens R. Hentschke

When Was Latin America Modern?
Edited by Nicola Miller and Stephen Hart

Debating Cuban Exceptionalism
Edited by Bert Hoffmann and Laurence Whitehead

Caribbean Land and Development Revisited
Edited by Jean Besson and Janet Momsen

Cultures of the Lusophone Black Atlantic
Edited by Nancy Naro, Roger Sansi-Roca and David Treece

The Republican Party and Immigration Politics

From Proposition 187 to George W. Bush

Andrew Wroe

First published in 2008 by
PALGRAVE MACMILLAN™
175 Fifth Avenue, New York, N.Y. 10010 and
Houndmills, Basingstoke, Hampshire, England RG21 6XS
Companies and representatives throughout the world.

PALGRAVE MACMILLAN is the global academic imprint of the Palgrave Macmillan division of St. Martin's Press, LLC and of Palgrave Macmillan Ltd. Macmillan® is a registered trademark in the United States, United Kingdom and other countries. Palgrave is a registered trademark in the European Union and other countries.

ISBN-13: 978–0–230–60053–9
ISBN-10: 0–230–60053–0

Library of Congress Cataloging-in-Publication Data

Wroe, Andrew.

   The Republican party and immigration politics : from Proposition 187 to George W. Bush / Andrew Wroe.
      p. cm.—(Studies of the Americas series)
   Includes bibliographical references and index.
   ISBN 0–230–60053–0
      1. Illegal aliens—Government policy—United States. 2. United States—Emigration and immigration—Government policy. 3. Illegal aliens—Government policy—California. 4. California—Emigration and immigration—Government policy. 5. Republican Party (U.S. : 1854–) I. Title.

JV6483.W76 2008
325.73—dc22   2007034163

A catalogue record for this book is available from the British Library.

Design by Newgen Imaging Systems (P) Ltd., Chennai, India.

First edition: April 2008

10 9 8 7 6 5 4 3 2 1

Printed in the United States of America.

To My Family

Contents

List of Figures

List of Tables

Acknowledgments

Many friends, colleagues, and organizations have contributed to this book. Thanks are owed to the British Academy for its generous postdoctoral fellowship, which provided time to think and funds to travel, to the Department of Politics and International Relations at the University of Kent for a crucial sabbatical term, to members of the American Politics Group of the UK Political Studies Association who offered sharp criticism and support at its annual conferences, and to the staff, especially Sue Wedlake, at the U.S. Embassy in London who are so supportive of American Studies in the United Kingdom. The Embassy also provided research assistance and access to the U.S. Department of State's International Visitor Program. The editorial team at Palgrave, New York, helped pull the book together and their anonymous reviewer provided incisive comments and helpful suggestions. I would particularly like to thank the following individuals who have had a direct and positive influence on the manuscript: Edward Ashbee, George Conyne, Amanda Gosling, Jane Hindley, David Houghton, Anthony King, Desmond King, David McKay, Colin Sampson, Michael Smith, Maurice Vile, and the interviewees who gave their time generously. The faults are, of course, mine alone.

Chapter 1

Introduction

"America, at its best, is a welcoming society. We welcome not only immigrants themselves but the many gifts they bring and the values they live by." So said President George W. Bush at a naturalization ceremony for new citizens at Ellis Island in July 2001. The fifty million immigrants admitted legally to the United States in the twentieth century alone lends substantial credibility to Bush's words and to the old adage that "America is a nation of immigrants." Indeed, immigrants seeking their freedom and fortune and fulfilling the American dream have become part of the nation's mythology. No symbol of this is more potent than the Statue of Liberty and no words more poignant than those of Emmas Lazarus inscribed upon it:

> Give me your tired, your poor.
> Your huddled masses yearning to breathe free
> The wretched refuse of your teaming shore.
> Send these, the homeless, tempest-tost to me,
> I lift my lamp beside the golden door!

And yet the history of immigration to the United States is far from unambiguously positive, as Bush's "at its best" caveat recognizes. His qualification implies that Americans have ambivalent attitudes towards immigrants and immigration and that the broadly positive welcome afforded immigrants has been punctuated by a series of anti-immigrant episodes throughout American history. Many potential immigrants have been refused entry and many new immigrants persecuted because of their skin color or religion. Others have been excluded because the resident population decided they burdened schools, hospitals, and welfare rolls, because they took the jobs of native-born workers, and because they avoided taxes. What's more, each new wave of immigrants is regarded as less morally upstanding, hardworking, or assimilable than previous ones. In the mid 1990s, for example, the public debate revolved around how best to remove aliens illegally resident in the United States and how to prevent the entry of any more. The talk was of prison, of deportations, of digging trenches along the U.S.-Mexico border, of calling in the National Guard to stop the "alien influx," of barring undocumented children from public schools, of repealing the birthright citizenship provision of the Fourteenth Amendment, of withholding medical care and welfare help, and of Americans informing on "suspected" illegal immigrants.

Illegal immigration is a main theme of this book, but the story also involves legal immigration. Most Americans draw a distinction between legal and illegal immigration—the former is central to the United States' mythology while the latter is regarded much more negatively[1]—but hostility toward all forms of migration grew in the 1990s. Some prominent Republican Party politicians utilized the antipathy to argue for a reduction in the level of legal immigration and for deep cuts in legal immigrants' public benefits. A central aim is to explain why many Americans, both citizens and elites, turned against immigration in the 1990s. It is, in other words, to uncover how the United States turned from a nation that wanted foreign nations to "give me your tired, your poor" to one that told them to "take back your tired, your poor."

In the first decade of the twenty-first century, however, the terms of debate changed. While many ordinary Americans remained hostile to large-scale illegal immigration, elites in both political parties introduced legislation to legalize the status of millions of previously undocumented residents. President Bush was at the forefront of the campaign, yet in the previous decade his GOP colleagues led the anti-immigration agenda. The book aims to describe and account for the changes in the Republican Party's immigration discourse.

After decades of studying the phenomenon, social scientists and historians actually know quite a lot about why Americans periodically revolt against immigrants and immigration. There is, for example, an especially rich seam of scholarship on the anti-immigrant impulse of the first decades of the twentieth century when the United States shut it doors to Asians and to eastern and southern Europeans, while leaving the door ajar for (white, protestant) immigrants from northwestern Europe. The usual explanations for this restrictionist episode include the large increase in immigrants arriving on America's shores in the last two decades of the nineteenth century and first three of the twentieth; a cultural crisis about American identity and "foreignness," engendered in part by World War I; and a downturn in the economy in the early 1920s. In addition to the "usual suspects" of numbers, identity/racism, and the economy, more subtle analyses have shown how eugenicists' racist "science" dovetailed neatly with public and elite opinion about immigrants to produce an unstoppable momentum in favor of restricting immigration.[2]

Social scientists and historians also know quite a lot about the form and causes of the anti-immigrant episode in the 1990s. We know that while its form was different to that of the 1920s—the focus this time was largely on illegal immigration from Mexico, rather than legal immigration from southern and eastern Europe— it shared many of the same causes. We know that it was preceded by a large increase in the number of illegal and legal immigrants, by an economic downturn, and by debates about American culture and identity—especially in California where some in the white majority thought their economic and social hegemony was threatened by the fast-growing Latino population.[3] Not unreasonably, most attempts to explain the restrictionism of the 1990s have focused on the recession, racism, and numbers. And they are quite right to do so. Each was crucial to the growth of anti-immigrant sentiment. Without each, it is unlikely that the United States would have witnessed anything more than a latent, ill-defined ill feeling toward illegal immigrants.

However, these factors cannot account for either the timing or the intensity of the anti-immigrant impulse. The usual suspects are, in other words, necessary but insufficient explanations. They helped engender an environment that was conducive to increasingly negative attitudes toward immigrants, but they were not the factors that forced illegal immigration to the forefront of Americans' minds and to the top of the political agenda. That distinction belongs to a conflation and conjuncture of events, people, and processes that occurred in California in the early 1990s.

There, feelings of resentment toward illegal immigrants had been stirred initially by an especially deep and long recession. Sensing the public's growing unease and hoping to profit from it politically, some politicians, notably California's Republican governor Pete Wilson, began to speak out against illegal immigration, arguing that undocumented persons took jobs, burdened schools and hospitals, and avoided taxes. These arguments played on people's fears and further increased the saliency of illegal immigration. Seizing the political opportunity offered by this early politicization of the issue, a group of grassroots anti-immigrant activists came together to write and qualify for the November 1994 ballot a direct democracy initiative that became known as Proposition 187. Prop. 187, which denied public services to undocumented residents of California and required persons to report "suspected" illegal immigrants to the authorities, became the vehicle for Governor Wilson's reelection drive.[4] His focus on illegal immigration and support for Prop. 187 raised the initiative's profile, and it in turn further increased the salience of the illegal-immigration issue and Wilson's campaign against it. As we shall see, these symbiotic relationships helped propel Prop. 187 to victory, Wilson back to the governor's mansion, and illegal immigration onto the national agenda.

Simply stated, without Wilson and without the direct democracy process, the illegal-immigration issue would not have become as salient and explosive as it did. Yet scholars have until now treated Wilson's reelection strategy and the success of Prop. 187 as manifestations of the anti-immigrant backlash. I show that they are both cause and effect. As is so often the case in our history, it is the timely convergence of people, events, and ideas that brings change.

* * *

Proposition 187 is in many ways the most important direct democracy proposal of the last 25 years. The following chapters detail its conception, birth, life, and death. They show how it was a driving force behind the 1990s anti-immigrant impulse, how it helped engender changes to immigration law at the national level, and how, ironically, it helped inspire a new political activism among Latinos and encouraged some in the Republican Party to moderate their anti-immigrant, anti-minority rhetoric.[5] While several books provide aggregate-level analyses of direct democracy procedures,[6] few initiative-specific monographs have been published.[7] Given the relative absence of research, we actually know very little about the genesis of direct democracy proposals, the battle to qualify them for the ballot, their agenda-setting function, and the campaigns for and against the measures. The absence of scholarly work is especially surprising given the increasing importance of the initiative process as a tool to effect major and, some would say, invidious, even insidious, changes in public policy. There is plenty of circumstantial evidence to suggest that direct democracy proposals, especially those originating in California, ignite further significant reforms across the United States, but more systematic research is required.[8]

The direct democracy process was introduced in some U.S. states at the start of the twentieth century to allow citizens to bypass a political system dominated by entrenched interests and corrupt politicians, yet many modern observers suggest that today's initiative process is being manipulated by political elites for their own gain. If politicians are seen to be manipulating a process designed specifically to bypass them, this must raise questions about the functioning of democracy generally and direct democracy specifically. In the case at hand here, there was much controversy over the role of California's then governor, Pete Wilson, in the genesis of Prop. 187. While Wilson's and 187's critics have long-claimed that he was instrumental in its inception and qualification, the governor's advisers deny such close links. The following pages test these claims and counterclaims.

Another major dispute regards the extent to which racist attitudes contributed to the anti-immigrant impulse of the 1990s and, later, the rejection of liberal immigration reform during Bush's presidency. There are of course many legitimate reasons why people may want to restrict the numbers entering the United States. They may believe that large-scale immigration places unacceptable stresses on the receiving country's environment, resources, and structures; that immigration robs the often poor sending country of key workers (which it has spent scarce resources educating); that immigrants threaten the job security and wages of the receiving country's most vulnerable native workers; that immigrants receive more in public benefits than they pay in taxes; that they have a generally negative effect on the national economy; or, in the case of undocumented immigrants, that they broke the law by entering the country illegally. Nonetheless, while most immigration experts make no distinctions on racial, ethnic or nationality grounds between immigrants,[9] for many living in the south west of the United States the issue of illegal immigration is intimately linked with a specific nationality—Mexicans. To many, illegal immigrant means illegal Mexican, and the public "war" against illegal immigration takes place at the U.S.-Mexico border. It is easy to see why many commentators, politicians, and people of Mexican origin regarded the anti-immigrant impulse generally, and Prop. 187 specifically, as a racist attack on illegal Mexican immigrants[10]—even though Prop. 187's proponents denied it was aimed at a specific race or nationality. Indeed, readers of the initiative text (see appendix B) will find no mention of race or nationality, only the legality of people's residence in the United States. However, an ostensibly race-neutral law can be racist in its effects. The anti-alien land laws and English-only statutes introduced in the nineteenth and twentieth centuries in some states, including California, by initiative proposition were race-neutral, yet their effects were felt predominantly by particular minorities. Johnson has argued that English-only laws

> in the South West . . . are voted upon primarily with Spanish as the "competing" language in mind. Designation of English as the official language, though facially neutral, has a meaningful impact on the Latino community. In important ways, initiatives dealing with noncitizens are similar—though facially neutral, they may disparately affect immigrants from certain countries.[11]

A race-neutral law can win the support of a population for racist reasons. But it is always difficult to isolate the extent to which support for a policy is founded on racism. Johnson's analysis of the difficulties in demonstrating racial motivation in a court of law applies equally to social science research. His remarks are worth quoting at some length:

> One of the most vociferous, and serious, contentions made by Proposition 187 opponents in the heated campaign was that, at bottom, it is racist. This often is a damning claim in our legal culture. For a variety of reasons, however, including the difficulties of proving claims of discrimination under existing constitutional doctrine, the many lawsuits challenging Proposition 187 do not squarely raise the issue. Part of the reason is that it is difficult to separate the permissible from the impermissible motives for supporting Proposition 187. On the one hand, an anti-undocumented, or even anti-immigrant law is not necessarily suspect. On the other hand, anti-people-of-color or anti-Mexican laws generally are. Some Proposition 187 supporters were motivated by impermissible factors while others were not. Some were motivated by a mix of the two. In light of the difficulties in ascertaining the motives of the electorate, a court of law in all likelihood will never address the issue that immediately jumps into the minds of many who condemn the initiative . . . Only in the court of history will it be decided whether Proposition 187—like the alien land laws of yesteryear—was passed for invidious reasons and thus whether it is properly classified as racist and discriminatory.[12]

Some commentators argue that polling data support the contention that Americans are less racist than they were just fifty years ago. For instance, in 1942 only 30 percent of white respondents in a national sample thought white and black children should attend the same school. By 1976 84 percent thought they should.[13] However, some scholars argue that racism has not disappeared but merely changed its form. They point out that opinion poll data are of little use in measuring racial and racist attitudes because Americans will not express their beliefs honestly and openly on this issue, especially when asked directly. They will not do so because it is no longer acceptable to be openly racist, and therefore Americans' racism is not reflected in responses to opinion polls. Racism instead manifests itself in symbolic ways—for example, in fear of crime, in opposition to school busing and immigration, and in support for traditional American values such as liberalism, democracy, and veneration of the Stars and Stripes.[14] Moreover, symbolic attitudes reflected in subjective conceptions of national identity—what it means to be American—have been shown to be correlated with individuals' reactions to immigration and immigrants and policy preferences on ethnic/race questions.[15]

In this thinking, the 1990s anti-immigrant impulse was little more than a racist outburst against Mexican immigrants, whose racial identity facilitated their scapegoating and exclusion.[16] In a similar vein but different era, Guerin-Gonzales argued that it was Mexicans' racial identity that led to their expulsion from the southwest United States during the depression of the late 1920s and early 1930s.[17] And other scholars have shown that constructions of identity—and specifically whether an individual or group qualifies for citizenship—can determine acceptance in or exclusion from the political and social system.[18] All these works suggest that the significance of the construction of illegal immigrant as illegal Mexican in California.

However, other scholars criticize the above interpretation for conflating racism with legitimate group conflict.[19] They argue that conflicts between groups politicize certain issues, which in turn personalizes the issues for each group member—even if no real threat exists for the individual. Using this logic, interethnic group conflict should not necessarily be regarded as racism. Another part of this argument is that whites accept racial integration—and, by implication, immigration—in practice, so long as it does not threaten their majority status. This also seems to have some base in California history. The concentration of the Chinese population in San Francisco produced an ugly racism there in the late nineteenth century but not in other parts of the state where they were in a clear minority.[20] Moreover, it has been shown that economic competition between ethnic groups and the white majority produces conflict and racism; and that this conflict occurs most in cities with large populations of ethnic minorities because their salience makes them a visible threat to the white majority.[21] Given that the "threat" that whites would become a minority in California by the early twenty-first century was widely publicized and discussed during the 1994 election campaign, white Californians may have expressed anti-immigrant sentiments because of a threat to their majority status. Recent research suggests:

> A new populism has arisen in California politics, [which is] a product of white/Anglo concerns over the increased size and political influence of blacks and Latinos in the state. This new populism represents a voter backlash against the gains of minority groups in the 1970s to inhibit their access and influence in government. A clear manifestation of this new populism is the use of ballot initiatives to circumvent representative institutions, especially the state legislature, where blacks and Latinos have gained influence.[22]

I suggest that the backlash against illegal and, later, legal immigrants in the 1990s was driven in part, but not in the main, by racism. While many unpleasant things were said about immigrants, especially undocumented ones, many Californians were frustrated by the federal government's perceived inability to address the illegal-immigration issue. During the campaign there was much talk of "sending a message to the federal government" to do something, anything, about the illegal-immigration "problem." Moreover, at one point in the campaign, Prop. 187—supposedly the exemplar of unpleasant nativism—enjoyed the support of majorities of Latinos and Asians, as well as liberals and Democrats. Given that most undocumented immigrants are Latino and Asian, it would seem odd to label American Asian and Latino hostility as racism.[23] It is more likely that whites' hostility was at least in part driven by racism, but does this justify the racist tag when many other people's opposition to immigration was driven by other concerns? Of course, "the court of history" will ultimately determine the extent to which the 1990s anti-immigrant impulse was racist. The story of that impulse, as told here, will help inform that judgment.

The Chapters to Come

The next chapter begins by placing the contemporary immigration debate in its historical context. It draws parallels and pinpoints differences between the recent reaction against immigrants, especially the undocumented, and the many inter-mittent reactions in America's past. This review demonstrates how the racially based exclusionist immigration laws introduced from the 1850s to the 1940s were finally repealed by the passage of the 1965 Immigration Act. It then shows how the post-1960s liberal inclusionist discourse that dominated political thought and speech was challenged by the anti-immigrant impulse of the mid 1990s. Finally, it details the impulse's effects in terms of the changes to laws, programs, and the political and public discourse.

Polls show that many Americans for many years regarded illegal-immigration as an issue of concern, but that they rarely regarded it as a top priority. However, this changed in the early-to-mid 1990s, first in California and then across the United States. Chapter 3 explains why the issue was "politicized" for an elec-torally critical number of citizens in mid-to-late 1993. The number of undocu-mented persons, the recession, racism, and the role of politicians are all examined to see whether some or all of these can account for the early politicization of the illegal-immigration issue. As noted above, the analysis highlights the key role played by California governor, Pete Wilson.

The role of anti-immigrant grassroots activists is highlighted in chapter 4. It shows how a group of California-based activists, seizing the opportunity offered by Wilson's politicization of the illegal-immigration issue, came together to write Prop. 187 and qualify it successfully for the ballot. It then demonstrates how Prop. 187, offering a concrete policy "solution" to the illegal-immigrant "prob-lem," further fuelled anti-immigrant feelings and enhanced the issue's salience. It is argued that Prop. 187 may not have been written and probably would not have qualified for the ballot without Governor Wilson, because the initiative's propo-nents had very few financial resources that they could draw on for the signature-gathering phase. They had to rely on the energy of thousands of grassroots signature gatherers, and the issue's politicization energized or mobilized these individuals and made Californians amenable to signing the petition forms. In other words, Wilson's politicization of illegal immigration permitted and facili-tated the qualification of Prop. 187. However, Wilson could not alone ensure Prop. 187's qualification. Without the efforts of, first, a small group of Orange County-based anti-immigrant activists who came together to write the direct democracy proposition and, second, the thousands of grassroots signature gatherers, the initiative would never have made it onto the ballot and thus never have further increased the saliency of the illegal-immigration issue. In sum, its increased salience was a product of the symbiotic relationship between Governor Wilson and the architects and proponents of Prop. 187. With each helping the other, Prop. 187 qualified for the ballot and the real campaign could begin.

Chapter 5 tells the story of one of the most emotive, vituperative, divisive, and exciting initiative campaigns in California's history. It demonstrates how the involvement in the campaign of political big hitters such as Bill Clinton, Dianne Feinstein, William Bennett, Jack Kemp, and Pete Wilson raised the stakes even further. The referendum was no longer about the specific provisions of Prop. 187, but rather about the future role and place of illegal immigrants in California and the wider United States. It had become a "message" initiative. The chapter describes and analyses the strategy of the various actors in the Yes and No campaigns, and assesses the importance of the campaigns. It thus provides crucial insights into why California voters gave the initiative their support despite some impressive advantages enjoyed by the No campaign, which was run by professionals from the initiative "industry," and was well funded and widely supported by many respected interest groups and politicians. Many of the No campaign's problems stemmed from the broad nature of its coalition, which complicated strategic and tactical decisions and made it difficult to win over the white middle-class vote. For example, while the No campaign began to reduce Prop. 187's support in the last month of the campaign, it was ironically some No on 187 grassroots activists who halted the hemorrhaging in support for the initiative in the final weeks. Whatever the actual dynamics, there is little question that by the end of the campaign illegal immigration had become front-page news.

On November 8, 1994 Prop. 187 received the endorsement of the California electorate, winning by nearly 18 percentage points. However, it was immediately enjoined in several state and federal courts. Over the course of the next few years, this controversial direct democracy initiative would die a slow judicial and bureaucratic death. The sixth chapter details its demise. However, while Prop. 187 was interred in the courts, its electoral victory inspired significant changes to the nation's immigration laws. The new Republican majority in the U.S. Congress, marshaled by the charismatic and ambitious Newt Gingrich, passed the Personal Responsibility and Work Opportunity Reconciliation Act in August 1996 and the Illegal Immigration Reform and Immigrant Responsibility Act in September 1996. The first, better known as the Welfare Reform Act, slashed legal immigrants' welfare and healthcare benefits. The second sought to address the illegal-immigration "problem" by strengthening America's borders, by streamlining deportation procedures, by curtailing undocumented persons' already minimal access to public benefits, and by making it harder for them to find work. These fundamental changes to America's immigration laws are detailed in chapter 7.

The eighth chapter tells the story of the 1996 presidential election. Governor George W. Bush's success in winning reelection in Texas in 1994, in part a product of his popularity with Latino voters, offered his party a different model of electoral success than that promulgated by Pete Wilson in California. However, most GOP presidential primary candidates ran on right-wing platforms that sought to appeal to conservative voters on social and cultural issues. Even candidates previously regarded as centrist, such as Bob Dole, took hard-line positions on immigration and affirmative action. Dole eventually won the nomination after overcoming the populist paleoconservative, Pat "Pitchfork" Buchanan, but was easily defeated by the incumbent, President Bill Clinton.

While it was not exactly a secret that demographers had been predicting a large increase in the Latino population in the twenty-first century, few in the Republican Party took much note. Or if they did, they figured that the short-run advantages of playing the immigration card and antagonizing Latino voters outweighed the longer-term benefits of courting tomorrow's voters. Key Republican strategists began to take the demographic time bomb more seriously when they also realized that their party's anti-immigrant associations had driven minority voters further toward the Democratic Party. The last part of chapter 8 examines the demographics of immigration politics, concluding that the growth in the number of Latino voters is due in part to a reaction against the anti-immigrant climate.

The GOP changed tack after Bob Dole's lackluster presidential campaign and embarrassing defeat to Bill Clinton in November 1996. Congressional Republicans, with Democratic support, restored many of the public benefits only just denied to legal immigrants, and politicians from both parties competed with each other to be the most Latino- and immigrant-friendly. There was even talk of another amnesty for undocumented persons and a new guest-worker program—just months after Congress had nearly excluded undocumented kids from public schools. Governor Pete Wilson found himself demonized by Latinos and ignored by fellow Republicans who only a little while earlier had feted him as a prospective presidential candidate. Instead, George W. Bush emerged as the choice of the party's elite in 2000. As a (far from fluent) Spanish-speaking, pro-immigration, Latino-friendly Republican, they hoped he would help rebuild the party's damaged image among the new century's key emerging demographic group. Chapter 9 explores the changing politics of immigration reform during the Bush presidency.

Bush pushed hard for liberal immigration reform throughout his presidency. His pro-Latino strategy has not, however, been adopted by everyone in the Republican Party. Responding to widespread public concern about border security and the large number of illegal immigrants resident in the United States, many Republicans in the House of Representatives, led by Rep. Tom Tancredo of Colorado, continue to lobby vigorously for further legislation to solve the illegal-immigration "problem." In December 2005 the House passed a bill that would, in addition to tightening border security with an extra 700 miles of security fencing along the U.S.-Mexico border and increased penalties for smugglers, change the status of illegal presence in the United States from a civil to a criminal offense and require all employers to check with the Department of Homeland Security and the Social Security Administration that workers were not in the country illegally. And in mid 2007 President Bush saw his cherished immigration reform agenda, which included putting over ten million illegal-immigrants on the path to legal residency and citizenship, stall in the Senate, as moderate Republicans bolted from liberal solutions under intense pressure from conservative radio talk-show hosts and grassroots activists.

It would be wrong, however, to suggest that the Republican Party has forgotten the lessons it learned at the end of the previous decade. No senior Republican politician is proposing to expel undocumented children from public school, as Bob Dole did in the 1996 presidential campaign. Very few of even the most radical House Republicans are proposing to reduce the level of legal immigration or cut legal immigrants' benefits—both of which were key proposals in the mid 1990s. Moreover, the Senate version of the immigration bill, although stalled, with its guest-worker program and amnesty, is a remarkably liberal response to the immigration problem and very different from the conservative, restrictionist legislation passed a decade earlier. While Republican presidential hopefuls of course need to appeal to the party's more radical, conservative primary electorate, most now also recognize the need to appeal to Latinos in the national electorate with temporary-worker and amnesty programs. Senate Majority Leader Bill Frist's short-lived presidential ambitions received a blow when he misstepped badly by including a provision in his immigration bill that would have made undocumented residence in the United States a criminal rather than a civil offense. He backtracked quickly, as did House Republicans, proposing an amendment to make illegal residency a misdemeanor rather than a felony, although it would remain a criminal offense. The pro-immigration forces have also learned lessons from the battles of the 1990s. When around 100,000 people marched against Proposition 187 in Los Angeles in 1994, most protestors carried Mexican flags. Amid the thousands of flags in the photograph in the next day's Los Angeles Times, only one American flag could be seen, causing much consternation among the newspaper's readers. Twelve years later an estimated 500,000 protestors on the streets of Los Angeles and hundreds of thousands more in other U.S. cities marched against the House proposals in an impressive show of strength. This time most protesters carried American flags.

The events of the mid 1990s helped mobilize Latinos and other immigrants against perceived, albeit lesser, threats in the next decade. This mobilization, together with a significant growth in population, has helped establish Latinos as a key force in American politics and encouraged some in the GOP to champion their cause. Faced with a new political map, Republicans with national ambitions probably would have had to remodel their electoral strategy even without their party's close association with the anti-immigrant movement of the mid 1990s. However, the rejection of the GOP by Latino voters ensured that many Republicans' own rejection of anti-immigration and, by association, anti-Latino policies came earlier than it would otherwise have done. Ironically, then, the contemporary anti-immigrant episode has helped establish Latinos as a key force in American politics and encouraged more in the GOP to champion their cause.

Chapter 2

Learning from History

In antebellum America restrictions on immigration were virtually nonexistent, and immigrants already resident in the United States generally faced few constraints on their freedom or movement[1]—at least for those that came voluntarily. For slaves the context was of course horrifically different. This is not to say that there were no tensions among the early white settlers and between them and later newcomers. Many early Puritan settlers in New England were deeply suspicious of the non-Puritans. There were tensions between different religious groups. Puritans, Quakers, and Lutherans distrusted each other and all expressed anti-Semitic and anti-Catholic views. Although religion was the most significant factor in opposing new settlement, some among the native-born feared that the new immigrants would increase labor-market competition and thus drive down wages, and others expressed concern about the newcomers' supposed moral degeneracy. Still others, notably those descended from English stock, worried about the difficulties of assimilating those of a different nationality, especially non-English speakers. Of particular concern in the eighteenth century were German settlers. Their tongue and customs were alien, and tensions heightened further when they established their own schools.

In spite of the concerns of many people, however, immigrants were broadly welcomed first by the colonies and later by the federal government. The number of newcomers was absolutely and relatively small (as a percentage of the native population), and the need for labor and availability of land, especially in the west, neutralized what popular opposition to immigration existed. America's doors remained wide open.[2] Indeed, one of Thomas Jefferson's grievances in his Declaration of Independence was that George III of England had "endeavored to prevent the population of these States."[3] In a similar vein, predating but echoing Emma Lazarus's words on the Statue of Liberty, George Washington wrote, "let the poor, the needy and the oppressed of the Earth, and those who want Land, resort to the fertile plains of our west country, the Second Land of Promise, and there dwell in peace, fulfilling the first and greatest commandment."[4]

After the American revolution, early congresses made some minor efforts, in the form of the Alien and Sedition Acts of 1798, to curb the entry of political refugees fleeing the French and other revolutions in late eighteenth-century Europe.[5] They worried the refugees would bring revolutionary ideals that could threaten America's nascent democracy. Some Federalists were also concerned that the refugees would be natural supporters of their political opponents, the Democratic Republicans. Eligibility for citizenship was tightened but remained relatively easy to acquire—certainly by contemporary standards—and the federal government in the main demonstrated little interest in the number and type of immigrant arriving. Such was its lack of interest that it did not bother to count them before 1820, and even after 1820 the count remained inefficient and incomplete.[6]

Interest in immigration matters, however, increased from the mid nineteenth century onwards. For the first time the federal government intervened significantly in immigration policy and border patrol, introducing many restrictive and racist laws. By the end of the 1920s, Asian immigration had virtually ceased and eastern and southern European immigration severely curtailed. In contrast, the 1960s through 1990 saw the repeal of many restrictionist and racist immigration laws and their replacement with liberal, nonracial ones.

The First Backlash

In the middle of the nineteenth century the United States experienced a precipitous increase in immigration, as table 2.1 details. One hundred and fifty thousand arrived in the 1820s, increasing to 600,000 in the 1830s, 1.7 million in the 1840s, and 2.6 million in the 1850s. To put these figures in context, demographers often use the immigration rate, which calculates the number of new arrivals as a percentage of the resident population. The immigration rate was 1.1 percent, 3.9 percent, 8.4 percent, and 9.3 percent in each decade, respectively. Not only did the number and rate increase, but the composition changed too. In earlier decades immigrants from the United Kingdom made up the majority of new entrants, but from the 1820s the proportion of Irish and Germans increased

Table 2.1   Legal Immigration to the United States, 1820–2000

Year	Number	Rate (%)	Year	Number	Rate (%)
1801–1810	—	—	1901–1910	8,795,386	10.4
1811–1820	—	—	1911–1920	5,735,811	5.7
1821–1830	143,439	1.1	1921–1930	4,107,209	3.5
1831–1840	599,125	3.9	1931–1940	528,431	0.4
1841–1850	1,713,251	8.4	1941–1950	1,035,039	0.7
1851–1860	2,598,214	9.3	1951–1960	2,515,479	1.5
1861–1870	2,314,824	6.4	1961–1970	3,321,677	1.7
1871–1880	2,812,191	6.2	1971–1980	4,399,172	2.0
1881–1890	5,246,613	9.2	1981–1990	7,255,956	3.0
1891–1900	3,687,564	5.3	1991–2000	9,080,528	3.4

Notes. — indicates data not available (federal government made no systematic attempt to count the number of arrivals before 1820); rate is sum of annual immigration totals divided by sum of annual U.S. populations for same years.

Sources: U.S. Census Bureau, *The Statistical Abstract, 2006*; and Office of Immigration Statistics, *2005 Yearbook of Immigration Statistics.*

considerably, until they constituted over 70 percent of all newcomers in the 1850s.[7] We saw above how some native-born Americans reacted negatively to the arrival of a limited number of Germans in the eighteenth century. While the same causes—language, religion, and the economy—help explain the negative reaction in the nineteenth century, the big difference is in the number arriving. Tensions increased commensurate with the numerical increase. The spotlight also began to focus on the Irish. Suspicions were aroused by their poverty, the threat they posed to domestic wage levels, their Catholicism, and their supposed lack of decency and moral fiber. Despite the grassroots opposition to immigration—the Know-Nothings, for example, lobbied to increase the length of time before new arrivals could take up U.S. citizenship—the strong demand for labor outweighed the pressures for its restriction as the authorities and business continued, in the main, to welcome newcomers. Furthermore, the Civil War pushed the issue of immigration onto the backburner and reduced the United States' attractiveness as an immigrant destination.

In the Civil War decade, 2.3 million immigrants arrived in the United States, a rate of 6.4 percent compared with 9.3 in the previous decade. The number and rate remained steady through the 1870s, but increased again in the 1880s when over five million arrived, equaling the high rate in the 1850s. The composition of new immigrants also began to change around the same time. By the 1890s the United Kingdom, Germany, and Ireland were no longer the top sending nations. Immigrants from northern and western Europe were replaced by others from eastern and southern Europe. Italians, Russians, Poles, and Hungarians now dominated. In addition to practicing a different religion—most were Catholics and Jews, not Protestants—they also looked different to most Americans who were descended from Anglo-Saxon stock. Moreover, the assassination of President William McKinley in 1901 by anarchist radical Leon Czolgosz—native-born to immigrant parents—increased fears about the robustness of American democracy to agitation by foreign forces. These racial and religious differences, together with concerns about alien radicals, lay at the heart of the restrictionist movement that would eventually succeed in reducing dramatically the immigration of these peoples.

It was not only immigrants from southern and eastern Europe who were attracting suspicion, however. On the west coast, the young state of California, which entered the union in 1850, was pressing the U.S. Congress to act against Asian immigrants, and the Chinese in particular. Daniels estimates that about 300,000 Chinese arrived in the United States between 1848 and 1882. Most went to California to work in the gold mines and on the new railroads, but their "foreign habits," strange looks, and language combined with an economic depression to arouse great hostility, especially among workers and their trade unions. In essence, the hostility was classic racism borne of fear, ignorance, and competition. The Workingmen's Party, for example, "declare[d] that the Chinamen must leave our shores. We declare that white men, and women, and boys, and girls, cannot live as the people of a great republic should and compete with the single Chinese coolies in the labor market."[8] Partly in response to pressure from California, Congress passed its first meaningful restrictions on immigration in 1870. While the Fourteenth Amendment of 1868 guaranteed citizenship to all persons born in the United States, the 1870 Naturalization Act prohibited Asians being naturalized and thus excluded foreign-born Asians from citizenship.[9] Despite this restriction, many Californians feared the perceived growing economic power of the immigrant Chinese population. Specifically, they worried that Chinese contract, or "coolie," laborers were being imported into California to enrich U.S.-resident Chinese businessmen. An 1875 law made it an offense to supply Asian contract labor and for "Oriental" persons to be imported into the United States without their consent.[10] In addition to its anti-Asian provisions, the law gave immigration officials the power to exclude "undesirables" such as prostitutes, criminals, and those with communicable diseases. In these provisions, the law reflected growing concern about the type and character of immigrants arriving from Europe and Asia. However, the law proved largely ineffectual, especially in reducing European immigration.

As concern continued to grow, the anti-Chinese restrictions were tightened with the passage of the temporary 1882 Chinese Exclusion Act. The act prevented all Chinese laborers, but not merchants, emigrating to the United States for the next ten years. In 1887 more temporary legislation restricted land ownership to citizens and those who intended to become citizens. Because the Chinese were already excluded from citizenship, the effect of this law was to exclude them from land ownership too. These exclusion acts were made permanent federal law in 1902. Chinese persons were not the only targets. While few in number, Japanese immigrants also worried the native-born, but America's political elites were wary of antagonizing the militarily powerful Japan. Its leaders would have interpreted a Japanese Exclusion Act as disrespectful; Roosevelt even worried that it, and anti-Japanese violence and sentiments generally, could "plunge us into war."[11] Roosevelt instead reached a compromise in 1907, known as the Gentlemen's Agreement, in which the Japanese government would itself refuse passports to laborers seeking to emigrate to the United States. In turn, the agreement allowed the families of laborers then resident in the United States to join them and also allowed laborers who had previously visited the United States to enter again. The anti-Asian trend established since 1870 culminated in the passage of the Immigration Act in 1917. The act created a "barred zone" to exclude natives from the Asia-Pacific triangle, and curtailed the entry of most Asians to the United States.

While much of the focus was on Asian immigration, the public and the lawmakers had not forgotten about "undesirables" arriving from Europe. Epileptics, beggars, anarchists, together with the insane, the criminal, and the indigent were excluded in a series of acts passed in 1891, 1903, and 1907. Furthermore, an 1875 Supreme Court ruling and the 1891 act gave the federal government responsibility for assessing the desirability of new arrivals. The combined effect of these new laws was minimal, however. The 3.7 million new arrivals in the 1890s were dwarfed by the nearly nine million who came between 1901 and 1910—doubling the rate from 5.3 to 10.4 percent. Fortunately for proponents of restriction in the early twentieth century, a movement was building that would soon help alter dramatically the scale and composition of immigration to the United States for the next forty years. Today the movement would simply be labeled racist. Then, however, it had the veneer of scientific respectability and was called eugenics. Eugenicists believed that some human beings were genetically superior/inferior to others. They sought to determine scientifically the poor quality human "stock" and to eradicate it through selective breeding. Such goals were rarely questioned in the pre-Holocaust age. The desirability of selecting the fittest and best that the human race had to offer—determined by analyzing family histories—was commonsensical to many, including some of the best brains of the age.[12]

University of Wisconsin sociology professor Edward A. Ross, for example, claimed that "the Mediterranean peoples are morally below the races of northern Europe is as certain as any social fact," and that "It is unthinkable that so many persons with crooked faces, coarse mouths, bad noses, heavy jaws, and low fore-heads can mingle their heredity with ours without making personal beauty yet more rare among us that it actually is. So much ugliness is bound to work to the surface."[13] The Immigration Restriction League, the preeminent anti-immigrant pressure group founded in the late nineteenth century by Harvard academics, stated in 1910 that "A considerable proportion of immigrants now coming are from races and countries, or parts of countries, which have not progressed, but have been backward, downtrodden, and relatively useless for centuries. If these immigrants 'have not had opportunities,' it is because their races have not made the opportunities; for they have had all the time that any other races have had."[14] And Professor Carl C. Brigham, a leading thinker, stated conclusively: "The intellectual superiority of our Nordic group over the Alpine, Mediterranean and negro groups has been demonstrated."[15]

While the discipline of eugenics was not the child of the restrictionist move-ment and while restrictionism would have existed irrespective of eugenics, the eugenicists' pseudo-science and the restrictionists' hostility to the new immigra-tion "proved a felicitous match."[16] The match began with the eugenicists' submissions to the Immigration Commission between 1907 and 1910. Better known as the Dillingham Commission after its chairman, Senator William Dillingham, it finally published its multivolume report in 1910. The report dis-tinguished between the "old" immigrants of northern and western Europe and the "new" immigrants of southern and eastern Europe. The scientific evidence, the report concluded, showed that new immigrants were poorer than previous generations and that children of immigrants were more likely to commit crime than native children.[17] The evidence also purportedly showed that old immi-grants were of a high quality and "quickly assimilated" to established American cultural norms. The new immigrants, in contrast, were classed as more illiterate, less intelligent, and less assimilable. In addition, the commission found that "insanity is relatively more prevalent among the foreign-born than among the native-born, and relatively more prevalent among certain immigrant races or nationalities than among others."[18] The commission in response proposed a number of far-reaching recommendations. As desired by the eugenicists, it suggested that immigration officers should be stationed in sending countries to check potential migrants' mental health and criminal tendencies. Those found wanting would be refused passage. It also proposed the deportation of public charges, the exclusion of single unskilled males, a racial quota limit, a cap on the number admitted at each port of entry, an increase in the tax on each new immi-grant, and a literacy test.[19] While the literacy test was ostensibly race neutral—newcomers were not required to be able to read English but any recognized language—its effect would be to limit the immigration of undesirable stock from southern and eastern Europe where literacy was rare. Initial attempts to get the commission's recommendations onto the statutes failed, as Presidents Cleveland, Taft, and Wilson wielded their veto pens. The immigration bill finally became law in 1917 when Congress found the two-thirds majorities necessary to override President Wilson's veto, in a climate where the first world war had heightened nationalism and fear of foreigners. While the test did little to quell immigration, in large part due to improved literacy levels across Europe, it was an important symbolic victory for the restrictionists.

While immigration to the United States fell in the aftermath of World War I and the introduction of the barred zone, pressure for further restrictions did not dissipate. Most importantly, the argument for a liberal immigration policy was lost because:

> The [first world] war virtually swept from the American consciousness the old belief in unrestricted immigration. It did so, very simply, by creating an urgent demand for national unity and homogeneity that practically destroyed what the travail of preceding decades had already fatally weakened: the historic confidence in the capacity of American society to assimilate all men automatically. And with the passing of faith in the melting pot there perished the ideal of American nationality as an unfinished, steadily improving, cosmopolitan blend. Once almost everyone except immigrant spokesmen tacitly conceded that immigration might overtax the natural processes of assimilation, supporters of a "liberal" policy retired from grounds of fundamental principle to an uneasy, relative position.[20]

While the war had opened the road to restriction, its scale and form had still to be determined. Spurred by a recession in 1920, a Prohibition-inspired crime spree, another immigrant wave after the war lull,[21] the eugenicists, and his own hard-line restrictionist beliefs, the House Immigration Committee chair Albert Johnson began to hold hearings on these issues.[22] His first success was the 1921 act. It curtailed European immigration by awarding each country a quota, the size of which was determined by the size of its U.S. resident population in the 1910 census.[23] In effect, the act limited the "new" immigration from southern and eastern Europe while leaving open the door to the "old" immigration from northern and western Europe, because many of the former only arrived after the census. With President Coolidge on board, an even more restrictive, albeit temporary, law passed easily in 1924. Coolidge had written previously that "there are racial considerations too grave to be brushed aside for sentimental reasons . . . The Nordics propagate themselves successfully. With other races, the outcome shows deterioration. . . . Quality of mind and body suggests that observance of ethnic law is as great a necessity to a nation as immigration law."[24] Often referred to as the Johnson-Reed Act after its House and Senate sponsors, the 1924 law further reduced immigration from eastern and southern Europe by reducing the percentage size of the quotas and basing them on the 1890 U.S. census, when even fewer new immigrants were resident in the US.[25] The 1924 act was super-seded by 1929 regulations that based the National Origins Quota on the white population of the 1920 census. While this was more generous that the 1924 quotas, "its enactment was a triumph for a view of American people as racially homogenous, whose racial integrity should not be compromised by unsuitable immigrants."[26] For example, although about 150,000 Italians arrived annually in the United States in the early part of the century, Italy's quota was set at less than 6,000.[27]

The Quota Acts of 1921 and 1924, the 1929 regulations, and to some extent the 1917 literacy test represented a significant victory for the eugenicists. Led by Dr Harry Laughlin, the House Immigration Committee's eugenics expert, their arguments gave added impetus to the campaign to reduce the "new" immigration and clothed it with scientific respectability. The laws' effects were justified on the grounds that they excluded genetic degenerates, not racial groups. However, because genetic degeneracy was determined by membership of specific races and groups, the laws were clearly racist both in their design and their effect. While it hardly requires noting that the eugenicists' "science" was nothing of the sort, in the 1920s it was widely respected (and welcomed) by politicians and public alike. Some members of the scientific community were a little concerned about the close association between politics and eugenics, but few challenged the validity of the eugenicists' science. That public and elite opinion dovetailed neatly with scientific "fact" only exacerbated the confidence in, and effects of, each.[28] A century of high immigration was brought to an end. Indeed, in the early 1930s net migration was negative; more were leaving the United States than entering.

Interestingly, despite the large number of Mexicans living and working in the United States, especially in the southwest, and the considerable amount of racial prejudice directed toward them, they emerged from the 1920s restrictions relatively unscathed.[29] Indeed, the exclusion of eastern and southern Europeans increased the demand for cheap Mexican laborers and outweighed pressures to exclude them—or at least did so until the onset of the Great Depression in 1929. As the depression wore on through the early 1930s, over 500,000 Mexicans and Mexican Americans working in California left or were expelled. Further labor shortages in agriculture and industry during and after the second world war led the United States and Mexican governments to establish the Bracero program in 1942, which brought several million Mexican guest-workers to the United States. The program lasted until 1964, but faced significant interruptions, including in 1954 when over one million temporary Mexican workers were forcibly returned or fled to Mexico in the Immigration and Naturalization Service's Operation Wetback. The operation was approved by the National Association for the Advancement of Colored People and many labor unions.

Of course, California was previously Mexican territory and before that Spanish. And American Indians predated, and coexisted with, them all. The first groups of non-American Indian settlers to establish themselves permanently were Spanish Franciscan missionaries in the eighteenth century. Jesuit missionaries had earlier settled Baja California to the south. After Mexico won independence from Spain in 1821, California became a Mexican territory and more Mexicans, perhaps 20,000 of Spanish, mixed, and indigenous descent, settled there long before the Bracero program and the territory's annexation by the United States under the 1848 Treaty of Guadalupe-Hidalgo. The terms of the treaty were ostensibly generous to existing settlers, the "Californios," in terms of property rights and citizenship guarantees, but they soon found themselves treated as second-class citizens on territory previously theirs.

At the same time that the federal government was passing laws to restrict immigration to the United States, California adopted several of its own anti-immigrant laws, aimed first at the Chinese and Japanese and later at Latinos. Indeed, as has been noted recently by scholars,

> Discrimination against immigrants or anyone who seems "foreign" is not a new phenomenon in California. A brief glance at the state's history reveals an ugly cycle of nativism that repeats itself in periods of national anxiety provoked by economic recession, unemployment, or perceived external threats . . . "Wetbacks" were blamed for everything from diseases to labor strikes, "subversion" and crime along the border.[30]

In 1858 the nascent state prohibited the entry of all Chinese people and in 1862 it placed a $2.50 tax on each Chinese person already residing in the state.[31] And, as was noted above, lobbying from California congressional delegation was one of the main factors behind Congress's approval of the immigration acts of 1875 and 1882. The 1879 California Constitution decreed that Chinese and Mongolians should live in special segregated areas and forbade their public employment. These constitutional provisions were not repealed until 1952. In another precursor to congressional reform, 75 percent of California voters approved the 1920 anti-alien land law, Proposition 1, which excluded immigrants from land ownership if they were not eligible for citizenship under federal laws. In effect, this permitted Europeans to own land, but not the Chinese or Japanese who were the particular target of the initiative. Not until 1974 were noncitizens given the same property rights as citizens when the state constitution was amended.[32]

The final important piece of federal legislation passed during the exclusionist epoch was the 1952 Immigration and Nationality Act—also known as the McCarran-Walter Act after its congressional sponsors. On the one hand, it liberalized U.S. immigration law by amending the quota acts of the 1920s to allow immigration from all countries, including previously excluded Asian nations. On the other, however, each Asian country was awarded a maximum of just 2,000 visas, thus preserving the essentially discriminatory basis of U.S. immigration law. President Truman vetoed the bill because it failed to scrap the discriminatory national origins system, but Congress overrode his veto. The act also made it a criminal offence under the "Harboring a Native Provision" to smuggle people into the United States illegally or shelter them once in the country. However, the Texas congressional delegation lobbied hard for employers to be excluded from criminal prosecution if they hired, knowingly or not, undocumented workers. Congress accepted the Texan proposal, which became known as the "Texas Proviso." The legislation also gave the U.S. Border Patrol increased powers to investigate illegal immigration and immigrants.[33]

Repeal of Exclusionist and Racist Laws

The era of racial exclusion began to draw to a close in the 1950s when the 1952 McCarren-Walter Act formally allowed immigration from all countries. However, while a person's race or country of origin could no longer exclude them from obtaining U.S. citizenship, the quota system was still heavily biased in favor of northern and western Europeans and against Asians. This was to change in the 1960s.

The civil rights movement, which emerged in the 1950s and achieved most of its successes in the 1960s, changed the nature of American politics. One consequence was that the political discourse towards minorities and, later, immigrants became more liberal and accepting. No longer was it permissible or possible for politicians to make explicit racist appeals to their electorate; nor could employers, at least openly, refuse employment to women or minorities; nor could hotels or restaurants refuse service to minorities. Minorities saw their rights protected by the U.S. Supreme Court, especially by the two *Brown* decisions in 1954 and 1955, and expanded by Congress and the Executive in the form of the 1964 Civil Rights Act and the 1965 Voting Rights Act. The civil rights movement encouraged—because of its political impact and emphasis on equality and fairness—new thinking on immigration questions.[34] Consequently, the liberalization of immigration laws, which had begun in the late 1940s and gathered pace in the 1950s, was cemented into place with the passage of the Immigration and Nationality Act in 1965.

The 1965 act fundamentally changed what many critics saw as the racist nature of American immigration policy. National origins quotas, which discriminated against Asians and southern and eastern Europeans, were replaced with an annual 20,000 visa limit for all countries outside the western hemisphere and a 120,000 combined annual limit for all countries inside it. In total, 290,000 immigrants were allowed to enter the United States each year—although this was a permeable limit because some immigrants, such as immediate family relatives (spouses, children, parents), were off-quota. Within this total, the act gave priority to immigrants who already had family in the United States and to immigrants who had specialist and desirable job skills. The 1965 act was amended in 1977. The western hemisphere's 120,000 limit was replaced and each country was given its own 20,000 quota. With these two acts, racial and racist quota laws were finally removed from the statutes of the United States.[35]

The 20,000 visa-limit system was replaced in the Immigration Act of 1990. The new regulations allowed the entry of a maximum of 700,000 legal immigrants per annum between 1992 and 1994, followed by a flexible ceiling of 675,000 immigrants beginning in the 1995 fiscal year.[36] Special consideration was given to family reunification with 480,000 of the 675,000 places set aside for family-sponsored immigrants. While these provisions did not fundamentally affect the total numbers admitted to the United States, other provisions in the 1990 legislation emphasized the importance of skilled workers for whom 140,000 places were set aside. Special visas were also available for highly educated or trained professionals and for those prepared to invest money in the United States. Finally, the legislation provided 55,000 places for "diversity" immigrants—that is, immigrants from countries with previously low immigration levels who would therefore find it difficult to apply under the family reunification provisions. The 1990 act did not however fundamentally affect the nonracial system established in the 1965 legislation. In sum, from 1965 to 1990 the federal government changed its immigration laws by removing selective quotas that favored some countries and discriminated against others.

While the 1965 act established the basic parameters of legal immigration to the United States for the next twenty-five years, Daniels argues that "much of what it has accomplished was unforeseen by its authors, and had the Congress fully understood its consequences, it almost certainly would not have passed."[37] The key changes were a significant increase in the level of immigration; a decline in the European share of immigration and an increase in the Asian and Latin American share; and a substantial growth of chain migration due to the law's family reunification and off-quota provisions. A further consequence, one particularly pertinent to the discussion in this book, is that the 1965 act precipitated a large expansion in illegal immigration. The reasons are several. Because it regularized and placed limits on western hemisphere immigration for the first time and because supply (especially from Mexico) of potential immigrants exceeded available slots, it forced many migrants to enter the country illegally. Conversely, regularization also encouraged many families to put down permanent, legal roots in the United States, but they also in turn became important receiving networks for those entering later and illegally. In many household units, American citizens live alongside permanent and temporary legal residents and the undocumented. Linked to this are increased border surveillance and attendant difficulties in crossing borders. Historically, many Mexicans, especially agricultural laborers, would work in the United States for the picking season but return home each year. As it becomes more difficult to enter and leave the United States undetected, it increases the possibility that such workers settle illegally rather than sojourn.

At the same time that the federal government was liberalizing entry for legal immigrants, it was forced for the first time to address seriously the question of illegal immigration. The increase in undocumented migration to the United States, with approximately half coming from Mexico, along with a widespread torpor and loss of confidence about the American way in the 1970s led Congress to establish in 1977 the U.S. Select Commission on Immigration and Refugee Policy to review U.S. immigration policy generally and illegal immigration specifically.

The outcome of the committee's deliberations and the wider illegal-immigration debate was the passage of the federal Immigration Reform and Control Act (IRCA) in 1986. The philosophy underlying the IRCA is that undocumented persons come to the United States to find work and therefore displace native workers. A series of employer sanctions was thus introduced, imposing civil and criminal penalties on employers who knowingly employed undocumented workers or who did not check their employees' papers to establish eligibility for work. It was hoped that these checks and sanctions would curtail the employment of illegal workers. The IRCA therefore repealed the Texas Proviso of 1952, which had given employers immunity from sanctions even if they knowingly employed undocumented persons. Furthermore, the IRCA provided for increased border enforcement to prevent illegal immigrants entering the United States in the first place.

However, the more significant aspect of the IRCA was an amnesty offered to undocumented persons already resident in the United States. The amnesty applied to all illegal immigrants who could prove they had been in the United States from before January 1, 1982. The amnesty allowed the undocumented to apply immediately for temporary resident status. Nineteen months after this was granted, they could apply for permanent legal status. Five years later immigrants could apply for citizenship, which in most cases was automatic providing applicants could demonstrate a basic understanding of U.S. history and the English language or show they were in the process of acquiring these "skills."

The IRCA provided a more lenient amnesty for a special category of worker—the Special Agricultural Worker (SAW). SAWs had to prove they had done seasonal agricultural work in the United States for at least ninety days in the year preceding May 1, 1986. They acquired permanent resident status immediately, rather than waiting nineteen months. Both SAWs and other IRCA applicants could, on receiving permanent residency status, petition for their immediate families to be admitted to the United States, thus creating the foundations for an increase in legal immigration, much of it off-quota. These new entrants could then, in turn, apply for permanent residency and citizenship.

A short-term consequence of the IRCA amnesty was that the number of illegal immigrants residing in California dropped dramatically—from 2.4 million in 1986 to less than one million in 1988—as the undocumented took advantage of the act's provisions to become legal residents and, later, citizens. However, the number of illegal immigrants resident in the state soon began to increase—reaching 1.4 million in 1992 and 1.6 million in 1994—as many more continued to cross the border illegally. The employer sanctions and increased border patrols were having little effect on the flow of illegal immigrants into California.[38] In this sense the IRCA failed because the number of illegal immigrants continued to rise. However, despite the employer sanctions and increased border patrol efforts, the legislation was in no way a draconian response to the perceived problem. It was, rather, an inclusive, liberal law. The amnesty in particular was a humanitarian solution to a serious population problem. Of course, the law incorporated both carrot (the amnesty) and stick (the employer sanctions and increased funds for the Border Patrol) to solve the illegal-immigration problem, but the stick part proved especially ineffectual. Despite the Border Patrol turning away hundreds of thousands of illegal entrants annually, the flow of migrants was so large that further hundreds of thousands managed to make it safely to the United States. A crackdown at one porous part of the two-thousand mile border would produce a "balloon effect" elsewhere as immigrants simply changed their place of crossing. Furthermore, the employer sanctions proved to be particularly toothless. Federal attorneys were reluctant to prosecute and employers began to subcontract their labor needs to avoid what minimal threat of prosecution existed.[39] Such problems combined with the continuing huge disparity in wealth north and south of the border, and with established sending and receiving communities, to ensure that large-scale migration from Mexico to the United States continued.

*   *   *

In sum, from 1965 onwards immigration quotas and/or visa limits were generous and did not discriminate on the grounds of ethnicity or country of origin. Moreover, safeguards were put in place that protected ethnic-minority rights. A liberal discourse largely dominated acceptable political thought and speech in the post-1960s period. Politicians and commentators who favored tighter immigration controls and selective quotas or spoke of controlling the border were viewed by other political elites—especially in the liberal press and the East Coast establishment—with suspicion at best or as racist at worst. However, this changed in the 1990s. The electoral success of Proposition 187 specifically and the rise of anti-immigrant sentiment generally demonstrated to politicians, mainly but not exclusively on the right, that talking about illegal immigration and, perhaps more sinisterly, playing the race card could be effective ways of winning public support and elections. For example, as the following chapters will show, Pete Wilson's successful 1994 gubernatorial reelection campaign was symbiotically linked to his anti-illegal-immigration stance generally and support for Prop. 187 specifically. However, only a decade earlier when a U.S. senator, Wilson had sent an open letter to President Reagan appealing to him to let undocumented Mexican agricultural workers into California because "the crops are rotting in the fields." On the same issue, Senator Wilson also threatened to vote against the IRCA unless an amendment was added to the bill that permitted the entry of hundreds of thousands of crop pickers into California. The machinations of political leaders like Wilson on the IRCA led Wayne Cornelius, an immigration specialist at the University of California, San Diego, to later suggest that mass illegal immigration "is partly a self-inflicted problem. And here we are in this morass today . . . [A] close examination of the record shows that to a significant degree California has brought its immigration problems on itself. Policies promoted by the state's leaders in the 1980s actively encouraged illegal immigration into California, and as a result hundreds of thousands of illegal immigrants came."[40]

On the one hand then, widespread restrictionist sentiments encouraged politicians to use illegal immigration as a means of garnering support. On the other, politicians had to address the illegal-immigration "problem" in a way that voters found convincing. Because of the increasingly vehement anti-immigrant attitudes, voters would not have found another liberal, IRCA-type amnesty convincing. In the aftermath of Prop. 187, therefore, "tough" talking and direct action against illegal immigrants and illegal immigration became the norm, at both the federal and state levels. In California, Governor Wilson used executive orders to implement changes in the welfare and social service benefits of undocumented persons. Nationally, the Immigration and Naturalization Service saw a dramatic increase in its budget and thousands of new Border Patrol agents were appointed. More liberal politicians began to recognize that immigration was a key concern for the American people—and therefore an electoral concern that could not be ignored. President Clinton, who expressed his opposition to Prop. 187 on many occasions, began to speak of controlling the borders and cracking down on illegal immigration. He agreed to exclude even legally resident permanent immigrants from SSI, Medicaid, and food stamps when he signed the 1996 Welfare Reform Act.[41] Clinton also signed the Immigration Act in 1996, which sped up the expulsion process for illegal aliens and for asylum applicants whose application for asylee status had been denied. The act also provided more funds for increased border enforcement and forced immigrants to find a "sponsor" in the United States. While previous legislation had introduced sponsorship, the provisions were neither stringent nor rigorously enforced.

Important changes have been made to immigration policy since the passage of Prop. 187, in part because its success helped engender an anti-immigrant climate. It increased the saliency of the illegal-immigration issue for millions of Americans. Prop. 187, in other words, helped politicize the issue. This story is told in chapter 4 and later chapters. It is, however, important to stress that Prop. 187's success was itself in part a product of an earlier politicization of the illegal-immigration issue. It was borne into the world in a context that could already be labeled anti-immigrant. It was not yet a vehemently anti-immigrant climate—that would require Prop. 187 itself—but the path had been cleared and the first steps towards restrictionism had been taken. The following chapter will explain this early politicization of the illegal-immigration issue.[42]

Before it does it is worth pausing on the relationship between party politics and immigration reform. The anti-immigration story that follows is to a large extent a narrative about the Republican Party, yet the discussion above makes little reference to the political affiliations of the various actors, in large part because such affiliations would have provided few cues about actors' likely positions on immigration issues. Historically, and to some but lesser extent today, immigration politics cuts across partisan affiliations. Some trade union leaders, especially in the service sectors, line up alongside business leaders in support of more liberal immigration laws, as do other unlikely couplings such as liberal intellectuals and free-market economists, and civil rights organizations and pro-family Christians. On the other side, some environmentalists and nativists share a similar desire to restrict immigration, as do industrial trade unions members and cultural conservatives. Within parties, then, there are deep fissures on the immigration issue as, for example, cultural conservatives line up against economic conservatives in the Republican Party, and environmentalists against civil rights organizations in the Democratic Party.

The trade union case highlights well the crosscutting currents that swirl around the immigration issue. Most trade union leaders and their members for most of American history have sought to curtail the entry of new foreign workers into the labor market because they threaten native workers' wages and security. More recently, however, as membership has declined toward only one in ten workers, trade union leaders have targeted as new recruits first- and second-generation immigrants in low wage service sector jobs. A pro-immigration position helps them do so, but it may be antithetical to the interests of existing members. It has been pointed out, not only by restrictionists, that those with most to lose from future high levels of immigration are the most recent newcomers specifically and those at the bottom of the employment pyramid generally, including African Americans.[43] Some Americans threatened economically by immigration may however express support for it because of ethnic solidarity with the newcomers, or because they believe the oppressed must stand shoulder to shoulder. The union elites who distribute millions of dollars annually to Democratic candidates and causes and the many liberal union members who are tireless grassroots activists may support liberal immigration policies, but there are millions of other members and Democratic voters who do not. The Democratic Party must therefore tread cautiously. The path is made more uncertain once *illegal* immigration is thrown into the mix.

The IRCA discussed above won bipartisan support. Democrats were concerned that undocumented itinerants, because they were in the county illegally with little or no recourse to law, could be subject to mass exploitation by farm owners. The protection of farm workers was a key Democratic motivation for supporting the SAW program, yet Republicans with close links to agricultural interests supported SAW to ensure a large supply of cheap farm labor. While the liberal IRCA passed with majority bipartisan support, so did the racist and restrictionist Chinese Exclusion Act of 1882 and the quota acts of the 1920s. The quota acts' congressional champions were Republicans—Dillingham, Johnson, and Cabot Lodge—but a majority of Democrats were fully committed to the dominant racist ideology of the eugenicists. So prominent was the Ku Klux Klan and racist, anti-Catholic, and anti-immigrant attitudes at the 1924 Democratic convention that it became known as the Klanbake. President Franklin D. Roosevelt was no nativist and he repealed the Chinese Exclusion Act in 1943, but he made no serious attempt to revoke the national origins quotas, despite the large number of prominent immigrants in his administration and the importance of ethnic voters to his New Deal coalition. More damningly, Roosevelt did not push Congress or use executive orders to help Jewish refugees feeling Nazi Germany, and he authorized in 1942 the internment of 120,000 persons of Japanese ancestry—two thirds of whom were native-born Americans—in ten camps in the west of the United States. President Harry Truman vetoed the McCarran-Walter act because it did not abolish the discriminatory national origins framework, but his veto was overridden with the help of Democratic members of Congress, including the future President and champion of liberal immigration reform, Lyndon B. Johnson. Neither Truman, nor Eisenhower or Kennedy pushed hard for liberal immigration reform despite their professed, and the latter's prominent, support for the cause. Kennedy's ghost-written book, *A Nation of Immigrants*, set out the arguments, but Daniels questions his willingness to do battle on its behalf: "Those who loved him assure us that, had he lived, immigration reform would have surely come. The historian can only wonder."[44]

Gimpel and Edwards argue that divisions on immigration issues became increasingly partisan—indeed, "fiercely partisan"—from the late 1960s onwards as the post-1965 surge in immigration reinforced existing party divisions on government spending and civil rights issues.[45] Immigrants, they argue, came to be seen by Republicans as a potential financial burden and by Democrats as potential members of their political coalition. While it is true that party affiliation is today a more useful heuristic for determining a politician's immigration position, it is far from an infallible guide and the partisanship is often less than fierce. There was little movement on immigration reform during the Nixon and Carter years, but President Reagan happily put his name to the IRCA in 1986 and President George H. W. Bush's 1990 immigration act was generally an expansionist, liberal affair. The restrictionist movement of the mid 1990s had many prominent Republican opponents—witness the maneuverings of Senator Spencer Abraham in opposition to Senator Alan Simpson's attempt to reduce the level of legal immigration in 1996—and President George W. Bush has worked tirelessly in support of another amnesty (while eschewing the word) for millions more illegal immigrants, in opposition to a majority of his own party in Congress. However, while party affiliation is not a good historical guide to a partisan's position on the immigration issue, it certainly became more so in the mid 1990s. The next chapter sets out the early causes of that decade's turn against immigration.

Chapter 3

The Early Politicization of the Illegal-Immigration Issue

The concern of this chapter is the genesis of the backlash against immigration, and illegal immigration in particular, which began in California in the early 1990s and later spread to the wider United States. Many intersecting factors contributed to the backlash, including a deteriorating economy, environmental worries, crime, the perceived welfare burden imposed by immigrants, and concerns about immigrants' assimilability and threat to whites' numerical and cultural dominance.

The United States' and especially California's demographic profile changed rapidly in the late twentieth century, mainly in response to the changes wrought by the 1965 immigration act discussed in the previous chapter. In the early part of the century immigrants from Europe constituted nearly 90 percent of new arrivals to the United States; by the century's end it was less than 20 percent, with four out of every five coming from Latin America and Asia. By 1990 California was more than a quarter Latino, with around eight million persons of Latino origin living in the state. Latinos concentrated in the south of the state, with nearly 3.5 million in Los Angeles County alone. The Asian population also increased dramatically and by the early 1990s one in ten Californians was of Asian descent. Some of course were descended from old stock that came in the nineteenth and early twentieth centuries before racist legislation closed the door on Asian immigration, but more were post-1965 arrivals from China, Japan, the Philippines, Vietnam, India, and Korea. Demographers predicted, and Californians discussed widely, that whites would become a minority in California in the early twenty-first century. Many whites that saw this as a threat blamed immigration as the cause. While the vast majority of Latino and Asian residents were citizens or legal immigrants, some, perhaps a million persons, were there illegally. Most of the undocumented were from Latin America, most of these were Mexican, and most arrived in the United States having slipped illegally across the 2,000 mile U.S.-Mexico border. America's southern border became in the 1990s the site and symbol of the battle and failure to control illegal entry. It was, and remains, notoriously porous. The inability of the federal government to curtail illegal entry created considerable resentment among citizens, hundreds of whom took to parking their cars at night on a hill overlooking the border near San Diego, with headlights illuminated to pick out the desperate figures darting into El Norte. In the next decade such direct action became more organized in the form of Arizona's Minuteman Project, an armed citizen militia which took border control into its own hands.

The numerical increase in the nonwhite population, which some commentators referred to dramatically as the Latinoization of California, helped engender a new cultural insecurity among the dominant Anglo group. On one everyday level, whites were confronted with different cultural practices: pets such as chickens, roosters, and goats, pastimes like cockfighting and sports such as soccer; street vendors selling Mexican food and trinkets; and a significant increase in Spanish-language books, newspapers, magazines, and television and radio stations.[1] The sounds, sights, and smells of southern California were changing, and many white residents found it strange, difficult, threatening even. On another level, the perceived Latinoization encouraged larger existential questions about California's future. The fall of communism in Europe at the turn of the decade produced an upsurge in ethnic tensions and fighting, including genocide, as historic rivalries long suppressed by leftwing dictatorships burst bloodily forth. Commentators worried that California too could become Balkanized if its ethnic populations continued to expand while rejecting the dominant Anglo culture. In this debate, the apparent reluctance or inability of new immigrants to learn English figured large. Based more on supposition that fact—indeed, opinion polls show that a large majority of immigrants want to learn English—the perception was reinforced by California's bilingual education program, in which non-English speaking schoolchildren were taught in their native language and only a small section of the day given over to formal English language instruction. Critics argued, and would later change the law in their favor by passing Proposition 227 in 1998, that bilingual programs risked ghettoizing students by stymieing their chances of learning English early and quickly.

In universities debate raged about what it meant to be American. The old descriptive and normative metaphor of the melting pot where immigrants assimilated to American culture while adding a little of their own to the mix was denounced by some academics as nothing less than racist. The intellectual driving force behind such ideas were the postmodern and post-structural turns in political thought, which argued that all cultures, races, ethnicities, genders, sexualities, and so on were of equal value and that membership in one or more of these groups defined individuals' identity. But a multicultural society, where diversity is eulogized and different cultures sit side by side, challenges the process of Americanization. Affirmation action programs provided a further challenge to America's philosophical foundations. Originally designed in the 1960s, affirmation action recognized that African Americans had been held back by institutional racism and that a helping hand was needed to give them a fair chance in life. Over time, however, the programs were widened to include women and other racial and ethnic minorities, but the motivations also changed. Were once it was about righting past wrongs, the rise of the multiculturalism encouraged proponents to justify affirmative action in terms of promoting diversity, but a diversity defined by individuals' membership of certain demographic groups. Multiculturalism and group identities, critics argued, posed a fundamental challenge to the idea of America as e pluribus unum—from many, one.

Arthur Schlesinger provided one of the highest profile critiques of multiculturalism, or separatism as he called it, in his 1991 book *The Disuniting of America*. He argued that the United States offers a diverse people a "common purpose" and a strong sense of national identity based on shared values that transcend ethnic, racial, and national origins. He lists some "facts of history: that Europe was the birthplace of the United States of America, that European ideas and culture formed the republic, that the United States is an extension of European civilization, and that nearly 80 percent of Americans are of European descent." While acknowledging that the shared values of democracy, rule of law, and liberty are unquestionably Anglo-Saxon in origin, Schlesinger worried that the foundations upon which America was built and had served it well were threatened by the new "cult of ethnicity" and its attendant separatism and the bilingual lobby. Whether their motivations were philosophical or political, it is certainly the case that some self-styled Latino community leaders, although rarely *el hombre de la calle*, began to speak the language of separatism in the early 1990s. Some radical irredentists, and indeed anti-immigration activists, even suggested that California would one day secede from the union or be annexed by Mexico, further reinforcing and exacerbating fears about Balkanization. Raising the assimilationist argument heard so often at the start of the century, some white activists and commentators suggested that Latino culture was too different from American culture and that, anyway, Latinos either rejected or were not capable of assimilating existing cultural norms—arguments that of course would only inflame ethnic sentiment and encourage further talk of separatism.

A general malaise hanging over California in the early 1990s, a feeling that the Golden State had lost its way, also drove anti-immigrant sentiments, and anti-Latino sentiments by extension. A key ingredient in the malaise was the 1990–1993 recession. As Kevin Starr, California's state librarian and premier historian, notes, "more and more Californians began to blame immigrants for the tough times and the pervasive perception that the quality of life had declined."[2] In 1990 California had a gross state product of $745 billion, the highest in the Union, but in the same year entered its deepest and longest recession since the Great Depression and by 1993 had the second highest unemployment rate in the country at 9.2 percent, with 1.5 million people out of work. Between 1990 and 1993 personal disposable income per capita increased by 7.4 percent, the lowest rate of increase in the country, and two-thirds of all U.S. jobs lost were in California—519,000 out of 810,000. The state also had the highest rate of business failures of any state in 1993.[3] What made this recession different and more problematic was its nature: it was both cyclical and structural. The structural element was that the post–cold war job losses in the aerospace and military industries—about 375,000—were permanent and hit California particularly hard. Starr notes that in the fifty years after the second world war, California was on "defense steroids."[4] Cold turkey hit in the 1990s as the state lost military bases and defense contracts, jobs were shed, and tax revenues plummeted by

40 percent, forcing politicians to slash public spending, increase taxes, and lay off more employees. Other companies relocated outside California because of its tough regulatory climate and high corporate taxes, further exacerbating the recession's effects. So, while the whole of the United States went into recession in 1990, the structural changes ensured that California's recession was especially deep and lengthy. Moreover, Californians had little experience of economic hardship; the state's postwar history was until 1990 one of considerable prosperity and opportunity, and is itself the key reason why the state attracted and absorbed so many immigrants.

Academics, think-tanks, pressure groups, and government agencies produced dozens of reports analyzing the relative costs and benefits of immigration. While there was no consensus on whether immigrants were a burden or a benefit, a slight majority probably came down on the pro-immigration side of the argument. But Californians weren't listening. The shrinking economy focused their minds clearly on the costs rather than the benefits. The equation looked very one-sided in the 1990s. Immigrants were accused burdening hard-pressed taxpayers by living luxurious but idle lives on California's generous welfare payments, by committing crimes and filling up prisons, and by requiring expensive bilingual programs for their many children, hundreds of thousands of whom were undocumented.

More generally the malaise was deepened by a sense that California's infrastructure was crumbling. Its once great education system was in crisis. Spending per pupil and test scores raced each other to the bottom of the state-by-state league and its two university systems, the twenty campus California State University and the prestigious nine campus University of California, hiked fees and laid of staff. Freeways were packed, commuting times horrendous, efficient public transport nearly nonexistent. Prisons were bursting at the seams. Even the natural environment seemed to groan in despair. Forest and bush fires, droughts, torrential rains, mudslides, and, most dramatically, earthquakes in San Francisco and Los Angeles in 1990 and 1994 respectively brought terrible destruction, took hundreds of lives, and cost billions of dollars. The 1992 Los Angeles riots, the 1993 abduction and murder of Polly Klass, the continuing destruction, misery, and death wrought by warring gangs fighting battles over turf, drugs, and honor, and corrupt and violent law-enforcement agencies reinforced the perception of California as a state on the edge of self-destruction.[5]

The United States and California appeared to be in turmoil ideologically and politically, too. Spurred by the publication of James Davison Hunter's 1991 book, *Culture Wars*, learned weeklies were full of stories about the clash between two apparently irreconcilable views of the world.[6] On the traditional side sat conservatives aghast at the perceived moral abyss that America had fallen into since the 1960s with the breakdown of the traditional family and the erosion of religious values, the explosion of pornography and "deviant" sexual practices, the supremacy of environmental protection over workers' jobs and families, the rise in violent crime and drug use and its glamorization and glorification by a decadent, liberal media establishment, and, perhaps most saliently, abortion—"the Bosnia of the cultural war" according to Pat Buchanan—and in particular the constitutional protection offered to "abortionists" but not "unborn children" by the Supreme Court of the United States of America. As Buchanan orated at the 1992 Republican Party convention:

> My friends, this election is about much more than who gets what. It is about who we are. It is about what we believe. It is about what we stand for as Americans. There is a religious war going on in our country for the soul of America. It is a cultural war, as critical to the kind of nation we will one day be as was the Cold War itself. And in that struggle for the soul of America, Clinton & Clinton are on the other side, and George Bush is on our side.[7]

More recent scholarship on the cultural war between Democrats and Republicans, liberals and conservatives suggests that the differences have probably been overplayed, especially, as Fiorina has eloquently demonstrated, at the level of the average citizen.[8] Nonetheless, it is also true that the ideological space between the parties has widened to the extent that it is valid to talk about polarization, especially at the elite level on cultural and social issues.[9] The new cadre of Republican activists and aspiring office holders staked out increasingly conservative positions on abortion, gay rights, feminism, civil rights, the environment, and American identity, as well as a hard-line stance on taxes and government spending, while Democrats increasingly take liberal positions. The consequence is that liberal Republicans and conservative Democrats are endangered species, as are civility and comity in Congress and between the legislature and executive when control is divided between the parties. A further consequence is that trust in government and authority declines as ordinary Americans are stranded in the middle of a high-pitched, saber-rattling confrontation between two groups that have little to say to the moderate majority.[10] Ross Perot's barnstorming and popular 1992 presidential campaign, George H. W. Bush's unceremonious ejection from the White House only a year after winning a quick and widely supported war in the Persian Gulf, and the Democratic Party's stunning loss of control of Congress in 1994 after forty years' hegemony confirms the disenchantment and discontent of many Americans toward the established political parties and the governmental institutions. This is the context in which the illegal-immigration issue was politicized, but context alone is an insufficient explanation.

The Level and Intensity of Anti-Immigrant Sentiment

While the United States is widely regarded as a "nation of immigrants," Americans have ambivalent attitudes toward immigration. On the one hand, Americans revere past immigrants and the idea of immigration but, on the other, say that fewer immigrants should be admitted to the United States. Some Americans' antipathy toward immigration and new immigrants is reflected in many opinion poll surveys conducted over the years. Table 3.1 and figure 3.1, for example, highlight mid-to-late twentieth-century thinking on the number of immigrants that should be admitted. Most notable is the high level of support over time for restrictionist policies. Rarely do more than one in ten Americans think the number should be increased, and sometimes as many as two-thirds think the number should be decreased. Indeed, after an extensive review of public opinion from 1880 to 1990 toward legal and illegal immigration, Simon and Alexander noted that

> It is something of a miracle that so many immigrants gained entry to the United States between 1880 and 1990. Going back to recapture the tone of the debate in the print media, examining the bills proposed and passed by Congress and the statutes enacted into federal law, and reviewing the national poll data lead to wonderment and bewilderment at how more than 40 million people gained admittance during a century and to a country that at best was ambivalent toward them and at worst erected barriers to their entry.[11]

The trend line in figure 3.1 shows that the number of Americans wishing to see a reduction in the number of immigrants entering the United States increased in the 1970s, declined in the 1980s, and increased again in the first half of the 1990s. Yet what is more notable about the 1990s is that in addition to increasing *numbers* of people expressing restrictionist views—what may be called the *level* of anti-immigrant sentiment—the *intensity* of people's opinions also increased. In fact, it did so precipitously; the change in intensity is much more marked than the change in the number expressing restrictionist sentiments. While it is always problematic to measure the intensity of people's beliefs on any issue, consider

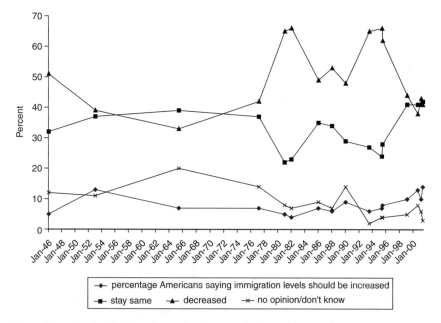

Figure 3.1. Level of Anti-immigrant Sentiment in the United States, 1946–2001

Sources: Gallup Polls and Simon and Alexander, *The Ambivalent Welcome.*

the following evidence. Various opinion polls, including *Gallup*'s surveys of Americans and the *Los Angeles Times* (*LA Times*) surveys of Californians, have for many years asked respondents to name the "most important problem facing the country/state today." Tables 3.1 and 3.2 present Californians' and Americans' most important concerns. Unsurprisingly, jobs, the economy, crime, and education are perennial worries. In most years, immigration, whether legal, illegal or both, rarely figures. Indeed, in the wider United States between 1939 and 1979 never more than one half of one percent of Americans said immigration was the most important problem facing the country. Even during the recession of the early 1990s the number saying immigration was the most important problem was too small to register. The peak in 1980 reflects a short-lived concern about the Mariel boatlift, which resulted in 125,000 Cubans arriving in the United States. The politicians and public were particularly anxious over the large number of criminals and mentally ill who arrived; Castro had deliberately released from jail and hospital large numbers of undesirables in order "to bring havoc to the United States."[12]

In California, meanwhile, where immigration has always been more of an issue than in the wider United States, a similar pattern is repeated. As table 3.1 shows,

Table 3.1   Intensity of Anti-immigrant Sentiment in California Compared with Other Issues, May 1991–May 1994

Month and Year	Crime/ Gangs	Economy/ Jobs	Education	Immigration	Drugs	Notes
May 1991	11	12	16	2	7	CA AA 1
Dec. 1991	9	35	6	3	3	CA AA 1
May 1992	9	30	9	2	3	CA AA 1
Oct. 1992	44	46	13	3	10	LA AA 2
Mar. 1993	10	34	10	2	2	CA AA 1
Aug. 1993	52	16	6	5	7	OC AA 2
Sept. 1993	16	32	7	9	1	CA AA 1
Sept. 1993	27	48	14	16	4	CA AA 2
Oct. 1993	30	54	18	11	5	CA AA 2
Mar. 1994	42	38	14	12	5	CA AA 2
May 1994	38	46	14	15	5	CA AA 2

Notes. All entries are percentages.

CA = California sample; LA = Los Angeles city sample; OC = Orange County sample; AA = All Adults; RV = Registered Voters; 1 = 1 reply accepted; 2 = up to 2 replies accepted.

Questions: (Of California sample:) What do you think is the most important problem facing California today? Is there another problem you feel is almost as important? (Of LA city sample:) What do you think is the most important problem facing the city of Los Angeles today? Is there another problem you think is almost as important as this one? (Of OC sample:) What's the most important problem facing your community today? Is there another problem which is almost as important?

The September 1993 survey distinguished between first and both replies. Immigration was rated as the most important problem by 9 percent of the California-wide sample, and 16 percent said it was either the first or second most important problem. The latter statistic clearly overestimates the "politicization" of the immigration issue compared with the two percent who rated it the most important problem in the previous *LA Times* poll in March 1993. However, the increase from 2 to 9 percent is nevertheless significant, representing an increase of 350 percent. All *LA Times* polls after September 1993 record Californians' top two concerns.

Sources: *LA Times Polls*; see appendix A for details.

Table 3.2 Intensity of Anti-immigrant Sentiment in United States Compared with Other Issues, Selected Years, January 1939–June 2001

Month and Year	Crime	Economy/ Recession	Jobs	Education	Immigration/ Illegal Aliens
Jan. 1939	0.5	6	39	0	0.5
Mar. 1945	0.5	12	20	1	0
Mar. 1950	1	16	9	0.5	0
Mar. 1954	2	13	16	0	0
Sept. 1960	0	5	6	1	0
Sept. 1965	2	5	3	2	0
Sept. 1970	5	9	2	2	0
Oct. 1975	4	53	21	1	0
June 1980	1	55	14	0	3
Oct. 1984	0.5	3	5	1	0.5
Oct. 1990	2	10	3	2	0
Sept. 1993	16	26	20	7	3
July 1995	15	6	9	4	2
Aug. 1997	16	8	8	12	3
Jan. 1999	13	6	6	13	1
June 2001	9	10	4	12	2

Notes. All entries are percentages.
Question: What do you think is the most important problem facing this country today?
Only one reply accepted.
Sources. Gallup Polls.

the intensity of anti-immigrant sentiment—as measured by responses to the "most important problem" question—was low before mid 1993. As in the wider United States, immigration hardly registered on Californians' policy problem radar, despite the recession and the widespread malaise outlined above. For example, in December 1991, only 3 percent of Californians cited immigration as the most pressing problem facing the state. In contrast, 35 percent mentioned the economy and jobs, 9 percent said crime and gangs and 6 percent education.[13] And in May 1992, only 5 percent of San Diego–city residents said immigration was "the one issue [they] would most like to see the San Diego mayoral candidates address," despite the city's large legal and illegal-immigrant population. Crime at 22 percent, education and schools also at 22 percent, and jobs and unemployment at 18 percent were cited as the most important issues.[14] Finally, in October 1992, only 3 percent of Los Angeles–city residents said immigration was a serious concern.[15]

But in mid-to-late 1993 the percentage of Californians placing immigration as their top concern increased dramatically. In March 1993 only 2 percent of California adults had said immigration was the most important problem facing their state, but by September 1993 9 percent said so, more than a threefold increase. In the same September poll, fully 16 percent of Californians rated immigration as one of the state's two most important problems.[16] And in Orange County 19 percent of adults rated "foreign immigration" as their county's "most serious problem."[17] Likewise, the intensity of anti-immigrant sentiment also increased in the rest of the United States, although from a lower base and to a lower peak. While failing to register in the very early 1990s, the percentage of Americans saying immigration was the country's most important problem increased to 3 percent in September 1993, before settling down to between 1 and 2 percent for the next few years. The objective of this chapter is to examine the potential causes of the increasingly intense anti-immigrant sentiment—in other words, to explain why the immigration issue became "politicized" in late 1993. California's malaise cannot account for it, although it provided the context in which politicization was possible.

Before pursuing these causes, however, it is wise to pause on the relationship between the *level* and *intensity* of sentiment and the slightly messy concept of politicization. Politicization is used here to refer to the increased political character or saliency of the immigration issue. Two potential measures of politicization are the level and the intensity of anti-immigrant sentiment. While these measures are related, they are different things. It is possible for an individual or a population to have negative views about an issue *and* for that issue to be unimportant to them or for it to be overshadowed by other concerns. In terms of politicization, it is the intensity of the sentiment that matters more than the level. An individual may come to feel very strongly about immigration, and this is certainly politicization, but it would be wrong to say she was politicized solely because her position changed from favoring open doors to favoring closed doors; opinions can change without passions being aroused. Similarly, at the societal level, the immigration issue can be said to have been politicized when a critical number of citizens feel very strongly about it. This matters more than an increase in the proportion of people saying they prefer more restrictions because the American political system is more responsive to intensely held opinions than to widely held, but thinly spread ones.[18] Precisely this happened on the immigration issue in California and the United States in the late 1980s and early 1990s. Latent hostility toward immigrants was reflected in polls showing high support for restricitonist policies, but Americans did not feel strongly about the issue. In other words, the issue had not yet been politicized. We need to explain why it was so in late 1993.

So, politicization refers at the micro level to the intensely held anti-immigrant views of an individual and, with one important caveat, at the macro level to the aggregation of all individuals' intense passions. The caveat is that it makes little sense to describe an issue as politicized at the societal level if only a few people are passionate about it. Thus the issue must be politicized for a critical number of people. But how many is critical? There is no definite social scientific answer to this question. However, researchers should expect to see, in addition to the increasing intensity of opinion, an increase in the issue's press coverage, politicians discussing and addressing the issue, individuals mobilizing and perhaps forming together into groups to promote their views, or, if a group already exists, its mobilization on the issue. In the case of the immigration issue, all these things happened. And they did so first in California and later in the wider United States. California was first for several reasons, the most obvious being that it is the legal- and illegal-immigration capital of the United States. The now disbanded Immigration and Naturalization Service estimated that 100,000 undocumented persons entered California successfully every year, in spite of the Border Patrol turning away hundreds of thousands annually.[19] Furthermore, California is a bellwether state. In part, this is because of its national political significance. With 53 of the 435 seats in the U.S. House of Representatives and 55 of the 270 electoral college votes needed to win the presidency, California's sheer political clout forces politicians with national ambitions to listen to its residents.[20] Its bellwether status also derives from the widespread use, and some would say abuse, of direct democracy procedures. Initiative propositions are especially significant in this respect. They allow citizens to place before their fellow voters a proposal to change the law or state constitution, bypassing the traditional law-making institutions and their checks and balances. The free exercise of the passions, while horrifying modern-day Madisons, sends irresistible signals to the finely tuned antennae of the modern politician. It also sends important signals to residents and activists in other states. The 1978 victory of the anti-property tax measure, Prop. 13, set off a wave of tax revolts in other states and paved the way for Reagan's presidential election victory and tax cuts. The successful Prop. 209 of 1996 helped stoke the anti-affirmative action fires. And, most relevant here, the large Yes vote on the anti-illegal-immigration initiative in 1994 helped further deepen passions in California and propel the issue onto the national agenda. That story is, however, for a later chapter. The object of this one is to examine and explain the first stage of the politicization of the illegal immigration. The story begins in the Golden State.

The Number of Illegal Immigrants

The restrictionist laws of the first decades of the twentieth century were introduced, at least in part, in response to the large number of immigrants entering the United States at that time.[21] In this light, it makes sense to suggest that Californians may have become increasingly concerned about illegal immigration in the 1990s because of an increase in the number of undocumented persons in the state. Before examining this connection, it is necessary to establish the numbers involved. While it is impossible to know with certainty either the number of undocumented persons in California and the United States or the number attempting to enter each year—they, after all, do not enter through the official channels—the U.S. Immigration and Naturalization Service (INS) released estimates from time to time. Table 3.3 presents these estimates between 1980 and 1996.[22]

In 1980 there were an estimated two million illegal residents in the United States, half of whom resided in California. By 1986, the undocumented population had risen to 2.4 million in California—an increase from 1980 of 132 percent. Between 1986 and 1988 the undocumented population dropped dramatically to under one million as 1.6 million illegal aliens took advantage of the 1986 Immigration Reform and Control Act (IRCA) amnesty. From 1988, the number of undocumented persons rose steadily to 1.1 million in 1990, 1.4 million in 1992, 1.6 million in 1994, and 2 million in 1996.

One way of looking at these figures is to say that in 1986 illegal residents constituted nearly 9 percent of California's population of 27 million, while in 1994 they constituted 5 percent of 31.5 million people.[23] Another way is to say that the absolute (660,000) and percentage (70%) increase in the number of illegal

Table 3.3   Estimated Illegal Immigrant Populations (in Thousands) in United States and California by Origin, 1980–1996

Type of Estimate[a]	Place		Origin	
	United States	California	Mexico	Other
Estimated number of illegals in *1980* U.S. Census	2,057	1,024	1,131	926
Percent of total	—	50%	55%	45%
Estimated number of illegals in *1986* (at passage of IRCA)	4,774	2,374	2,907	1,867
Percent of total	—	50%	61%	39%
Total number of IRCA applications	3,041	1,622	2,271	770
Percent of total	—	53%	75%	25%
Percent of total who applied under IRCA[b]	64%	68%	78%	41%
Estimated number of illegals, October *1988*	2,182	940	823	1,359
Percent of total	—	43%	38%	62%
Estimated number of illegals in *1990* U.S. Census	2,631	1,128	1,009	1,621
Percent of total	—	43%	38%	62%
Estimated number of illegals, October *1992*	3,379	1,441	1,321	2,059
Percent of total	—	43%	39%	61%
Average annual growth, 1988–1992	299	125	125	175
Percent of total	—	42%	42%	58%
Ratio of 1992 population to total at passage of IRCA	.71	.61	.45	1.10
Estimated number of illegals, *1994*	4,000[c]	1,600[d]	—	—
Percent of total	—	40%	—	—
Estimated number of illegals, *1996*[e]	5,000	2,000	2,700	2,300
Percent of total	—	40%	54%	46%

Notes. — = not applicable or not available.

[a] All entries in thousands unless stated.

[b] Denominator is total population at beginning of IRCA legalization, not the number eligible to apply NB. Those who entered (illegally) later than January 1, 1982, were not eligible to apply unless satisfied criterion of Special Agricultural Worker Program.

[c] INS estimate, reported in *New York Times*, January 3, 1995, p. A-1 and B-4.

[d] Warren estimated that the 1994 illegal population in California was "about 1.6 million" (see Warren, "Undocumented Immigrants in California," p. 15).

[e] INS estimate. See "Illegal Alien Resident Population," archived at http://www.dhs.gov/xlibrary/assets/statistics/illegal.pdf (accessed October 25, 2007).

Sources: Warren, "Undocumented Immigrants in California," pp. 11–23 and Appendix G; *New York Times*, January 3, 1995, pp. A-1 and B-4; INS, "Illegal Alien Resident Population: Estimates of the Undocumented Immigrant Population Residing in the United States (October 1996) (Updated December 2001)," archived at http://www.dhs.gov/xlibrary/assets/statistics/illegal.pdf (accessed October 25, 2007).

immigrants residing in California between 1988 and 1994 was roughly half the earlier 1980–1986 increase (1.3 million or 132%). However, while the 1988–1994 increase was followed by a significant nativist backlash and the passage of Proposition 187, the larger 1980–1986 increase did not produce an exclusionist legislative response. In comparison to Prop. 187, the IRCA of 1986 was a liberal, inclusionist remedy to the illegal-immigration problem; it offered an amnesty to certain categories of illegal immigrants in the form of legal resident status and, later, citizenship.

This suggests that illegal-immigrant numbers per se cannot explain the nature of the anti-immigrant discourse and the politicization of illegal immigration in late 1993. The timing is wrong. The sharp upturn in the intensity of anti-immigrant sentiment in late 1993 cannot be explained by the smooth increase in undocumented numbers between 1988 and 1994. However, this is not to claim that illegal-immigrant numbers are not important. It is unlikely that the issue's saliency could have increased without a large illegal population; there would simply have been very little for people to get upset about. A "critical" number of illegal immigrants, then, provides a necessary but insufficient condition for the politicization. It is possible that Americans were more concerned about the growing numbers of nonwhite residents generally than about their illegal or legal status. Again, however, the timing is not right. Legal immigration to the United States was about 600,000 per year in the mid 1980s, spiked between 1989 and 1991, and then fell off between 1992 and 1995.[24] This historically high level of legal entry could have contributed to a general dissatisfaction with immigration policy, but the decline in legal immigration from 1992 onwards suggests that it cannot explain the dramatic increase in the intensity of anti-immigrant sentiment in mid-to-late 1993. It is also possible that white Americans and Californians were concerned not specifically about illegal and legal immigrant numbers but more generally about Anglos losing their numerical and cultural dominance. As discussed above, it is highly likely that such worries contributed to a growth in the level of restrictionist sentiment, but they cannot account for the sharp upturn in the intensity of that sentiment that occurred in late 1993. Another likely candidate is the recession.

The Recession

The California recession could have had an indirect and/or direct effect on the politicization of the illegal-immigration issue. The indirect effect is linked to the role of politicians and is expressed best in a number of statements. Elective politicians were worried about their election prospects because the state was in a deep recession, for which the voters blamed the politicians. The politicians therefore needed a scapegoat to blame the recession on, and they also needed an issue around which they could build an electoral coalition. Illegal immigrants provided the scapegoat and illegal immigration provided the issue. If this proves to be the case, then we could say that the recession provided the motivation for politicians to politicize the issue. In other words, the recession had an indirect effect. In addition, the recession could have had a direct effect, and there are two possible ways in which it could have done so. In the first case, the recession personalizes the perceived negative impact of illegal immigrants. Californians could have felt personally threatened by illegal immigrants because of a perception that the undocumented posed a threat to their jobs, or because they thought their taxes would increase because it was perceived that undocumented persons were likely to live on welfare or be high users of state-provided health care. In the second case, Californians could have believed that illegal immigrants had a negative effect on the economy generally—as distinct from a personal effect on their own well-being. These general concerns are usually referred to as sociotropic considerations.

Is there any evidence in previous research suggesting that financial self-interest should be expected to have played a part in motivating anti-immigrant attitudes? The concept of self-interest certainly provides a major premise and research tool across intellectual disciplines.[25] For example, psychology, economics, philosophy, and political science all emphasize its importance.[26] Yet, recent studies on gender, government spending, taxation, welfare, crime, and foreign policy have found little role for self-interest in opinion formation.[27] Self-interest has also been shown to be a weak predictor of Americans' racial attitudes—especially on the issue of school busing to achieve integration.[28]

However, some scholars looking specifically at contemporary events in California have argued that the 1990–1993 recession, and the attendant budget crisis and unemployment, brought the issue of illegal immigration to the fore—although their arguments are largely anecdotal and nonquantitative.[29] More rigorous studies have demonstrated that economic concerns are the most important explanations for restrictionist sentiments toward both legal and illegal immigrants.[30] These results are further supported by studies showing that more people think that immigration should be restricted as an economy slides into recession; and that people with a pessimistic view of the national economy are more restrictionist than people who think the economy is performing well.[31] Moreover, economic competition between whites and ethnic minorities has been shown to produce conflict and racism,[32] and economic downturns, when combined with increasing immigration levels and a national crisis of confidence, are associated with nativist outbursts.[33] Others emphasize that it was unemployment caused by depression, in conjunction with a construction of immigrants' identity as "birds of passage," that led to an increase in nativist resentment and ultimately deportations of Mexicans and Mexican Americans in the early 1930s and between 1939 and 1954.[34] In addition, at the micro level, Citrin et al. and Espenshade and Calhoun found that individuals who thought legal and illegal immigrants posed a threat to their jobs were more likely to view immigrants malignly.[35] Citrin et al. also found that people who thought their income would decline in the next year were more likely to favor restricting legal immigrants' access to government benefits than people who were optimistic about their future income,[36] and Espenshade and Calhoun found that individuals who believed that illegal immigrants pushed up taxes were likely to have negative attitudes toward them.[37] Overall, then, for most scholars, an economic downturn is a necessary condition for increasing nativist or restrictionist sentiment.[38] Other research, meanwhile, has identified the circumstances under which self-interest may be activated. These circumstances include: when there are clear and substantial costs and benefits[39]; when there are severe but ambiguous costs and benefits, so that individuals may imagine extraordinary threats or gains[40]; when self-interest is "politicized"[41]; when an issue is highly salient[42]; and when behavior rather than opinions are under examination.[43]

It is thus reasonable to suggest that economic self-interest should have played an important role in the politicization of the illegal-immigration issue. In addition, it is plausible that the politicization could have been influenced by the perception that the undocumented imposed a general burden on the California economy and, by implication, were responsible for, or in some way exacerbated the effects of, the recession.

To be sure, the recession was especially acute in California, which when combined with the evidence that its residents exhibited stronger restrictionist sentiments than did Americans generally suggests a correlation between economic circumstances and anti-immigrant attitudes. Indeed, the trend line in figure 3.1 indicates that more Americans express restrictionist views when the economy is doing poorly; the rise in the level of restrictionist sentiment clearly coincides with the downturn in economic performance during the late 1970s/early 1980s and the early-to-mid 1990s.

However, as noted above, the *level* of sentiment is not the best measure of the issue's politicization; that belongs to the *intensity* of sentiment. The data in table 3.1 show that the intensity of that negative sentiment remained constant and low during the early 1990s, with approximately 2–3 percent of Californians identifying illegal immigration as the most pressing problem facing California. The intensity of Californians' feelings only increased dramatically in late 1993, as the recession was nearing its end. This suggests that the economic downturn did not directly politicize illegal immigration because it did not coincide with the increased salience of the issue. As with the number of illegal immigrants, the timing again appears wrong.

Other evidence, also taken from opinion polls, supports this suggestion. For example, in January/February 1993, people living in the San Fernando Valley were the most economically pessimistic residents of Los Angeles city, yet they were no more likely than other Los Angeles dwellers to view illegal immigration as their most important concern.[44] Furthermore, evidence from an *LA Times* September 1993 poll shows that anti-immigrant views were held across incomes, and even by those with self-identified "secure" personal finances. Fully 68 percent of Californians who believed their personal finances were secure also believed illegal immigration was a serious problem. Of those with self-identified "shaky" personal finances, 72 percent thought the same. The difference is within the poll's margin of error. Furthermore, 62 percent of Californians who thought the state was in good financial health also thought that illegal immigration was a major problem, as did 77 percent of those with pessimistic evaluations of the economy—again, not a major difference.[45]

The evidence shows that there was little difference in attitudes toward immigrants between those with positive and negative evaluations of their personal finances and, to a lesser extent, the general economy. Furthermore, the timing of the recession can tell us little about the sharp increase in the intensity of anti-immigrant sentiment in late 1993. This all suggests that the proposition that the recession *directly* politicized the illegal-immigration issue can be rejected. However, this does not mean that the recession was unimportant; it had a very important *indirect* influence.

Political Opportunism, Race, and the Indirect Effect of the Recession

American political parties are generally considered programmatically, ideologically, and organizationally weaker than their counterparts in other western democracies. Parties are usually defined as "loose coalitions of diverse interests," and the nature of the political system forces politicians to be individuals attached to a political party rather than representatives of a party. Moreover, politicians cannot rely solely or even mainly on the party machine and party support when competing for elective office.[46] For this reason, Riker compares American politicians to entrepreneurs in the market place. Both must constantly develop new products/policy alternatives and place them before the people. The aim of the entrepreneur is of course to make a profit. The politician meanwhile must construct a winning electoral coalition.[47]

While parties in the United States are weak, they are even weaker in California. It is therefore even more imperative that California's politicians construct majority coalitions at each election. This is a more important imperative for Republicans because more Californians identify with the Democrats than the GOP. Consequently, Californian politicians and especially Republican politicians seeking reelection cannot rely on partisan advantage or the party machine. Cain argues that in California it is important to win over the conservative, white males—often referred to as Reagan Democrats—who make up an important segment of the state's swing voters.[48] Following the advice of Cain and Riker, politicians can succeed by offering policy options around which a majority (the natural support plus the swing voters) can coalesce. If politicians are in a perilous electoral position, they may well decide to use an issue or policy option that they would not have otherwise used. Certainly, issues revolving around questions of nation, race, and immigration have been used by politicians throughout history and across continents as a way of whipping up sentiment and constructing coalitions.

In California in the early 1990s, many incumbent politicians were facing difficult reelection contests. The economy was in a deep recession, and, as is often the case during such times, there was widespread discontent with the political class and the state's executive. It is possible that some politicians, facing a problematic reelection contest during a prolonged and serious recession, decided to focus on illegal immigration in order to form a winning electoral coalition. The question then is, did California's politicians, for the reasons outlined above, politicize the illegal-immigration issue? The short answer is yes, but the story is longer. It begins in part on April 29, 1992.

On this day, the Los Angeles riots ignited in response to the not guilty verdicts handed down to the Los Angeles Police Department officers in the Rodney G. King case. Although the riots were not directly linked to illegal immigration, once again race, ethnicity, and immigration became a central point of discussion and contention. Ethnic tensions were especially noticeable between the black and Korean populations in Los Angeles. A *LA Times* survey of Los Angeles County analyzed the ethnic conflict and found a depressing picture with blacks increasingly suspicious of nonblack groups and vice versa. In the riot's aftermath Patrick Buchanan tried to use the illegal-immigration issue to construct an electoral coalition during the California Republican Party's presidential primaries.[49] Buchanan called for a trench to be dug along the U.S.-Mexico border and military troops to be used to prevent illegal immigration from Mexico. He also suggested that there should be a constitutional amendment to deny U.S. citizenship to children born in the United States to undocumented parents. Buchanan argued that illegal immigration threatened to turn California into a third world nation because of the social and economic problems immigrants engender.[50] He also did not baulk from raising questions about new immigrants' potential to assimilate to the American way, albeit based on what many considered to be a crude ethnocentric vision of American identity: "If we had to take a million immigrants in, say Zulus, next year, or Englishmen, and put them in Virginia, what group would be easier to assimilate and would cause less problems for the people of Virginia?"[51]

Buchanan's populist appeal had little popular appeal, however, and he was easily defeated by George Bush in the June 2, 1992, California primary. Yet Buchanan did win a majority of those who said that immigration was the key issue—although this group represented only one in fourteen primary voters at the time. Californians still regarded illegal immigration as a relatively unimportant issue compared with crime, the economy/jobs, and education (see table 3.1). Despite Buchanan's failed attempt to make the issue work for him, other politicians taking their lead from Buchanan also began to focus on illegal immigration during late 1992 and early 1993 in an attempt to create their own winning electoral coalitions. For example, in May 1992 during the Republican primary contest for Orange County's 45th Congressional District, Republican congressman Dan Rohrabacher claimed that illegal immigrants came to California for health and social services and were bankrupting the state. In November 1992, Los Angeles county supervisor Michael Antonovich claimed that illegal immigrants were a fiscal burden on the county and were therefore to blame for its budget crisis. He called for increased Border Patrol funding, tamper-proof identity cards for legal immigrants, quicker deportation hearings, and strict enforcement of immigration law. In the 1993 Los Angeles mayoral primaries Tom Houston claimed illegal immigrants were a drain on the city's resources and that the federal government should contribute to their costs.[52] U.S. senator Dianne Feinstein also tried to draw attention to the issue. Her and the others' efforts, however, continued to have little impact on the intensity of the anti-immigrant sentiment, and the issue remained un-politicized. By February 1993 still only 3 percent of Los Angeles–city residents placed illegal immigration as one of their top two concerns. This is despite 61 percent who said there were too many "foreign immigrants" in Los Angeles and 50 percent who thought illegal immigrants were responsible for a "great deal or a good amount" of the crime and street violence in Los Angeles.[53] And in early August 1993 still only 4 percent of southern Californians said illegal immigration was one of the top problems facing their community, well below crime and gangs (at 54%) and unemployment and the economy (20%), and even below graffiti (8%).[54]

Politicians failed to politicize the illegal-immigration issue between 1992 and early-to-mid 1993. Californians continued to view the issue with relative apathy despite the serious recession and the attendant job losses and the widespread belief that there were too many illegal immigrants in the state. However, California's Republican governor, Pete Wilson, changed this in August 1993. His intervention politicized the issue for millions of Californians.

Pete Wilson, first elected governor in November 1990, never enjoyed particularly high approval ratings. An actual slide in his ratings began in the spring of 1992 when he had a belligerent and confrontational standoff with the Democrat-controlled legislature. The conflict resulted in gridlock on the budget and other important issues. And it was not just the Democrats that Wilson managed to upset; he alienated many on the right of his own party when he raised taxes during his first term. The recession, a weak party system, and a natural Democratic advantage all further threatened his support. It is not surprising that in 1993, with only a year to go before the next gubernatorial contest, Wilson's approval ratings were the lowest of any governor in the state's history.[55]

In a first attempt to assuage the conservative right, deflect attention away from the recession, revive his ratings, and construct a winning electoral coalition, Wilson attacked welfare recipients toward the end of 1992. This attack, however, had no effect on his support. After this failure, Wilson's approval ratings (see table 3.4) and the results of hypothetical gubernatorial contests (table 3.5) suggested that he would face a difficult campaign. For example, in September 1992 62 percent of registered voters disapproved of his performance as governor while just 33 percent approved, giving him a net rating of −29 points. His net rating dropped further in October 1992 to −33 points before recovering slightly to −29 points in March 1993—the same position he had been in the previous September. Also in March 1993, *LA Times* poll respondents were asked who they would vote for if there were a gubernatorial election tomorrow between Wilson and Democratic State Treasurer and future Wilson challenger Kathleen Brown. Wilson lost the hypothetical contest by a worrying 22 percentage points. Trailing badly with the election on the horizon, it was time to make a move on a new issue—Wilson chose illegal immigration.

Certainly, Wilson was not the first politician to use immigration in these circumstances. As Johnson notes, "[h]arsh immigration policies historically have been proposed by those searching for answers to the particular political, social, and economic woes of the day."[56] Part of the problem for Wilson was that as California's chief executive he was receiving a lot of the blame for the poor state

Table 3.4   Governor Wilson's Approval Ratings, May 1991–May 1994

Month and Year	Approve	Disapprove	Difference	Notes
May 1991	52	34	+18	CA AA
Oct. 1991	41	47	−6	CA RV
Dec. 1991	38	55	−17	CA RV
Apr. 1992	44	48	−4	CA RV
May 1992	43	52	−9	CA RV
Aug. 1992	38	55	−17	OC RV
Sept. 1992	33	62	−29	CA RV
Oct. 1992	28	61	−33	CA RV
Mar. 1993	30	59	−29	CA AA
Sept. 1993	37	45	−8	CA RV
Oct. 1993	34	56	−22	CA RV
Mar. 1994	42	50	−8	CA RV
May 1994	39	52	−13	CA RV

Notes. All entries are percentages except Differences, which are percentage points.

CA = California sample; OC = Orange County sample; RV = registered voters; AA = all adults.

Question: Do you approve or disapprove of the way Pete Wilson is handling his job as governor?

Sources. *LA Times Polls*, see appendix A for details.

Table 3.5 Results of Hypothetical Gubernatorial Contests, March 1993–March 1994

Month and Year	Wilson	Brown	Difference	Wilson	Garamendi	Difference
Mar. 1993	31	53	−22	34	51	−17
Sept. 1993	40	48	−8	39	49	−10
Oct. 1993	34	49	−15	31	49	−18
Mar. 1994	41	51	−10	42	47	−5

Notes: Entries are percentages except Differences, which are percentage points.
Question: If the general election were held today and the candidates for governor were Brown/ Garamendi and Wilson, who would you vote for?
Asked of registered voters.
Source: *LA Times Polls;* see appendix A for details.

of the economy. For this reason, the recession contributed partly to Wilson's precarious electoral position and, therefore, was an important motivation in his focus on illegal immigration. But, as the discussion above demonstrated, the recession on its own cannot be held directly responsible for the issue's politicization; its impact was more subtle and indirect.

On August 9, 1993, Wilson moved dramatically and decisively by sending a public letter to the federal government. In the letter Wilson proposed to deny U.S. citizenship to children born in the United States to undocumented parents; to introduce a "legal residency" card to stop illegal immigrants taking jobs or receiving welfare; and to deny public education and even emergency healthcare to illegal aliens. Furthermore, he encouraged the federal government to use its influence during the North American Free Trade Agreement (NAFTA) negotiations "as a tool to secure the cooperation of the Mexican government in stopping massive illegal immigration on the Mexican side of the border."[57]

Whether the measures would have stemmed the flow of illegal immigrants into the country generally and California specifically is debatable. Yet the question of whether his proposals would have provided a successful solution to illegal immigration to some extent misses the point. The reaction that the proposals produced rather than their feasibility is what mattered. The exercise got Wilson noticed, in his state and in the nation at large. Wilson ensured that he received maximum attention by publishing his letter in paid advertising space of the West Coast editions of the *New York Times*, *USA Today*, and the *Washington Post*.

In the event Wilson's letter increased the salience of illegal immigration and the intensity of anti-immigrant sentiment. As the *LA Times* noted on August 22, "the [illegal-immigration] issue had moved to the nation's front burner and loomed as an explosive topic for debate in the 1994 elections."[58] Moreover, Wilson's focus on the issue forced senior California Democrats to state their positions—against their political and electoral instincts.[59] For example, Democratic U.S. senator Barbara Boxer suggested on August 17 that the National Guard be brought in to assist the Border Patrol. While disagreeing with Wilson that illegal immigrants should be excluded from receipt of public services and rejecting the idea of a constitutional amendment, Democratic U.S. senator Dianne Feinstein proposed on October 20 a $1 border toll with the proceeds going to increase border security.[60] Democratic State Treasurer Kathleen Brown, future guberna-torial challenger to Wilson, proposed on September 29 that illegal aliens in state prisons should be deported. Even renowned liberal Democrats felt forced to put forward proposals for solving the "problem." For instance, Assembly Speaker Willie Brown proposed that businesses that hired illegal immigrants should have their assets seized.

Of the various proposals offered by high-profile politicians, Governor Wilson's were the least popular. Seventy-three percent approved of Senator Boxer's plan to use the National Guard, 73 percent Senator Feinstein's $1 toll, and 56 percent Speaker Brown's asset seizing idea. In comparison, only 54 percent supported Wilson's proposal to amend the Fourteenth Amendment to deny automatic citizenship to children born in the United States to undocumented parents, 39 percent supported his proposal to prohibit illegal immigrants from attending public schools, and just 23 percent supported his proposal to deny medical care to illegal aliens.[61] The actual support that his proposals garnered is less important, however, than the attention they generated—and in the latter Wilson certainly succeeded. His letter and the debate it engendered politicized the illegal-immigration issue for millions of Californians. In March 1993, only 2 percent of Californians had said immigration was *the* most important problem. However, in the next directly comparable *LA Times* poll in early September, 9 percent said it was the most important problem (a 350% increase) and 16 percent said it was one of the top two most important ones.[62]

The emphasis placed on illegal immigration by Wilson and public debate that ensued from August 1993 onwards had a knock-on effect. Other major politi-cians in California offered their own solutions, and these solutions were reported and discussed in the media. This, in turn, encouraged other politicians to focus on the issue, further reinforcing the issue's newly found importance. For example, thirty-eight immigration bills were introduced in the 1994 session of the California legislature, the majority by Republicans.[63] An *LA Times* editorial made a succinct point: "Surprised by all the sudden bills in Sacramento dealing with the hot-button issue of illegal immigration? Hey, it's an election year."[64]

Wilson's focus on illegal immigration achieved two ends. As noted above, it politicized the issue, as measured by the substantial increase in the *intensity* of negative sentiment toward illegal immigrants. Moreover, it played well for Wilson personally. Felix de la Torre, a policy analyst for the Mexican American Legal Defense and Educational Fund (MALDEF), commented:

> Wilson was coming at different issues at different times, trying to see what sparked a reaction with the public . . . Wilson hit an immigration note and saw [his polls] jump. From that point on, he kept at the immigration issue. He began to pick up on it as it was working for him.[65]

Although Wilson's focus on illegal immigration was not the sole reason for his improving fortunes,[66] he had found an issue around which he thought he could construct a winning coalition.[67] The polls bear this out. In the September *LA Times* poll, a net 14 percent of all respondents felt more favorable toward Wilson because of his proposals, as did a net 19 percent of registered voters, 15 percent of registered Democrats and 42 percent of the elderly. These net gains were repeated among Republicans and Independents as well as Democrats, and also amongst liberals, conservatives and moderates. Only Latino respondents, at −13 percent, viewed Wilson less favorably as a result of his proposals.[68]

Partly as a result of his focus on illegal immigration and its mainly positive effect on Californians' perceptions of him, Wilson's approval/disapproval rating improved to a net −8 percentage points in September 1993, compared to −29 points in March 1993 and −33 points in October 1992 (see table 3.4). This improvement was also reflected in the *LA Times* poll's "hypothetical" gubernatorial contests. In the September 1993 contest against Kathleen Brown, Wilson trailed by 8 percentage points compared to 22 in March 1993. Against Democratic Insurance Commissioner John Garamendi, he trailed by 10 points compared to 17 in the March poll (see table 3.5). Wilson's new issue clearly played well for him.

> [T]he 60 year old Mr. Wilson has succeeded not because voters have deep affection for him (they do not), but because he is smart, reaches out to moderates, thrives on the game of politics and is relentless in practicing it. That helps explain why, having presided over the biggest recession in California since the [Great] Depression and after being 20 points down in some opinion polls last summer, Mr. Wilson is rebounding in his race for a second term. He is helped by an economy that is beginning to emerge from a recession, but also by his own political acumen in shifting the debate to crime and immigration . . . The strategy of Mr. Wilson, who has long surrounded himself with the same close aides, is simple: set the agenda by seizing on highly emotional issues, and never let a rival get the upper hand.[69]

Wilson was always careful not to make illegal immigration a question of race or ethnicity. Instead, he tried to turn it into a financial issue. His argument had two strands: first, at the state level illegal immigrants took more in services than they paid in taxes, and, second, the federal government should reimburse California for the costs of educating, incarcerating, and providing health care to illegal immigrants. By implicitly blaming illegal immigrants for the recession and exacerbating the effects of it, Wilson was able to construct an argument that exonerated himself from culpability for the recession. Utilizing these financial arguments, Wilson provoked a high-profile standoff with the Democrat-controlled California legislature and launched a three-stage $2.5 billion claim against the federal government. He also conducted several "illegal immigration blitzes" during which he devoted most of his time over several days to the issue. The standoff, the claim, and the blitzes ensured the salience of illegal immigration throughout 1994.

Wilson's first blitz came in the last ten days of April 1994. He made a high-profile visit to the California-Mexico border, announced that more California National Guard troops would be deployed on the border, attended and spoke at conferences on immigration, and outlined the reasons why he was suing the federal government.[70] On May 13, 1994, Wilson launched his second blitz with a two-week advertising campaign costing one million dollars. The advertisement pictured a small group of Latinos illegally crossing the border, with a voice-over commenting:

> They keep coming. Two-million illegal immigrants in California. The federal government won't stop them at the border, yet requires us to pay billions to take care of them.[71]

The ad created uproar. Journalist John Marelius, writing in the *San Diego Tribune*, described the tone of the ad thus:

> [It] showed blurry black-and-white footage of people dodging cars as they dash through the San Ysidro border crossing . . . [accompanied by] pulsating cop-show-style music and an announcer who menacingly intones, "they keep coming."[72]

Wilson's campaign manager, John Gorton, claimed that Wilson was not trying to scapegoat anyone or whip up anti-immigrant hysteria. The ad, he argued, merely focused on a public issue and informed Californians how the governor proposed to address their concerns. Wilson had not created the issue, Gorton rather disingenuously claimed: "You don't create problems in politics. Problems are either there or they're not there. Picturing them is what you do."[73] Yet perhaps unsurprisingly, Wilson's ad, campaign, and message drew considerable criticism of immigrant bashing from civil rights organizations and his potential gubernatorial opponents. Darry Sragow, campaign director for potential Democratic gubernatorial hopeful John Garamendi, argued that the refrain "They keep coming" was specific enough to ensure that Wilson was referring to Mexican illegals. And Democratic U.S. representative Xavier Becerra from Los Angeles compared Wilson's ad to the infamous 1988 Willie Horton ad, which played on white voters' fears of black sexuality and violence. Becerra claimed that Wilson was playing the race card in a political maneuver that could not fail:

> How many immigrants can vote? None. How many do you find contributing massive amounts of money to campaigns? None. It's a no lose strategy for him.[74]

Other critics stressed that during his tenure as U.S. senator, Wilson had done nothing to help reduce illegal immigration. They argued that his support for the 1986 Immigration Reform and Control Act, and in particular his championing of its Special Agricultural Workers (SAW) provisions, made it easier for illegal farm workers to enter the country and to naturalize under the act's provisions. The SAW amendment resulted in 1.1 million immigrants being granted permanent residency, despite farmers' claims that they needed only 350,000 workers. Wilson later claimed that his version of the amendment would have required the guest-workers to return home after the harvest. Mr. Alan Nelson, then Commissioner of the INS and later coauthor of Proposition 187, clashed with Senator Wilson over the SAW program. Nelson wanted immigrants to prove they had been agricultural workers before they were allowed into the country, while Wilson opposed this in a letter to President Reagan, claiming that crops were "rotting in the fields" because the INS refused to let in farm workers. Wilson won the argument and the workers were allowed in on the condition that they later presented proof they had recently been agricultural workers.[75]

Such criticisms failed to dampen Wilson's enthusiasm for the illegal-immigration issue. On April 29, at the end of his first blitz, Wilson filed the first of three claims against the federal government to reimburse California's costs for providing services to illegal immigrants. The first suit called for a $377-million reimbursement of costs for incarcerating illegal-immigrant felons.[76] This was followed by a $370-million claim, announced on May 31, 1994, for reimbursement of costs for providing emergency medical care for illegal indigents. While the federal government already matched California dollar for dollar, Wilson wanted Washington to bear the full cost. A federal law, passed during President Reagan's tenure and for which Senator Wilson voted, mandated the states to provide limited health care for illegal aliens under the federal Medicaid program—known as Medi-Cal in California.[77] The third stage involved the filing of a $1.7-billion claim for the costs incurred educating illegal-immigrant children.[78]

Critics pointed out that Wilson's claims for reimbursement were based on gross estimates, thus highlighting the cost of providing services to illegal immigrants without balancing the tax income and economic benefits received from them. As well as inflating costs in this way, Wilson ensured that he would receive maximum press coverage over an extended period by filing each of the suits separately, thus keeping the issue on the agenda and in people's minds for longer. The claims also provided Wilson with the opportunity to make several high-profile trips to Washington to lobby the federal government for reimbursement. Furthermore, the suits were a no-lose strategy. If he got the money from the federal government, he could claim victory. If the money was not forthcoming, he could criticize an unresponsive central government and blame illegal immigrants for draining the state's resources.

In a further attempt to keep the issue on the political agenda, Governor Wilson provoked a high-profile clash with the Democrat-controlled California legislature. Wilson's proposed budget for the 1994–1995 fiscal year passed in both chambers of the legislature before the start of the fiscal year on July 1, 1994. While this was relatively quick compared with previous years, Wilson then refused to sign the budget until the legislature capitulated to his demand that they pass an additional bill removing state-funded prenatal care from undocumented pregnant women.[79] Wilson claimed the changes would save the state $50 million and discourage potential illegal-immigrant women from coming to California to give birth. The prenatal care bill passed in the Senate, but the Assembly refused to pass the measure. Wilson threatened to use his line-item veto to cut spending already targeted at legal residents if the Assembly continued to block its passage. Wilson's press secretary, Sean Walsh, making the issue a zero-sum game, argued "the citizens of the state of California, the legal residents, are not going to be pleased to see additional programs that benefit them cut. Legal residents are going to be cut at the expense of illegal immigrants."[80]

Democrats in the Assembly argued that Wilson was posturing for political effect and that he was being short-termist. They argued that money spent on prenatal care saves money later and, because any child born to an illegal immigrant on American soil is automatically a U.S. citizen, they would be automatically entitled to postnatal care anyway. They also pointed out that Wilson had used this same logic to defend his other preventive healthcare programs.[81]

Whatever the criticisms from Wilson's detractors, his reelection campaign provided and was built on a simple, powerful, and effective message: illegal immigrants committed crime, took jobs, and exacerbated the effects of the recession through their use of public services. The California public thought that Wilson had the best ideas on crime and illegal immigration, and crime was consistently one of Californians' top policy concerns (see table 3.1).[82]

By focusing on crime and illegal immigration and, by implication, linking these two issues, Wilson further strengthened his position. About half of

Californians already believed that illegal immigrants committed "a great deal or good amount of crime and street violence," and research has shown that such people are more likely to view illegal immigration as a serious problem.[83] Some scholars argue that fearing crime is actually a symbolic affect—that is, fearing and getting "tough" on crime, while ostensibly nonracial, symbolize whites' racial and racist attitudes toward nonwhites.[84] Whatever the scholarly debate, Wilson helped reinforce the immigrant-crime nexus by demanding the federal government reimburse the state's costs for incarcerating illegal immigrants. This made very public the notion that illegal immigrants committed crime; they must do so because it cost California $377 million each year to keep them in prison. The other part of Wilson's message was equally effective. Illegal immigrants exacerbated the effects of the recession and posed an additional threat to Americans' job security because the undocumented earned lower wages at a time when firms were seeking to minimize costs. The reality may have been different than the message, but the illegal immigration–crime-jobs triumvirate constituted a simple and powerful argument. Explaining his election strategy to reporters between rallies, Wilson said:

> In a state as large as this people don't have time for a lot of fine points. You have to be crystal clear. We think people are most deeply moved in three areas: crime and immigration—a real sense of rage about those—and jobs, which is their broadest, most long-lasting concern. So that's what we hit on, morning, noon, and night.[85]

It was noted above that many commentators and politicians viewed Wilson's emphasis on illegal immigrants with suspicion. After Wilson sent his August open letter to the federal government, a *New York Times* editorial used phrases such as "nativist demagogy" to describe his attack.[86] Writing in the same paper, Anthony Lewis argued in an op-ed piece that "much of what is going on in California today is old-fashioned nativism or xenophobia."[87] Lewis suggested that politicians such as Governor Wilson had whipped up anti-immigrant hysteria for political purposes. Wilson defended his letter to the federal government and his focus on illegal immigration, arguing that it had "nothing to do with race. This has to do with facts."[88] "No one is condemning illegal immigrants. It is those in Washington we should condemn."[89] Phil Romero, Wilson's chief economic adviser, repeated his boss's message, saying the focus on illegal immigration "has nothing to do with race. His sole concern is with lifting the financial burden caused by illegal immigrants."[90] The governor explained that illegal immigration cost the state $2.5 billion each year because of federal government mandates. He tried to turn the issue, at least ostensibly, to a question of federalism and economics and away from race. Wilson did enjoy a vigorous defense from Alan Nelson, former Commissioner of the INS and future coauthor of Prop. 187, in a *New York Times* op-ed piece. Nelson pointed to a dichotomy between the critics' venom and the widespread support—80 to 90 percent—for tighter immigration policies among the American public. He argued that

> [p]oliticians are taking heed: liberals and conservatives admit that the burden of the illegals is too heavy, in education, health and welfare benefits, and can no longer be

tolerated. . . . Let the public's voice be heard. It wants the rhetoric translated into specific and responsible actions.[91]

Despite Wilson's public protestations that race was not an issue, the context and subtext of the debate suggest otherwise. Many Californians conflate illegal immigrant and illegal Mexican; the public battle against illegal immigration takes place at the United States' southern border, not its northern one or at its airports or ports; and the vast majority of deportable aliens located are of Mexican origin.[92] Moreover, Wilson's letter to the federal government called specifically on the Mexican government to orchestrate a police crackdown to prevent illegal immigration from its territory. The governor's television ads featured a group of identifiably Latino people illegally crossing the border. And his joint focus on illegal immigration and crime in a state where a majority of people believed that Latinos were the most violent reinforced attitudes that Mexican illegal immigration was the problem that required action. Finally and perhaps most importantly, Wilson was closely associated with Proposition 187 throughout 1994. He used it and it used him. Although the symbiotic nature of Wilson's anti-immigrant strategy and the campaign for Prop. 187 are addressed in detail in the next two chapters, it is worth noting here that some Prop. 187 supporters were less timid than Wilson about addressing questions of race and nationality. For example, in a letter to the *New York Times*, Linda R. Hayes, Prop. 187's Southern California media director said:

> By flooding the state with 2 million illegal aliens to date, and increasing that figure each of the following 10 years, Mexicans in California would number 15 million to 20 million by 2004. During those 10 years about 5 million to 8 million Californians would have emigrated to other states. If these trends continue, a Mexico-controlled California could vote to establish Spanish as the sole language of California, 10 million more English-speaking Californians could flee, and there could be a statewide vote to leave the Union and annex California to Mexico.[93]

Wilson's close association with Prop. 187 further reinforced the importance of racial constructions in the illegal-immigration debate and should lead commentators to question Wilson's ostensibly race-neutral position. The important question here, however, is whether race was an important factor in the illegal-immigration issue's early politicization? While the available data do not permit a definitive answer, evidence from a September 1993 poll is instructive. Although 45 percent of Californians made no distinction between illegal-immigrant groups, 32 percent said that illegal Latino residents were a specific cause of problems in California while only 16 percent said Asians.[94] This difference suggest that racial prejudice, or at least animosity, contributed to the issue's politicization because a large number, although not quite a majority, of Californians identified a specific race or nationality of illegal-immigrant as the cause of the state's problems. However, as with the recession and the absolute number of illegal immigrants, there is little or no evidence to suggest that racial constructions of identity were central in the politicization of illegal immigration. Prejudice on its own did not politicize the issue. Race was, rather, probably a facilitator of politicization because it influenced some individuals' receptivity to the message that illegal immigration was a problem requiring remedial action.

Whatever the explanations for why Wilson succeeded in politicizing the issue, his focus on it had the desired effect by helping him over the first hurdle to reelection when he won easily the Republican gubernatorial nomination in the June 7, 1994, primaries.[95] After a surprising ratings slip in October 1993,[96] Wilson's support continued to increase through early-to-mid 1994 as he remained focused on illegal immigration and crime. Kathleen Brown meanwhile won the Democratic gubernatorial nomination to challenge Wilson.

The *LA Times* primary exit poll found that the issue of top concern to voters was crime, cited by 36 percent, followed by education (25%), immigration (23%), and the economy (20%). Wilson was best placed to capitalize on these concerns in the forthcoming contest. An earlier March poll showed that 37 percent of respondents thought Wilson had the best ideas on handling crime and 16 percent thought Brown. On immigration, 35 percent thought Wilson had the best ideas and 11 percent thought Brown. So Wilson led Brown on the issues of crime and immigration while Brown had the upper hand on education and the economy. Wilson was therefore best placed on the first and third most important issues (as expressed in the exit poll) and Brown on the second and fourth.

Even more encouraging for Wilson was the low level of support for Brown among moderate, independent, and elderly Democrats. Victory for Brown in the gubernatorial contest in November would be difficult with only strong support from liberal Democrats. Brown did poorly in the primary among Democrats who said crime and immigration were important issues. Only 36 percent of Democrats who voted for Brown's primary challengers said they would vote for Brown in November. In comparison, 46 percent of Republicans who voted for Wilson's challenger said they would vote for Wilson.[97] Furthermore, an article in the *LA Times* predicted "Wilson could extract some political benefit from his support of the [Prop. 187] measure. It is favored by majorities of independents, moderates, whites, the elderly and women—all groups Wilson must court aggressively in the fall if he is to win."[98] It appears then that Wilson's strategy of winning over moderate swing voters by using the illegal-immigration tactic was working.

In sum, Wilson first politicized the illegal-immigration issue, and this helped him in his primary victory. His August 1993 letter to the federal government engendered a high-profile debate on illegal immigration. This and his continued focus on it through his claims against the federal government and his immigration blitzes were responsible for the early politicization of the issue. While racism, the recession, and high immigrant numbers were not directly responsible for the politicization, it would be wrong to suggest that these three factors were unimportant. Without the recession, it is unlikely that incumbent politicians would have felt the need to focus on illegal immigration because they would not have been in such a perilous electoral position. Moreover, issues revolving around questions of nation, race and immigration have been used by politicians throughout history as a way of constructing coalitions and whipping up sentiment, especially during times of economic difficulty. Race and recession are intimate bedfellows, and Pete Wilson did nothing new by playing the immigration card; the tradition of using race as a wedge issue had already been well established. Without the recession, illegal immigrants residing in California, and possibly some racial prejudice, it is unlikely that the issue could have been politicized.

Thus, these factors were necessary but insufficient conditions for politicization. The catalyst was Governor Pete Wilson. Wilson was, therefore, central and instrumental in establishing an environment that energized anti-immigrant activists. Indeed, less than two months after Wilson sent his letter, Proposition 187 was written.

Chapter 4

The Increasing Salience of Illegal Immigration and the Qualification of Proposition 187

Direct democracy was introduced in many western states of the United States in the early twentieth century. The Progressives wanted to heal what they saw as the political system's deep wounds. They believed that special interests, notably the railroad companies in California, were manipulating and bribing politicians and corrupting the political system for their own selfish ends. "There was only one kind of politics and that was corrupt politics. It didn't matter whether a man was a Republican or Democrat. The Southern Pacific Railroad controlled both parties, and he either had to stay out of the game altogether or play it with the railroad," suggested a California journalist writing in 1896.[1] The Progressives believed that making the system more democratic could save democracy from itself. While the founding fathers had feared the tyranny of the masses, the Progressives sought to give more power to the people to provide a countervailing force to the special interests. To do so they introduced a number of reforms, including the secret ballot, the direct election of U.S. senators, women's suffrage, and primary elections. Another key reform was direct democracy, of which there are three main types: the recall, referendum, and initiative. Voters can use the recall to remove an elected politician from office before the end of his or her term. Referendums allow legislatures to place a law before the people for their approval or rejection. Initiatives, which are the most controversial of the three types of direct democracy, differ from referendums in that the citizens themselves write and adjudicate on the proposed change to the law. Initiatives are thus "tools of the people" because the people make the law directly, bypassing the traditional lawmaking institutions.[2] Or at least that is the theory. According to critics of initiatives, the practice is very different.

Part of the problem, critics argue, is that the initiative process is structured so as to exclude the very people that it was designed to serve: that is, ordinary citizens.[3] A quick review of the initiative process shows why. Somebody must first decide the law needs to be changed. But it is not only an individual citizen who can initiate a change—politicians, interest groups, corporations, and unions can also do so. Indeed, critics say, the initiative process today discriminates against ordinary individuals and in favor of special interests. The reason why has a lot to do with resources. Although the decision to try to change the law may be free, nothing else is. First, a proposed law must be written to replace or amend the old one, and it is usually necessary to employ lawyers to do this complex, detailed, often expensive work—and no state funding is available. The proposed law is usually then sent to state officials for "titling." Officials give the law a name and usually provide a brief summary of the measure. After titling is the stage at which about four-fifths of initiatives fail: qualification.[4] Proponents of the proposed initiative are required to collect, usually within three to five months depending on the state, a certain number of registered voters' signatures in order to qualify it for the ballot. The numbers in all states are daunting, but especially so in California, the most populous in the nation. There, about 400,000 signatures were required in the mid 1990s if the initiative proposed a change to statute law, and about 650,000 if constitutional law.[5] And these are the validated totals. Given that a proportion of the signatures will be ruled invalid by state officials, signature collectors have to gather an extra hundred thousand or so to be safe. Most organizations do not have anywhere near the capacity to collect so many signatures themselves. Instead, they pay professional firms to do it, which can be very expensive. The price depends to some extent on the initiative issue and the number of other initiatives trying to qualify for the ballot; while it averages about a dollar a signature, it can rise to three or four dollars. If enough valid signatures are collected within the allotted time frame the initiative is placed on the primary or general election ballot paper for the consideration of the whole electorate.[6] By this time the initiative will most likely have attracted a considerable opposition; thus, qualification usually signals the beginning of an expensive campaign as both sides seek to persuade the electorate of the merits or demerits of the proposition. Election day rarely signals the end of the campaign as most successful initiatives now face a judicial challenge. And so, as the lawyers who wrote the initiative are drafted in to defend it in court, the wheel turns full circle and the costs continue to escalate.

It is little wonder then that critics of the initiative process agree with former California governor Jerry Brown's analysis: "The initiative was an instrument to give the people the power to make their own laws, but it is very rapidly becoming a tool of the special interests."[7] And Brown was speaking in the 1970s when the costs were much lower. Today's costs are such that the initiative process is beyond the means of most ordinary citizens and grassroots organizations. It is, say critics, only the wealthy who have pockets deep enough to fund an initiative campaign. For example, $29.6 million was spent by business organizations and labor unions in favor of and against California's Prop. 226, a 1998 initiative that proposed unions must get their members' authorization before spending money for political purposes (it lost). In the same year $92 million was spent on Prop. 5, which sought to liberalize gaming on Indian reservations in California (it won). In total over one quarter billion dollars was spent on initiative campaigns in 1998 alone.[8]

The above evidence is rather anecdotal, however. More systematic analyses show that while money is positively correlated with votes,[9] it can rarely buy a victory.[10] In other words, wealthy special interests are effective using their monetary resources to defeat initiatives that threaten their interests, but are not particularly effective at changing the status quo in their favor. However, these analyses in turn fail to take into account that many grassroots groups fail to get their initiative onto the ballot in the first place because they have neither the monetary resources to pay a professional signature-gathering firm nor the organizational capacity to collect the signatures themselves. In this light, grassroots groups appear greatly disadvantaged.[11]

As we shall see in detail below, there was considerable debate during the campaign about who was "behind" Proposition 187 and what their motives were. Some critics of the initiative argued it was the product of special interests—this time, elective politicians (mis)using for their own ends the "people's process." In particular, California's Republican governor, Pete Wilson, was accused of being the brainchild of the initiative and the California Republican Party its financial sponsor. Wilson, they argued, facing a difficult election contest during an economic downturn, needed an issue around which he could construct a winning electoral coalition. Thus, he created a hysterical anti-immigrant climate, funded Prop. 187's qualification, and rode it back to the governor's mansion.[12] While Wilson's use of direct democracy procedures to support his political ambitions has been well documented by Ellis,[13] Proposition 187's sponsors and supporters deny that he was involved in its genesis and qualification, as did Wilson himself and his campaign managers.[14] The extent to which Prop. 187 was a product of special interests is an important question. Prop. 187 may be viewed by history more benignly if it was a genuine grassroots mobilization based on Californians' legitimate fear of the consequences of large-scale illegal immigration than if it was a vehicle for elective politicians to hold onto office. Another important question is the extent to which the most contemporary backlash against illegal immigrants was the product of a genuine, organic concern of the American public or a product of elite manipulation of mass opinion. Surprisingly, given the historical and political significance of Prop. 187 and the wider anti-immigrant impulse, neither question has received a comprehensive answer. One aim of this and other chapters is to suggest answers to these questions.

Before moving on to the birth of Prop. 187, it is worth noting that initiatives—whether grassroots or elite led—have also been criticized for threatening minority rights. Prop. 187 was no exception. The white majority was accused of targeting Latinos (including those living legally in California) and immigrants (the undocumented especially, but the legally resident too). California has witnessed many initiatives that have sought to exclude, discriminate against, and generally make life unpleasant for racial, sexual, or political minorities. The problem according to critics is that the majoritarian nature of the process combined with the absence of the checks and balances found in the traditional lawmaking process means that minority rights have little protection against majority tyranny.

Several scholars have shown that minority rights are particularly subject to abuse by the initiative process.[15] For example, Barbara Gamble found that "Citizen initiatives that restrict civil rights experience extraordinary electoral success: voters have approved over three-quarters of these, while endorsing only a third of *all* initiatives and popular referendums."[16] Moreover, the courts are less likely to strike down laws made directly by the people than those made by politicians because they fear the wrath of popular disapproval.[17] However, other scholars have argued that anti-minority initiatives actually make up a small proportion of those placed on the ballot,[18] and that it is not direct democracy per se that threatens minority rights but the size of the constituency in which the vote is taken.[19] The logic, following that of the founding fathers, is that small homogeneous constituencies threaten minority rights more than larger heterogeneous ones. Moreover, scholars have also shown that racial minorities—Latinos and African and Asian Americans—in California usually find themselves on the winning side of an initiative.[20]

The evidence, then, is mixed. On one side, it suggests that we should not be surprised to discover that Prop. 187 is a child of special interests who sought to persecute California's minorities for political gain. On the other side, however, the evidence suggests that we should be cautious about accepting such a story. The remainder of this chapter tests these competing claims. It investigates the characters and groups that came together to write Prop. 187 and it examines how the initiative qualified successfully for the ballot.

The Characters behind Proposition 187

Prop. 187's life began in inauspicious circumstances. It is doubtful that its authors could have imagined the political and cultural impact it would go on to have in California and the nation at large. The person who started it all was Ron Prince.[21] Prince, like many other characters behind Prop. 187, resided and worked in Orange County, California.[22] According to some sources, he first became interested in the illegal-immigration issue when an alleged illegal immigrant defrauded him of $500,000. The person in question was Leonard Thomas Chornomud. In fact, court records show that Chornomud was not an illegal immigrant, but a legal U.S. resident immigrant of Canadian birth. Chornomud and Prince were friends and business partners but both relationships turned sour when each made accusations of fraud against the other. The resulting court case saw Prince file a claim for a $70,000 loss—not the $500,000 he had stated. The case ended in May 1993 when Prince was awarded $32,000 from Chornomud.[23] Interestingly, Prince's first lawyer on the case, William Baker, sued Prince for $9,643 when he refused to pay Baker's costs. After Prince had dropped Baker from the case, Prince filed a petition with the California secretary of state for an initiative proposition that would have required every member of the bar to be recertified every four years. Prop. 187 then was not Prince's first attempt to use the initiative process to right a perceived wrong.[24]

However, Prince later denied that the Chornomud incident was important in persuading him that something needed to be done about illegal immigration. He said that he first started paying attention to the "problem" after the passage of the Immigration Reform and Control Act (IRCA) in 1986. Prince suggested that an amnesty was not an appropriate solution:

> You have a situation were millions of people are committing a crime [by crossing the border illegally]. The government says it can no longer control the situation so it says the situation is no longer illegal.[25]

For Prince, though, it was not just a matter of principle. Prince lived in

> Tustin, which is next to Santa Ana, the illegal immigration center of Orange County. We are talking about such a mass of people. It's like a street festival. You have people

on the street with no work just milling around. There are too many people for too few jobs.[26]

Prince clearly thought there was a problem that needed addressing, but why did he choose to use the initiative process? As with some other proponents of what was to become Proposition 187, Prince decided

> To go the initiative route after failing to get anything done in the state legislature. The answer kept coming back that no one will touch this with a barge pole. At that point, it was evident that the only way any legislation would get passed was through the initiative process. [I thought,] "If I can't find a legislator willing, I'll have to do it."[27]

Once Prince had decided that something needed to be done, he approached Robert and Barbara Kiley in mid-to-late 1993—after Wilson had sent his letter about illegal immigration to the federal government.[28] At the time, Barbara Kiley was mayor of Yorba Linda in Orange County and Robert Kiley (her husband) was a self-employed political consultant who had worked mainly with Republican candidates.[29] Although Robert Kiley was a political consultant, he claimed that he "believe[d] in this [immigration] issue. This was not a thing about money . . . We're consultants and we like to be paid, but that's not what this is about."[30] Prince and the Kileys had lunch and Prince talked to them about illegal immigration. Robert Kiley suggested to Prince that before they did anything else they should see if there was any public interest in the issue. Consequently, Prince and the Kileys sat down together and wrote a simple question that they would consult ordinary Californians on:

> "Do you believe that illegal immigration is a problem in California?" Ron went and stood in front of a market—just picked the market out of the blue—for one hour and got over one hundred signatures. And with each signature came a story. They thought [illegal immigration] was affecting California in the areas of education, crime, welfare—[in fact,] it was affecting California just about everywhere they could see.[31]

This test of public opinion convinced Prince and the Kileys to move forward. Their next step was to approach Harold Ezell. Ezell had previously been the Immigration and Naturalization Service's (INS) Western Commissioner and was a moderately well known figure in California because of his sometimes-controversial statements on illegal immigration and his media-friendly persona. Ezell had once created a storm of controversy for suggesting that illegal aliens should be "caught, skinned and fried."[32] And another key proponent of Prop. 187 joked that Ezell had never met a television camera he didn't like.[33] In spite of this, Ezell was approached because:

> With his expertise and knowledge—not only with the issue but also of the people who might have been involved with this issue for quite a while—we thought he would have been a great source of information and contacts that we could basically build the campaign from or around.[34]

Ezell fulfilled their hopes by bringing the Orange County anti-immigrant activists Bill King and Barbara Coe on board.[35] By her own admission, Coe first became concerned about illegal immigration after the 1986 IRCA amnesty when she was working for the Anaheim police department. She claimed that police officers she spoke to said the post-1986 increase in "violent crime, gang activity and narcotic activity . . . was primarily due the illegal-immigration problem."[36] However, the issue was not politicized personally for Coe until late 1991. At the time, she was

> Responsible for a crippled World War II veteran. He was getting Medi-Cal . . . As a veteran, he was also getting SSI, which of course he had paid into over all his years. Out of the clear blue sky, I was called into social services and told at that point in time that he would be denied these benefits. And I was further told that billions of tax dollars were being put out to illegal aliens for these same benefits that he was being denied. That was really what got me started.[37]

Coe consequently decided that she was going to try to do something about the "problem" and formed the anti-illegal-immigrant group Citizens for Action Now (CAN) in early 1992 with Bill King, a retired Border Patrol chief. Shortly afterwards Coe and King formed an anti-immigrant umbrella organization in June 1992 to bring together the small and disparate anti-immigrant groups already active in Orange County and California. This group was named the California Coalition for Immigration Reform (CCIR).[38] When Coe met Prince for the first time in mid-to-late 1993 Prince wanted an assurance from Coe that if he got the initiative off the ground she would ensure that the CCIR would "spearhead the [signature-gathering] effort."[39]

Ezell also contacted Alan Nelson. Nelson had been the INS Commissioner (the top official in the federal agency) during Reagan's presidency, and he had appointed Ezell to his position as Western Commissioner.[40] At the time Ezell approached him, Nelson was working as a lobbyist in Sacramento, California, for the Washington-based restrictionist group Federation for American Immigration Reform (FAIR) and had recently had some minor successes pushing four anti-immigrant bills through the California legislature. Nelson was to become one of the most important proponents of the Prop. 187.

Writing the Proposition

After the preliminary meetings between Ron Prince, Robert and Barbara Kiley, and Harold Ezell, the first major meeting of what was to become the Prop. 187 committee took place on October 5, 1993. The meeting took place at the opulent, members-only Center Club in Costa Mesa, Orange County. As well as the characters already mentioned one other person of note was present: Republican California Assemblyman Dick Mountjoy. Mountjoy had introduced several anti-illegal-immigration bills into the California legislature—with no success. At the meeting, the people named themselves the Save Our State (SOS) committee. Until June 1994, when the secretary of state officially named the initiative as Proposition 187, the committee, campaign, and prospective initiative were labeled SOS. However, for consistency and stylistic reasons, I will use the label that was later applied: Proposition 187.

The reports of what happened at the October 5 meeting are slightly contradictory, with each participant having a somewhat different recollection about the details.[41] However, it is possible to draw some conclusions about the discussion and the dynamics of the meeting.

The meeting began in the morning with a general discussion about illegal immigration and possible ways to address the problem.[42] Some of those at the meeting were not initially convinced that the initiative route was the best way forward. Nelson in particular was concerned that qualifying an initiative would prove prohibitively expensive. He argued that all available resources should be used to continue the progress he had made pushing legislation through the California legislature.[43] However, Prince and Mountjoy were convinced that an initiative was the best way to address the issue.[44] Nelson was eventually persuaded that an initiative was a good idea, because it would receive "massive public attention" that could not have been achieved through the legislative process. Furthermore, by writing their own law they could address issues—such as excluding undocumented children from public schools—that the legislature would never consider.[45]

The issue of denying education to undocumented children worried some participants at the meeting because it directly challenged the U.S. Supreme Court's 1982 *Plyler v. Doe* decision, in which the Court stated that undocumented children were entitled to a public education.[46] The case came to the U.S. Supreme Court from Texas, which in 1975 had passed a law refusing undocumented persons a free public education. The Mexican American Legal Defense and Educational Fund (MALDEF) brought a suit against Texas to have the law overturned. On appeal, a Texas judge ruled that James Plyler, Superintendent of Tyler (Texas) schools, should permit undocumented persons to return to school. Texas appealed to the Supreme Court, but the Court ruled against Texas. The decision was a clear case of interpretative policymaking according to both critics and Chief Justice Warren Burger who wrote the dissent.[47] Justice William J. Brennan, writing for the majority, argued that "By denying these children a basic education, we deny them the ability to live within the structure of our civic institutions, and foreclose any realistic possibility that they will contribute in even the smallest way to the progress of our Nation." Even Burger acknowledged in dissent that failing to educate the undocumented is "senseless for an enlightened society . . . It would be folly—and wrong—to tolerate [the] creation of a segment of society made up of illiterate persons, many having a limited or no command of our language."

Prince, Nelson, and others at the meeting realized that including the education provision in the initiative text would likely provoke a constitutional challenge if Prop. 187 was victorious at the polls. It was decided, however, that the time was right to force the Court to revisit the issue. But it was also feared that the education provision might not play well with the wider California electorate if it thought that the initiative was targeting innocent children. Ultimately, it was deemed necessary to include the provision to keep the grassroots anti-immigrant activists on board—who would be so important in the signature-gathering phase.[48]

It was also decided in the general discussion before lunch, largely at the insistence of Assemblyman Mountjoy, to include a provision dealing with the fraudulent use of documents, such as driving licenses and green cards. It was also believed that questions of welfare, heathcare, and the reporting of illegal immigrants to the authorities should be addressed by the initiative, along with the education and fraudulent document provisions. After lunch, the meeting broke up into a number of smaller groups of two or three people. Each group discussed in detail one of the specific provisions identified earlier in the day. After these discussions, each group wrote a short paragraph proposing a way to address their problem. When the full meeting reconvened later that day, each group's work was circulated among the others for further discussion and/or criticism.[49]

Prince took the work of the smaller groups and combined them into one draft. Alan Nelson, a trained lawyer and the group's preeminent immigration expert after his time in charge of the INS, also wrote a separate draft that addressed some of the finer legal points and language. Nelson's and Prince's drafts were synthesized and the rest of the committee did some minor "tinkering."[50] Assemblyman Mountjoy then used his legislative position to send the new draft to the legislative counsel's office, so it could review the proposed legislation to ensure it was legal. One change suggested by the counsel—which would cause much controversy later in the campaign—and accepted by the Prop. 187 committee was to include a phrase that "any public entity" (schools, hospitals, police, and so on) should report to the INS and the California attorney general any person it "reasonably suspects" is an illegal alien. The justification for including the reasonably suspects clause was that it would remove liability from informers. However, opponents of Prop. 187 would later use the phrase to justify their claim that the initiative was racist because Latinos would be suspected, not Anglos. Nelson later claimed that "people misunderstood [the clause]. If we knew we'd get all this flak, it would have been very easy to say the definition of suspect is failure to provide documents."[51] Ezell also later claimed that when he saw the wording of the clause he exclaimed: " 'Holy Toledo, what is this?' It won't be in any other propositions that [I] have anything to do with . . . There's no need to run red flags up like that. It fanned the flames of the opposition . . . To me, the word should have been better defined."[52] Despite his concern, Ezell failed to persuade the group to change the wording. When the proposed initiative was sent to the attorney general for titling and a summary, Nelson and Ezell were named as the authors. However, according to Prince, Ezell was only included as an author because of his name recognition in California; actually, "Ezell wrote six words."[53]

In sum, the writing of the initiative was a group effort, with Nelson and Prince taking a leading, first-among-equals role. Nelson in particular was heavily criticized for his involvement. Because he had worked as a lobbyist in the California legislature for FAIR, Nelson was accused of being a political opportunist using the people's initiative process for his employer's advantage. However, Nelson attended the meeting as a private individual, not as FAIR's representative. Nor was FAIR involved in the genesis of Prop. 187 in any other way, despite claims made by critics to the contrary.[54] Kiley noted that Nelson

Came in at the invitation of Hal Ezell basically to give us a background, some history, some sage advice—seen as he'd been involved with the issue for quite a while—and to try to help us avoid some of the pitfalls. He was very helpful, although at that time he was in very poor health so we didn't really want to exercise his position on this thing. But then he got so excited about what we were trying to accomplish that he started writing it.[55]

Similarly, Ron Prince, the driving force behind and architect of Prop. 187, was not a politician searching for an issue around which to construct a political coalition. Nor were the Kileys, Ezell, or Coe. The only elective politician on the Prop. 187 committee was Assemblyman Mountjoy, and he was neither rich enough nor sufficiently important to make any significant difference to the qualification or the campaign. If he had not sent the initiative to the legislative counsel and had the "reasonably suspects" clause not been included, Prop. 187 and its proponents would probably have had an easier ride during the qualification and campaign stages.

However, while the majority of the Prop. 187 committee members were not elected politicians, neither were they mainly grassroots activists. Of the major players, only Barbara Coe was a true activist.[56] Yet, as Prince, Robert Kiley, and Ezell expected, anti-immigrant grassroots activists were to play a significant role in the qualification of the measure—and for this reason Coe was invited to become involved.[57]

The Qualification of the Proposition

The Proposition was given a title by the attorney general on January 10, 1994, and the proponents had 150 days to collect 385,000 verifiable signatures. The next day the first petition forms were sent out to the signature gatherers. The petition drive got off to a slow start, however, because Prop. 187's proponents did not have any significant financial backing early in the qualification stage. Nelson thought they would not be able to qualify the measure because they did not have the money to employ a professional signature-gathering firm.[58] However, the immediate problem was to find enough money to print and mail the petition forms (on which the signatures would be recorded) to the volunteer signature gatherers. It was the chairman of the campaign, Ron Prince, who provided the first notable contribution with a $2,500 donation.[59]

Although Prop. 187's proponents claimed that the petition drive was a grass-roots mobilization, this is not strictly the case. In the first three months of the qualification stage (January–March 1994) the drive was largely, but not totally, a grassroots mobilization. It was, as suggested by the evidence presented below, a grassroots mobilization in the sense that volunteers collected the vast majority of signatures during this period. But it was not a grassroots effort in the sense that some but by no means all of the donations received were from "establishment" politicians and institutions such as the Republican Party. For example, during the January–March period the committee received a $15,000 loan on March 28 from Republican California senator Robb Hurtt's Container Supply Company. The committee also received just over $105,000 in nonmonetary contributions. Most notably, Assemblyman Mountjoy gave nearly $26,000 to the committee to pay for printing, mailing, telephone calls, and office rent. And the California Republican Party gave $76,500 for mailing-list rental, mailing, and postage.[60] However, of the $55,000 received in monetary contributions, $35,000 or 65 percent were donations of less than 100 dollars. If this is compared to the tobacco industry-backed Prop. 188, it becomes clear that the qualification of Prop. 187 began as a relatively grassroots operation. Of the two million dollars spent to qualify Prop. 188, 0 percent of donations were contributions of 100 dollars or less and 100 percent were 10,000 dollars or more.[61]

Of the little money that was received, none was used between January and March to pay a professional signature-gathering firm. The nonmonetary contributions detailed above were used for standard office expenses, such as mailing out petition forms, printing and telephone calls. Indeed, for most of the qualification and campaign periods the committee ran a deficit on its account.[62] During the January–March period Prop. 187's proponents relied on grassroots volunteers to collect signatures. Apart from thirty-three thousand signatures collected from a mail-shot paid for by the Republican Party, the vast majority of signatures were collected by grassroots activists.[63] Nelson estimated that they had fourteen thousand volunteers out on the streets who collected about 400,000 in total.[64]

Most of the signature gatherers can be placed in one of three groups: the grassroots anti-immigrant group California Coalition for Immigration Reform (CCIR), Ross Perot's United We Stand America party supporters (UWSA), and Republican Party supporters. Bill King commented that "Barbara Coe's [CCIR] organization did a great job in gathering signatures."[65] Coe coordinated the signature gathering of CCIR members through her *911* newsletter and by phone and fax with other group members.[66] The essence of their signature-gathering strategy, according to Coe, was to "follow the crowds": "Wherever there were going to be heavy-duty crowds of people, then we'd contact the [CCIR] people in those areas and get X number of them to be there [to collect signatures]."[67] One of Coe's CCIR members was also a member of Perot's UWSA party and this "really opened the door to [the party]. And really, really, we owe them so much because they really went forward on the issue. UWSA came through like champions."[68] King was equally fulsome in his praise of USWA's members: "United We Stand, I have always said, were the key to the success of this thing because they had so many people out on the streets collecting signatures."[69] The final group of volunteers was California Republican Party supporters. However, as Prince stressed, "the signature-gathering effort . . . did receive help from California Republicans. But they contacted us directly; they did not come through the California Republican Party."[70]

Despite the efforts of the grassroots volunteers, the Prop. 187 campaign was still short of the required 385,000 signatures as the deadline for the submission of petitions neared. In mid April Ezell reported that they had collected 310,000 signatures.[71] There was some suspicion that petitions and checks that had been mailed to the campaign headquarters in Tustin had not been delivered by the Santa Ana post office.[72] The suggestion was that someone in the post office was storing the mail in order to sabotage the campaign and prevent the proposal being placed on the ballot. Robert Kiley said that his solution to the alleged tampering was to trick their opponents in the post office. He claimed that he released to the press an "official" but false deadline date for the collection of signatures.[73]

> The next two weeks we got buckets and buckets of mail delivered all of a sudden with postmarks from way back when. It was a riot. It was funny. We wanted to see what would happen. What I expected would happen happened. They [in the post

office] just said "It's over with, so now they can have their mail." So we got all our mail, checks, money . . . petitions. The whole thing started coming across.[74]

Only in April did Prop. 187's proponents employ a professional firm to collect signatures. In the event, American Petition Consultants provided about 200,000 signatures as an insurance against invalid signatures collected by the grassroots activists, at a cost of $153,507.[75] But Nelson argued, "We basically got all the needed signatures by volunteers and probably would have sustained it with just volunteers."[76] The major reason why American Petition Consultants was only employed in April is that before this time the committee could not afford to pay for signatures. However, as the signature-gathering phase continued and qualification looked increasingly likely, many Republican politicians made monetary and non-monetary contributions and endorsed the initiative.[77] For example, at a press conference on February 15, Republican U.S. congressmen Ron Packard and Dana Rohrabacher gave their support.[78] Both argued that illegal immigrants were a drain on the state because they consumed public services, especially during recession when the state could least afford to subsidize them. Rohrabacher rejected accusations that the measure was racist because it was targeted at a specific race, arguing "those who suggest that this is racist are trying to obfuscate honest discussion of the problem. You will find the vast majority of Mexican Americans will support the initiative."[79] Mountjoy also rejected claims that the measure was racist: "We don't want any illegals here, regardless of where they come from. . . . What is racist about wanting to protect our borders? Nothing. It [Prop. 187] will pass because it is right and because it is supported by all races, religions, and creeds."[80] Governor Wilson, meanwhile, despite his focus on the illegal-immigration issue had yet to take a definite position on the initiative. However, on May 26 he gave Prop. 187 his tentative backing, saying, "I *think* I'd *probably* vote 'yes' on it."[81] The Republican Party continued to provide some help behind the scenes, meanwhile. In addition to the $76,500 for a mail shot in the January–March period, the party gave $10,000 for an absentee-ballot mailing on May 20.

Despite Wilson's equivocation on Prop. 187, his focus on illegal immigration and the initiative's qualification became entwined as the signature-gathering process proceeded. Wilson's emotive anti-illegal immigration May television ad described in the previous chapter reinforced his position on illegal immigration at a time when Prop. 187 was enjoying increasing publicity and a high level of support. Furthermore, both Wilson and Prop. 187's proponents made the same arguments about illegal immigration and faced the same criticisms. Both emphasized that their focus on illegal immigration had nothing to do with race, while their opponents accused them of whipping up nativist and racist sentiment. Both also claimed that illegal immigrants took more in public services than they paid in taxes and were therefore a financial drain on the state. Critics counterclaimed that their figures were inaccurate because they did not include contributions—for example, in sales taxes—made by undocumented persons. In other words, the estimates were not net estimates but skewed gross estimates. But such nuances were generally lost on the public. The only thing that researchers did generally agree on was that the federal government enjoyed a surplus and state and local governments a deficit on tax revenue versus spending costs for legal and illegal immigrants combined.

While many Republicans leaders endorsed Prop. 187, most Democratic politicians did not support it. They were in a difficult position, though. As George Skelton correctly predicted in a June 1994 *LA Times* op-ed piece, Prop. 187 would become the central issue in the November elections, and all politicians would have to make their position clear on the issue, otherwise they would be branded cowards. Moreover, he argued, because the measure was a wedge issue only a yes or no position would suffice—there would be no middle ground. Skelton also suggested that the measure "has the potential to join a list of historic ballot props [sic] that have influenced voting for elective office and swayed national policy-makers." For example, Pete Wilson when mayor of San Diego opposed Proposition 13 in 1978 and lost votes in his quest for the Republican gubernatorial nomination. Governor Edmund G. "Pat" Brown opposed Proposition 14 in 1964 (the initiative overturned a law banning discrimination in housing) and suffered politically, although the Supreme Court later overturned the initiative. And in 1982 the anti-handgun measure Proposition 15 helped increase turnout among white males who voted heavily in favor of Republican George Deukmejian in the closely contested gubernatorial contest (he won).[82]

The Democrats' position was made more difficult still by opinion polls showing that the vast majority of Californians thought there were too many illegal immigrants in the state, and because early support for Prop. 187 was high. Denying that illegal immigration was a problem or opposing Prop. 187 may therefore have damaged Democrats electorally. Yet supporting Prop. 187 may also have proved damaging because of the significance of Latino support and donations to Democratic campaigns.[83] The Democrats were in a double bind, and yet as Skelton argued the issue had become too important to ignore. Pretending it did not exist would allow conservatives to set the agenda and the tone of the debate, to manipulate it for its own purposes, and, possibly, to produce some form of legislation objectionable to moderates and liberals. The strategy most Democrats therefore adopted was to say "No on 187" while acknowledging that illegal immigration was a legitimate concern and offering alternative, less punitive solutions. For example, California Democrats in the U.S. Congress introduced six bills dealing with illegal immigration in March 1994, but none of the bills addressed the issue of amending the Fourteenth Amendment. Nor did they propose to remove education entitlements or non-emergency healthcare from illegal immigrants. U.S. representative Anthony C. Beilenson's (D-Woodland Hills) bill proposed to add 2,500 Border Patrol officers to the existing 3,500 and to increase training and improve equipment. Representative Sam Farr's (D-Carmel) bill proposed to speed up the naturalization process, and Representative Lucille Roybal-Allard's (D-Los Angeles) proposed education and outreach services for illegal immigrants seeking citizenship. Representative Xavier Becerra (D-Los Angeles) introduced three bills: one to require the federal government to reimburse states for the cost of incarcerating illegal-immigrant prisoners, which he estimated at $18,000 per inmate; one to expand the federal government's power to investigate discrimination in hiring workers; and another to establish a review board to investigate civil rights abuses by federal agents.[84] Although Becerra was a congressional freshman, his presence on the House Judiciary Subcommittee on International Law, Refugees and Immigration gave him considerable influence in Congress, especially as he was the only one of the eighteen member Congressional Hispanic Caucus on the committee. Moreover, as a third generation Latino from California, he was the only member of the caucus who spoke the language of immigrants' rights *and* border control. The caucus appeared incapable of adjusting to the new debate, reflected in the position of the immigration issue at number seven on its 1994 agenda.[85]

While some Democrats made clear they were against Prop. 187 and offered alternative ways to combat the perceived immigration problem, organized opposition to the initiative was minimal during the signature-collection phase. A new organization called Proponents for Responsible Immigration Debate and Education (PRIDE) was established in January 1994 by some politicians and Latino organizations. Run from the offices of the MALDEF, PRIDE wanted to bring together disparate Latino and other ethnic groups to advance the arguments for immigration and to challenge the anti-immigrant forces that had dominated and framed the debate so far. While a lack of funds seriously curtailed its ability to mobilize opinion and to advertise on television and radio,[86] some representatives of PRIDE secured a private meeting with Governor Wilson on January 7, 1994. During the meeting, which was deemed a success by both sides, Wilson and PRIDE agreed it was necessary to improve the economy of sending countries and to retain civilian control of U.S. borders. Both also said the new dialogue over illegal immigration was helpful and constructive, but disagreed over Wilson's proposals to change the Fourteenth Amendment and to remove publicly funded healthcare and education from illegal immigrants.[87] However, Wilson benefited more from the meeting. On the one hand, the publicity surrounding the meeting ensured illegal immigration remained in the news, which could only help Wilson given his close association with the issue and the widespread popular support for his position. On the other, in meeting PRIDE Wilson was able to look amenable to dialogue and receptive to reasoned argument, allowing him to rebuff to some extent the allegations of racism that had begun to be aired by critics of Prop. 187 and the governor.

In addition to PRIDE, which was an elite organization, there was also a modest grassroots mobilization against Prop. 187 during the qualification stage. Immigrant-rights activists formed the Proposition One Coalition to push for an extension to the IRCA amnesty and to protest against immigrant-bashing rhetoric and Prop. 187.[88] The coalition was a radical organization whose goals— especially the aim of another IRCA-style amnesty—and language were extreme when compared to that of even liberal Democrats. The coalition organized a march on Los Angeles City Hall on February 26.[89] Only 1,500 attended, but the coalition and its leaders were to become very significant in the campaign against and, paradoxically, the success of Prop. 187—as we shall see in the next chapter.[90]

Overall, the opponents of Wilson and Prop. 187 were not particularly well-organized or funded during the signature-gathering phase. Nelson argued that the absence of an well-organized opposition was a deliberate plan.[91] In Nelson's thinking, groups in opposition to Prop. 187 thought that a vocal opposition during qualification would only increase publicity for the issue. Other supporters of the initiative thought along similar lines. Prince, however, argued conspiratorially that there was virtually a press blackout during the qualification stage because "the worst thing they can do with a petition drive is to ignore it."[92]

> It is something that can not be proven, but something I believe, that the media in California were so vitriolically opposed to 187 to the point of being outright vicious about it. [They] were not just opposed after we qualified for the ballot, they were opposed to it before we got on the ballot. We considered that there was a press blackout on 187. You just didn't see anything about it. Subsequent to my initiative, I can tell you, I've seen a number of others where a person files an initiative and gets a great deal of publicity about it because the press for whatever reason seems to be interested in it, and primarily in supporting it. We had very little money and we had no way of letting people know that we were here. If ten million Californians knew we were trying to circulate petitions to put 187 on the ballot . . . we would have gotten on the ballot very easily. We had very little money and it was very difficult. That's why so many initiatives are backed by big-money special interests. If you have the money you can get on the ballot in a couple of weeks. We weren't a special interest. We were a bunch of people trying to do something. It started off very small, but by the time it got up the hill it was very large.[93]

A more likely explanation for the absence of a coherent, strong opposition was that, at least early in the qualification stage, there was a feeling that the initiative would not qualify. This is not especially surprising given that there are dozens of proposed initiatives trying to get on the ballot each year, the vast majority of which fail. It therefore makes sense not to spend resources attacking something that most likely will fail anyway. Furthermore, because the Prop. 187 campaign was widely considered to be a relatively impoverished unprofessional operation run by a group of Orange County "nut cases,"[94] many potential opponents had good reason to believe it would not qualify in a state where the initiative process had become very professionalized.[95] Another likely explanation was touched upon above. For many groups that would have been natural opponents of 187, it was a very difficult issue on which to position themselves.

A better organized mainstream opposition began on June 22, 1994, with the formation of a fund-raising committee, "No on SOS," constituted from some leading Democratic politicians and powerful interest groups, including California Assembly speaker Willie Brown and Latino-caucus leader Richard Polanco, the Roman Catholic Church, the California Medical Association, and the California Teachers Association.[96] "No on SOS" quickly mutated into Taxpayers Against 187, which was to become the main opposition against Prop. 187 during the campaign stage. The establishment of the No campaign, however, came too late to kill the proposed initiative. The illegal-immigration issue was not about to go away for Democrats, and the difficulties they faced during the qualification stage would continue during the campaign. In a press release on June 23, the secretary of state's office announced that Prop. 187 had qualified for the November ballot and support looked promising.

Assessing the Impact of Wilson and the Republican Party

In total the Republican Party gave $86,500 in nonmonetary contributions to the Prop. 187 petition drive, but no monetary contribution. This sum represents a quarter of all monetary and nonmonetary contributions received during this stage. However, it is difficult to quantify how important the party's help was. Indeed, even the members of the Prop. 187 committee were divided on its importance. For example, Ron Prince declared that "we got very little help from the California Republican Party," while Robert Kiley and Alan Nelson were more fulsome in their praise.[97] Nelson, who attended the party's state convention in February 1994 when the qualification stage had just begun, commented, "They were very helpful. They got people involved in the signature gathering. They sent out a lot of literature."[98] It seems, however, that while the Republican Party did aid the signature-gathering effort, this help was not crucial or even significant; the qualification probably could have succeeded without the party. More important than the party was the number of signatures provided by Republican supporters. But, as Prince stressed, the supporters helped Prop. 187 independent of their party.

It is also difficult to assess Wilson's importance during the qualification stage. On balance, Wilson's emphasis on the illegal-immigration issue probably helped Prop. 187 to qualify. The previous chapter showed how Wilson's politicization of the issue created an opportunity to qualify an initiative (and Prop. 187's proponents used the opportunity), which was certainly important. Yet Wilson did not endorse Prop. 187 until September, well after qualification, although he did say he may vote for it. Nevertheless, he continued to focus on illegal immigration throughout the qualification stage, and this too was important.

This view is not universally held, though. Ron Prince argued that Wilson, and especially his May television ad, harmed the petition drive. Prince's argument was that Wilson's ad engendered emotion and "racialized" the issue, therefore losing Prop. 187 the support of Latinos. Prince called the ad "damaging . . . It may have served the governor's purpose of getting re-elected, but it did 187 no good."[99] Prince's argument is supported to some extent by an *LA Times* May poll showing that almost three-fifths of Latinos and a small majority of African Americans opposed the measure, whereas they had previously approved it.[100] Overall, though, Prop. 187 remained very popular: 59 percent of respondents expressed support, 32 percent opposition and 9 percent responded don't know in May. Whites were heavily in favor by 64–26 percent. Support for the measure was high across ideological lines, with conservatives most likely to support the measure. A majority of moderates also expressed support, while a small majority of liberals were against it.[101] There is little evidence to suggest that Wilson harmed Prop. 187's qualification chances overall.

While it is possible to make some inferences about the impact of Wilson's public emphasis on illegal immigration, it is more difficult to quantify the importance of the behind-the-scenes link between Wilson and the qualification of Prop. 187. Quantifying the relationship is difficult partly because there is no official record and partly because, as with the link with the Republican Party, different members of the Prop. 187 committee have different recollections. Furthermore, members of Wilson's team were keen to distance their campaign from Prop. 187. For example, George Gorton, Wilson's campaign manager, recalled that

> We had nothing to do with qualifying 187, zero, zip. In fact, there were a lot of people in our campaign who thought it would be bad to have it on the ballot. We

had nothing to do with qualifying it; we had nothing to do with writing it; we didn't change one comma in it; we had nothing to do with it. We had a yes/no decision, which came to us after it qualified.[102]

Dick Dresner, Wilson's pollster, echoed Gorton's remarks:

Proposition 187 hooked onto Pete Wilson. Pete Wilson had been talking about immigration for a year, two years, prior to that. Pete Wilson did not circulate petitions for the initiative, he didn't put any money into the initiative, and in a number of our internal discussions, we thought we'd be a lot happier if it wasn't on the ballot. It wasn't like the situation of Jan Van de Kamp with Big Green: he put it on the ballot, he campaigned on it, and he lost. This issue was something that the governor raised, it excited a lot of people, and that excitement created Prop. 187. Anyone who thinks you go out and create this the other way doesn't know what they're talking about.[103]

Similarly, Prince recalls that during qualification:

There was never a time when we sat down with the governor or the governor's people and coordinated, consulted, or had really any kind of contact in that way at all . . . Every once in a while, some contact of ours would make an appeal to the governor's office for help—all of which were denied. In fact, we got nothing from the governor's office until September 1994—by which point the governor was 20 points behind in the polls.[104]

However, Kiley's recollection is very different and is worth quoting at some length:

I knew everybody on Wilson's staff. Wilson and I go way back to when I was working for Bob Finch's U.S. Senate campaign in '76. I got a call from a couple of Pete Wilson's operatives—and talk about people that didn't really have a clue about what was going on. They had heard a bunch of stories that this [187] was being run by a bunch of nut cases, a bunch of right-wing crazies, bigots—you name it. So they called me and said, "We want to have lunch." And I said "Fine." So we had lunch behind the scenes with the Wilson people. That was about April '94 [before Prop. 187 had qualified for the ballot] . . .

We had lunch and they said "What do you need?" I said "I need money—what do you think I need." They said "We can't give you money, so what else do you need?" I said "I'd like a mailing. Can you pay for a mailing?" They said they could probably do that. I said "I need a clipping service; I need to know what's going on in the other parts of California, but I don't have the money for a clipping service." They said "You've got it, it's yours." I said "I need polling information." They said "It's yours, no problem." They asked if there was anything else I needed. I said "I'll think about it, but that's about it right now" . . .

This is Wilson's people . . . Some of the guys that I've been working with that were Wilson's operatives were friends of mine for years. We've been in different campaigns and different wars for over ten, fifteen years . . . There was honesty at the table.[105]

It is possible that Prince may not have known that Kiley was going to meet Wilson's people, but it hardly likely that Kiley would have failed to tell Prince—the central character behind Prop. 187—that he had met them. It is likely that political consultant Kiley was keen to play up his connections with the Republican Party. Wilson's people on the other hand may have been keen to downplay any connection with Prop. 187 during the qualification stage because they did not want Wilson, who had political ambitions beyond California, to be too closely associated with an initiative that was widely regarded, especially outside California, as nativist and even racist by some.

Prince, meanwhile, perhaps for some personal and/or political reasons that have never been made public, felt extremely hostile toward both Wilson and his party and was thus reluctant to admit that Prop. 187 received any help from them, even though his own statements suggest ambiguity about what exactly constitutes help:

> Trying to draw parallels between Wilson and [Prop. 187] would be inaccurate. There was virtually no connection between the two. We did not look to Governor Wilson for anything other than financial support, or political support during the petition drive, endorsements, a little publicity . . . There was literally no connection. There were a few requests made to which there was no reply. That does not establish a connection.[106]

One possible explanation for his hostility may be that he wished to retain the credit for "his" initiative's success. Nelson, who described Prince as a "strange character,"[107] probably best articulated the *direct* connection between Wilson and Prop. 187. For Nelson, the connection lay somewhere between the poles offered by Prince and Kiley:

> The Republican Party was on board pretty early, but that was not Pete Wilson . . . The governor has a lot of impact, but he doesn't control it [the Republican Party]. But I'm sure his people weren't discouraging the Republican Party. It's just that they weren't controlling this behind the scenes. I think a lot of the conspiracy theories would have us believe that this was always Wilson, that this was always lined up for him to use as a vehicle; that they orchestrated it the way they did so he could keep a low profile for a while—that just isn't the case. The fact is that his people were not involved *particularly*. The bottom line: Pete Wilson had nothing to do with putting 187 together. A lot of people think it was a grand conspiracy; now that's the popular thought that 187 was Pete Wilson from the get-go, it was all his, it was all figured out. Not at all. He had nothing to do with the thing being developed, designed, quoted [titled], approved/qualified.[108]

Nelson was right that Wilson had nothing to do with Prop. 187 being written. However, Nelson was wrong when he suggested that Wilson did not have anything to do with the initiative's qualification. As demonstrated in this and the previous chapter, Wilson had an important, perhaps crucial, effect on Prop. 187's qualification. His focus on illegal immigration politicized the issue for millions of Californians and provided an opportunity to qualify an initiative. Furthermore, his continued focus on the issue throughout the qualification stage helped the qualification because it kept the issue on the agenda. Finally, his election team provided some minimal backroom help in the form of polling data and a clipping service.

The qualification of Prop. 187 was, at least in part, a grassroots mobilization. It would not have qualified for the November ballot without the signature-gathering efforts of the grassroots activists. However, while the petition drive was relatively unprofessional in its execution, the qualification was not a truly grass-roots effort because a significant proportion of the monetary and nonmonetary contributions it received came from elective politicians and the Republican Party. Moreover, later in the qualification stage, the Prop. 187 committee did employ a professional firm, although it only provided 200,000 of 600,000 signatures. Finally, the campaign received a great deal of indirect help from Wilson in the form of free publicity through his focus on illegal immigration, although the direct help he provided was negligible.

In sum, then, the qualification of Prop. 187 was an unprofessional quasi-grassroots effort. However, the initiative's proponents were fortunate because there was no effective organized opposition during qualification. After the initiative qualified, this changed. The mainstream campaign against the initiative was professional, well funded, and widely supported by many respected interest groups and politicians. The next chapter details how the opposition fought back. It describes and analyses the strategy of the Yes and No campaigns, assesses the importance of various actors in those campaigns, and examines why Californians' opinions on Prop. 187 changed dramatically in such a short time.

Chapter 5

The Campaign

On June 23, 1994, California's secretary of state officially announced that Proposition 187 had qualified for the November general election ballot. With opinion polls showing Prop. 187 leading in May by 27 percentage points and in July by 37 points, the campaign began with opponents of the illegal-immigration initiative facing a difficult contest. They had not yet lost the war, but their enemy was well entrenched before a shot had been fired. The story of the campaign is essentially the story of how the opposition to Prop. 187 fought back in an exceptionally emotive and bitter contest.

The No campaign was in essence an amalgamation of disparate mainstream, grassroots, and ad hoc oppositions. The coalitional nature of the No campaign is significant because it created problems for the opposition itself. In particular, strategy formation, tactical choices, and attracting the white middle-class vote were made problematic by the odd mix of groups and people fighting the initiative. However, a planned tactical shift by the mainstream opposition in September 1994, combined with a number of high-profile politicians expressing their opposition, started to erode Prop. 187's support in the last month of the campaign. These factors, though, ultimately proved insufficient as some grassroots opposition forces beyond the control of the mainstream opposition halted the hemorrhaging in support for Prop. 187 in the campaign's last weeks.

The Opposition

The mainstream opposition to Proposition 187 was Taxpayers Against 187, a coalition group established by and including many of the large, wealthy, and politically entrenched pressure groups in California, such as the California Parents and Teachers Association (PTA), the California Teachers Association (CTA), the California School Boards Association, the American College of Emergency Physicians, the California Medical Association (CMA), the Mexican American Legal Defense and Educational Fund (MALDEF), and the Roman Catholic Church. Some important California public officials and personalities also joined the Taxpayers coalition. For example, Richard Polanco, Latino-caucus leader in the California legislature, Gloria Molina, Los Angeles county supervisor, and Sherman Block, Los Angeles County sheriff, were important voices for Taxpayers.

As well as including many of California's political "big hitters," the Taxpayers coalition received and controlled most of the anti-187 financial contributions. Some of the money was used to employ the political consultancy firm Woodward and McDowell to run the anti-187 campaign. Owned by Richard Woodward and Jack McDowell, the firm built its reputation helping the successful 1984 initiative campaign to establish a state lottery in California. It also enjoyed a notable success helping defeat Proposition 128, better known as Big Green, in 1990. Karen Kapler, an employee of Woodward and McDowell, was Taxpayers' campaign manager responsible for the day-to-day running of the campaign. Jackie Steinman, research director at Woodward and McDowell, was responsible for developing the strategy and message. And Scott Macdonald, also of Woodward and McDowell, was Taxpayers' communications director responsible for news-media relations and strategy and getting the message out to voters.[1] The analogy of a company describes well the relationship between Taxpayers and Woodward and McDowell: Woodward and McDowell was the staff and Taxpayers was the board of directors. The staff developed the message and was responsible for getting it out. Those involved said that the board and staff worked well together, and that the board was supportive of the staff's strategy and message, although the board retained the right to approve/veto decisions taken by the staff. Kapler and Steinman thought that the staff and the board worked well together partly because there was little time for dissent and partly because both were committed to victory.[2]

While Taxpayers was the "elite" opposition to Prop. 187, the main grassroots opposition was Californians United Against Proposition 187 (CUAP 187). Like Taxpayers, CUAP 187 was a coalition group, constituted from a number of grassroots civil rights organizations. These organizations were themselves often coalitions of even smaller grassroots groups. For example, groups representing the Asian community in California—such as the Chinese American Citizens Alliance, the Japanese American Citizens League, the Thai Community Development group, and the United Cambodian Community—formed a coalition called Asian Pacific Americans Opposed to Proposition 187 in July 1994. Asian Pacific Americans Opposed to Proposition 187 then affiliated with the larger coalition of CUAP 187. Despite the large number of groups affiliated to CUAP 187, it had few financial resources and had little impact on the strategy and tactics of Taxpayers' and Woodward and McDowell's No campaign.

Although CUAP 187 did not spearhead the public No campaign, it worked hard to encourage ethnic-minority Californians to register to vote against Prop. 187. For example, in the heavily Latino Pico-Union district in downtown Los Angeles, CUAP 187 worked with Coalition '94, an outreach and education organization. The idea was to assign a trained local leader to each precinct in Pico-Union. Each precinct leader was responsible for encouraging residents to register to vote. Voting guides were distributed to inform people about Prop. 187 and to encourage them to cast a No vote. CUAP 187 also held a conference in the summer of 1994 in Fresno to discuss and teach direct-action mobilization techniques to anti-187 groups and individuals.[3] Hundreds of student leaders attended the conference and, as we shall see, the direct-action techniques discussed at the conference had an important, albeit negative, impact on the No campaign.

The third element in the opposition to Prop. 187 was a disparate collection of individuals, groups, and coalitions not aligned to either the mainstream or grass-roots campaigns. As the campaign progressed an eclectic mix of individuals from across partisan, ideological, religious, and ethnic lines expressed their opposition to the illegal-immigration initiative. For example, Democrats such as Jesse Jackson, President Clinton, Dianne Feinstein, Barbara Boxer, and Kathleen Brown announced their opposition. More surprisingly, so did Republicans such as William Bennett, Jack Kemp, and Ron Unz. Unz's opposition to Prop. 187 was especially significant as he ran against Wilson for the 1994 Republican guber-natorial nomination on a conservative platform that was anti-multiculturalism, antipolitical correctness, and anti-bilingual education. He claimed he was about to endorse Prop. 187 but on reading the proposed law carefully discovered its provisions were "crazy."[4]

Others in the ad hoc opposition included important California law-enforcement officials and organizations such as the Los Angeles Police Commission; Willie Williams, chief of the Los Angeles Police Department; Gil Garcetti, Los Angeles County district attorney; James Hahn, Los Angeles City attorney; and Arlo Smith, San Francisco district attorney. Enrique Hernandez Jr., president of the Los Angeles Police Commission, described Prop. 187 as "immoral. It's going to make it almost unbearable for police to do their job in this city." Deidre Hill, vice president of the commission, was even more forthright, calling the initiative "racist and divisive."[5]

Most minority-group leaders from the Latino, Asian, and African American communities also tried to persuade their constituents to vote No. For example, in an emotive article in the *LA Times* two African American leaders, Joe Hicks and Constance L. Rice, evoked the memory of Martin Luther King Jr. and other civil rights heroes to persuade African Americans to unite with Latinos in opposition to Prop. 187:

> As champions of equal justice who crusaded for racial equality, they would reject a law that will subject Latinos and Asians—but not Europeans—to suspicion and stigma . . . As crusaders for young people blocked at the school doors by Orval Faubus and George Wallace, they would reject a law that turns teachers into INS agents and children away from school to the streets. As warriors for economic equality who defended poor Southern black migrants seen as a threat to white union jobs, they would reject a law that scapegoats the poorest Latinos and Asians . . . As foes of racial hatred, they would oppose a law born of racial resentment.[6]

Most religious groups that expressed a position on Prop. 187 came out against it, including the Episcopalian General Conference, the Presbyterian Synod of Southern California, and the Evangelical Lutheran Church of America. Cardinal Roger M. Mahoney, leader of America's largest Roman Catholic archdiocese and California's most important Catholic cleric, was especially active. Describing Prop. 187 as "punitive . . . [and] a devastating assault on human dignity," he encouraged Catholics to oppose the measure.[7] A coalition of Jewish organiza-tions claiming to represent over 50,000 families in southern California formed the Jewish Community Coalition Against Proposition 187 to oppose it. The Board of Rabbis of Southern California also came out against it. Furthermore, sixty religious organizations formed the Interfaith Coalition for Immigrant

Rights (ICIR) in July 1994. This interfaith umbrella group coordinated most of the religious opposition to Prop. 187 from its headquarters in San Francisco. With few financial resources available, the ICIR and other religious oppositions relied on their extensive church networks to disseminate anti-187 material and messages, but faced particular problems in poorer white neighborhoods where there was widespread support for the initiative.[8]

Many business leaders and business organizations also made public their opposition. On October 21, 1994, Michael Rossi, vice-chairman of the Bank of America, Bruce Corwin, president of Metropolitan Theatre Corporation, Michael George, managing director of JP Morgan Securities, Michael Peevey, former president of Southern California Edison Company, and Benjamin M. Reznik, former chairman of the Valley Industry and Commerce Association, all spoke out. In addition, the Valley Industry and Commerce Association, the most important business coalition in the Los Angeles Valley, voted to oppose it on October 27.[9]

It was noted above that the California Medical Association and the American College of Emergency Physicians affiliated to the mainstream Taxpayers coalition. Other groups of doctors and medical researchers also expressed their opposition. A group of medical scholars from the University of Southern California and the University of California, Los Angeles released a report on October 19 claiming that Prop. 187 could, if passed, lead to the spread of tuberculosis in Los Angeles County. They argued Prop. 187 would discourage undocumented residents from immunizing themselves against TB because of increased fears that they would be reported to the Immigration and Naturalization Service (INS). The disease would then spread into the wider Los Angeles community as illegal immigrants were exposed to other members of the public. And on November 3, just days before the vote, another group of medical scholars issued an anti-187 statement. Dr. D. Johnston, secretary of Los Angeles County Medical Association, claimed that:

> If we do not immunize undocumented children, we will increase the incidence of measles, whooping cough, mumps, rubella, diphtheria and hepatitis B in all children, not just the undocumented . . . Every dollar spent on prenatal care saves between $3 and $10 later on in caring for babies who are born with medical problems that could have been prevented. Every dollar spent on immunizations saves between $10 and $14 in future disease and disability costs.[10]

Finally, most individuals and groups involved in education expressed their opposition to Prop. 187. In addition to the already noted oppositions, the National Education Association, Los Angeles Board of Education, Los Angeles Unified School District, Santa Ana Unified School District, and Laguna Beach Unified School District all publicly expressed their opposition.[11]

In sum, the opposition to Prop. 187 was impressive in its scope and depth, with small groups of citizens, powerful and wealthy interest groups, and important politicians all expressing their opposition. However, the nature of the opposition in many ways also proved a handicap for the No campaign. The next section identifies the problems engendered by the conflicts within the opposition and shows how these hurt the No campaign.

Strategy, Tactics, and Problems

Messages of, and Conflicts within, the No Campaign

There were several aspects to the mainstream message promulgated by the Taxpayers coalition and its employees, Woodward and McDowell. The thinking of the strategists was that they had to construct a winning coalition by attracting the support of the white middle-class swing voters who decide elections.[12] Scott Macdonald, Taxpayers' communications director, said:

> I would say that we were trying to talk to white middle-class voters with messages that resonated with them, because they are the people who vote. We wish it were different. We wish everyone participated to the fullest extent. But when you're trying to win an election campaign you have to deal with the realities of it.[13]

Thus, because the polls and Taxpayers' focus groups showed the white majority was concerned about illegal immigration, the core message was an admission that illegal immigration was a problem but that Prop. 187 was not an appropriate solution. In other words, there was a right way and a wrong way to address the problem and Prop. 187 was the wrong way. For example, an October 1994 press release by Taxpayers noted:

> Illegal immigration IS a problem, but <u>187</u> won't fix it. 187 will only make a bad situation worse . . . We've got an illegal immigration problem, but 187 is DEFINITELY not the way to solve it.[14]

Another part of the message was that Prop. 187 would not solve the problem because it would do nothing to curb illegal border crossings, nor stop employers hiring undocumented workers. Kapler and Steinman argued that it was not possible in just four months to educate Californians about the benefits of undocumented migration, but it may have been possible to educate Californians to believe that Prop. 187 was not the solution.

The mainstream opposition also tried to appeal to white middle-class voters by arguing that Prop. 187 would remove children from school, thus placing them on the streets where they would commit crime. In a further attempt to appeal to the middle class, Taxpayers estimated that Prop. 187 would put at risk $15 billion of federal money because it violated various federal laws. This in turn would lead to annual tax rises of $1,600 per family to make up the shortfall, they claimed.

There was little or no mention of the humanitarian impact on illegal immigrants that Prop. 187's passage could produce. Nor did Taxpayers directly attack the measure as racist, at least early in the campaign. There was no focus on the "reasonably suspects" clause, or on the link between Prop. 187 and the Pioneer Fund, an allegedly white supremacist organization, which could have implied more sinister motives behind the initiative and the potential for increased harassment of nonwhite Californians. However, as we shall see, later in the campaign Taxpayers did raise these "racist" issues, which seemed to have had a positive impact on their support. They were deliberately holding back on the racist message until later in the campaign because, they thought, it was important to build a base of opposition to the initiative before using the Pioneer Fund scare tactic. The thinking was that no one would pay attention to the Pioneer Fund message early in the campaign because they did not have people's attention.[15]

The mainstream message may have appealed to some white voters and pleased conservative opponents of Prop. 187 such as Sherman Block, but it antagonized liberals and minority-group leaders, especially those in CUAP 187.[16] Macdonald later conceded that admitting illegal immigration was a problem "drove the people who were supposed to be our allies right through the roof."[17] Kapler and Steinman also admitted that their message made some immigrant groups go "ballistic." Consequently, too much time was spent trying to calm people down, which could have been better spent trying to defeat Prop. 187.[18] These conflicts also meant that CUAP 187 and Taxpayers were not united in their public facade and in the arguments they placed before the people.

CUAP 187 was further antagonized by the Taxpayers tactic—which remained unspoken at the time—of keeping Latino faces in the background. Because Taxpayers believed that constructing a winning No coalition meant that the anti-187 forces had to appeal to the white majority, it acknowledged that illegal immigration was a problem, kept ethnic-minority faces from view, and gave leading roles to white conservatives such as Sherman Block. Macdonald admitted that this was a very hard decision to take: "All of a sudden, the world is paying attention to something they [the activists] have spent their life on, and we're telling them they're not the ones who can talk about it . . . It's just that there are better people to carry the message."[19] While some Latino activists agreed with this tactic, they admitted it was not easy to accept. One anonymous Latino involved in the No campaign commented, "[s]ometimes it's difficult to hold your tongue. But it would be irresponsible not to do it now." Another noted that "[t]he fact is, if you go up [to speak publicly] and you have brown skin on this issue, people aren't going to listen to you. . . . They don't look beyond the messenger to the message."[20]

While the message and tactics of Taxpayers antagonized CUAP 187, the message of CUAP 187 and other ad hoc opponents of Prop. 187 in turn unsettled Taxpayers because it did not bring white middle-class swing voters into the No camp. In fact, it antagonized them. Scott Macdonald accused CUAP 187 of being politically naive, commenting:

> We are convinced that we [at Woodward and McDowell] know how to evaluate the polling and come up with messages. And everything about the campaign must reflect those messages and further the public's understanding of them, or it is a waste. Anything that any other organization did, as well meaning as they might have been, that did not concentrate on those messages—and believe me, those people did not concentrate on those messages—was a waste and in fact counterproductive. We're talking about winning an election. Of course, it breaks your heart. They've been in this issue all their lives. Now people are paying attention and telling them they can't say certain things or do certain things or whatever, and it makes them crazy. But [when] you want to win the election . . . you can't introduce other issues. You need to beat up the initiative and make everybody focus on just this initiative, not on any other solutions to the problem or anything else—just the initiative. And it was a battle.[21]

In a similar vein, *New York Times* writer William Safire commented:

> Many opponents of [Prop. 187] are seeking to redress centuries of North American "Imperialism" through imposing bilingualism and "group rights" for Latinos and other minorities. They view immigration as a kind of affirmative action program for the third world . . . [P]eople are not likely to be turned against the measure by the pronouncements of self-proclaimed community spokesmen such as Xavier Hermasillo of Los Angeles, who has called for Latinos to take back Southern California "block by block." Some advocates even call for granting voting rights to noncitizens. "At one time only white males could vote," says Leticia Quezada, a Los Angeles School Board member. "My position is that it's time we cross that line in terms of citizenship."[22]

This type of language, as Safire argued, frightened both white moderates and legal immigrants who had been through the naturalization process and assimilated to the American way. It is easy to see why Kapler and Steinman thought that the grassroots movement provided their greatest problem. They even went so far as to suggest that they could have defeated Prop. 187 if CUAP 187 and other immigrant-rights groups had kept quiet.[23]

It is certainly the case that some grassroots activists tried to use the controversy surrounding Prop. 187 as a means of establishing a homogenous political consciousness among and between ethnic-minority groups. However, the creation of a new civil rights movement was not, to say the least, the primary concern of the mainstream opposition. As we will see later, Taxpayers was rightly worried about ethnic political activism. Opinion polls in October 1994 showed that the No campaign had seriously eroded Prop. 187's lead, but the decline in support stopped as the grassroots protests began to dominate news coverage.

In sum, the conflicts created by the coalitional nature of the No campaign produced an inchoate, incoherent, and contradictory strategy and message. Early in the campaign the conflicts obfuscated the issues and each side cancelled out the other's message. And the actions of the anti-187 grassroots activists later in the campaign actually proved detrimental.

Time and Money Problems

Opponents of Prop. 187 also confronted a time problem. The mainstream opposition only employed Woodward and McDowell in July 1994. At the time Prop. 187 enjoyed a 37-point lead yet the consultancy firm had just four months to get the Taxpayers message across to the voters (see table 5.1 and figure 5.1).[24] As late as September Karen Kapler commented that Prop. 187's remedy was "the only solution on the blocks right now and we (must) communicate that it's not going to solve the problem, it's going to make it worse."[25]

The problem of getting the message across was further compounded by evidence that voters did not seem interested in Prop. 187's specific provisions. Political scientist Sherry Bebitch Jeffe commented that Prop. 187 is "a message initiative, and those people who support it will do so no matter what and aren't susceptible to reasoned economic or social debate."[26] Moreover, many Californians who were members of groups affiliated to the No campaign were

Table 5.1   Support for Prop. 187, March–October 1994

	Mar. 26–29 LA Times Poll[RV]	May 21–25 LA Times Poll[RV]	July 12–17 Field Poll[AA]	Aug. 19–29 UCI Poll[AA]	Sept. 8–11 LA Times Poll[RV]	Oct. 8–11 LA Times Poll[RV]	Oct. 22–25 LA Times Poll[RV]	Oct. 21–30 Field Poll[AA]
Yes	62	59	64	65	62	61	51	47
No	32	32	27	26	28	32	39	46
Don't know	6	9	10	9	10	7	10	7
Difference	+30	+27	+37	+39	+34	+29	+12	+1

Notes: Enteries are percentages; AA = all adults; RV = registered voters; Some columns >100 due to rounding.
Sources: See appendix A.

reluctant to heed the advice of their political leaders to oppose the initiative. As academic and keen observer of Latino-Anglo relations Peter Skerry noted, "there's been a disconnect between the political elite and just rank-and-file Americans . . . The dam has broken and people feel they can express these feelings that kind of pent up."[27]

A further problem was money. Woodward and McDowell estimated that between three and four million dollars were required to run a successful initiative campaign.[28] However, while many business leaders came out against Prop. 187, they were reluctant to donate money. Even the California Farm Bureau Association (CFBA), an organization representing large employers of undocumented labor, refused to take a position on the initiative or donate money.[29] Yet the same organization lobbied hard in the 1980s to ensure that illegal immigrants were allowed into California to harvest crops. Surprisingly, most farm organizations remain neutral despite claiming they were facing a severe labor shortage during 1994. A representative of an agricultural packaging company noted that "[immigrant bashing] plays well as a political issue, but if the politicians get their way, we're going to be in trouble. If you removed every illegal from this state tomorrow, you'd see the businesses—and not just the agricultural business—start to crumble."[30] Other pressure groups in the Taxpayers coalition were also unwilling to give money. For example, the California Medical Association, a big-name opponent of Prop. 187 and one of the state's largest political donors, made no financial contribution to the No campaign.

Why were Prop. 187's wealthy opponents reluctant to donate? Part of the explanation lies in the politically explosive nature of the initiative and the whole illegal-immigration issue. As Roy Gabriel, legislative director of labor affairs for the CFBA, noted, 187 "was so controversial on both sides we'd make enemies no matter what position we took."[31] Another part is Prop. 187's large lead in the polls. It looked as if the initiative's success was assured when the campaign began, and as late as September 1994 a Taxpayers supporter declared, "I believe without question [Prop. 187 is] going to pass."[32] What therefore was the point giving money? Confirming this interpretation, a spokesman for the CMA noting Prop. 187's large lead in the polls argued that money spent trying to defeat it would be wasted. His association therefore planned to wait until after the election and spend its money on defeating Prop. 187 in the courts. Unsurprisingly, therefore, in July, August, and September Taxpayers raised just $821,000 and was in debt by $125,000. The California Teachers Association was the largest donor during this period, giving $321,000. The No campaign also received $139,000 from the State Council of Service Employees and $100,000 from Univision. Univision was a New Jersey–based television conglomerate and owner of several California Spanish-language television stations. In an unusual move, several California Spanish-language television and radio stations and newspapers donated free advertising space to the No campaign. The editor of La Opinion, the Los Angeles–based Spanish-language newspaper, made a personal donation of $5,000. La Opinion also offered advertising space to the No campaign at a reduced rate.[33]

Prop. 187's supporters were in an even worse financial situation than their opponents, having raised just $124,000 in the same three-month period.[34] Yet the Yes campaign's lack of funds was less of a disability. Partly this was because at the start of the campaign Prop. 187's proponents already enjoyed a healthy lead in the polls. Also, they did not have to publicize their initiative because of the existing salience of the illegal-immigration issue, and could rely on others to encourage Californians to vote Yes. As during the qualification stage/primary races, Governor Wilson continued to use illegal immigration as the cornerstone of his reelection campaign, pumping millions of dollars into anti-illegal-immigration ads.

Wilson's role in promoting the illegal-immigration issue was vital to the Yes campaign. Wilson made yet another well-publicized trip to the California-Mexico border at the end of August 1994 and published a letter to President Clinton castigating his administration for turning its "back on California's illegal immigration crisis" while moving decisively to keep Cuban refugees out of Florida.[35] The reference was to Clinton's decision earlier in 1994 to use the U.S. Military to intercept illegal immigrants heading for Florida on rafts and to intern them in Guantanamo Bay naval base in Cuba. The Clinton administration had also allocated more funds for more Border Patrol officers and equipment at El Paso on the Texas-Mexico border, which helped reduce illegal crossings there by 73 percent.[36] On September 14 Wilson began to show a short, ten-second television ad that continued the theme of his letter to Clinton, berating the president for acting on the Florida-Cuba immigration problem while doing nothing about California's. The ad gave the White House–switchboard telephone number and encouraged Californians to call the president and register their views on illegal immigration. At the end of September Wilson sent three letters in ten days to U.S. attorney general Janet Reno, again criticizing the Clinton administration for failing to close the California-Mexico border. Reno argued in response that California politicians and officials, notably Pete Wilson, were partly responsible for their state's illegal-immigration problem as they had previously encouraged undocumented workers from Mexico to migrate north to work in California's fields.

Despite his continuing focus on illegal immigration, Wilson had still not formally endorsed Prop. 187 by mid September. He did, however, take a position on the provision of the initiative that would expel undocumented children from

California's public schools—one of the measure's most controversial clauses. Wilson said that if Prop. 187 passed he would enforce the provision so long as it was legal. He also stated that he was in favor of forcing a constitutional challenge to *Plyler*, the 1982 Supreme Court ruling that strongly suggested Prop. 187's expulsion provision would be found unconstitutional.[37] After some prevarication Wilson finally endorsed Prop. 187 at the California Republican Party convention on September 17.[38] As well as giving Prop. 187 his support, Wilson also stressed his anticrime and antiwelfare messages. These positions and his new silence on gay rights and environmental concerns, which he had previously supported, combined with his no-new-taxes pledge, allowed Wilson to reposition himself closer to the conservative Republicans who dominated the state party. When Wilson ran for governor in 1990 he was pro-choice, a defender of gay rights and the environment. Moreover, he raised taxes in response to a fiscal crisis in 1991, much to the chagrin of conservative colleagues.

The No campaign, then, faced a series of substantial difficulties, especially during July, August, and September 1994. Conflicting messages from, and conflicts between, Taxpayers and CUAP 187 hampered the No campaign. Taxpayers also suffered from a lack of money and time to get its message across. Furthermore, Californians did not seem to be paying attention to their leaders' advice to oppose the initiative. Thus, when Wilson officially endorsed Prop. 187 in mid September, all the evidence pointed to an overwhelming victory for it in November. In July, it had a statewide lead of 37 points.[39] In August, in populous and conservative Orange County, its lead was 39 points.[40] And by early September, it still enjoyed a considerable statewide lead of 34 points (see table 5.1 and figure 5.1).[41]

Moreover, support for the initiative came from across political, ideological, social, and racial groups. In September, majorities of Democrats and Republicans, self-identified conservatives and moderates, males and females, all age groups, all income groups, and all education levels expressed support for the initiative. Even Latinos were in favor by 52–42 percent. Furthermore, 90 percent of registered voters said illegal immigration was a problem. John Brennan, director of the *LA Times Poll*, argued that the data demonstrated frustration over illegal immigration was high and "something, anything" had to be done.[42] The anti-187 coalition that could have been expected to form—including liberals, Democrats, and members of minority groups—showed no sign of doing so by early September. All the evidence suggested that the No campaign would not be able to overcome its deficit in the polls in the last month and a half.

A Twist in the Campaign

Taxpayers Play Hardball

Executing a preplanned tactical shift, Taxpayers Against 187 held a press conference on September 9 to draw attention to the link between Prop. 187 and an allegedly racist organization called the Pioneer Fund. According to Taxpayers, the Pioneer Fund in its first charter had called for the encouragement of the "reproduction of individuals descended predominantly from white persons who settled in the original 13 states or from related stock." Taxpayers also claimed that the fund supported racist research, including that of notorious scientist

William B. Shockley.[43] In a press release, Taxpayers described the Pioneer Fund as a "white supremacist" organization. What was the racist link between Prop. 187 and the Pioneer Fund? Taxpayers claimed that the Federation for American Immigration Reform (FAIR) had received $600,000 in grants since 1988 from the Pioneer Fund, and that Alan Nelson was FAIR's lobbyist in Sacramento when he coauthored Prop. 187. According to Scott Macdonald, this demonstrated "a very direct link from the Pioneer Fund to Proposition 187."[44] He did, however, stop short of saying that any members of the Prop. 187 committee were racists.

Unsurprisingly, Prop. 187's supporters and committee members denied the allegations. Harold Ezell, Alan Nelson, and FAIR's executive director Daniel A. Stein all said FAIR had no link with Prop. 187.[45] Although the Pioneer Fund story did not produce big headlines—making only page three of the second section of the *LA Times*—it did push Prop. 187's proponents on to the defensive. They were forced to defend their motives publicly, while their opponents were clearly on the offensive.

Taxpayers kept up the pressure when it aired its first radio spot on October 10. In addition to repeating the old message that Prop. 187 would lead to increased crime and taxes, the ad referred to the link between the Pioneer Fund and Prop. 187, claiming that "white supremacists are behind 187."[46] At an October 11 press conference Karen Kapler again stressed that the Pioneer Fund sponsored racist research, that it had donated money to FAIR, and that Alan Nelson was working as FAIR's lobbyist in Sacramento when he coauthored Prop. 187. While claiming the commercial was not inferring that any of the Prop. 187 committee was racist, Kapler said, "trace the trail down. I think it's a legitimate thing to be

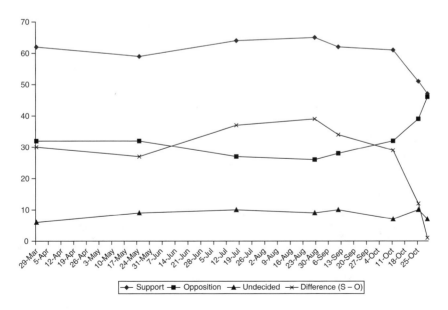

Figure 5.1 Support for Prop. 187, March–October 1994

Sources: See appendix A.

raised. Is there a kind of convergence of ideas and thoughts?"[47] Proponents of Prop. 187 were again quick to deny the allegations. Ezell called the ad a "total lie" and Nelson denied any connection to the Pioneer Fund, calling the allegations "total bullshit".[48] Professor Bruce Cain of the Institute of Governmental Studies at UC Berkeley agreed that the argument linking Prop. 187 with racist organizations was "probably a non sequitur." However, this would not necessarily mean that the advertisement would be ineffective: "the opposition strategy is to create doubt in people's minds," and it would have fulfilled its objective by doing so, argued Cain.[49]

Brown Attacks Too

Kathleen Brown, Wilson's gubernatorial opponent, also changed strategy in September 1994, and this too probably helped the No campaign. Early on, Brown had expressed her opposition to Prop. 187 and offered alternative solutions. However, like Taxpayers, she did not want to antagonize members and potential members of her electoral coalition—especially moderate and conservative Democrats who early on heavily favored Prop. 187—so her condemnation of the initiative and Wilson's connection with it was always muted. Her campaign, however, was weak and her message was not getting across. Wilson closed the gap throughout 1994 (see table 3.5 in chapter 3 and figure 5.2). He trailed Brown by 4 points in July but started to build up a lead though August and September.

The September 8–11 *LA Times Poll* shows that Brown was trailing Wilson by 2 points among registered voters and a worrying 9 points among likely voters. With the trend clearly against her, Brown's responded by going on the offensive,

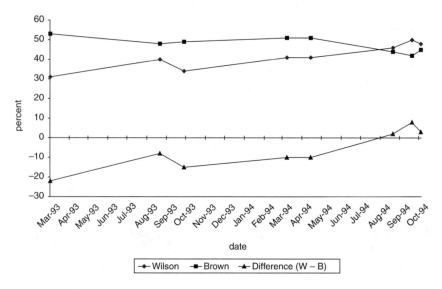

Figure 5.2   Governor's Contest Poll Ratings, March 1993–October 1994

Sources: See appendix A.

attacking—rather than just opposing—Prop. 187 and Wilson's association with it. In mid September, and not for the last time, she accused Wilson of using "inflammatory" language and "scapegoating" illegal immigrants. She also focused on the reasonably suspects clause. Although she fell short of describing Prop. 187 as racist, the implication of her attack was clear: "What it [Prop. 187] fails to tell you is exactly how you're supposed to determine that reasonable suspicion. Is it by the color of one's skin? Is it by the accent? The last name maybe?"[50]

At a campaign rally in Los Angeles the day after Wilson endorsed Prop. 187, Brown claimed her opponent was a hypocrite. She produced letters that the then Senator Wilson had written to President Reagan claiming that the INS was stopping Mexican farm workers from entering the country when there was a shortage of labor to harvest crops. Moreover, Wilson while senator had, she said, voted for a federal law that provided health services to illegal immigrants, yet now he opposed this provision. Wilson had "cut a hole in the fence to allow millions of illegal immigrants in, and now he wants to patch that hole because that's what the polls tell him to do."[51] It seems that Brown's new tactics, combined with those of Taxpayers, helped erode the initiative's lead. Equally importantly, other high-profile Democrats throughout September and October attacked Prop. 187.

Other Oppositions

The Clinton administration became increasingly involved as the battle over Prop. 187 intensified. Because of the importance of California to Clinton's reelection prospects, he could not sit back and let California Republicans make the running on the highly emotional illegal-immigration issue. Officials from his administration therefore expressed their opposition to Prop. 187 and proposed alternative measures. On September 17 Attorney General Janet Reno visited California and announced a new federal program, "Operation Gatekeeper," to "shut the door on illegal immigration." Operation Gatekeeper would immediately assign one hundred more Border Patrol agents to the San Diego-Mexico border at the notoriously porous Imperial Beach area, with a further 700 agents arriving in the 1995 fiscal year. She also announced a program to fingerprint all illegal entrants to the United States; an increase in the deportation target from 3,000 to 6,000 a year; tougher penalties for those caught smuggling undocumented persons into the United States; and improved border security, comprising better lighting and fences. Operation Gatekeeper was put into effect on the first weekend in October 1994, one month before election-day.[52] Reno also announced that $130 million would be transferred from the federal government to California to help pay for the incarceration of undocumented felons.

On September 20 Education Secretary Richard Riley threatened to stop federal aid to California schools if Prop. 187 passed. He argued that the initiative violated privacy rights established in the U.S. Family Education Rights and Privacy Act because school administrators would have to verify the residency status of pupils and their parents and report suspected illegal immigrants to the INS. The Los Angeles Board of Education predicted that California as a whole could lose $2.3 billion in federal grants for education and the Los Angeles Unified School District alone could lose $450 million if Prop. 187 passed and

Riley implemented his threat.[53] Ron Prince denied that California would lose any federal money, accusing Prop. 187's opponents of using scare tactics to confuse voters.[54] Indeed, California's electoral importance made it unlikely that any president or Congress would try to implement such punitive reprisals. Nevertheless, the attacks on the initiative continued, and the administration continued to offer alternative solutions. INS Commissioner Doris Meissner argued that the way to deal with illegal immigration was to enhance border enforcement and ensure that undocumented residents were prevented from working. She announced that the Clinton administration would introduce various legislative initiatives into the next Congress to do this.[55]

By October 19 Vice President Al Gore, INS Commissioner Doris Meissner, Attorney General Janet Reno, and Clinton's chief of staff Leon E. Panetta had all spoken out against Prop. 187. Then on October 21 President Clinton and Senator Feinstein added their voices to the opposition. At a televised press conference at the White House, Clinton reinforced many of the arguments put forward by the No campaign, arguing that the passage of Prop. 187 would produce more crime and health problems. Without mentioning him by name, Clinton also criticized Governor Wilson for voting for the Immigration Reform and Control Act of 1986, which led to millions of illegal aliens being given legal residency and, later, citizenship, and argued that "I don't think as a matter of practice it's a good thing to condition an election referendum, much less other elections in California, on a measure that even the supporters say is unconstitutional."[56]

Dianne Feinstein announced her opposition to Prop. 187 the day after Michael Huffington, her Republican opponent in a vituperative and expensive U.S. Senate race, endorsed it. In a speech to the Commonwealth Club in San Francisco, Feinstein said,

> I simply do not believe it will work. I read the polls and know that a majority of Californians support it. No way do I question the sincerity of working Californians, for I'm as fed up with the situation as they (are). But I believe that Proposition 187 won't solve the problem, it'll only make things worse.[57]

While criticizing Huffington's endorsement as "the politically expedient thing to do," Feinstein admitted that her opposition "could cost me votes, quite possibly the election."[58]

Both Feinstein and Huffington had already run hard on illegal immigration during the campaign. Each candidate ran television ads attacking the other's position while promoting their own tough stance. Surprisingly then, on October 11, Huffington did not know what the illegal immigration initiative was called or what it was about. In response to a question at a fund-raising event in San Francisco, Huffington replied, "I have not yet made a public stand on 170, er [stammering], what was that?" to which the crowd chanted, "One, Eighty, Seven."[59] Only nine days later, on October 20, Huffington announced his support for Prop. 187, arguing "It's time to send a message to those illegal immigrants who disregard our laws and take advantage of our government's misplaced generosity. Equally importantly, it is high time we send a message to Washington. The taxpayers of California are sick and tired of paying for Washington's federally imposed mandates while Washington ignores their federal responsibility at the border."[60] Pat Buchanan also endorsed the initiative on October 20. He called Prop. 187 "pro-family and pro-American" and rejected accusations that it was racist, adding "[i]t is not bigotry to put your own country and own family first. That is the essence of true charity and patriotism."[61]

Huffington's and Buchanan's endorsements were counterbalanced by the opposition of two other prominent Republicans, Jack F. Kemp and William Bennett. Kemp, previously President George H. W. Bush's housing and urban development secretary, and Bennett, President Ronald Reagan's education secretary, had joined forces in the 1990s as codirectors of the Empower America think tank. Their announcement to oppose Prop. 187 on October 18 was significant because they were the first national Republican figures to come out against it, although Bennett had earlier expressed support based, he claimed, on the faulty understanding that the initiative did no more than bar illegal immigrants from welfare services. They noted in a press release that, "For some, immigrants have become a popular political and social scapegoat. But concerns about illegal immigration should not give rise to a series of fundamentally flawed, constitutionally questionable 'solutions' which are not consistent with our history."[62] Both men expressed the belief that the passage of Prop. 187 would lead to similar attempts to legislate against illegal immigration in other states, encourage the rise of nativist sentiment, and perhaps ultimately produce a reaction against even legal immigration. They warned the Republican Party against adopting an anti-immigrant platform that could lead to strong Democratic support among the new generation of Asian and Latino voters, noting that the Republican Party's hostility to "the last generation of immigrants from Italy, Ireland and the nations of Central Europe . . . helped to create a Democratic base in many of America's cities . . . Can anyone calculate the political cost of turning away immigrants this time?"[63] As an alternative to Prop. 187, they proposed that the government close the border, prevent the use of bogus immigration documents, and reform the INS. More importantly for the No campaign, they also raised the specter that the measure could lead to racial discrimination, thus reinforcing the message of Taxpayers and Brown. The initiative was, they said, a "mandate for ethnic discrimination. Does anyone seriously doubt that Latino children named Rodriguez would be more likely to 'appear' to be illegal than Anglo children named, say, Jones?"[64] Kemp, an early front-runner for the 1996 GOP presidential nomination, warned against nationalizing the immigration issue and turning "the party away from its historic belief in opportunity and jobs and growth, and . . . inward to a protectionist and isolationist and more xenophobic party. That would be something around which the soul of our party would be decided."[65]

Appealing to conservative values, Kemp and Bennett argued that encouraging teachers and others officials to report illegal immigrants could produce a Big Brother state and another layer of bureaucracy that conservatives should oppose. Following the Kemp-Bennett statement, several conservative think tanks—including the Alexis de Tocqueville Institution, the Reason Foundation, and the Heritage Foundation—issued a joint press release condemning the initiative. The statement, issued on November 3, five days before the election, reiterated Kemp and Bennett's concern that the passage of Prop. 187 could lead to Big Brother government by "promot[ing] government intrusion into the lives of individuals." School administrators and other public officials would become "de facto INS agents and Border Patrol guards, forc[ed] . . . to investigate the citizen status of every child and parent."[66]

Kemp's opposition to Prop. 187 produced much consternation among his conservative brethren, especially in the pages of the *National Review* where William F. Buckley argued "he was just offbeat a hemidemisemiquaver on developing conservative orthodoxy [because] he did not endorse Proposition 187."[67] Surely, Buckley thought, all good conservatives should support an initiative that promised to reduce the welfare burden at the expense of people who should not even be in the country?

Prop. 187's Proponents and Wilson Play Softball

The second half of October 1994 was not a good time for Prop. 187. Alan Nelson noted that the Yes campaign was being "outspent and outgunned, so [the No campaign] was getting a lot more attention. As [the Yes campaign was] sliding back, [the No campaign] was feeling pretty cocky that the trend was against 187."[68] Nelson's comments captured a general feeling that the swathe of opposition announcements from politicians of different partisan and ideological persuasions was swinging the campaign against the initiative. In response, Prop. 187's proponents tried to assure voters that any problems would be ironed out in the courts. Some even went so far as to suggest that the specific provisions of the initiative did not matter because "this is a message initiative and we're sending a message to Washington, to Sacramento: Enough's enough."[69] Supporters of Prop. 187 also began to use language that was more conciliatory toward immigrants. Wilson's two new television ads launched on October 24 both made a distinction between legal and illegal immigration and their tone was much less hard edged. While his May ad intoned "They keep coming," one of his new ads said,

> *there's a right way and a wrong way,* (and) to reward the wrong way is not the American way. . . . American citizenship is a treasure beyond measure. But now the rules are being broken. . . . Join Governor Wilson in sending a strong message to Congress and to the courts to stop illegal immigration[70]

Wilson also backtracked on some radical remarks he had made to the *San Francisco Chronicle*. In an interview with the paper, Wilson had proposed the introduction of an official identity card that someone seeking a job, emergency medical care, or schooling should present as a way of preventing illegal immigrants receiving services to which they were not entitled. Wilson's campaign team quickly realized that its charge had overstepped the political mark; no one had yet suggested the introduction as anything as radical as an identity card to which Americans have longstanding and intense antipathies. In response to the adverse criticism and worries of his campaign team, Wilson backtracked. He claimed he had always opposed the introduction of a national identity card that must be carried at all times, but was in favor of a proof-of-residence card to be shown only when applying for jobs, healthcare, or education services.[71] One political analyst commented:

> Wilson's polling must be indicating that his harsh rhetoric on immigration is beginning to backfire. If Wilson ratchets up the rhetoric to point where he mobilized the right, he may well risk losing the moderate liberals and Democrats to Brown.[72]

In sum, the polls suggest that Taxpayers' and Brown's attacks combined with the swathe of opposition announcements from high-profile Democratic and Republican politicians had a negative effect on Prop. 187's support. The 34-point advantage among registered voters enjoyed by Prop. 187 in early September 1994 declined to 29 points in early October and then to just 12 points in late October. The No campaign had clawed back 17 points in just two weeks and, if this trend continued in the two weeks remaining before election day, victory for Prop. 187 no longer looked assured. As *LA Times Poll* director John Brennan commented, "what seemed inevitable two weeks ago is inevitable no longer. As people pay more attention to this thing, they seem to like it less and less."[73] Indeed, as the contest entered its final week, the final *Field Poll* of the campaign showed that Prop. 187 led by just 1 percentage point among all adults, and Woodward and McDowell's private polls showed the contest was too close to call.[74]

A Shot in the Foot

At the same time that Taxpayers and Woodward and McDowell looked as though they had begun to turn the campaign around, events outside their control halted them in their tracks. Toward the end of October 1994, when the No on 187 campaign surged in the polls, and through early November, the mainstream message of Taxpayers began to be crowded out by direct-action grassroots protests against Prop. 187. The first major anti-187 grassroots protest was a march and rally that took place in Los Angeles on October 16—"the largest demonstration in recent Los Angeles history" according to the *LA Times*.[75] Starting in Los Angeles' Eastside and proceeding nearly four miles to the City Hall downtown, the column of mainly Latino marchers stretched for over a mile; the police estimated that between 60,000 and 70,000 people took part, and CNN up to 150,000.[76] At the rally outside City Hall some speakers denounced Pete Wilson as a racist and protesters burned the governor in effigy.

As well as helping to defeat Prop. 187, the march's organizers also hoped it would prove a catalyst for the development of a new homogenous political consciousness among Latinos. They hoped, in effect, to create a new civil rights movement.[77] Their agenda thus differed markedly from that of the mainstream opposition, which consisted solely of defeating Prop. 187. There was, unsurprisingly, conflict between the mainstream and the grassroots opposition even before the march took place. Taxpayers took no part in organizing the march, and nor did any of its representatives or affiliates attend. Even MALDEF representatives expressed their unease at such a large Latino march so close to polling day. Both Taxpayers and MALDEF actively lobbied for the event to be postponed, arguing that a mass of Latino faces would only alienate the white electorate. One anti-187 activist commented, "the last thing we need is a sense that Los Angeles is truly overrun by all these immigrants. A lot of this is about image."[78]

In the event, the fears of the mainstream opposition were fully realised. Many newspapers and television news bulletins featured the march prominently. Macdonald later described the march as a "huge blow." He noted that the march was pictured on the front page of the *LA Times* and commented:

> People used to make jokes just because it was so funny to see how many
> Mexican flags there could possibly be in this picture. It was on talk-radio for

weeks . . . [People who supported 187 think illegal immigrants] come here not in the traditional concept of immigrants to America—that they want to start a new life—but they don't relinquish their old ways or their citizenship. They [think illegals] live off the social programs of California, then go back [home] when they have the opportunity. And this picture just kind of screamed that to everybody.[79]

The images it projected are captured in a reader's letter to the *LA Times*, which noted "the sea of red, green and white Mexican flags and, in the foreground, one tiny lone American flag." Another letter said:

> It was sad to glimpse only a single U.S. flag amid a sea of Mexican flags . . . I think it illustrates the frustrations that many Californians feel about this issue. Why should Californians support a foreign welfare state on its own soil? I would like to see all those Mexican flag-wavers go back to Mexico and demand free health care, education, aid to dependent children and welfare.[80]

Ironically, proponents of Prop. 187 were delighted with the march. Nelson commented that "[a]ny time they're flying Mexican flags, it helps us." Political analyst Sherry Bebitch Jeffe concurred, arguing "In the cold reality of politics, the pictures that went out on the front pages and on television may have energized proponents of the proposition." Even some Latino activists and central figures in the No campaign were pessimistic about the march's potential effect. One Latino activist commented, "Some people felt the more visible we [Latinos] are, the more difficult it may be to beat this initiative." Scott Macdonald, clearly wanting to put a brave face on events, said, "It's difficult to assess whether it helps or hurts us at this point. It's time to move on."[81] The direct-action protests of the anti-187 grassroots activists did not however stop, much to the dismay of the mainstream opposition. In late October, energized by the march and drawing on knowledge gained during a summer 1994 conference organized for student leaders by CUAP 187 to discuss mobilization techniques, Latino-student protests against Prop. 187 took place all over California, mainly in the form of school walkouts.[82]

Latino-Student Walkouts

The "success," as the organizers perceived it, of the October 16 march encouraged them to continue with large-scale direct-action protests. To the horror of the mainstream opposition, Juan Jose Gutierrez, who had helped organize the march, organized a countywide school walkout in Los Angeles County for November 2. Taxpayers and some Latino activists were again faced with the prospect of a high-profile Latino protest that could hurt the No campaign and lobbied for the walkout to be abandoned. Gutierrez said he would call off the planned protest if all school principals in Los Angeles County followed the advice of Los Angeles Unified School District officials and organized alternative in-school protest events. In the event, the November 2 walkout was cancelled after discussions with parents and an agreement that the Los Angeles Unified School District would encourage in-school events and discussions. However, many of the walkouts, sit-ins, and other student protests were ad hoc, spontaneous responses to Prop. 187, and these continued unabated. In a snowballing effect, when one school in a district staged a walkout or sit-in, others followed, and the protests were soon dominating news coverage of the initiative despite the abandonment of the November 2 walkout.[83]

Macdonald from Taxpayers publicly admitted at the time that the student protests had "[d]istracted the voters. We believe that anything that keeps people from taking time to understand the initiative is not helping our side." On November 1 Macdonald claimed that his private tracking polls showed that, for the first time, Prop. 187 was losing. But on November 3 he admitted that he had not looked at the polls since the first because the student protests had made him too "terrified." Macdonald later commented that the walkouts might have been the central reason why their poll numbers dropped in November:

> It was every night on the news and it was a nightmare. You could see the polling numbers change as the kids ran. They were trying to do what they thought they could do to make a point—although some of them were just running out of class. Overall, they wanted to do something, and they were trying to do what they could, and it was a disaster. It was a disaster . . . All hell broke loose. Of course, what drives you crazy is all hell didn't break loose because the other side came up with some [good] idea.[84]

Professor Bruce Cain agreed that the protests were "probably a break for the pro-187 people. It would be very easy for everybody to become fixated on the events and sort of ignore the issues." Alan Nelson was not surprised that his opponents were so worried about the Latino-student protests: "people can draw their own conclusions" about the student demonstrations and waving of Mexican flags, "but I would say that's un-American."[85]

By early November the contest was too close to call. As we have seen, the polls showed that the initiative's lead had been cut substantially, and Woodward and McDowell's private polling apparently showed that the No campaign had taken a narrow lead. However, the mainstream No campaign was extremely concerned that the anti-187 Latino-student walkouts would halt their ascent in the polls. On the other side, Prop. 187's proponents drew some comfort from the Latino protests, but their confidence was diminishing quickly and defeat seemed a real possibility. So as the campaign entered its final week, with neither side confident of victory, a frantic and feverish finale looked likely.

The Final Week

The October improvement in the No campaign's poll ratings encouraged donors—previously unwilling to donate to a losing cause—to commit money for a final effort in November. In the final week, the No on 187 campaign received one million dollars in donations, nearly equal to what it had raised previously.[86] Joel Maliniak, spokesperson for Taxpayers, claimed that the new influx of money was "significant and part of the momentum that's been happening."[87] The new money enabled the No campaign to air several anti-187 commercials, although not as many as they would have liked. Macdonald later pointed out that it is difficult to buy airtime so late in the campaign because most of it has already been booked. Macdonald also observed that the money could have been used more effectively if it was available early in the campaign. His reasoning was that people's opinions become more fixed and harder to change as the campaign progresses; early advertising works best.[88]

Surprisingly, there was little organized and coordinated activity by the whole Prop. 187 committee. Barbara Coe said, "we're not doing anything, if you will, organized. But we feel very good."[89] Moreover, both Harold Ezell and Alan Nelson had become somewhat detached from the committee. And in early October Ezell announced that he would refuse all future speaking requests after he was confronted by anti-187 protesters while speaking to the Encino Republican Women Federated Group.[90] There was, however, an ad hoc flourish of activity from some Prop. 187 supporters. Coe and her California Coalition for Immigration Reform (CCIR) planned an election-day protest outside polling stations to discourage noncitizens from voting. They planned to post flyers outside polling stations that read "Only citizens can vote." Coe claimed in a letter to CCIR members that "[s]ince there are no safeguards (to) ensure citizenship (of voters), this is our greatest fear—that illegal aliens will 'stuff' the ballot boxes!"[91] More importantly, the Federation for American Immigration Reform (FAIR) sponsored a series of pro-187 radio ads in the final week, costing $132,568.[92] As well as FAIR's new ads, Wilson was still running his anti-illegal immigration television commercials, which began on October 24. The Yes campaign was also buoyed by Brown's poor gubernatorial campaign. Brown ran desperately short of money in the final few days of the campaign and had to pull several planned television ads.

Essentially, the Prop. 187 committee was relying on others to promote its message and on the Latino-student protests to damage the No campaign. It is likely that FAIR's ads and Wilson's commercial helped check the slippage in Prop. 187's support that had begun in mid October. Moreover, the continuing Latino-student protests also probably helped stop the downturn. Eight Los Angeles schools staged walkouts on November 1. Around 8,000 students took part in the walkouts on the second. Between 4,000 and 10,000 did so on the third, and around 3,500 on the fourth.[93] Coe argued in response "that loyal Americans will come forward and support Proposition 187 . . . If [the student protests have] been anything like some in the past, if you're a loyal American and you love your country, they will hurt [you] real bad."[94] However, her committee colleague Ron Prince did not think that the march and the walkouts had much impact on Prop. 187's support. He attributed any overall drop in support to Wilson's anti-illegal immigration ads, arguing that they turned off Latino voters.[95]

The publicity produced by the school walkouts also started to worry school administrators. Los Angeles County Unified School District officials had originally followed a lenient policy to those organizing and involved in the school walkouts—there would be no suspensions so long as the protests were peaceful. However, as the protests grew increasingly emotional and frequent, district officials and school principals changed tack. Expounding the district's new position, spokesman Bill Rivera said the "whole emphasis [now] is to try to persuade the kids to stay in school." On November 7, the day before the election, the school district announced that students participating in walkouts would be regarded as truants. Officials also liaised with schools and colleges to encourage them to stage in-house demonstrations as a way of channeling frustration. However, over 2,500 students walked out of Los Angeles District schools on the seventh. Other anti-187 protesters also staged rallies and marches, and over 1,000 people converged on Los Angeles City Hall. Unfortunately for the No campaign, the flag issue was again prominent. While Mexican and other flags from Latin American countries were highly visible at previous marches, on the City Hall march some protesters were carrying American flags—but upside down.[96]

Law-enforcement agencies also grew increasingly worried about the walkouts and the possibility that they could turn violent if Prop. 187 was passed. Police in Los Angeles County held an emergency meeting on November 1 to plan and coordinate the emergency services' response if violence flared after the vote. The Los Angeles Police Department (LAPD) decided to open its emergency operations center in East Los Angeles. Extra police officers were stationed on the streets, all leave was cancelled, and the force was placed on a tactical alert. Police officers also met with student leaders to encourage them to remain calm and to stage in-school protests rather than walkouts. Gloria Molina, Los Angeles county supervisor and a leading Latino in the No campaign, visited schools and colleges across Los Angeles County and appeared on Spanish-language television to promote the same message.

Ventura County law-enforcement agencies also made contingency plans in case of unrest. The county's Sheriff's Department cancelled all leave and drafted additional officers into uniform for election and postelection day. Uniformed officers were stationed at every school in Oxnard, Ventura County, and a helicopter was made available for surveillance. Community groups joined the police in appealing for calm.[97]

Even the Mexican government—usually unwilling to engage in the other countries' domestic disputes—became embroiled in the controversy. In a formal protest to the U.S. State Department, the Mexican government argued that California's interference in the migration of Mexican laborers was an affront to Mexican sovereignty. President Carlos Salinas de Gortari defended the rights of Mexican migrant workers and called Prop. 187 inherently xenophobic in his state of the union address. And Andreas Rozental, Mexico's Deputy Foreign Minister, said the controversy created by Prop. 187 would make "immigration . . . the number 1 issue between the United States and Mexico for the next few years."[98] Some Mexicans boycotted American goods, and in Mexico City demonstrations against Prop. 187 took place outside the U.S. Embassy and forty masked-men attacked a McDonald's restaurant.[99]

By this time Prop. 187 had become the most important initiative referendum in California since Prop. 13 in 1978. Voters considered the contest more important than both the U.S. senatorial and the California gubernatorial elections, with 37 percent saying it would motivate them to vote—more than twice the number citing the governor's contest and four times the senatorial one.[100] And the *New York Times's* William Safire suggested that Prop. 187 could

provide impetus for groups [such as FAIR] that seek to curtail legal immigration drastically . . . [Prop. 187's] fate may ultimately determine the economic future of California and other hard-pressed areas such as New York City that depend increasingly on the entrepreneurial energy and ambition of legal immigrants. Yet until those who favor immigration face up to the storm over illegal entrants, this latest California tidal wave could end up extinguishing one of the greatest sources of American renewal.[101]

However, opinion polls at the end of October suggested that the passage of Prop. 187, once seemingly inevitable, was no longer certain. The various denunciations of it in the last month, and the emotion released on both sides by the student protests in the final week of the campaign, only added to the uncertainty. With law-enforcement agencies bracing themselves for violence, voters cast their ballots on November 8, 1994. In the event, the initiative's supporters need not have worried. Californians gave Prop. 187 their backing, with 59 percent voting Yes and just 41 No.[102]

Conclusions

Prop. 187 continued to enjoy a considerable lead in opinion polls during the early stages of the campaign as neither the mainstream nor the grassroots opposition made much impact. It was always unlikely that the No campaign would have a significant effect while its messages were contradictory and incoherent. The message promoted early in the campaign was ineffective precisely for this reason. However, when the mainstream opposition went on the offensive, drawing connections between racist organizations and Prop. 187, and when Brown started to attack Wilson and his association with the initiative, the No campaign reduced its poll deficit by 5 points between early September and early October 1994. Despite this reduction, Prop. 187 still enjoyed majority support from most demographic groups. Despite the involvement of the Catholic Church and unions in the No campaign, Catholic voters favored it by 56 to 37 percent and union members by 55 to 34 percent. The initiative also enjoyed majority support amongst Republicans (75-19), Democrats (52-40), independents (57-34), and whites (64-28). However, Latinos now opposed the measure narrowly by 48-46.

The change from majority Latino support in early September to opposition in early October was significant and encouraging for the No campaign. It highlighted that Prop. 187 had become increasingly "racialized" and suggested that the focus of Taxpayers on the "racist" link between the Pioneer Fund and Prop. 187's authors was working. The move away from attacking the specific provisions of the initiative was a wise choice because Californians did not seem interested in its provisions. For example, when opinion poll respondents were informed that Prop. 187 could produce savings of *millions* of dollars 58 percent said this would make them more likely to vote Yes, yet when they were read the argument that it could lead to losses of *billions* of dollars in federal aid only 26 percent said this would make them less likely to vote Yes.[103]

Prop. 187's lead was further reduced during mid October when officials from the Clinton administration, Senator Feinstein, and Republicans Jack Kemp and William Bennett announced their opposition. Their attacks together with the continuing efforts of Taxpayers and Brown probably had some impact on the further reduction in Prop. 187's lead from 29 to 12 points between early and late October.

During this time Latino support for Prop. 187 fell further, from −2 points in early October to −43 points in late October (see figure 5.3). Support for Prop. 187

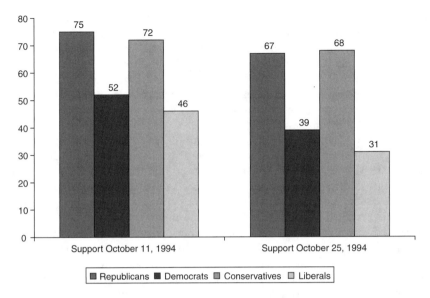

Figure 5.3 Support for Prop. 187, Various Groups, October 1994

Sources: LA Times Polls. See appendix A.

also fell significantly among liberals and Democrats. While it is impossible to say definitely which groups found which arguments most persuasive, it is probable that liberals and Democrats, like Latinos, were influenced by the attacks implying Prop. 187 was driven by racial considerations and would have an inequitable effect on certain racial groups. The logic is that before the racialized attacks on Prop. 187 the Taxpayers tactic of emphasizing the impact of the initiative in terms of increased crime, health risks, and taxes had little effect on support for the initiative. Only when Taxpayers and others began to racialize Prop. 187 did its support erode.

Interestingly, the racialized arguments of the No campaign had less effect on support for Prop. 187 among conservatives and Republicans than among Latinos, liberals, and Democrats. Conservative and Republican support decreased only marginally during October. It would be wrong however to con-clude that conservative and Republican support for Prop. 187 was driven by racism merely because these groups were not susceptible to the arguments that the initiative was racist. An alternative and more satisfactory explanation is that conservatives and Republicans were more committed to it and therefore less likely to withdraw their support. They were more committed in part because of a combination of factors revolving around the gubernatorial contest. Conservatives and Republicans overwhelmingly supported Wilson, and Wilson had champi-oned illegal immigration reform generally and Prop. 187 specifically. Thus, while Wilson continued to support Prop. 187, so would these two groups. Moreover, Wilson's support may have legitimized Prop. 187 in face of the attacks on it. This interpretation of conservative and Republican commitment to Prop. 187 allows us, in turn, to understand why the arguments of Kemp and Bennett (and some other conservative groups such as the Alexis de Tocqueville Institution) had little impact on their target groups. It appears that the conservative attacks on Prop. 187 instead had a greater effect on liberals and Democrats. But why? The fact that even the political opponents of liberals and Democrats—whom some may well have viewed as extremists—came out against Prop. 187 may have led liberals and Democrats to question the morality of supporting it and the motivations of those behind the initiative.

Turning to the other side of the opposition, what effect did the grassroots mobilization against Prop. 187 have? It was suggested earlier in the chapter that the grassroots direct-action protests—particularly the large October 16 march, the Latino-student school walkouts, and the accompanying Mexican flags— probably had a significant but detrimental effect on the No campaign. The fear of Taxpayers that the protests would alienate important swing voters appears justified. Support for Prop. 187 dropped dramatically in October when some high-profile politicians expressed their opposition, but this decline stopped as the march and then the school walkouts began to dominate news coverage of the contest in the final week. However, Wilson continued to run his anti-illegal immigration television ads and FAIR started to run some pro-187 radio spots in the final week, which also helped stop the slippage in its support. These commercials alone cannot account for the significant turnaround in support that occurred. Between the poll and the vote, the dominating issue surrounding Prop. 187 was the school walkouts. The direct-action grassroots mobilizations were mainly responsible for the dramatic increase in Prop. 187's support during the final week of the campaign.

Chapter 6

The Judicial Death of Proposition 187

Proposition 187's victory made headlines across the United States.[1] Many stories focused on the initiative's impressive margin of victory, on how it would change immigration policy in California and possibly the wider United States, and on how it had helped propel Governor Wilson to an unexpected second term. Other reports, meanwhile, concentrated on the deleterious consequences of the radical initiative. They examined the angry reaction of Latinos, the street protests, the student boycott of schools and their participation in demonstrations and civic unrest.[2] They reported the anecdotal evidence that pointed to an increase in racial abuse of Latinos—whether American citizens, legal residents, or undocumented—by (white) Californians who interpreted the initiative's success as a liberation from social mores regarding public expressions of racism.[3] Still other reports suggested that attendance decreased at medical centers as undocumented persons missed appointments because of fears about deportation.[4] Health officials worried that if undocumented persons did not seek early treatment for communicable diseases such as TB and measles, a health crisis could develop as the diseases spread quickly to the wider California population.[5] One of the most shocking reports told of the death of an undocumented twelve-year-old boy, Julio Cano, on November 19. Julio had fallen ill with chest and bowel pains on November 16, one week after Prop. 187's electoral victory. Julio's father, also an undocumented resident, told reporters how he had been afraid to take his son to the community clinic or hospital because he thought staff there would inform the immigration authorities about his illegal status. Instead, the family raised $60 to send Julio to a private physician on November 18. The doctor gave the boy an enema and some antibiotics. The next day he was dead.[6] Although it is unclear whether earlier medical treatment could have prevented Julio's death,[7] his parents' concern about being reported to the authorities was ill-founded, thus making their son's death even more tragic. His parents need not have worried about seeking medical assistance because most of Prop. 187 never became law. Immediately after its approval by the California electorate it was enjoined in various state and federal courts, where it would remain until its formal death in 1999.

It would be wrong to infer from its legal demise that Prop. 187 was a short-lived populist reaction against undocumented immigrants that had no long-term policy consequences. Its passage provided the inspiration and blueprint for a number of significant changes to federal immigration law, most notably in the form of the 1996 Illegal Immigration Reform and Individual Responsibility Act and the immigration provisions in the 1996 Personal Responsibility and Work Opportunity Reconciliation Act—better known as the Immigration Act and the Welfare Reform Act, respectively. In addition, it opened up an opportunity for the passage of two more "anti-minority" initiatives. The first in 1996 ended affirmative action in California; the second in 1998 ended bilingual education in the state's schools. Prop. 187, then, was much more than a high-profile example of the 1990s backlash against illegal immigrants. Rather, its electoral success further increased the saliency of the illegal-immigration issue and proved the catalyst for further changes to immigration policy. It defined the nature of the debate about illegal immigration in the United States in the last decade of the twentieth century, and it structured the policy choices made by politicians in response to the public's anti-immigrant outburst. Later still, it would force the GOP to reconsider its anti-immigrant and, by association, anti-Latino stance and ultimately strengthen Latinos' position in the political community. That, however, is the story of the forthcoming chapters. The story of the present one is Prop. 187's unceremonious death in the courts.

The Early Judicial Challenges

As was widely expected by both its proponents and opponents, Prop. 187's electoral victory engendered a series of legal challenges. Four separate cases were filed in the federal District Court and several others in various state courts. California Superior Court judge Stuart R. Pollak struck the first blow on November 9, 1994—the very day after Prop. 187's victory—by issuing a temporary restraining order on the initiative's education provisions. Federal District Judge Matthew Byrne Jr. also struck an early blow, agreeing with the plaintiffs that the implementation of all its most important provisions should be halted temporarily until a proper hearing could be held. To simplify the legal challenges to Prop. 187 the federal cases were quickly consolidated as the *League of United Latin American Citizens et al. v. Wilson* and placed on the docket of Judge Mariana R. Pfaelzer's LA-based Federal District Court. The first action of Pfaelzer, taken in a court hearing on November 22, 1994, was to extend Judge Byrne's temporary restraining order on Prop. 187 until a further hearing on December 14 could determine whether a preliminary injunction should be issued. Pfaelzer also emphasized that the state should not make public any regulations relating to the implementation of the initiative in the meantime.[8] Only the provisions regarding the sale and use of false identity and citizenship documents were permitted to go into effect.

A wide variety of organizations joined the legal effort to defeat Prop. 187. Many of those involved in the electoral campaign also joined the legal effort as plaintiffs, including the Mexican American Legal Defense and Educational Fund (MALDEF), the League of United Latin American Citizens (LULAC), the American Civil Liberties Union (ACLU), the Pacific American Legal Center of Southern California, and the Center for Human Rights and Constitutional Law.

In addition to these and other civil rights groups, many local governments, school boards, and quasi-governmental agencies joined the fight. For example, the California School Boards Association, Los Angeles Unified School District, Sacramento City Unified School District, and LA City Council all joined the legal actions, as did religious and medical groups such as the Californian Association of Catholic Hospitals and the Catholic Health Association of the United States.

However, many organizations opposed to Prop. 187 chose not to enter the judicial fray immediately. For example, the LA County Board of Supervisors and the Antelope Valley Union High School District did not, despite having ideological and logistical objections to Prop. 187.[9] And the thirteen-member LA City Council spent many meetings debating how best to proceed. City attorney James M. Hahn—later mayor of Los Angeles—finally recommended to the council that it should proceed with its legal challenge but avoid using public money to finance it.[10] Hahn suggested the council seek free counsel from private lawyers.[11] Other organizations waited many months before joining the suits against Prop. 187—including unions such as the California Teachers Association, the California Faculty Association, the Service Employees International Union, and the American Federation of State, County and Municipal Employees, and religious groups such as the California Council of Churches and the Muslim Public Affairs Council.[12] One explanation for these groups' late arrival in the judicial arena is that they feared the disapproval of large sections of the California population. Many Californians were angry that the citizen-approved initiative had not been implemented immediately on its passage, but instead had been snarled up in the courts by elective officials and bureaucrats perceived to be thwarting the will of the majority. Others were further riled because they thought that most of the legal challenges to Prop. 187 were funded with "taxpayer dollars." Faced with a torrent of phone calls from irate taxpayers and with some elected officials facing the threat of recall, many agencies and politicians tried to duck the issue.[13]

Meanwhile, Governor Wilson, on a high after being swept back to office on the pro-187 tide, and Attorney General Dan Lungren began preparing the legal defense of Prop. 187 and the grounds for the state's implementation of the initiative. Wilson issued an executive order barring "as soon as legally possible" undocumented persons in California from receipt of prenatal-care services and nursing-home care, and he directed various state agencies to draft the necessary regulations to facilitate the initiative's implementation.[14] Wilson also sent a letter to President Clinton asking for his and the Immigration and Naturalization Service's (INS) help in implementing Prop. 187 and pleading that the federal government should not follow up its threat to cut California's grant if the initiative passed—always an unlikely prospect given California's political clout at the national level. Lungren's office issued forms to various state agencies, including those dealing with law enforcement, on which they could report the names of suspected illegal aliens.[15] However, the various cases making their way through many different courts rendered moot the actions of Wilson and Lungren. Prop. 187 had been thrown to the courts, where it would be mauled and suffer a long, drawn-out, unglamorous death. Wilson's high would not last long.

The strategy and arguments of each side in the legal dispute changed over time. In the first instance, the state argued that the court should not prevent Prop. 187 being enforced until regulations relating to its implementation were drawn up. Lawyers for the state suggested that well-written regulations could help circumvent many of the legal problems inherent in the initiative's language, thus safeguarding the will of a majority of voters. Unsurprisingly, the plaintiffs did not want the state lawyers to defend the regulations, but Prop. 187 itself.[16] As one ACLU lawyer said, "it's like giving a face lift to Frankenstein [sic] to turn it into Mother Teresa."[17] The defendants also wanted the case transferred from the federal to the state courts, where they believed they had a greater chance of success. This is because the appointees of Republican governors dominated the state appellate courts, because the state courts are generally regarded to be more accountable and responsive to public opinion in California than the federal courts (because state judges can be recalled), and because the state courts had a history of deferring to citizen-approved propositions.[18] Furthermore, the state defendants regarded the Carter-appointed federal district judge allocated the case, Mariana Pfaelzer, as a liberal likely to be sympathetic to the plaintiffs.

Their worries were well founded. At the hearing on December 14, three weeks after extending Judge Byrne's temporary restraining order, Pfaelzer ruled in favor of the plaintiffs, issuing a preliminary injunction to block implementation of the initiative's most significant provisions until a full trial could determine its legality. Pfaelzer argued that Prop. 187 raised enough serious constitutional issues to warrant a trial. Most significantly, the initiative appeared to encroach on the federal government's power to regulate immigration. Furthermore, the initiative's educational provision barring undocumented persons from attending public schools clashed with the U.S. Supreme Court's 1982 ruling in *Plyler v. Doe*. While *Plyler* did not establish a right to education, it said denying undocumented children access to public schooling violated the Constitution's equal protection clause. Because it "imposes a lifetime hardship on a discrete class of children not accountable for their disabling status," states can only deny undocumented children education if it serves a "substantial" state interest.[19] As Justice William J. Brennan noted in his majority opinion in *Plyler*:

> It is difficult to understand precisely what the State [of Texas] hopes to achieve by promoting the creation and perpetuation of a subclass of illiterates within our boundaries, surely adding to the problem and costs of unemployment, welfare and crime . . . It is thus clear that whatever savings might be achieved by denying these children an education, they are wholly insubstantial in light of the cost involved to these children, the State, and the Nation.[20]

Pfaelzer also argued that the number of practical issues raised by Prop. 187 warranted a full trial. For example, she suggested that "the loss of medical services for illegal aliens could result in greater health risks for the general population."[21] In sum, Pfaelzer's ruling gutted the main provisions of Prop. 187, leaving in place only the section on the manufacture, sale, and use of false citizenship documents and the provision barring undocumented persons from attending universities and public colleges. The latter provision, however, had already been held invalid in a temporary restraining order issued by Judge Pollak in November.[22]

Moreover, the false citizenship provision contained a loophole that would render meaningless its penalties. Prop. 187 mandated that those found guilty of manufacturing or selling fake documents be imprisoned for five years or fined

$75,000. However, in the first case to reach the California courts after Prop. 187's passage the guilty defendants were sentenced to six months in jail with a further three years' probation, apparently violating the initiative's sentencing requirements. The authors, however, had mistakenly permitted the option of a fine, which under California law meant that the offense could be regarded legally as a misdemeanor, which in turn meant that prosecutors could enter into plea bargains with defendants. Guilty persons therefore did not have to receive the mandatory sentence or fine. Further, Prop. 187 actually reduced the penalties for persons found guilty of manufacturing *multiple* fake documents. California law already allowed for persons found guilty of this crime to be imprisoned for more than five years, whereas Prop. 187 imposed a maximum of five years no matter how many forgeries were involved. A further loophole came to light during a court case in April 1995. Because the illegal immigrant was found guilty of carrying just *one* false citizenship document, he received a much lower sentence than that mandated by Prop. 187. The reason was that the initiative's authors had unwittingly written that their new law applied to those carrying "false documents."[23]

Legal commentators noted in response that Prop. 187 had been "sloppily drafted" by a committee of nonlawyers.[24] While its authors expected some of its provisions would be challenged in court—and wisely included a severability clause—it is unlikely that they foresaw the extent to which it would be enjoined. The architects of Prop. 187, and Ron Prince especially, reacted angrily to the court cases. On the one hand, Prince and others attacked their opponents and the courts for ignoring the will of the people and being undemocratic. On the other, Prince turned against those defending the initiative in court—Pete Wilson, Dan Lungren, and lawyers from the attorney general's office—accusing them of incompetence and hinting that they were not fully committed to the cause.[25]

Civil rights lawyers were jubilant after Pfaelzer issued her preliminary injunction, while defense lawyers from Lungren's office were forced to rethink their strategy. They could try to appeal Pfaelzer's ruling to the U.S. Ninth Circuit Court of Appeals but would have to demonstrate that she abused her discretion. In addition, the defendants had to consider the length of time that an appeal would take; it may be quicker to go straight to trial rather than getting caught up in a potentially lengthy appeal, which had little chance of success. However, there was a good political reason for appealing. In not doing so the state defendants would send a clear message to the California public that the initiative has lost its first significant judicial battle, and thus hand a political victory to the plaintiffs. Conversely, in appealing, even if victory was unlikely, Wilson especially and Lungren could keep both the illegal-immigration issue and themselves firmly in the public eye. Given that the issue had worked so successfully for Wilson in the 1994 gubernatorial election and that he was then contemplating running for the presidency in 1996, a legal appeal seemed the obvious political, if not judicial, choice. Similarly, for Lungren, elected as attorney general in 1994 and harboring gubernatorial ambitions in 1998, the evidence suggested that in the contemporary political climate a hard-line on immigration would help secure the Republican nomination in the primaries and possibly play well with voters in the general election four years hence. It had worked spectacularly well for Wilson, after all. Yet Prop. 187 presented an ideological problem for Lungren. A

Republican proud of his links to the Latino community, he only endorsed Prop. 187 late in the campaign and with little enthusiasm. That he did endorse it, however, highlights the strength of public feeling on the issue in 1994; Lungren's short-term political instincts trumped his longer-term ideological position. In early 1995, with public sentiment still intensely anti-immigrant and with anger mounting over Prop. 187's judicial interment, it made political sense for Lungren to continue to push hard in the courts.

In the event, several appeals were filed. Lawyers for Wilson did appeal, but not to the U.S. Appeals Court. Rather, reviving an earlier tactic, Wilson filed a suit in the California Superior Court in San Francisco on January 27, 1995, requesting that the state courts uphold Prop. 187 and prevent the federal courts ruling until after the state courts had determined its legality.[26] The suit argued that "Under California law, the state courts have a 'solemn duty to jealously guard the precious initiative power' and to interpret a ballot proposition. Allowing the state courts to thoroughly rule on the law will demonstrate once and for all that the proposition can and should be interpreted to conform with federal law."[27] A spokesperson for the governor defended the appeal strategy, arguing, "Rather than doing it quickly, we want to make sure it's being done right. While the time factor is very important to us, being successful is more important."[28]

Lawyers from the attorney general's office appealed Pfaelzer's preliminary injunction on January 30, 1995, to the U.S. Ninth Circuit Court of Appeals, arguing that Pfaelzer had abused her discretion in blocking Prop. 187's implementation. They also requested, as had the governor's lawyers in their January 27 suit, that the federal courts abstain from the case until the state courts had ruled on the initiative.[29] The appeals court rejected this application on July 14, saying that Pfaelzer did not abuse her discretion.[30] On February 3, 1995, state lawyers also filed suit in Judge Pfaelzer's U.S. District Court, asking that she stand aside from the case until the state courts had ruled on Prop. 187's legality—even though Pfaelzer had already rejected an application that she abstain. An ACLU lawyer rightly called the state's machinations "a bizarre [judicial] strategy."[31] Pfaelzer dismissed the state's request to stand aside in a March 13 ruling: "A state court determination of the state issues presented by these actions would not terminate the controversy, nor would it obviate the need for a constitutional adjudication by the federal court."[32] In the same ruling, she also said that there would be a full trial by September 5, 1995, and that the state could continue to draw up privately regulations for the implementation of Prop. 187, which must be submitted to the court by April 15. Unsurprisingly, Wilson reacted angrily to the judgment. Claiming that the "patience of Californians will soon wear thin if their will is not carried out," Wilson promised to appeal Pfaelzer's decision not to abstain from the federal suits.[33] In a picket of Pfaelzer's LA courthouse, Barbara Coe, one of the key grassroots figures behind Prop. 187, carried a placard reading "5 Million Americans vs. One Corrupt Judge." Another protester's sign read "The Only Difference Between Hitler and Pfaelzer is the Mustache."[34]

Wilson received a further setback in the courts on February 13, 1995, when his suit against the federal government for reimbursement of $4 billion in state costs for incarcerating, educating, and providing healthcare to undocumented citizens was thrown out by U.S. district judge Judith Keep. The suit, filed in April 1994 during the gubernatorial campaign, constituted an important part of

Wilson's reelection strategy of keeping the illegal-immigration issue at the top of the political agenda. Keep's judgment elicited little surprise as Florida had had a similar suit dismissed in December 1994. Keep rejected the arguments that California faced an "invasion" of illegal immigrants who threatened "national security." In addition, Keep argued that there was no precedent for the federal government being sued by the states for its failure to enforce immigration laws.[35]

Governor Wilson responded to the many judicial setbacks by suggesting that the legislative route would prove more productive in the future. In particular, he believed that he could work with Republican congressional leaders in Washington—especially new House speaker Newt Gingrich and Senate majority leader Bob Dole—to reimburse the states for their immigration costs. He pointed to a bill already passed by the House allocating $600 million to the states for costs incurred incarcerating illegal immigrants and urged Clinton to sign it.[36] He also suggested that the federal government consider deporting illegal-immigrant felons—estimated by Wilson to number 20,000, or 15 percent of California's prison population—so they could complete their prison terms in their own countries.[37] As the law stood, such transfers required both the agreement of the individual prisoner and both countries. Attorney General Lungren, like Wilson, was also becoming increasingly pessimistic about the chances of victory in the courts, recognizing that the process could take "months and [possibly] some years."[38]

Nevertheless, his and Wilson's offices continued to pursue in early 1995 all possible legal avenues, including trying to take the cases out of the federal and into the state courts, even though most legal scholars thought this strategy had little chance of success.[39] Meanwhile, opponents of Prop. 187 were trying to effect the same strategy, but in reverse. MALDEF lawyers applied in late February to have the case before Pollak's San Francisco Superior Court transferred to U.S. district judge Lowell Jensen's courtroom, also in San Francisco. The next step was to have it transferred from there to Pfaelzer's Los Angeles–based federal court, where they believed they would receive a more sympathetic hearing.[40] On April 17, 1995, Reagan-appointee Judge Jensen ruled that the lawsuit should indeed be sent to Pfaelzer's court to be incorporated with the four other cases due to be tried in September, saying simply, "federal courts have jurisdiction over the case."[41]

About the same time that the Prop. 187's lawyers failed to persuade the courts to try the case solely in the state courts, they also decided to drop their argument that tightly drawn state regulations could circumvent some of the initiative's legal and logistical problems. The state, which had previously suggested that "surgically" precise regulations would nullify any legal problems in Prop. 187's language, was now suggesting that "the best strategic course . . . [is] to force the plaintiffs to attack the proposition on its face, which the Supreme Court says is the most difficult challenge to make,"[42] adding, "we felt the courts had enjoined us from issuing these regulations and we couldn't publish them, so we chose not to put them before the trial."[43] Consequently, state lawyers did not file the regulations with Judge Pfaelzer, a decision that legal scholars once again thought "very puzzling. With some aspects of the law, like due process before cutting off benefits to suspected illegal immigrants, the state's only hope is to say regulations will deal with it. I don't see how they can answer that issue except to provide for it by regulations."[44]

In response to the state's decision not to file the "surgical" regulations, opponents of Prop. 187 filed a motion for summary judgment with Pfaelzer on May 1, in effect asking her to declare the initiative unconstitutional without a full trial. Opponents reasoned that the state's decision not to submit the regulations was an admission that the law could not be salvaged and thus was "tantamount to throwing in the towel."[45] At the summary judgment hearing on July 26, 1995, the anti-187 lawyers argued that Pfaelzer should throw the case out of court because Prop. 187 was a state scheme to regulate immigration and thus preempted federal prerogatives in this area. State lawyers again tried to persuade Pfaelzer that the initiative did not preempt federal prerogatives but merely sought to withdraw public benefits from undocumented persons. They also again tried to persuade Pfaelzer that any problems with the initiative could be solved by writing appropriate implementation regulations, even though the state had earlier failed to submit such regulations to Pfaelzer. And once again Pfaelzer appeared unimpressed by the state's arguments. Even the state's lawyers admitted that things had not gone well for them, observing that "Some of her questions and comments suggested she was not leaning our way on certain issues."[46]

Pfaelzer did not make an immediate decision on the summary judgment motion. On September 7 she asked lawyers for the state to submit up to forty pages of arguments by October 10 on the question of Prop. 187's severability. As civil rights lawyer Stephen Yagman observed, the judge's concern about whether some provisions of Prop. 187 could be preserved if others were found unconstitutional suggested that she has "tentatively . . . decided that at least one section . . . is unconstitutional."[47] If the state could not persuade Pfaelzer that the initiative was severable, all of it would fall if just one section was judged unconstitutional. At the full hearing on the severability issue on October 23 both sides presented their opinions, but Pfaelzer once again declined to issue her opinion on the plaintiffs' motion for summary judgment. The full trial first scheduled for September 5, 1995, had already been postponed while arguments were heard for and against summary judgment, and now Pfaelzer seemed reluctant to make the summary judgment.

Finally, on November 20, 1995, Pfaelzer issued a seventy-two-page partial summary judgment ruling, granting in part but also denying in part the plaintiffs' summary judgment motion. On balance, her judgment was a defeat for the state defendants. Pfaelzer struck down Prop. 187's most important provisions because they preempted federal authority on immigration:

> The California voters' overwhelming approval of Proposition 187 reflects their justifiable frustration with the federal government's inability to enforce the immigration laws effectively. . . . [However,] no matter how serious the problem may be . . . the authority to regulate immigration belongs exclusively to the federal government, and state agencies are not permitted to assume that authority.[48]

Regarding the initiative's individual sections, Pfaelzer struck down the provision barring undocumented children from public elementary and secondary schools because it clashed directly with federal law as established in *Plyler v. Doe*; ruled unlawful the scheme to report "suspected" illegal immigrants to the authorities because it was a state attempt to regulate immigration, which is the sole province of the federal government; and said that California cannot exclude illegal immigrants from health and welfare services funded by the federal government under federal law. Pfaelzer did not, however, rule unlawful the state's attempt to deny undocumented persons access to health and welfare services funded by the state and to which they are not entitled under federal law—although few such services existed. Further, she did not rule the forged documents provision invalid—although problems with the initiative's language had already severely curtailed its impact in this area. Nor did she rule invalid the provision excluding undocumented persons from the state's public colleges and universities— although this provision had already been enjoined in the Judge Pollak's California Superior Court.[49]

Opponents of Prop. 187 viewed Pfaelzer's ruling as a major victory, while proponents knew it was significant setback. Attorney General Lungren tried to put a brave face on the ruling, arguing that he was more concerned about what would happen when Prop. 187 reached the U.S. Supreme Court than in minor setbacks in the lower courts: "We are in the first round of a 10-round heavyweight fight and at this point we are about even on the score card. I am confident that when this case is finally resolved in the courts, my office will be successful in defending the will of the people."[50] Lungren was already making plans to appeal Pfaelzer's decision to the U.S. Ninth Circuit Court of Appeals, with the expectation that it would reach the Supreme Court. And he also suggested that the provisions not ruled unlawful in Pfaelzer's summary judgment could still win at trial.[51] Governor Wilson, however, suggested that the judicial setback would "shift the focus [of the immigration debate] properly to the Congress. . . . California taxpayers should know that Congress has heard our outrage, and they are acting. We are very encouraged by federal law changes advancing through the Congress, and are hopeful that when they pass, much of Proposition 187 will become law despite the court's ruling."[52] Harold Ezell, one of the architects of Prop. 187, commented that his initiative

> may have been given a blow to the body, [but] it sure hasn't been a fatal blow, because we have had a major impact on the national debate on immigration. . . . It has caused the House and the Senate to take a serious look at reforming legal and illegal immigration.[53]

His colleague on the Yes on 187 committee, Robert Kiley, agreed: "We did what we set out to do and that was to bring illegal immigration to the table of the federal government."[54]

Pfaelzer's November 1995 ruling closed another chapter in Prop. 187's life. The attorney general's lawyers decided after some vacillation not to appeal Pfaelzer's partial summary judgment, arguing that appealing could have intimated that the state had conceded defeat on those provisions not yet ruled invalid by Pfaelzer.[55] Lawyers for the state decided instead to focus on removing undocumented persons from those state welfare and healthcare programs not protected by federal laws, and in particular illegal aliens' access to prenatal care.[56] Prenatal care was a first choice for the state because lawyers thought they could promptly write and implement a plan that would abide by those conditions established by Judge Pfaelzer. In the event, however, the hope of the lawyers proved misplaced. The plan proved controversial and attracted its own legal challenges. But, as Pfaelzer and the two sides in the dispute sought a solution, national-level events rendered the argument irrelevant.[57]

Prop. 187–inspired Federal Laws Return to Haunt Prop. 187

The national momentum on the immigration issue generated by Prop. 187 resulted in the passage of the Immigration Act in September 1996 and the inclusion of anti-immigrant provisions in the Welfare Reform Act (WRA) in August 1996. Both changed in important ways the legal framework governing the responsibilities and entitlements of legal and illegal immigrants. While the next chapter details these changes and how Prop. 187 inspired them, these new federal laws in turn influenced significantly Prop. 187's journey through the courts. For example, it seemed the WRA would permit California to implement its planned cuts in health services to undocumented persons, including prenatal care, because it specifically outlawed state-funded programs to illegal immigrants. After the enactment of the WRA, the individual states could only provide prenatal care to undocumented persons if they passed new laws specifically authorizing illegal aliens' eligibility for such programs—something unlikely given the widespread anti-immigrant feeling at the time.[58] Thus, under the provisions of the new law, Pfaelzer ruled on November 1, 1996, that Wilson could introduce emergency regulations to cut prenatal aid to an estimated 70,000 pregnant undocumented women per year from December 1.[59] However, Wilson's joy over the first significant legal victory for the pro-187 forces proved short-lived. Superior Court judge William Cahill ruled on November 26 that the emergency regulations—designed to protect the public's health and safety in a crisis situation—could not be invoked because there was no crisis. Instead, Cahill ruled that the standard procedures should apply, which in effect meant that prenatal care would remain in place for all residents of California, whether documented or not, until mid 1997.[60]

Further legal confusion arose when Pfaelzer did not respond to a request by the state and the plaintiffs for a status conference to clarify the post-WRA rules on reporting illegal aliens to the relevant authorities. At the end of 1996 both sides in the dispute were concerned and frustrated about Pfaelzer's silence on the request and about her delay in resolving the legal challenges to the Prop. 187 provisions not enjoined in the November 1995 partial summary judgment.[61] Lawyers in the attorney general's office now argued that they could not appeal Pfaelzer's partial summary judgment to the U.S. Appeals Court because the "single final judgment rule" prevented the appeal of partial rulings in the federal courts. Other proponents of the initiative were skeptical of such legal reasoning, suggesting that Lungren was delaying for his own political purposes. Such was the frustration of the authors and supporters of Prop. 187 that they decided to try to intervene directly in the lawsuits to move them quickly towards a final resolution. Backed by California state senators Richard Mountjoy, Ray Haynes, and Ross Johnson and with legal help from the conservative Pacific Legal Foundation, the Alan C. Nelson Foundation of Americans for Responsible Immigration (ARI) filed a motion to intervene in *League of United Latin*

American Citizens et al. v. Wilson.[62] Although unsuccessful, the motion indicated that important backers of Prop. 187 were unhappy with the state's progress in pushing Pfaelzer toward a full and final decision. And, although Senator Mountjoy specifically said that Attorney General Lungren should not be blamed for the case's slow progress, others were less politic in their comments. The Federation for American Immigration Reform's (FAIR) Dan Stein attacked Lungren as a fair-weather supporter of Prop. 187 who was trying to "keep the whole matter quiet long enough for him to pursue election to the governor's office without generating the kind of controversy that an aggressive defense of 187 would certainly create."[63]

Pfaelzer finally responded to Wilson's request to clarify the post-WRA reporting of illegal aliens on March 3, 1997. Wilson had argued that, because the WRA had improved the institutional links between the INS and governmental agencies in order to increase the number of undocumented immigrants reported to the immigration service, his administration should be allowed to put into effect the provision of Prop. 187 that required teachers, doctors, law-enforcement officers, and others to report to the INS suspected illegal aliens. Pfaelzer ruled, however, that while the state could freely implement those policies and reporting regulations established by federal law, the state could not implement its own, no matter how similar the policies and regulations.[64] Pfaelzer's reasoning was again clear: immigration policy is the domain of the federal government.

Governor Wilson became more irate with each of Pfaelzer's rulings against the state, as did other supporters of Prop. 187. They argued that Pfaelzer was delaying her final judgment for political purposes: she did not want the initiative implemented because she thought it poor policy and politics, not poor law. In comparison, they pointed to the legal challenge to Prop. 209, the anti-affirmative action initiative of 1996, which had lasted just one year, including the U.S. Supreme Court's dismissal of the case. Opponents of Prop. 209 initially won in late 1996 a temporary restraining order and then a preliminary injunction from federal Judge Thelton Henderson on the grounds that it "probably" violated the Fourteenth Amendment's equal protection clause, but the Ninth Circuit U.S. Court of Appeals swiftly overturned his decision in April 2007. One of the three appellate judges, Diarmuid O'Scannlain, wrote: "A system which permits one judge to block with the stroke of a pen what 4,736,180 state residents voted to enact as law tests the integrity of our constitutional democracy."[65]

On November 7, 1997, just four days after the Supreme Court let the decision of the appeals court stand, Governor Wilson ratcheted up the political pressure on Pfaelzer, accusing her of "an abuse of discretion beyond any justification" and declaring his intention to ask the U.S. Ninth Circuit Court of Appeals court to force the federal district judge to set a trial date.[66] Wilson was not alone in responding to what he called Pfaelzer's "unprecedented" behavior.[67] The U.S. Congress began to examine changes to the legal process itself, considering in particular Republican congressman Sonny Bono's previously unsuccessful Prop. 187-inspired proposal to prevent a single federal judge enjoining a direct democracy proposition. It was proposed that a panel of three judges should be required to give its assent before an injunction could be issued.[68]

Pfaelzer eventually published the draft of her final ruling, known as a memorandum of law, on the whole of Prop. 187 (rather than just a partial ruling on some of its parts) in *League of United Latin American Citizens et al. v. Wilson* on November 14, 1997.[69] The judgment was a clear victory for the plaintiffs, and was expected given Pfaelzer's previous rulings. Pfaelzer stated that Prop. 187 violated the U.S. Constitution *and* the 1996 WRA, arguing the WRA

> effectively ended any further debate about what the states could do in this field. . . . California is powerless to enact its own legislative scheme to regulate immigration. It is likewise powerless to enact its own legislative scheme to regulate alien access to public benefits. It can do what [the law] permits, and nothing more. . . . The states have no power to effectuate a scheme parallel to that specified in [federal law], even if that parallel scheme does not conflict with [the law].[70]

Except for the increased penalties for the manufacture, sale, and use of false citizenship documents—which, anyway, were seriously flawed—Pfaelzer declared all other provisions of Prop. 187 unlawful. Proponents of the initiative expressed mixed emotions about the ruling. On the one hand, they were angry that Pfaelzer had ruled against them and had taken so long to do so. On the other, there was a sense of relief. The initiative was now out of Pfaelzer's "liberal" court and could be appealed to the U.S. Ninth Circuit Court of Appeals, and probably to the Supreme Court after that, where they believed it stood a better chance of success. Wilson commented that, "Her analysis of Proposition 187 is as flawed and error-prone as the 1962 New York Mets. We look forward to this measure going to a higher court that has a better understanding of the law." Ron Prince said simply, "We're free at last."[71]

The opponents of Prop. 187 were understandably delighted by Pfaelzer's ruling, labeling it the "tombstone" for the initiative.[72] There was particular satisfaction over the emphasis that Pfaelzer had placed in her ruling on the 1996 WRA. After the passage of the law, which itself was a significant victory for Newt Gingrich and his conservative Contract with America agenda, Wilson and Lungren had tried to persuade the judge that Prop. 187 should be declared legal because many of its provisions were replicated—or, more accurately, imitated—in the federal legislation. Instead, Pfaelzer used the law to reinforce her argument that Prop. 187 was an impermissible state scheme to regulate immigration, which was the sole responsibility of the federal government. As one lawyer for the plaintiffs said, "Governor Wilson has been hoisted on his own petard."[73]

A Changing Political Landscape

Pfaelzer's November 14 memorandum of law was finally made permanent on March 18, 1998. While the ruling itself surprised nobody, merely reiterating her November 14 decision, it finally permitted the supporters of Prop. 187 to appeal.[74] FAIR's Dan Stein, aware of the attorney general's increasing reluctance to associate himself closely with Prop. 187, called on Dan Lungren to "take time out of his busy campaign schedule for the governor to carry out the job he has already been elected to do. The people of California have a right to have the U.S. Supreme Court issue a final ruling on whether they will be forced, against their wills, to pay for social service for illegal aliens, or whether they will be allowed to determine how their tax dollars are spent."[75] Lungren, like Wilson, said the state would appeal Pfaelzer's permanent injunction to the U.S. Appeals Court, but his language was more conciliatory and moderate than it had been after the judge temporarily enjoined the measure immediately after the 1994 elections.

The political landscape in California in 1998 was very different to that four years earlier. Lungren's gubernatorial ambitions in 1998 did not sit easily with his personal and his party's association with the anti-immigrant message. Rumors that California Latinos had responded to Prop. 187 by upping their rate of voter registration encouraged Lungren to be careful about alienating further an increasingly significant voting bloc, representing about 14 percent of registered voters and nearly one-third of California's population. Moreover, the improving economy ensured that it would be harder to sell an anti-immigrant message to voters in 1998. Recognizing this, Lungren described Prop. 187 as a "very flawed proposal" during a debate between the potential Republican and Democratic gubernatorial nominees.[76] He even opposed Prop. 227, the successful initiative that repealed California's bilingual education provision, which won the support of 37 percent of Latinos.[77] This did little for his Latino support in the June 1998 open primary, however.[78] While he won 34 percent of the overall vote, he took just 17 percent of the Latino vote, well below Republicans' pre-Prop. 187 level.[79] After winning the Republican nomination Lungren continued his campaign to win back some share of the Latino vote from the Democratic Party. He acknowledged that he had "a long road to travel. . . . I know my party has not done what it should do to open itself up over the last several years. But that doesn't mean I'll give up."[80] He stressed that during his time in the U.S. House of Representatives he had been a major sponsor and supporter of the 1986 Immigration Reform and Control Act (IRCA), and threatened to "take issue with anyone who says they've had a longer relationship with the Latino community than I have. . . . I went to school with those people. I went to school with people named Heredia and Contreras and Morales and Ortega. I played football with them. I sat side-by-side with them."[81]

Lungren argued throughout the campaign that the Republican Party, as the pro-life, family values party, should be the natural home of Latinos. He also hoped that his Catholicism would further recommend him to Latinos in a potentially tight race. In one television ad his daughter Kathleen spoke of how important religion and family were to her father, and how he helped millions of immigrants become citizens through his support of the IRCA.[82] Democratic nominee Gray Davis, meanwhile, sought to link Lungren to Prop. 187 and Pete Wilson, especially when talking to Hispanic audiences. One Davis television ad, fronted by prominent Latino Assembly speaker Antonio Villaraigosa and run mainly in Latino districts, reminded voters that Lungren had endorsed Prop. 187.[83] However, with little evidence that immigration was a top concern of most voters in 1998, neither candidate made the immigration issue the centerpiece of their campaign, as Wilson had done four years earlier. To do so would have been a dangerous strategy for both candidates. Lungren was desperate for a slice of the Latino vote (and was genuinely lukewarm in his endorsement of Prop. 187 anyway), and thus did not want to antagonize the Latino community by talking about cracking down on illegal aliens. For the Davis campaign, meanwhile, the immigration issue was a potential double-edged sword. While tarring Lungren with the Wilson/Prop. 187 brush probably would help bring Latinos into the Davis camp, it could possibly have driven moderate and/or conservative whites to Lungren, especially if the candidates' focus on immigration had the effect of politicizing the issue once more for millions of California voters—as happened in 1994. Immigration still had the potential to be a wedge issue, but neither candidate was totally confident that it would be *his* wedge issue.

On November 3, 1998, Lungren failed in his bid to become governor, winning just 38 percent of the overall vote and 23 percent of the Latino vote. Davis, in contrast, took 58 percent and 71 percent respectively. In addition, 18 percent of Republicans and 60 percent of independents voted for Davis, while only 9 percent of Democrats and 28 percent of independents chose Lungren.[84] On his inauguration on January 4, 1999, the pragmatic but uncharismatic Davis became the first Democrat in the state house since Jerry Brown vacated it in 1983. Only six months before the election few political commentators gave him much chance of victory. Davis ran a steady if unspectacular campaign, which suffered from early fund-raising problems. Fortunately, he benefited from a fair slice of luck in the primary when high-spending Democratic millionaires Al Checchi and Jane Harman each brought the other down in an unpleasant media war from which Davis, once trailing behind in third place, escaped relatively untarnished and victorious.

In the general election campaign Davis focused on education, the environment, abortion, and gun control. He worked hard to paint Lungren as a radical extremist who opposed abortion rights and an assault weapons ban. Lungren, in turn, ran a poor campaign. Always behind in the polls, he failed to find an issue that resonated with Californians. Having tried tax cuts and school vouchers with little conviction or success, Lungren settled on crime as his major weapon. It failed. Not only did Californians not rate crime as a top issue this time around, unlike in 1994, they actually thought Davis had the better policies on this traditional Republican issue, in part because they increasingly associated being tough on crime with improved gun control. And, although Lungren tried hard to win over Latino voters, he actually polled a smaller percentage than in his 1990 race for attorney general. But the fault was not all Lungren's. Many problems were not of his own making, and 1998 was not a Republican year, or certainly not a year for Republicans who the public regarded as radical—governors Jeb Bush in Florida and George W. Bush in Texas both came out against Prop. 187 in 1994 and polled well in 1998 having run inclusive, minority-friendly campaigns that emphasized the "compassionate" side of their conservatism. Meanwhile, Democrats retained control of the state assembly and senate and took all three of the statewide constitutional offices that were up for grabs. Indeed, Cruz Bustamante's victory in the lieutenant governor's race made him the first Latino in a century to win statewide office.[85]

Davis's success, together with the election of Democratic California senator Bill Lockyer as attorney general, would have important consequences for the future of Prop. 187. After Pfaelzer issued her permanent injunction against Prop. 187, Governor Wilson had filed an appeal in U.S. Ninth Circuit Court of Appeals. Subsequently the state and the original plaintiffs in the case filed briefs with the court, but final written arguments were not submitted. After the election of Davis the court issued a temporary delay in proceedings. Because the new governor had the power to abandon the appeal, the court argued that the governor's position must be clear before the case could proceed. During March and April 1999 Democratic assembly speaker Antonio Villaraigosa and the lieutenant governor Cruz Bustamante pressured Davis to drop the appeal and let Prop. 187 expire. The attorney general's office, meanwhile, made it clear that the governor must make the decision about the appeal, and that it would play a fairly passive role, acting as his attorney.

The main problem for Davis was that whichever decision he took—to continue the appeal or to abandon it—would alienate some important electoral groups and/or break a campaign promise. On the one hand, he had courted the (expanding) Latino vote and promised more harmonious relations between the races. In his first inaugural address, he reminded his audience that,

> Throughout my campaign, I pledged that the day I took the oath of office, the era of wedge-issue politics in California would be over. Well, my fellow Californians, that day is here. That time is now. And you can finally bring down the curtain on the politics of division. . . . [W]e can either allow society to be torn by factions and disunity, or we can demonstrate to the world how a heterogeneous people can live and prosper together. Our vast diversity is our strength.[86]

On the other hand, he had promised to execute the laws and to uphold the will of the electorate, which had approved Prop. 187 by a large margin.[87] Such competing interests and uncertainties inevitably led to confusion in Davis's thinking. On March 25, 1999, he said both that he would like to see the U.S. Supreme Court rule on Prop. 187 *and* that he had not decided whether to continue the appeal. But without the latter, the former was impossible.[88] Davis later admitted he faced "two conflicting obligations. I opposed 187. I personally think it is unconstitutional. I also believe I have certain obligations as the chief executive to support the law."[89]

Davis Takes the Middle Path

On April 15, 1999, Governor Davis surprised many people by announcing that he would neither drop nor continue the appeal. Instead, adopting a third way compromise, he said he would ask the Court of Appeals to appoint a mediator to settle the case.[90] In doing so Davis hoped to claim that he had not neglected the will of the people, while signaling to the Latino community that he was not prepared to pursue a hardheaded formal appeal. He argued that under the state constitution he could only refuse to enforce the law if it was deemed unconstitutional in the courts—although constitutional scholars suggested this was probably not the case, intimating that Davis was using this interpretation of the law to send a signal to the Latino community that he took the decision against his will. Predictably, Davis's third way solution, designed to cause least offense to the most people, actually pleased neither Prop. 187's proponents nor opponents. Its supporters argued that this was at best a delaying tactic by Davis, and that he was at worst trying to kill the initiative by the backdoor. Its detractors, in contrast, argued that Davis should have the courage of his convictions and fulfill his campaign promise to end "divisive wedge politics" by dropping the case. Lieutenant Governor Bustamante, a fellow Democrat and Davis's constitutional deputy, went so far as to warn that he would "as a matter of principle" petition the appeals court to throw out the Wilson-instigated appeal without the need for the Davis-inspired mediation.[91] While Bustamante's "friend of the court" petition was rejected, it nevertheless caused a divisive rift at the top of the California Democratic Party. Much to the chagrin of the governor, it allowed his deputy to portray himself as an alternative leader, especially on Latino issues.[92] It also made Davis's mediation decision appear politically cowardly and threatened his minority support. Davis's office reacted on a professional level by meeting the legislative Latino caucus to discuss the issue, and on a petty level by revoking nine of the Lieutenant Governor Office's prime Capitol parking permits.[93]

Despite all the intraparty machinations, political bluster, and power games, Davis's decision to go to mediation actually represented a considerable victory for the initiative's opponents. Unlike during the Wilson years, the state defendants in the case were now opposed to Prop. 187. With both sides in the case ideologically against it, it would be unlikely that a court mediator would not be able to find common ground between the parties—ground which would be unkind to Prop. 187's supporters, who had been prevented in various judgments from becoming a party to the case. Although Davis suggested in his press conference announcing the mediation decision that he would press for the Pacific Legal Foundation—representing the Alan C. Nelson Foundation for Americans for Responsible Immigration Reform—to be consulted, lawyers for the plaintiffs were much less conciliatory: "If that's what he envisions, that won't happen. We will not agree to be involved in any formal process with someone who is not a party to this case."[94]

While Davis's decision to ask the court to find a compromise in the dispute reflected well his cautious, pragmatic, anti-ideological approach to politics, it was also an unusual step. Never before had an initiative proposition gone to mediation.[95] Moreover, mediation was not commonly used to determine constitutional and legal issues such as those raised in the Prop. 187 case. The process, which is not open to public scrutiny and can take several months to complete, is usually used to settle disputes over facts and/or money. Thus, while many legal commentators regarded Davis's decision as a novel and interesting solution, most also questioned the efficacy of mediation in this case. As one constitutional law professor noted, "You can compromise on money, but how can you compromise on a constitutional challenge?"[96] But Davis was playing politics, and mediation suited his purposes.[97] It would likely produce the outcome he desired—the death of Prop. 187—and permit him to claim he had fulfilled his constitutional obligations, but it would also help guard against the possibility of a further Prop. 187-style initiative. In refusing to pursue the case Davis could have reignited anti-immigrant sentiments; in fudging the issue through mediation he hoped to avoid any landmark or symbolic decision that could act as a rallying point for grassroots activists and again politicize Californians' anti-immigrant sentiments. Perhaps Californians no longer felt as intensely as they did about illegal immigration, but Davis's private polling told him clearly that another Prop. 187-style initiative on the ballot would win 60–40.[98] One colleague noted wisely, "Our friends are trying to say, 'Wait a minute, Pete Wilson's out of office. No way could this thing go back on the ballot.' But Pete Wilson did not put this thing on the ballot. This was as close to a citizens' movement as you can get. Wilson jumped on this horse about 40 feet from the finish line."[99]

After more than three months of negotiations both sides in the mediation agreed a compromise, which was filed with the Court of Appeals on July 29, 1999. While the settlement would require ratification by Judge Pfaelzer, there was little question her assent would be a formality as the compromise mirrored almost exactly Pfaelzer's earlier ruling.[100] Both parties agreed to drop their appeals, and the state agreed to implement the (flawed) provisions regarding the manufacture, sale, and use of false citizenship documents. All other provisions would be set aside. Prop. 187 was effectively dead.

Dead or not, Governor Davis and the participants in the negotiations tried to portray the agreement as a win-win. On the one hand, Davis appealed to Latinos by arguing that the mediation had "resolve[d] a divisive wedge issue . . . [and] avoided years of divisiveness."[101] His deputy and one-time nemesis Cruz Bustamante even rushed to support Davis and the negotiated solution: "Today's action signals that the era of hate politics is truly over. It's time to stand together and say in one loud voice that Californians are tired of wedge issues and culture wars."[102] On the other hand, Davis tried to shore up support among moderate and conservative white voters by suggesting that he had done his constitutional duty by the electorate. He suggested that the "spirit of 187" was very much alive because the state must, as a result of the negotiations, "deny welfare benefits, all health benefits except for emergency care, unemployment insurance, public housing, postsecondary benefits, granting of professional licenses, and on and on to people who cannot verify they are in this country legally."[103] Of course, such exclusions were not a consequence of Prop. 187 and the mediation process; they were established by the welfare and immigration acts of 1996. Davis, though, was also keen to portray the mediated outcome as a hard-won battle against determined pro-immigrant opponents (while at the same time singing a different tune to the Latino community). While neither side in the supposedly secret negotiations could talk openly, Davis's aides briefed the press under the cloak of anonymity, arguing their boss had fought long and hard to save Prop. 187—despite his earlier public comments that he would "never be a party to an effort to kick kids out of school."[104] One journalist reported that, "The final agreement on Proposition 187 was hammered out during three months of often-intense meetings, telephone conferences, exchanges or drafts and other discussions between the governor's representatives and attorneys for the opponents."[105] The governor's aides said he was particularly determined to save the provision that required law-enforcement officers to report to the INS suspected illegal aliens, and only backed down when faced with insurmountable opposition from the civil rights lawyers.[106] The lawyers, too, also sought to portray the negotiations as hard-fought "on every issue, tooth and nail. As recently as several days ago, it was unclear to every lawyer involved whether or not there would be an agreement."[107] Despite the governor's efforts to emphasize the hard bargaining on behalf of California voters, ex-governor Pete Wilson put it well when he said, "This is not mediation, this is like negotiating with yourself."[108] And his former press secretary Sean Walsh noted, the "fix is in."[109]

Pacific Legal Foundation lawyers representing Americans for Responsible Immigration appealed the mediated settlement on August 4 on the grounds that it violated the legal doctrine of "case and controversy." The doctrine holds that the federal courts can only hear a case in which the two parties have genuine opposing legal interests. As both Davis and his "opponents" were certified foes of

Prop. 187, PLF lawyers argued there could be no controversy between the parties. Furthermore, "When the governor abandoned the defense of Proposition 187, the will of the people was frustrated by the very representative government that the initiative process is designed to prevent."[110]

In response, and in addition to the PLF appeal, Ron Prince proposed another initiative that would prevent governors sending initiatives to arbitration and instead mandate them to defend it in court, all the way to the U.S. Supreme Court if necessary.[111] Prince and Barbara Coe also sought to qualify another initiative for the ballot that would bring Prop. 187 back from the dead. The nascent initiative, submitted to the attorney general for titling and summary on November 2, 1999, did not contain the controversial provision to bar undocumented children from public schools. It would, however, mandate schools to count the number of undocumented students; establish a bureau to help government agencies to identify undocumented persons and thus prevent them receiving services to which they are not entitled; mandate the state to check that those applying for driving licenses are legal residents; and allow residents to sue state agencies that violated the provisions of the initiative. As a constitutional initiative, Prince would have to collect 670,816 verified signatures (or about 900,000 raw signatures) by the end of April 2000 for it to qualify for the November ballot. And Glenn Spencer, chair of the small but very active anti-immigrant group Voices of Citizens Together, called Davis a "traitor . . . [assisting a] Mexican takeover of California"[112] and started a petition for his recall. Spencer needed to collect 1,006,224 verifiable signatures (or about 1.3 million raw signatures) by February 23, 2000, to get his recall petition onto the ballot. There was little chance he would succeed—although others would later.[113]

PLF's appeal, Prince's new initiative, and Spencer's recall all failed. The political landscape had been changed by an improving economy, by increased Latino participation, and by the Republican Party's response to these. The new terrain was highlighted by George W. Bush, then the Republican presidential nominee, who made several trips to California in mid-to-late 2000 to preach the new Republican orthodoxy to minority and moderate voters. In one speech to the National Hispanic Women's Conference Bush implicitly distanced himself from Pete Wilson and Prop. 187:

> It's so important to have leadership that tears down political barriers, leadership that offers a future hopeful for everybody, leadership that rejects the politics of pitting one group of people against another, leaders that stand up and say we will not use our children, the children of immigrants, as a political issue in America.[114]

Bush refused to give Wilson a role in his 2000 presidential campaign, and Wilson was not among the California delegation to the national Republican convention in Philadelphia in August 2000—both of which were extremely unusual given Wilson's record as the most successful and best-connected California Republican of his generation. At the convention, Republicans worked hard to portray themselves as a multiethnic party, giving primetime slots to Latinos and African Americans. The Democrats responded in a similar fashion at their Los Angeles convention, where Cruz Bustamante, the country's highest elected Latino official, heaped sarcasm on Bush: "You know, this guy in Texas speaks a little

Spanish, goes to a Cinco de Mayo parade, and thinks he represents Latinos"[115] Even though many Republicans acknowledged privately that Wilson was not a racist and had raised legitimate concerns over illegal immigration, the reason for his exclusion was simple: his support of Prop. 187 and his demonic status among California Latinos. Wilson had played immigration politics better than anyone in 1994. Just six years later, his reputation was in tatters among Latinos and he was considered persona non grata among ambitious Republicans. While Bush had expressed his opposition to Prop. 187 in 1994, even some Republicans who supported and funded it were reluctant to support Prince's "son of 187" in 2000. No money was forthcoming from the national or state Republican Party. Even state Senator Richard Mountjoy, a major supporter and financial contributor, said he could not contribute in 2000 as he was still paying off the debt from the 1994 campaign.[116] Still other Republicans actively sought to persuade Prince to abandon his new initiative. Michael Capaldi, president of the Lincoln Club in Orange Country, a Republican and pro-187 organization in 1994, wrote Prince arguing that the new initiative would be a step too far toward identity cards, would distract from core educational values in schools, would not reduce illegal immigration, and would "excite division among Californians."[117] Republican congressman Tom Campbell, in his campaign against Dianne Feinstein for her U.S. Senate seat, tried to portray himself as more liberal on immigration matters than his Democratic opponent, arguing in a television spot that Feinstein only announced her opposition to Prop. 187 late in the 1994 campaign whereas he had announced his opposition much earlier.[118]

While anti-immigrant activists responded angrily to the new immigrant- and Latino-friendly Republican Party, saying it "is paralyzed by fear . . . [and] has turned into cowards,"[119] the Democrats tried to play up Bush's and the Republicans' past connections to Prop. 187 and Wilson as both parties fought for the new middle ground. Joe Andrew, national chair of the DNC, accused Bush of "still clinging to the divisive politics of Pete Wilson and the Republican Party. Bush's recent attempts to distance himself from Wilson is just a façade."[120] And DNC general cochair Loretta Sanchez argued that "Bush's lack of leadership on opposing anything like Proposition 187 points to his lack of understanding of the Latino community. He cannot expect to gain any credibility among Latino voters when he does not actively fight policies that have harmed Latinos in the past."[121]

Supporters of Prop. 187 now faced defeat at every turn, and its foes were greatly emboldened after several years fighting the anti-immigrant tide. In the California legislature members introduced bills to expand the services and benefits available to undocumented residents, and legislators openly blamed Davis when they did not pass.[122] Nor did Davis receive much credit for his pro-immigration efforts—including reintroducing prenatal care for undocumented pregnant women and nursing-home care for the undocumented elderly, and scrapping a Wilson program that had stationed fraud investigators at border-entry points to pressure undocumented immigrants suspected of receiving Medi-Cal benefits into repaying the costs.[123] Civil rights advocates also mauled Davis, arguing they could no longer trust him. Oren Sellstrom of the Lawyers Committee for Civil Rights argued, perhaps unfairly, that "It's becoming increasingly clear that Davis is following directly in Pete Wilson's footsteps."[124]

And, having vetoed a Richard Polanco–sponsored outreach bill, Davis was accused of putting himself "to the right of Dan Lungren. He's now sided with the foes of affirmative action."[125] If Davis continued to neglect the increasingly powerful Latino vote, his critics warned, he could risk losing the Democratic Party the 2000 presidential election and put his own reelection in doubt in 2002.[126] His critics were wrong on the details, but right about his demise. Davis was removed from office in 2003 in a spectacular recall effort and replaced by Hollywood star Arnold Schwarzenegger. While many different factors, most notably California's energy crisis in 2000–2001 and underwhelming economic performance, explain the success of the recall drive against Davis, at least some of the hostility toward him from the right was a consequence of his decision to let Prop. 187 die by mediation. Davis failed to implement the will of the people as expressed through the direct democracy process and the same process was used to remove him from office.

In chapter 4 we reviewed the arguments of the critics and defenders of direct democracy. The Progressives of the early twentieth century worried about the influence of special interests on elective politicians and the democratic process. To overcome what they perceived as the corruption in the political system, they introduced direct democracy procedures to allow citizens to circumvent established institutions and make the laws directly themselves. Ironically, a key complaint of modern-day critics is that initiatives are increasing tools of special interests rather than ordinary citizens, in large part because of the contemporary cost of the initiative process. Another complaint, echoing the founding fathers' concern about democratic tyranny, is that initiatives permit the majority to undermine minority rights.

What about the case of Proposition 187? As to the question of the influence of special interests, the evidence presented in this and the proceeding chapters is mixed, but on balance probably breaks in favor of direct democracy's supporters. To be sure, Prop. 187 was lucky that Pete Wilson's focus on the illegal-immigration issue in 1993 helped create a political environment conducive to the qualification of a ballot initiative and was fortunate to have the governor of California as its most visible spokesperson during the campaign. The Republican Party also provided some help with office costs and mailings and some Republican politicians made monetary contributions. However, at its inception Prop. 187 was a grassroots, or at least quasi-grassroots, effort, and grassroots activists would also shoulder the largest burden during the initiative's qualification. Indeed, Prop. 187 is one of the very few initiatives to have qualified for the ballot in recent years relying mainly on volunteers to gather signatures rather than professional firms. Prop. 187 should not be used as an example, then, of the overweening and malign influence of special interests on the direct democracy process. It is more difficult to defend Prop. 187 against the charge that it allowed the majority to trample on a vulnerable minority. It stirred up intense passions, especially among many Latinos who saw the initiative not just as an attack on illegal immigrants but on Latinos generally. Passions remain raw today. The revelation during the Davis recall effort that the gubernatorial candidate and future governor, Arnold Schwarzenegger, had voted for Prop. 187 sparked heated protests from Latinos and liberals. His appointment of Pete Wilson as cochairman of his campaign further inflamed them. However, it should be remembered that Prop. 187 did not become law. Direct democracy does not operate in a political or legal vacuum. Despite the worry of some scholars that judges are reluctant to overturn the will of the majority expressed through the ballot box, they had no such aversion in the case of the illegal-immigration initiative. The initiative was roundly defeated in the courts and left to die in mediation by Governor Davis. Of course, that was not the end of the matter. Even in its death throes Prop. 187 helped inspire significant changes to U.S. immigration law. The next chapter examines these changes.

Chapter 7

The Legislative Revival of Proposition 187

The architects of Prop. 187 believed that a national version of the illegal-immigration initiative, enshrined in federal law, would offer a permanent and effective way to control undocumented migration. The initiative's judicial interment by Judge Pfaelzer only further increased the attractiveness of the legislative option. Thus, while members of the Yes on 187 committee were keen to see other states with direct democracy procedures introduce "son of 187" initiatives and gave much of their time to help the start-up efforts, they also encouraged legislators to take up the cause. "There's no need for another Proposition 187 in any other state if Congress does its job: a law that says you will ask and determine the alienage of people before you give them any government handouts," argued Harold Ezell.[1] Governor Wilson, on a high after his reelection, also expressed support for a national version of Prop. 187 before an audience at the conservative Heritage Foundation in Washington, DC, on November 18, 1995.[2] He argued that the federal government should allow the states to curtail the provision of education and medical and welfare benefits to illegal immigrants, or it should reimburse the states for those costs. Moreover, with the Republicans winning control of Congress in 1994 for the first time in forty years, it looked probable that Prop. 187 would help inspire a significant reform of federal immigration laws. The only question seemed to be the extent to which Prop. 187 would serve as the blueprint for the new law.

After the Republicans' remarkable congressional victory, Newt Gingrich of Georgia was elected speaker of the House of Representatives and Bob Dole of Kansas majority leader in the Senate. Their positions on the immigration issue would be crucial in determining the nature and success of the reform agenda. In a meeting with Governor Wilson on November 17 to discuss illegal immigration, Prop. 187, and other issues, Gingrich said that he thought the federal government should reimburse the states for the costs of educating, incarcerating, and providing emergency medical treatment to undocumented residents. Such reimbursements would not halt the flow of illegal immigrants into California and other states, however. "The best response is to eliminate the mandates (to provide services) because the welfare magnet (is) drawing people into the United

States," argued Gingrich.[3] He later said that while he did not support a national version of Prop. 187 he probably would have voted for it had he lived in California "out of frustration" at the federal government's failure to secure the borders.[4]

Two other key players in Congress were Representative Lamar Smith of Texas and Senator Alan Simpson of Wyoming. As the newly selected chairs of the House and Senate immigration subcommittees, Smith and Simpson together with the Republican leadership could control the reform agenda and thus the content of future immigration bills.[5] Smith noted soon after the November 1994 elections that the "passage of 187 by such a large margin created a tidal wave . . . washing up on the steps of the Capitol,"[6] and that "the thrust of 187 is going to be seriously considered by Congress."[7] However, he had previously rejected the idea of overturning the Supreme Court's *Plyler* decision and now warned that the initiative's controversial education provisions "would make it difficult" to attract the bipartisan support.[8] Senator Simpson, a Republican widely respected on immigration matters, joined Smith in opposing the exclusion of undocumented children from schools.[9]

Thus, the early maneuverings showed the Republican majority in Congress was keen to address the immigration issue, although clear differences were also evident between the key players about the nature and extent of reform. As we shall see, forces hostile to reform exploited these differences, particularly on legal immigration. Despite the efforts of those opposed to reform, however, Congress passed and President Clinton signed in late 1996 the Illegal Immigration Reform and Immigrant Responsibility Act (PL 104–208). In addition, Clinton also signed the 1996 Personal Responsibility and Work Opportunity Reconciliation Act (PL 104–193), better known as the Welfare Reform Act (WRA), which cut dramatically legal immigrants' access to federal benefits. This chapter examines Prop. 187's impact on the reform agenda in the 104th Congress and details the process by which the legislature came to pass such reforms.

The Jordan Commission I

As the new Congress formally convened in January 1995 eager to reform U.S. immigration laws, it found waiting a newly published report by the bipartisan U.S. Commission on Immigration Reform. The commission—widely known as the Jordan Commission after its chair, Barbara Jordan, a former U.S. representative from Texas—was authorized by the 1990 immigration act to review U.S. immigration policy and to report its findings to Congress. Its first report, *U.S. Immigration Policy: Restoring Credibility*, focused almost exclusively on illegal immigration. Written as the conflagration in California over Prop. 187 began to make headlines across the country, and presented to Congress on September 30, 1994, the report opened with a tribute to legal immigration:

> The Commission believes that legal immigration has strengthened and can continue to strengthen this country. . . . [I]mmigration presents many opportunities for this nation . . . [and] the tradition of welcoming newcomers has become an important element of how we define ourselves as a nation.[10]

However, the tone changed notably when the commission began to discuss illegal immigration:

> The Commission is mindful of the problems that also emanate from immigration. In particular, we believe that unlawful immigration is unacceptable. . . . The credibility of immigration policy can be measured by a single yardstick: people who should get in, do get in; people who should not get in are kept out; and people who are deportable are required to leave. . . . The immediate need is more effective prevention and deterrence of unlawful immigration.[11]

The report called for radical measures to control illegal migration. It argued that the borders, especially the U.S.-Mexico border, must be strengthened to prevent illegal entry, "because prevention is far more effective and cost-efficient than the apprehension and removal of illegal aliens after entry."[12] To this end, it recommended the appointment of more and better-trained Border Patrol agents utilizing more sophisticated technology and unbreachable fences. It proposed a border-crossing fee with proceeds to be used to improve border management, and increased coordination between the U.S. and Mexico governments to combat the smuggling of people and goods, especially drugs, across the border. It also criticized interagency coordination between the Immigration and Naturalization Service (INS) and Customs Service at entry ports, and suggested that one might have to be designated the lead agency to overcome the problems.

The Jordan Commission's most radical proposals, however, concerned work-site enforcement of immigration law. It argued that

> reducing the employment magnet is the linchpin of a comprehensive strategy to reduce illegal immigration. The ineffectiveness of employer sanctions, prevalence of fraudulent documents, and continued high numbers of unauthorized workers, combined with confusion for employers and reported discrimination against employees, have challenged the credibility of current worksite enforcement efforts.[13]

A litany of reforms was proposed to address these myriad problems, but the most significant was a computerized national registry of social security numbers. A potential employee would have to provide a prospective employer with a unique social security number, which the employer would check against the register to determine if the individual was permitted to work or not. The commission argued that this would reduce fraud and discrimination, while saving time and resources. It recommended that the president should authorize immediately a pilot study to examine its effectiveness in the five states with the most undocumented residents. The commission also proposed that the federal and state governments should work together to stamp out fraudulent documents—especially "breeder documents" such as birth certificates—that could be used to create a false identity and thus provide the basis for fraudulent access to benefits and employment. In a further move to prevent the unlawful employment of ineligible workers the commission iterated its support for the "vigorous enforcement of labor standards and enforcement against knowing hire of unauthorized workers," which it regarded as currently inadequate.[14] To improve enforcement, it proposed appointing additional staff, targeting industries known to employ significant amounts of unlawful labor, applying the employer sanctions to the hitherto exempted federal government, the "full use of current penalties" against those knowingly employing undocumented workers, and better coordination and cooperation between the INS and the Labor Department, who were jointly responsible for enforcing employment laws.

The commission recommended that undocumented residents should be ineligible for all public benefits, except emergency aid. While this was not an especially radical proposal—most federal and state programs were already out of bounds for unlawful residents—the commission controversially recommended that the pilot programs on workplace eligibility should also be utilized to test new procedures for verifying recipients' benefit eligibility. The commission also recommended that a sponsor's financial commitment to a legal immigrant be legally binding and that a legal immigrant's use of public benefits within five years of arriving in the United States should constitute grounds for deportation.

The commission also announced a list of recommendations aimed at speeding the deportation of illegal aliens, especially those convicted of a serious felony. It argued that increased resources were required to identify and deport aliens, that Mexican aliens should be deported far away from the border to deter reentry, and that criminal aliens should serve sentences in their own countries where possible. Finally, the commission recommended that the federal government reimburse the states for at least some of the costs incurred schooling, imprisoning, and caring for unlawful residents, and that better data were needed to estimate the impact of immigrants and immigration policies.

The report drew praise from Prop. 187 supporters—Bill King said that "It will certainly give (187) a boost"—although there was disappointment that it did not recommend the exclusion of undocumented children from school.[15] The Clinton administration's response to the Jordan Commission's report was also generally positive. "We agree with the commission on a number of significant steps, and we are heading in the same direction. . . . Very useful," said one senior White House official.[16] And Attorney General Janet Reno praised Jordan and the other commission members, which included Harold Ezell of Prop. 187 fame, for "their superb work."[17]

However, the administration also made public its distaste for Jordan's key proposal: a national registry of social security numbers designed to help prevent illegal immigrants getting jobs. Some in the administration argued that the government's databases were not up to the task. "The feeling is that there is a real serious problem with the databases right now. They aren't in a condition to be useful. . . . We're putting a lot of money into improving them, but they aren't there yet," argued a spokesperson for White House chief of staff Leon Panetta.[18] Others argued that the cost alone was prohibitive. Lawrence J. Haas, the associate director for communications at the Office of Management and Budget, suggested the registry "would cost billions of dollars to construct and [anyway] we don't see the need for it at this point."[19] The proposal also came under fire from civil rights and pro-immigration groups. The American Civil Liberties Union (ACLU) and American Bar Association (ABA) worried that the registry would invade people's privacy, give too much power to the federal government, and be one step closer to a national identity card.[20] The Mexican American Legal Defense and Educational Fund (MALDEF) and League of United Latin American Citizens (LULAC) argued that the registry could discriminate—sometimes intentionally, sometimes not—against nonwhite workers.[21] These opponents would find the Gallegly Commission's report even more odious.

The Gallegly Taskforce

U.S. representative Elton Gallegly, a California Republican, was a longtime advocate of immigration reform and a prominent supporter of Prop. 187 during the 1994 election cycle. He had previously introduced bills into Congress to deny birthright citizenship to children born to undocumented parents and to create a system of ID cards for resident aliens. Although these early efforts met with little success, Gallegly thought the post-187 environment was ripe for immigration reform.

> For probably the first time since I've been in Washington, we have an opportunity to enact real immigration reform. The resounding approval of Prop. 187 in California and the increased focus on this issue . . . sends a clear message that Americans want us to do something about the people who come here illegally.[22]

On reelection to the House in 1994 Gallegly hoped to chair the immigration subcommittee, and that it would give him the prominence and power to help frame a new immigration system. To his disappointment, Representative Lamar Smith was given the job. However, on December 16, 1995, Gingrich appointed Gallegly head of the Speaker's Congressional Task Force on Immigration Reform as compensation. Gallegly, with the help of Lamar Smith and Speaker Gingrich, initially selected seventeen members of Congress (eleven Republicans and six Democrats) to join him on the taskforce. This quickly swelled to fifty-four as politicians clamored to be part of a high-profile review of a problem set to be a top issue in the 1996 elections. Although officially bipartisan, the taskforce was dominated by California Republicans, reflecting the force of feeling in the state and GOP. Of the fifty-four representatives on the taskforce, forty-seven were Republicans and twenty-three represented California districts.[23] None were Latino.[24]

Inspired by the anti-immigrant revolt in California in late 1994, the taskforce's remit was to examine the options for reform during the 104th Congress, and specifically to "develop recommendations to end illegal entry and to encourage those residing in our country illegally to return to their homeland. . . . It has become apparent to many Americans that the federal government has failed in its efforts to enforce existing laws, to enact new laws or adopt effective policies to prevent illegal immigration."[25] Gingrich envisioned that the taskforce's recommendations would help shape the GOP's immigration policy and feed into the reform agenda being developed in Lamar Smith's immigration subcommittee.

As a member of the immigration subcommittee and chair of the immigration taskforce, Gallegly was well positioned and eager to play a prominent role in immigration reform. As soon as the new Congress convened he proposed several initiatives to combat undocumented migration. One, introduced on January 19, 1995, proposed that illegal immigrants should not receive any federal welfare payments, that the green card should be made tamper proof, and that the Border Patrol should employ 2,000 more agents. He went further in April, introducing a bill based on Prop. 187's controversial provision to allow the states to deny education to undocumented children.[26] He argued that,

> When illegal immigrants sit down in public school classrooms, the desks, textbooks and blackboards in effect become stolen property—stolen from the students rightfully entitled to these resources. . . . Just because someone has succeeded in breaking into your house, that does not entitle him to a seat by the fireplace, a warm meal and a good night's sleep. Only in the case of illegal immigration, it seems, is illegality so rewarded, condoned and encouraged.[27]

Although Gallegly's legislative proposals were largely symbolic at this time—the ten Contract with America provisions dominated the House floor's timetable, Lamar Smith was directing the immigration subcommittee's investigations, and the taskforce did not begin its investigations until March—they were indicative of a new activism. Californians, and Republican ones especially, were determined that the 104th Congress would witness major reform. For example, Dana Rohrabacher (R-CA), another longtime proponent of immigration reform, vowed to continue his campaign against illegal immigration. His specialty was to attach riders to appropriations bills denying funds to unlawful residents. "This year, I expect that every appropriations bill will have written into it the provision that I was being condemned as a radical for only three years ago," said Rohrabacher, reflecting the new Prop. 187-inspired anti-immigration discourse.[28] "The United States has had a huge 'Come on in' sign that has been seen all over the world. We mean business. We're taking down that 'Come on in' sign," he added.[29] Another California Republican, Representative Ron Packard (R-CA), a member of the prestigious appropriations committee, introduced legislation seeking to ensure that illegal immigrants did not receive any federal disaster aid. The measure was approved by the committee on March 2, 1995.[30] Even Gallegly's more moderate colleagues wanted to stake out their position on the new hot-button issue. For example, Representative Anthony C. Beilenson (D-CA) proposed a raft of reforms, including a constitutional amendment repealing birthright citizenship, a counterfeit-proof social security card to ensure that bosses did not employ illegal workers, and plans to make the Border Patrol independent of the INS.[31] And representatives Howard L. Berman (D-CA) and Carlos Moorhead (R-CA) presented a bill for consideration by the House judiciary committee to reimburse the states for the cost of incarcerating undocumented felons. It easily passed the committee, with bipartisan support.[32] Gingrich threw his weight behind the bill, even though the General Accounting Office (GAO) estimated the reimbursements could cost the federal government $630 million. "The flood of illegal immigrants is such a budget-buster that they can destroy California's economy, Arizona's economy, New Mexico's economy and Texas' economy. We have a federal obligation to solve it," said Gingrich.[33] Freshman Sonny Bono (R-CA) introduced a bill on March 8, 1995, to prevent a single federal judge serving an injunction on a citizen initiative, as Judge Pfaelzer had done on Prop. 187. Bono proposed that only a three-judge panel, appointed by the Circuit Court's chief judge, could do so.[34]

Gallegly delivered the taskforce's report to Speaker Gingrich on June 29, 1995. The report, which took just three months to complete, concluded that radical measures were required to control illegal immigration. Echoing the provisions of Prop. 187, the report proposed excluding undocumented immigrants from public education; denying illegal aliens all federal welfare and health benefits, except emergency medical care; matching birth and death records and federalizing birth certificates to guard against document fraud; increasing the penalties for possession and production of fraudulent documents from five to fifteen years; mandating hospitals to report to the INS all undocumented patients (or lose the federal reimbursement for the cost of the care); and allowing the states to report illegal aliens to the INS and for the INS to deport them.

In addition to these Prop. 187-style proposals, the taskforce proposed several other radical and controversial reforms, including repealing birthright citizenship, requiring illegal recipients of public benefits to pay back the full cost, plus interest, and using closed military bases to detain unlawful aliens. The report also reiterated some ideas floated earlier by the Jordan Commission, including implementing pilot studies designed to prevent the employment of undocumented workers (one would create a tamper-proof social security card and the other a computerized registry of eligible workers), strengthening the penalties on firms employing illegal labor, and paying back the states for the costs of incarcerating criminal aliens. Other important, albeit less controversial proposals, included doubling the number of Border Patrol agents; reinforcing the border fence at strategic points; expanding visa pre-inspection in foreign airports; fining those entering illegally and prosecuting those reentering illegally; increasing the penalties for smuggling aliens; expanding INS detention space; streamlining the deportation procedure for illegal aliens and those denied asylum; and developing systems to identify and deport visa overstays.[35] Rohrabacher, a taskforce member, argued that the report was

> even better than Prop. 187. This is the type of package that screams out: "We're serious about this problem." This again confirms that when California starts the ball rolling, it rolls east until it reaches the Capitol and then it lands with a big thud.[36]

After receiving the report, Gingrich passed it to the House immigration subcommittee. Many of its 100 proposals dovetailed neatly with those being discussed by subcommittee chair Lamar Smith. Indeed, Gallegly claimed he and Smith worked together "hand-in-glove" in drawing up the report, and Smith noted "the taskforce has been supportive and diligent about keeping us informed [of its activities and thinking]. I expect much of what they recommend to be in the final bill."[37] This was certainly the way that Gingrich planned it. It was his aim to have the taskforce recommendations influence the agenda of Smith's own investigations and thus the content of any bills originating in his committee. To this end, Gallegly's taskforce worked feverishly during the second quarter of 1995, listening to testimony from immigration experts and interest groups and conducting field trips to porous parts of the U.S.-Mexico border, in order to present its findings to Smith prior to any legislative markup. However, Gallegly always intended that his recommendations would be "even more aggressive" than Smith's.[38] He knew that Smith had already ruled out some of his more controversial ideas, such as excluding undocumented children from public schools and repealing birthright citizenship, but included them in the taskforce report nonetheless. By publishing a set of hard-line proposals, Gallegly could help frame the debate and make any future Smith recommendations look moderate in comparison, thus aiding their passage. Smith, meanwhile, was equally determined to overhaul immigration law, but wanted to do so with bipartisan support. He knew that Gallegly's most radical proposals would be unacceptable to most Democrats and even many in his own party, and would thus have to be jettisoned in the search for a political compromise. Nonetheless, Smith was well aware that the taskforce would provide momentum for his own proposals and act as a bulwark against moves from the left to water them down.[39]

Not everyone in the Republican Party was enamored of Gallegly and Smith's radical agenda. For example, Pete Wilson's old foes Jack Kemp and William Bennett still feared that the Republican anti-immigrant agenda would turn ethnic and racial minorities and recent immigrants against the GOP. They were particularly worried that the proportion of Latinos and Asians in the population and on the electoral register was increasing rapidly at the same time that the GOP seemed to be doing everything possible to alienate them. To try to turn the anti-immigrant tide they held another pro-immigration press conference sponsored by their Empower America think tank and the Manhattan Institute on November 21, 1994. They argued that the anti-immigrant agenda would "turn the party inward to a protectionist and isolationist and more xenophobic party. . . . We are willing to concede that tossing logs onto the anti-immigration fire might result in short-term gains, but believe that in the medium and long term, this posture is a loser."[40]

Kemp and Bennett found themselves increasingly isolated as the Republican Party moved to the right on immigration. In the postwar period, the party had in the main supported large-scale legal immigration and often turned a blind-eye to undocumented migration. Why then were 104th Congress's Republicans, especially those representing border states, so unenthusiastic about immigration? It was due in part to the success of Prop. 187, which indicated to Republicans the (short-run) political advantages to be had from promulgating a hard-line. It was also part of a wider shift to conservative positions on social and cultural issues, including abortion, family values, sexuality, pornography, and so on. Linked to increasing conservatism was the growth of what has been labeled popular or populist conservatism, which championed economic protectionism and military isolationism/unilateralism, as well as a closed-door immigration policy. Probably the most radical exponent of this philosophy was Patrick Buchanan, who by 1994 was well versed in populist oratory. It would be wrong, however, to say that conservatism was the wholly dominant force within the party. Many Republicans, especially those from the east coast and New England, still regarded themselves as free trade, pro-immigration, and internationalist. Nevertheless, the number of Republicans subscribing to these views diminished during the 1980s and 1990s as the party's elected officials and support increasingly came from the south and west rather than the north and east.

Another segment of the GOP supported immigration reform for electoral reasons. Newt Gingrich, the first Republican speaker for forty years, personified this. The mastermind of the party's stunning 1994 congressional victory had said nothing about immigration in his Contract with America. Intellectually from the libertarian wing of the Republican Party, Gingrich was not naturally anti-immigrant.

Nor was he a protectionist or isolationist.[41] Gingrich's conversion to the anti-immigrant agenda was a product of, first, his reading of public opinion and, second, his desire to reform the welfare system.[42] Because immigrants were politically unpopular and because many received federal benefits, he saw an opportunity to reduce welfare costs while strengthening the party's support. However, Gingrich faced a notable problem. Despite much campaign rhetoric, illegal aliens actually received very little welfare support from the federal government. The largest costs associated with undocumented persons were education and incarceration, both of which were politically and logistically difficult to cut. And, anyway, state and local governments largely shouldered those costs. One solution to Gingrich's problem was to widen the net on the type of immigrants to be excluded from welfare programs. The Yes on 187 committee, and Governor Wilson especially, had been careful to distinguish illegal from legal immigration. To cut welfare costs and to play the popular anti-immigrant card would mean Gingrich would have to blur that distinction and go after the welfare benefits of legal aliens. This he did, and the savings looked impressive. The Congressional Budget Office (CBO) estimated that Congress's March 1995 welfare reform proposals would render 670,000 immigrants ineligible for Aid to Families with Dependent Children (AFDC) and Medicaid, 520,000 for SSI and Medicaid, 500,000 for Medicaid alone, and 1.1 million for food stamps, and result in a saving of $21.4 billion over four years.[43] We will return to welfare reform below.

The White House Responds

The Clinton administration was keen to ensure that California Republicans in the House did not set the reform agenda on the immigration issue unopposed. As Gingrich and Gallegly were putting together the immigration taskforce in late 1994 and early 1995, INS chief Doris Meissner announced that the administration was examining a number of proposals to shore up the border and crack down on undocumented workers. Although no decision had yet been taken, Meissner let it be known that a national registry of employees, ID cards, stricter employer sanctions, and more Border Patrol officers were all under consideration.[44] Clinton even addressed the immigration issue in his January 1995 State of the Union address:

> All Americans, not only in the states most heavily affected, but in every place in this country, are rightly disturbed by the large numbers of illegal aliens entering our country. The jobs they hold might otherwise be held by citizens or legal immigrants. The public services they use impose burdens on our taxpayers. That's why our administration has moved aggressively to secure our borders more by hiring a record number of new border guards, by deporting twice as many criminal aliens as ever before, by cracking down on illegal hiring, by barring welfare benefits to illegal aliens.
>
> In the budget I will present to you we will try to do more to speed the deportation of illegal aliens who are arrested for crimes, to better identify illegal aliens in the workplace as recommended by the commission headed by former Congresswoman Barbara Jordan.
>
> We are a nation of immigrants. But we are also a nation of laws. It is wrong and ultimately self-defeating for a nation of immigrants to permit the kind of abuse of our immigration laws we have seen in recent years, and we must do more to stop it.[45]

The administration made official its proposals when it submitted to Congress on February 6, 1995, the budget bill for the 1996 fiscal year.[46] Although it stood little chance of winning the approval of the Republican Congress, the bill's contents are indicative of the administration's political concerns. Included in it were proposals to hire a further 370 INS and 200 Labor Department staff to ensure that firms did not hire undocumented workers. "If we turn off the stream for illegal workers, far, far fewer of them will risk the difficult journey here," stressed President Clinton.[47] He suggested that firms employing undocumented workers could have their assets confiscated, and announced a number of pilot programs to keep illegal aliens out of the workforce, including INS verification of workers' status and more accurate and efficient checking of social security cards. In effect, the administration had accepted the Jordan Commission's argument that U.S. jobs attracted unlawful workers and that the employer sanctions established by the 1986 Immigration Reform and Control Act (IRCA) had been nullified in part by weak enforcement and too many loopholes. However, even with the White House's proposed increase in personnel, the number of investigators would remain low relative to the seven million employers they were supposed to oversee. Interior enforcement would continue to rely significantly on firms' voluntary compliance. Still, very few resources had been previously allocated to enforcing the laws on employing illegal aliens, and the administration's proposals represented a 29 percent increase.[48] In addition, the budget proposed 700 additional Border Patrol agents; 1,055 more INS and Customs agents to be stationed at border crossings; a border-crossing fee of $1.50 per pedestrian and $3 per car; double the number of deportations; and $300 million reimbursement to the states for incarcerating undocumented felons and $150 million for emergency medical treatment and Medicaid costs.[49] Overall, the administration was proposing a $1 billion increase in funds allocated to curbing illegal immigration and ameliorating its effects.

Although little would come of these proposals—Gingrich was now in control of the legislative agenda and was loathe to let the White House take credit for any popular reforms—a spokesperson for Governor Wilson nevertheless criticized the administration's emphasis on employer sanctions because it "refuses to acknowledge that government services are a magnet."[50] The Clinton administration was still firmly of the opinion that jobs were pulling illegal immigrants to the United States. The jobs versus public benefits debate would be at the center of the partisan squabbles in the 104th Congress. On one side, Republicans did not believe that employers should be responsible for enforcing immigration law. Less altruistically, some Republicans did not want to reduce the flow of cheap labor to their major campaign contributors. On the other side, Democrats thought it immoral to exclude an already oppressed group of persons from the few public benefits they were still entitled to. Less benignly, some Democrats did not want to rock the welfare boat. They regarded recipients of public benefits as a key part of their electoral coalition. In this thinking, to reduce benefits was to shrink their constituency; to increase benefits was to expand it.[51]

The administration introduced another bill in early May 1995 sponsored by senators Edward Kennedy (D-MA), Paul Simon (D-IL), and Barbara Boxer (D-CA), again targeting workplace violations of the IRCA by increasing the penalties for those found guilty of employing undocumented labor.[52] To coincide with the bill being sent to Congress, Clinton ratcheted up his anti-immigrant rhetoric to new heights in his Saturday May 6, 1995, radio broadcast to the nation:

> Our nation was built by immigrants. But we won't tolerate immigration by people whose first act is to break the law as they enter our country. . . . Every day, illegal aliens show up in court who are charged. Some are guilty and surely some are innocent. Some go to jail and some don't. But they're all illegal aliens. And whether they're innocent or guilty of the crimes they were charged with in court, they're still here illegally, and they should be sent out of the country. . . . We are a nation of immigrants, but we are also a nation of laws. And it is wrong and ultimately self-defeating for a nation of immigrants to permit the kind of abuse of our immigration laws we have seen in recent years.[53]

In early 1995 the administration sought to improve cross-border cooperation with the Mexican government and law-enforcement agencies to reduce the flow of undocumented migrants. Mexico had traditionally been reluctant to cooperate with the United States on such matters, partly for political reasons (it did not want to be seen working with a foreign government to oppress its own citizens) and partly for constitutional reasons (the Mexican constitution guarantees free movement for migrants). However, America's $12 billion bailout of the Mexican economy in late 1994 came with strings attached, including a requirement to help stem the flow of migrants. One way in which Mexico tried to do so was by doubling the personnel of the Grupo Beta border police unit in Tijuana, which sought to disrupt the operations of "coyotes"—people who smuggle immigrants illegally across the border. The Mexican government also agreed to participate in a pilot program that would transport into the Mexican interior illegal Mexican migrants discovered in the United States. The program was announced jointly by President Clinton and Mexican president Ernesto Zedillo on October 10, 1995, during Zedillo's second visit to the United States. Some commentators thought Zedillo agreed to the plan because he was rewarding Clinton for bailing out the Mexican economy, and because he recognized immigration was an issue that the administration had to be seen to be addressing in the face of more radical proposals in the Republican Congress. During the same week, Attorney General Janet Reno announced the appointment of San Diego–based U.S. attorney Alan Bersin as "border czar" to oversee and coordinate law enforcement at the U.S.-Mexico border, with specific reference to immigrant smuggling and drug trafficking.[54]

Building on Zedillo's visit to the United States, Defense Secretary William J. Perry visited Mexico in late October and proclaimed a "new era of friendship" between the armed forces of the two nations. Of particular note was the agreement of Mexico's armed forces to cooperate with their northern neighbors in the fight against illegal immigration and drug running. Such bilateral cooperation had often floundered on Mexico's suspicion that its neighbor was threatening its sovereignty and on the Mexican army's reluctance to become involved in the contraband war. The army still enjoyed considerable public prestige, but feared that joining the war on drugs would open it up to corruption by the drug cartels—as had happened with other law-enforcement agencies. Recognizing the new glasnost, Perry toasted the "new U.S.-Mexican security relationship based on openness, trust and cooperation. . . . The ideas and proposals being discussed today in our hemisphere would have been unthinkable even 10 years ago."[55]

The administration's commitment to immigration reform and controlling the borders was in the main politically motivated. The upcoming 1996 presidential election focused sharply Clinton's need to court California voters on the hot-button issue of illegal immigration. Most political commentators gave Clinton little chance of reelection without California's fifty-four electoral college votes. The administration had already spent over $350 million bailing out LA County's bankrupt healthcare system in late 1995, and it was now demonstrating its sensitivity on immigration matters. To this end, Attorney General Reno announced that the administration was redeploying 200 Border Patrol agents to the California/Arizona-Mexico border for the post-Christmas rush north, as well as 350 soldiers and 135 police officers. While denying that this represented a militarization of the border because the soldiers would be working in a support role, it sent a strong message to Californians that Clinton was taking the issue very seriously. But the significant increases in (new) border and enforcement personnel was only possible because Congress had voted to increase substantially the INS's budget. Although most federal agencies witnessed a budget cut, the new Republican majority increased the INS budget by 24 percent on the previous year to $2.6 billion. Such was the scale of the increase in personnel that the Border Patrol had to build new training facilities to cope with supply of new personnel. The INS employed about 19,000 people in 1995. In 1996, that increased by 4,125.[56]

In sum, the White House, while keen to be seen cracking down on illegal immigration, did not want to alienate members of one of its core constituencies: ethnic-minority voters, especially Latinos. As noted above, many Republicans—Jack Kemp, William Bennett, and George W. Bush excluded—seemed little concerned about these voters, but the Democratic Party recognized Latinos' increasing electoral significance. Thus, it tried to portray itself as both tough on illegal immigration and as the party immigrants could trust. For example, to reach out to Latinos, Vice President Al Gore visited Pasadena in the San Fernando Valley on July 14, 1995, to bestow posthumously the Presidential Medal of Freedom to Willie Velasquez. Velasquez was a prominent California Latino activist and founder of the Southwest Voter Registration Education Project in the 1970s. Gore used the award ceremony to articulate his and Clinton's vision of a more inclusive California and to distance the administration from Wilson and the Republican Party: "We must create a future in which our children can look back on the demagoguery of this day and time, and lightly pass it off with an amused shake of the head. We will create the future by the sweat of our brow, by registering voters. . . . We stand for the proposition that men and women of different ethnic, national origin, and language groups can live together in harmony."[57]

1995 Subcommittee Action

Prop. 187's victory had given warning to politicians that the public wanted to bring illegal immigration under control. The Jordan Commission, Gallegly's taskforce, President Clinton and others in his administration, Patrick Buchanan, Kemp and Bennett, Speaker Gingrich, and many interest groups all jockeyed for position during 1995. Each knew that immigration reform was likely, and thus wanted to influence its parameters. Some wanted major reform while others desired only moderate change. Some wanted to concentrate on illegal immigration while others saw the backlash against illegal entry as an opportunity to reduce the level of legal immigration. For example, the new Republican chairs of the House and Senate immigration subcommittees, Lamar Smith and Alan Simpson, regarded Prop. 187 as a vanguard for their own proposals to cut documented entry into the United States. Still others, such as Gingrich, were not true believers but saw immigration reform as a vehicle for, or complement to, other reforms. Gingrich's primary goal was the reform of the welfare system, which he thought eroded recipients' motivation and self-belief while costing the government billions of dollars. His key role in the GOP's congressional victory ensured that other players in the reform process took Gingrich's position very seriously indeed, and his control of the House gave him the power to make or break reform. The only other congressional players with comparable power on the immigration issue were Smith and Simpson. Both were long-term advocates of tighter immigration policies who thought the 104th Congress offered bright prospects for reform.

Lamar Smith held immigration hearings between February and June 1995, and presented a bill to the House immigration subcommittee in late June. His bill (HR 2202; formerly HR 1915) sought to reduce legal immigration, further control illegal entry, and restrict both groups' access to public benefits.[58] Smith wanted to limit legal entry to about 600,000 immigrants per year. The official limit was 675,000, although the number of entries regularly neared one million because some categories of entrant were not subject to strict numerical limits.[59] Smith particularly wanted to curtail the entry of unskilled migrants and the siblings and adult children of U.S. citizens and legal permanent residents allowed in under the family reunification scheme.[60] Like others, he did not believe the U.S. economy needed more unskilled workers and was concerned about the effects of the family reunification scheme on chain migration. Other significant provisions of his bill included making illegal immigrants ineligible for all public benefits except emergency medical care and emergency relief aid; toughening up the rules on sponsoring legal migrants; adding a further 5,000 Border Patrol agents over five years and reinforcing the border defenses; increasing by 500 the number of INS and Labor Department inspectors enforcing the employment law; and establishing a pilot-study toll-free telephone hotline for employers to verify the status of prospective employees.

Although the full House judiciary committee approved Smith's bill 23-10 on October 24, 1995, it attracted considerable opposition from across the interest group spectrum. On one side, ethnic groups, unions, immigration lawyers, and religious organizations lined up against it, arguing the legislation was anti-immigrant, immoral, racist even. On the other, business groups argued that it would reduce the supply of labor, push up wages, impose additional costs, and thus hurt the U.S. economy. In addition, some Republicans were unsure about conflating the issues of legal and illegal immigration. Although few denied there were good political and practical reasons for cracking down on illegal entry to the United States, many Republicans did not think that legal immigration should be reduced. There was some disquiet about addressing both issues in the same bill, and pressure grew for it to be split into two. Some Republicans worried that the bill would fail if the legal immigration provisions were not addressed separately, because legal immigration reform was not as popular. Others didn't want to restrict legal immigration at all. Smith argued in response, successfully on this occasion, that the public was demanding action on both legal and illegal entry and that the number of unskilled legal migrants had to be reduced because of competition with native workers. The bill remained one, although it was subject to some minor amendments in full committee.

Simpson was also keen to tackle legal immigration. His Senate bill (S 1394) sought to reduce the level of legal immigration to about 540,000 a year, restrict the entry of siblings and adult children of U.S. citizens and legal permanent residents, reduce the number of permanent and temporary workers admitted, and tighten legal immigrants' access to public benefits. Simpson initially addressed illegal immigration in a separate bill (S 269), but later folded it into S 1394 because he believed that legal immigration reform would have a greater chance of success if it was combined with the more popular illegal-immigration bill. S 269, like Smith's bill, proposed restricting illegal immigrants' eligibility for federal programs, piloting an employee-verification scheme, and increasing the INS's and Border Patrol's budgets. It also proposed introducing a border-crossing fee, expediting the deportation of undocumented felons, strengthening the government's investigative powers to combat gangs who smuggled immigrants into the United States, giving greater powers to INS and customs officials to refuse entry to those claiming asylum, and repealing the Cuban Adjustment Act, which gave Cubans permanent residency status after only one year's residency in the United States.[61]

As Congressional Quarterly Almanac noted, "The Smith and Simpson proposals represented the most ambitious congressional rewrite of immigration law in years. . . . The 103rd Congress produced much sound and fury on questions of illegal and legal immigration but not much action. . . . With the Republican takeover, the new [104th] Congress began to consider much stronger measures."[62] However, the number of bills vying for time meant Smith's and Simpson's bills were not considered on the floor of the House and Senate before the end of the legislative session in late 1995. Nonetheless, the bills would be reintroduced in the next legislative session and form the basis of immigration reform in 1996.

The Jordan Commission II

The Jordan Commission's September 1994 report on illegal immigration had already given momentum to the pro-reform forces by helping to legitimize the idea of reform. The report also provided a number of concrete policy proposals, which would help frame the reform agenda. Its argument that undocumented migrants were drawn to the United States by the "job magnet" rang true with Smith and Simpson, who included in their bills the commission's policy solution of a national registry of eligible workers. In June 1995 the commission published its second report—this one on legal immigration. The commission concluded that

> a properly regulated system of legal immigration is in the national interest of the United States. . . . Immigrants often create new businesses. . . . [They] can strengthen America's economic and political ties with other nations, and, thus, enhance our ability to compete in a global economy and provide leadership in international and humanitarian affairs. . . . Immigration further strengthens American scientific, literary, artistic and other cultural resources, . . . promotes family values and ties . . . [and] can demonstrate to other countries that religious and ethnic diversity are compatible with national civic unity in a democratic and free society.[63]

The commission also noted, however, that legal immigration imposed costs on society. It was especially concerned that low-skilled immigrants competed for jobs and benefits with the most disadvantaged and vulnerable Americans. It was also concerned that high concentrations of recent immigrants in certain areas could over-burden communities' schools, roads, and public services and "exacerbate tensions among ethnic groups."[64] The solution was "major reform" of the immigration system to ensure that future admissions served the interests of the United States.

In particular, the commission recommended that legal immigration should be reduced from about 725,000 in 1996 to 550,000. This would require a five-to-eight year transition period to clear the backlog of hundreds of thousands of spouses and children of U.S. citizens and permanent residents who had been waiting years for visas. To achieve the reduction it proposed cutting the number of family reunification visas from 480,000 to 400,000, with the most dramatic reductions reserved for the siblings and adult children of U.S. citizens and permanent residents. Siblings and adult children were not considered by Smith and Simpson to be part of the nuclear family, but were usually blamed for chain migration because, after achieving permanent residency status, they too could petition for their nuclear and extended family to be admitted. By reserving visas for the spouses, parents, and children of U.S. citizens and legal immigrants the commission hoped to sever the migration chain.[65] It also hoped that making migrants legally dependent on their sponsor, not the government, for financial support would help reduce the welfare burden.[66]

The commission recommended that additional cuts in the level of legal immigration could be achieved by revoking the 50,000 visas available under the diversity program, which had been designed to promote immigration from countries that had sent few migrants to the United States in recent years. And to protect the jobs of domestic workers, the commission suggested cutting from 140,000 to 100,000 the number of immigrants admitted under the skills-based employment program. The commission stressed that while highly skilled immigrants contributed significantly to the U.S. economy and did not take native workers' jobs, unskilled immigrants did little for the economy and increased competition for low-paid, insecure jobs. Such immigrants should therefore be excluded from the employment visa program, the commission concluded. It also proposed that the number of refugee admissions should be capped at 50,000.

Finally, the commission noted that it "support[ed the] effective Americanization of new immigrants, that is the cultivation of a shared commitment to the American values of liberty, democracy, and equal opportunity."[67] This was controversial because the Americanization program of the 1920s had been tinged by racism and nativism and because the multicultural discourse dominant in the late twentieth century held that no culture or ethnic group was superior to any other. Nonetheless, the commission argued strongly that all immigrants should be taught to read, write, and speak English and have a good understanding of American history and values.[68]

President Clinton met with Barbara Jordan on June 7, 1995, and she outlined her proposals. Later in the day, Clinton welcomed the Jordan Commission's second report, calling it a "road map for Congress to consider. . . . Consistent with my own views, the commission's recommendations are pro-family, pro-work, pro-naturalization. . . . [The report] appears to reflect a balanced immigration policy that makes the most of our diversity while protecting the American workforce so that we can better compete in the emerging global economy."[69] Many commentators were surprised by Clinton's endorsement of the report. While he had earlier voiced his determination to control illegal immigration, Clinton had always expressed support for legal immigration. Now he was associating himself with a report suggesting it should be reduced—a position that threatened to alienate many of his core supporters. Others were surprised by the report's recommendations. Barbara Jordan, like Clinton, had been a vocal supporter of legal immigration, but now her commission was suggesting it should be cut. Why? Those close to Jordan knew that she wanted to produce a unanimous report, which she believed would have a greater impact, and this in part led her to compromise her support for legal immigration. That she was keen to influence the agenda in Congress was no secret.[70] It was also rumored at the time that the agenda in Smith's and Simpson's congressional committees in turn influenced the commission's thinking. At the least, Smith and Simpson were encouraged by the commission's findings and often quoted them in defense of their own bills.[71] It is most likely that the arrows of causation run both ways: the commission wanted its report to be relevant, and Smith and Simpson needed all available support. There was of course no surprise over Lamar Smith's support for Jordan's findings. He commented that the report "makes our job easier" because it provided extra evidence for the need to reform the legal immigration system.[72] Smith was concerned that pro-immigration groups would try to scuttle his reform agenda: "The interest groups should be reminded that, for the last 20 years, 75 percent of the American people have consistently wanted to reduce immigration."[73]

In sum, the Clinton administration, the Jordan Commission, and the chairs of the two most important congressional subcommittees agreed that there should be some reduction in the level of legal immigration, although there were differences regarding the extent. They also agreed on the need to control illegal immigration and were broadly in agreement about the best ways of doing so. Pro-immigration forces were rightly worried. As one lobbyist noted,

> In the spring of 1995, we didn't think we could turn the restrictionist tide, could stop the reform juggernaut, and it looked like something close to zero immigration

was on the verge of being enacted. The current system would be gutted, the safety net for legal immigrants would be shredded, and a national work verifications system would be imposed.[74]

1996 Congressional Action

Simpson introduced his two immigration bills—S 269 on illegal immigration and S 1394 on legal immigration—to the Senate judiciary committee in February 1996 as a single bill: S 1664, the Immigration Control and Financial Responsibility Act. However, the prospects for major reform, which looked a certainty in 1994 and 1995, began to ebb in 1996.

Pro-immigration business interests—especially high-tech firms such as Intel, Microsoft, and Sun Microsystems—formed a pressure group called American Business for Legal Immigration (ABLI) with the aim of destabilizing the effort to reform legal immigration. There was particular concern over the proposed restrictions on hiring foreign workers and the employee-verification schemes. Labor unions, religious and civil rights groups, and those representing ethnic interests, including the American Immigration Lawyers Association (AILA), also opposed the legislation, although for different reasons than the ABLI. They were little concerned about the employer provisions and more about the proposal to cut siblings and adult children from the family reunification scheme. In terms of political leverage, however, it would be important for these groups to work with business groups such as ABLI, which had better access to the Republican politicians holding the reigns of power in Washington.[75] The White House also began to soften its support for reductions in legal immigration as civil rights and ethnic groups began to lobby hard against the plan. For example, the vice president said in late June 1995 to the National Association of Latino Elected and Appointed Officials that the Jordan Commission report "is not the final word. It is a framework, not a blueprint. . . . We want to deter illegal immigration, but we are all descendents of immigrants."[76] Gore promised that Latino leaders would be consulted over any changes to immigration policy.

The most significant opposition, however, came from within the Senate judiciary committee. Most Democrats on the committee—including Edward Kennedy (D-MA), but not Dianne Feinstein (D-CA)—and two junior Republicans opposed Simpson's efforts to curtail legal immigration. The opposition of freshman senator Spencer Abraham (R-MI) would prove especially significant. He worked with business and pro-immigrant groups to divide S 1664 once again into two separate bills, arguing that legal and illegal immigration were "two distinct areas of law and ought to remain that way." Although he denied that he was "trying to kill legal immigration reform," to Senator Simpson and other observers it looked very much like he was.[77] And splitting the bills was certainly an effective way to do so. Simpson had united the two bills because he knew the chances of reforming legal immigration would be improved if it were bundled together with the more popular illegal-immigration reform. Thus, Abraham's effort to split the bill once again would, if successful, ease the process of killing legal reform.

Simpson, however, opposed Abraham. He decided to try to weaken the pro-immigration coalition by splitting it into two factions. He appealed directly to business interests by offering to remove the employment-oriented provisions from his bill, which included the employee-verification scheme and reductions in permanent and temporary employment visas.[78] Simpson hoped that business groups would support such a move while civil rights and pro-immigration groups would oppose it. However, his machinations came too late; both left and right were committed to defeating all efforts to curb legal migration. On March 14, 1996, the judiciary committee voted 12-6 to split the bill, and then approved a number of significant amendments excoriating the provisions curtailing legal immigration and those increasing sanctions on firms employing illegal workers.[79]

On the illegal-immigration bill, the committee approved amendments to ease the provisions on the deportation of immigrants convicted of serious crimes; to expand the INS's detention facilities by 800 places; and to introduce federal standards for birth certificates to discourage counterfeiting.[80] The more significant amendments were made to the legal immigration bill (introduced as S 1665), as Abraham had hoped. Simpson had wanted to reduce the number of family reunification visas to 300,000 from 450,000 and to exclude adult children and siblings from the visa program in order to combat chain migration. However, the committee approved 11-4 on March 28 an amendment from across the partisan divide that effectively ended Simpson's hope of reducing legal migration. Kennedy and Abraham's amendment actually increased the number of family reunification visas to 500,000 for 10 years before dropping to 425,000 thereafter. It also reinstated adult children's and sibling's access to the visa program and resurrected the diversity program. Simpson responded dejectedly that the amendment represented the "virtual maintenance of the status quo."[81]

Moreover, faced by opposition from business interests, Simpson was also defeated on his attempt to reduce the number of visas for workers with needed skills from 140,000 to 90,000. Two happier notes for Simpson were the approval of a Abraham-Specter amendment increasing the penalties on employers who abused the H-1B temporary skilled worker program by bringing in cheap foreign workers at the expense of qualified native workers, and the elimination of the 10,000 permanent visas for unskilled workers.[82] But these victories were largely pyrrhic given the scale of the retrenchment on legal migration levels.

As the Senate judiciary committee approved the amended bill 13-4 on March 21, the House bill had already progressed to the floor. The pro-reform forces were stronger in the House than in the Senate, and had the backing of Speaker Gingrich and the House Republican Policy Committee, which had declared its support for reforming legal migration. Nevertheless, the pro-immigration coalition, so effective in the Senate, was also increasing its influence in the House. Moreover, there was little effective lobbying by interest groups in support of legal immigration reform. Only the Federation for American Immigration Reform (FAIR) made any concerted effort to persuade members of the practical and electoral benefits of reform, yet it was considered an extremist group by many.[83]

Strangely, however, business and civil and immigrant rights groups would not prove the major cause of damage to Smith's legislation. That would come from inside his own party, from one of his most vocal supporters: Representative Elton Gallegly. Gallegly introduced an amendment that threatened to change the nature of the legislation and upset Smith's precarious pro-reform coalition.

Modeled on Prop. 187 and hoping to make irrelevant Judge Pfaelzer's interment of the citizen initiative, Gallegly's amendment proposed that the states should be permitted to deny public education to undocumented children. He argued in debate that forcing states to educate undocumented children amounted to "a federal unfunded mandate. Come to America for opportunity. Do not come to America to live off the law-abiding American taxpayer."[84] Many representatives reacted angrily. Floyd Flake (D-NY) said the amendment "was one of the most dangerous, damaging pieces of legislation we've considered in my 11 years here," and Gary Ackerman (D-NY) commented, "After I got over my initial reaction, I decided to be civil and not go out and commit any crimes of violence." Others called it variously "stupid," "hideous," and "immoral."[85]

Despite the extreme emotion engendered by Gallegly's amendment—which was similar to that in California in 1994 over Prop. 187's education provisions—it enjoyed enough support to win easily 257-163 on March 20, 1996. Speaker Gingrich praised the amendment, saying "There is no question that offering free taxpayer goods to illegals attracts more illegals. . . . It is wrong for us to be the welfare capital of the world."[86] Governor Wilson estimated the amendment would remove nearly 400,000 undocumented students from classrooms and save an estimated $2 billion per year in California alone.

Smith defeated two further proposals that would have watered down the bill's anti-immigrant provisions. The Pombo and the Goodlatte amendments sought to make it easier for agricultural interests to import migrant labor by easing the certification process. Opponents easily portrayed the amendments as new Bracero programs, and they lost 180-242 and 59-357 respectively. As one farm lobbyist noted, "We got our asses kicked pretty soundly. This is an increasingly urban Congress that doesn't care about the 3 percent of the country that feeds the other 97 percent."[87]

Although the House strengthened the bill in approving the Gallegly and defeating the Pombo and Goodlatte amendments, it weakened it significantly on March 21 in accepting an amendment offered by represenatitives Dick Chrysler (R-MI), Howard Berman (D-CA), and Sam Brownback (R-KS). The amendment struck down the key provision to reduce legal immigration, namely the ending of family reunification visas for siblings and adult children of U.S. citizens and permanent legal residents, which Smith had hoped would cut legal migration from 480,000 to 330,000 a year. The amendment enjoyed the support of 75 Republican members and President Clinton, who only weeks earlier had expressed his support for some cuts to legal migration and his opposition to visas for siblings and adult children. Gimpel and Edwards suggest that the Asian American Democratic activist John Huang lobbied Clinton to oppose the elimination of the sibling and adult children visas, and that Ralph Reed, director of the Christian Coalition, also lobbied against a change to the status quo.[88] Overall, the bill's anti-illegal-immigration provisions fared well on the floor, while those limiting legal immigration were gutted. HR 2202 passed the House 333-87 on March 21, 1996. However, the Gallegly amendment would return to haunt Smith.

It was considered in the Senate in mid April 1996. Senators faced considerable lobbying by educationalists and law-enforcement groups opposed to the measure. A spokesperson for the International Union of Police Associations asked, "How can anyone advocate throwing thousands of children onto the streets without supervision, where they will become both victims and criminals? Local law-enforcement officers, our members, will be overwhelmed at a time we can ill afford the extra pressure."[89] Many teaching unions—such as the National School Boards Association, and the Council of Great Cities and Schools—said their members would not enforce the amendment if it became law. Both California senators also expressed their opposition, as did many other groups and individuals, such as Roger Mahony, archbishop of Los Angeles.

Nevertheless, Senate majority leader Bob Dole endorsed the amendment. Dole had one eye on Pat Buchanan in the race for the Republican presidential nomination and the other on Bill Clinton in the race for the U.S. presidency. He hoped that his support for it would help court primary voters in California and elsewhere, create some policy distance between himself and President Clinton, and possibly put Clinton in the unenviable position of vetoing the whole immigration bill before the 1996 presidential election. Dole hoped that a veto would demonstrate to Californians that Clinton was not serious about immigration reform. The White House recognized the potential dilemma and worked hard to kill the amendment. "We're trying to keep it out of the final bill, and I will do everything I can to keep it out. . . . They're adopting a strategy to say that, 'We're going to use the lawmaking process of the United States to force the president to veto a bill where the main subject of the bill he's really for, because we'd rather have the veto. And I think that's wrong,' argued Clinton."[90] Gallegly was incredulous: "I cannot believe that he would be that stupid—or should we say politically naïve? He may talk a lot about it and play a poker-faced game, but I don't think it's a wise thing politically, especially in California, to veto this immigration bill."[91]

Despite Dole's support, the final version of the Senate bill, which was approved 97-3 on May 2, did not include the Gallegly amendment or any compromise measure.[92] Governor Wilson attacked the decision, arguing that "no illegal-immigration reform will be complete in addressing the concerns of Californians unless it includes the Gallegly amendment, which would allow states to set their own public education policies toward illegal immigrants."[93]

Also excluded from the final Senate bill was any cut in legal immigration levels. The bill did, however, strengthen the concept of sponsorship for legal immigrants and dramatically reduce their access to federal benefits, which attracted Clinton's ire: "While this bill strongly supports our enforcement efforts, it still goes too far in denying legal immigrants' access to vital safety net programs, which could jeopardize public health and safety."[94] Also controversial was a pilot program to allow employers to use government databases to check the legal status of employees, which critics argued would help create a monolithic, overbearing federal government, threaten Americans' civil rights, and be a first step toward a national ID card. Less controversially, the bill reduced the number of documents used to demonstrate employment status from nearly forty to just six, increased the number of Border Patrol agents from 5,100 by 1,000 a year for four years, equipped them with the latest technology, and refenced a particularly porous fourteen-mile stretch of border. Penalties for smuggling immigrants and for manufacturing fake citizenship documents were also increased and deportation procedures speeded up.[95] In addition to Gallegly's amendment, another significant absentee was a guest-worker program. Clearly, the time was not yet right for agriculture-friendly Republicans to move on this one. Nor did the Senate version include the requirement that hospitals identify and count undocumented patients. The House bill said sponsors must earn at least 200 percent of the poverty level, while the Senate version set a figure of 125 percent. The House bill also barred legal immigrants and even U.S. citizen children with undocumented parents from receiving most federal benefits, while the Senate version had no such provision.[96] These differences—and the Gallegly amendment—would have to be reconciled in conference committee.[97]

By the time both chambers were ready for the conference, Dole had resigned from the Senate on June 11 to campaign full time for the presidency. Although he had earlier expressed his support for the Gallegly amendment, the Republican congressional leadership was unsure whether its presidential candidate wanted the amendment in or out. If it was in and Clinton vetoed, Dole could portray his opponent as soft on illegal immigration and unresponsive to the states' financial burden. However, if Clinton did not veto, hundreds of thousands of children could be expelled from school. Although everyone knew it would be one of the most important changes in public policy for many years, no one was sure what the consequences of expelling so many children would be, only that it would be major. So concerned were forty-two Democratic and five Republican senators that they sent Dole a letter urging him to oppose the "highly controversial and ill-advised provision."[98] Dole was further plagued by the growing influence of the pro-immigration forces and by uncertainty about how the amendment would play outside California and the other half-dozen states with large undocumented populations.

Dole responded during another visit to California in mid June. He sent a message to congressional Republicans once again stating his support for the Gallegly amendment, arguing it was about "fairness. . . . [The teaching of illegal immigrants is] one of the most expensive mandates of all time. . . . The states provide a free education to people who by our own laws should not be in the United States. I don't believe it's fair to impose these burdens on the states."[99] Dole argued that not educating illegal minors would free up $1.8 billion, which "could hire 51,000 new teachers, . . . could reduce the pupil-teacher ratio to less than 20 to 1. Or you could build over 2,340 new classrooms in California. Or you could put 3.6 million . . . computers in the schools. So that's the choice."[100] Dole tried to soften the edges of his rhetoric by insisting that he was compassionate and cared deeply about the United States' immigrant history—although he mangled his lines, referring to America as "a boiling pot," rather than a melting pot. Earlier in the week he claimed, to great astonishment, that nicotine was probably not addictive.[101] Clinton also visited California in mid June, and used the opportunity to express, eloquently of course, his outrage over the burning of black churches in the south, which had recently occurred. He compared the (racist) motives of the arsonists to those activists and politicians who had whipped up anti-immigrant sentiments in California. At the same time, he praised his own efforts to stem the tide of illegal entrants.[102]

Despite Dole and Gingrich's support and his own dogged efforts, Gallegly's amendment did not survive the conference committee.[103] Informal and formal discussions began in May 1996 and continued through September. The GOP strategy was for Republicans to reach agreement first and then present a united front to Democratic conferees, thus making it more difficult for them to influence the two bills' reconciliation. Representatives Smith and Gallegly and senators Simpson, Orin Hatch (R-UT), and Arlen Specter (R-PA) were the key Republican negotiators. The latter two had previously expressed opposition to the Gallegly amendment.[104] A compromise watered down the amendment to apply only to children enrolling in school after September 1996 and appointed the General Accounting Office (GAO) to monitor the new law's impact. Although this was acceptable to Hatch and Specter, Clinton reiterated his intention to veto and Feinstein appealed to the Republican leadership to remove Gallegly's killer amendment. Even some California congressional Republicans came out against it, preferring an immigration act without the Gallegly amendment over no act. Most surprising, however, was Ron Prince's opposition. Although he had once been a vocal supporter, Prince changed his position because he feared the amendment would kill the bill.[105] Gallegly was angry when told the news: "If he wants to undermine the bill, let him undermine the bill. The last time I looked, Ron Prince does not have a vote in Congress. I respect his right to express his opinion, but we have a lot to do. Ron Prince can say what he wants."[106] Harold Ezell was also far from pleased: "I don't think Prince has any credibility on the immigration issue. I don't think anyone pays attention to him. I don't think he has any following but his own."[107]

With the end of September approaching and members wanting to return to their states and districts to campaign, Smith and Simpson recognized there was too little time to overcome the opposition even within their own party and began to lobby against the amendment. Simpson stated that he would not sign a conference report if it remained in the bill—"If the national interest is subverted by Machiavellian mumbo jumbo, I'm not going to play that game"—and Smith argued that the public did not support kicking undocumented kids out of school.[108] With enough Republicans threatening to join a Democratic filibuster in the Senate, the GOP leadership decided to kill the amendment. Even the watered down version of Gallegly's controversial proposal was not included in the conference report. They also reconciled more minor but still important differences on asylum applications, verification of employees' eligibility to work, and sponsorship before the bill was presented to the conference committee.

The Democrats were fuming because they had been frozen out of the reconciliation process, and complained bitterly when the full conference committee finally met on September 24. Still, the conference report was approved by the full House 305-123 on September 25. Seventy-six Democrats voted in favor of the bill, and only five Republicans against.[109] However, internal divisions within the Republican Party, especially over the Gallegly amendment, had taken too long to overcome. Members were desperate to return to their constituencies to campaign, but the reconciled bill had not yet been approved by the Senate. And, with time running out, Senator Kennedy was threatening to tie up the bill for days unless the Republican leadership further weakened its provisions. This further fortified the White House; Clinton and his advisers again threatened to veto the bill unless further amendments were made. Although they did not get everything they wanted, Clinton's lobbyists persuaded Gingrich to weaken the sponsorship requirements, rescind the requirement to deport immigrants who used benefits for more than a year, and include the bill as part of HR 3610, an omnibus spending bill. HR 3610 was approved by the House on September 28. The Senate approved and Clinton signed it into law on September 30.[110]

Restrictionists attacked the bill because it failed to reduce legal immigration, omitted the Gallegly amendment, and abandoned any robust sanctions or procedures to prevent employers taking on undocumented workers. Nevertheless, it did represent the most important change to immigration law since 1986 and, possibly, 1965. The 1996 immigration act did not represent the only reform of the immigration system in the 104th Congress. As Congress grappled with the immigration bill, and in particular the question of legal entry to the United States, another bill received the president's signature and changed fundamentally legal immigrants' access to federal benefits. Although the immigration act would prove something of a damp squib in terms of its implications for legal immigrants, the welfare act represented the most radical change in the relationship between legal immigrants and the government in thirty years.

Immigration Reform and the 1996 Welfare Act

The main impetus for welfare reform came from Bill Clinton who, while running for the presidency in 1992, promised famously to "end welfare as we know it." Four years later on August 22, 1996 he signed the Personal Responsibility and Work Opportunity Reconciliation Act, or Welfare Reform Act, and made good his promise. However, candidate Clinton could not possibly have envisaged that the Republicans would take control of the reform agenda or that he would put his name to such radical legislation. Nor could he have envisaged that the welfare act would impact so dramatically on legal immigrants. The passage of Prop. 187, the Jordan Commission, the wider anti-immigrant climate, and the Republican takeover of Congress made possible such radical reform. In the final section of this chapter we examine the passage of the WRA and detail the changes it made to legal immigrants' eligibility for public benefits.

President Clinton was consumed by healthcare reform, the crime bill, and NAFTA during the 103rd Congress (1993–1995). Welfare reform received little attention, despite his earlier promise. Only on June 14, 1994, nearly two years after his election victory, did the Clinton administration publish a detailed reform plan. "We propose to offer people on welfare a simple contract. We will help you get the skills you need, but after two years, anyone who can go to work must go to work—in the private sector if possible, in a subsidized job if necessary. But work is preferable to welfare. And it must be enforced," said Clinton.[111] The cornerstone of the bill was the requirement for welfare recipients to work within two years of first receiving AFDC, but this would apply initially only to those born after 1971. Moreover, welfare recipients who could not find work would be placed in jobs subsidized by the federal government. The cost of Clinton's plan to get people off welfare and into work was estimated at $9.3 billion over five years, with job training and childcare accounting for most of that amount. Some savings of $4 billion over five years would be made restricting legal immigrants' access to AFDC, SSI, and food stamps, but Clinton refused to entertain the idea that they should lose all entitlements—as many Republicans and several Democrats had proposed.[112] Instead, Clinton proposed that noncitizens should be reliant on the income of their sponsors for five years. They would be eligible after that, unless their sponsor earned above the national median family wage. If so, noncitizens would have to obtain citizenship before receiving federal benefits.[113] Bob Dole teased Clinton that his unambitious proposals represented only "the end of welfare reform as we know it." Newt Gingrich added, "The president is brilliant at describing a Ferrari, but his staff continues to deliver a Yugo."[114] Yet those to the left of Clinton in Congress were horrified by the harshness of the proposals. There was no significant congressional action on the administration's proposals before legislators went home to run for reelection in 1994.

On their return to Washington, the political map had changed radically. With the Republicans now in charge of both the House and Senate, Clinton's welfare proposals ceased to matter—although his opinion still did. The GOP's proposals, as set out in the Contract with America and introduced into Congress as HR 4 on January 4, 1995, were much more radical. Families would only receive AFDC for a maximum of five years. It would not be paid to single mothers under 18 years of age, or for additional children born to mothers already on welfare. Moreover, mothers would have to demonstrate paternity to receive AFDC. The federal government would hand over to the states the responsibility for managing many food and nutritional programs—such as food stamps, school lunch programs, and the nutritional program for women, infants, and children (WIC)—and give the money to the states in the form of block grants. The states would also be given considerable leeway to design job training programs to move people off welfare. The bill also proposed ending immigrants' and other noncitizens' eligibility for sixty federal benefit programs—including SSI, AFDC, food stamps, and housing subsidies—although elderly refugees, those who had lived in the United States for five or more years, and those admitted lawfully to the United States were exempted from some of the proposed restrictions. The legislation thus distinguished between different categories of legal immigrant, and some were deemed more worthy of receiving benefits than others. For example, legal immigrants amnestied under the IRCA's provisions originally entered the country illegally and would thus be denied benefits granted to legal entrants. However they arrived in America, all noncitizens would remain eligible for emergency medical care. Overall, the bill would save $40 billion over five years, of which $22 billion would derive from cutting welfare to noncitizens.[115]

After discussions with Republican governors in early 1995—particularly Massachusetts' William Weld, Michigan's John Engler, and Wisconsin's Tommy Thompson—the GOP leadership in the House moved toward making their proposals even more radical. Under the new proposals the federal government would abandon its guarantee of a minimum level of income for poor families. AFDC, the key entitlement program (received by fourteen million people at a cost of $25 billion in 1995), would be abolished and replaced by a block grant to the states. The states would be given the power to administer their own welfare programs and to determine eligibility.[116]

President Clinton criticized the proposals in his January 1995 State of the Union address for "punishing poverty," although he did not promise a veto. Senator Dole also expressed his unease about excluding legal immigrants from federal benefits.[117] Nevertheless, the House was keen to push on and pass a reform bill in the session's first 100 days, as promised in the Contract. The legislation began its journey in three separate committees—ways and means, economic and educational opportunities, and agriculture—and each produced slightly different versions. Under the bill marked up by the ways and means subcommittee on human resources, legal immigrants were excluded from thirty-five federal programs, including Medicaid, child welfare and care programs, SSI, food stamps, and subsidized housing. In the full ways and means committee, legal immigrants with children were reinstated in the child welfare program and those who were veterans were exempted from many of the cuts. However, the committee rejected amendments to reinstate benefits to legal immigrants who had paid taxes for five or more years and to those under eighteen years of age. It also rejected a proposal that immigrants should retain Medicaid eligibility. In the version of the bill marked up in the economic and educational opportunities committee, legal immigrants were excluded from nineteen federal benefit programs and illegal immigrants from twenty-three. Unlike in the ways and means bill, legal immigrants were eligible for school meals and emergency food programs, WIC, and housing grants. The ways and means bill did, however, permit legally resident immigrants to participate in the education and training programs, whereas the education committee version did not. The agriculture committee version also excluded legal immigrants from most federal benefits, but made exceptions for veterans and those seventy-five years or older. The committee rejected amendments to reduce the age exception to sixty-seven years and to exempt pregnant women and minors from the restrictions.[118]

Once the three committees had finished marking up their bills the different versions were combined into one bill by the House Republican leadership and the rules committee. The new bill (HR 4) was slightly more generous to legal immigrants than the committees' versions as it allowed greater access to some federal programs. However, it tightened the rules concerning sponsorship, as did the immigration bill progressing though the House at the same time. The whole House approved HR 4 on March 24 by a mainly partisan 234 votes to 199.[119]

The immigration provisions of the welfare bill attracted surprisingly little opposition from Democrats and civil and immigrant rights groups. In part, this was because it was thought that the public strongly supported the effort to restructure the welfare system and particularly to exclude immigrants from public benefit programs. Another part was that the pro-immigration forces had focused most of their efforts on mitigating the radical provisions in the immigration bill, which was making its way through Congress at the same time. Still another part was that some provisions of the welfare bill were so radical and controversial that its immigration sections seemed moderate in comparison. Understandably, its foes focused their energy on the bill's most radical aspects. For example, Democrats worked hard to publicize and portray as wrongheaded and mean-spirited the willingness of the GOP to "destroy the programs that protect hungry children and pregnant women"[120]—and to do so in order to cut the taxes of the rich. Clinton called it "weak on work and tough on children."[121] There was also great concern that the federal government was abandoning its commitment to provide a safety net for America's poorest and most vulnerable families and was turning the responsibility over to the states. Senator Daniel Patrick Moynihan

(D-NY) called it a "constitutional moment, something I could not imagine 10 years ago, even five years ago."[122] Moynihan later encouraged the president to veto the bill: "If this administration wishes to go down in history as one that abandoned, eagerly abandoned, the national commitment to dependent children, so be it. I would not want to be associated with such an enterprise."[123]

Democratic congressman Nathan Deal (GA) introduced an alternative welfare reform bill (HR 1267), which proposed cuts in public benefits to legal immigrants and strict limits on the length of time that could be spent on welfare. In comparison with the existing law it was a radical piece of legislation but nevertheless won the support of most congressional Democrats, demonstrating how far the welfare debate in Congress had moved to the right since the Republican takeover. It also demonstrates that even pro-immigration Democrats accepted that legal immigrants were almost certain to have their public benefits cut; their fight was to protect the benefits of America's poorest from the Republican onslaught. Immigrants stood little chance. Even so, the Democratic bill failed 205-228 on another partisan vote.

The Senate's version of the welfare reform bill was marked up in the finance committee. Similar to the House bill in most respects, it too proposed ending AFDC and turning its replacement, Temporary Assistance for Needy Families (TANF), over to the states to administer. It also had the same five- and two-year welfare limits as the House bill. It did not, like the House version, mandate ending cash aid to single teenage mothers, children born to existing welfare recipients, and legal immigrants. Instead, it allowed the individual states to deny such aid if they so wished. However, in mid June 1995 the bill reached an impasse. Some Republican senators thought it did not do enough to discourage pregnancy outside marriage, while others thought the federal government should hand over control of even more programs to the states. There was also an intraparty dispute between senators representing small and large states over the formula for allocating federal funds to the states.[124]

Majority Leader Bob Dole spent the early summer rewriting the bill to take account of the criticisms of both conservative and moderate GOP senators. After a failed attempt to pass the bill in early August, senators returned after the recess to approve it easily 87-12 on September 19. Several moderate Republicans joined forces with the Democratic minority to force some significant changes to the bill on the Senate floor. They succeeded in removing the provisions that would have mandated the states to deny welfare help to single teenage mothers and to any additional child born to a single mother already receiving benefits. The Senate chose to reserve these decisions to the states. They also succeeded in winning more money for childcare funding, and put a lower limit on what states could spend on welfare over the next five years.[125]

The lopsided roll call does not, however, demonstrate any strong support for the legislation from Democrats or moderate Republicans, despite the moderating amendments described above. The bill was more moderate than the House version, but still represented a radical overhaul of the welfare system. As Minority Leader Tom Daschle said with little enthusiasm, "It is the best bill that we are going to get under the circumstances."[126] The problem for Republican leaders, however, was what would happen at the conference committee. It would be difficult to keep on board conservative Republicans in the House without losing moderate Republicans in the Senate. Moreover, Clinton had made plain his disapproval of the House bill and would likely veto anything similar.[127]

The House-Senate conference began on October 24 and continued through November and into December, and, like the conference on the immigration bill, excluded the Democrats. As expected, the conference report relaxed some of the more radical provisions in the House bill. For example, the House version had proposed to exclude legal immigrants from SSI, food stamps, Medicaid, cash welfare, and block-grant funded social services, while the Senate version excluded immigrants from SSI but gave the states the power to decide on their welfare and food stamp eligibility and only barred immigrants from social services for five years after arrival. The CBO estimated the House bill would save $102 billion over seven years and the Senate bill $56.5 billion. The reconciled bill adopted the Senate's five-year rule on social services, and also excluded from its restrictions veterans, refugees, and asylees and legal immigrants who had worked for at least ten years. However, the conference report excluded legal immigrants from SSI and food stamps.[128] On December 21 the House voted 245-178 in favor of the report. On the 22nd the Senate approved it 52-47—a long way from the 87-12 vote in favor in September, as Democratic senators withdrew their support. Clinton vetoed it on January 9, 1996, as expected, although White House press secretary Mike McCurry said that Clinton may have signed the pre-conference Senate version as it was "within striking distance" of the president's position. Clinton himself called on Republicans to work with him in a bipartisan effort, saying welfare was "broken and must be fixed."[129]

Although Clinton opposed the radical reform agenda in the House, he did not want welfare reform to die. He had promised major reform and wanted to make good that promise, preferably before the November 1996 presidential election. In his January 23, 1996, State of the Union address Clinton said,

> We know big government does not have all the answers. We know there's not a program for every problem. We have worked to give the American people a smaller, less bureaucratic government in Washington. And we have to give the American people one that lives within its means.
>
> The era of big government is over. But we cannot go back to the time when our citizens were left to fend for themselves . . . .
>
> I say to those who are on welfare, and especially to those who have been trapped on welfare for a long time: For too long our welfare system has undermined the values of family and work, instead of supporting them. The Congress and I are near agreement on sweeping welfare reform. We agree on time limits, tough work requirements, and the toughest possible child support enforcement. But I believe we must also provide child care so that mothers who are required to go to work can do so without worrying about what is happening to their children.
>
> I challenge this Congress to send me a bipartisan welfare reform bill that will really move people from welfare to work and do the right thing by our children. I will sign it immediately.
>
> Let us be candid about this difficult problem. Passing a law, even the best possible law, is only a first step. The next step is to make it work. I challenge people on welfare to make the most of this opportunity for independence. I challenge American businesses to give people on welfare the chance to move into the work force. I applaud the work of religious groups and others who care for the poor. More than anyone else in our society, they know the true difficulty of the task before

us, and they are in a position to help. Every one of us should join them. That is the only way we can make real welfare reform a reality in the lives of the American people.[130]

However, Republicans in Congress were now less enthusiastic about reform than previously; they wanted legislation on their terms, not Clinton's, and they also worried about the political capital Clinton would reap from making good on his promise to "end welfare as we know it." Again, it was the governors who spurred Congress to action. At a February 1996 meeting of the National Governors Association (NGA) bipartisan agreement was reached on a broad outline to reform both welfare and Medicaid—the main health program for America's poorest families—in a single bill, which in turn caught the imagination of congressional Republicans. The governors' major concerns were the cost of Medicaid and the onerous federal rules regulating the states' role in the program. They had little say in the way money was distributed but had to bear half the cost. The governors suggested they would be willing to trade federal dollars for a greater say in the design and delivery of the program. This appealed to Republican congressional leaders who were looking for ways to cut the federal budget and devolve power back to the states. However, Clinton had vetoed the Republicans' budget reconciliation bill (HR 2491) in 1995, which included in it Medicaid cuts totaling $163.4 billion over seven years, and he immediately threatened to veto any joint welfare-Medicaid bill.[131] This did not discourage the Republicans and it increased its attractiveness for Bob Dole, the likely Republican presidential candidate, who wanted to use Clinton's vetoes against him in the campaign.

Although the bipartisan governors association had agreed a broad outline, it could not agree on the details of reform. Republican governors then began to work with the Republican congressional leaders to draw up new, detailed proposals, which they published on May 22. The Democratic governors disassociated themselves from the plan, arguing in a May 29 letter to Bill Archer (R-TX), chair of the House ways and means committee, that "your Medicaid proposal is far from the NGA agreement and appears to be more like the proposal vetoed by the president last year."[132] Nevertheless, congressional committees began to consider the joint welfare-Medicaid bill in June.

Its welfare provisions were very similar to those in HR 4 introduced the previous year. The federal government would end its commitment to providing welfare to America's poorest families, and instead give the states the power to determine eligibility and the level of welfare benefits. The federal government would still contribute to welfare programs by giving the states block grants, but the states would have considerable leeway to spend the money as they saw fit and have more freedom to decide how much to spend themselves. More specifically, legal immigrants were to be excluded from SSI and food stamps unless they had worked in the United States for at least ten years. Immigrants arriving after the bill's passage would in addition be excluded from most other federal programs aimed at those on low incomes, although exceptions were made for veterans, refugees, and asylees. The Medicaid proposals followed a logic similar to that exhibited in welfare reform. Those on low incomes would no longer be entitled to federally assisted healthcare. The states would take over the responsibility and be given the power to design and implement their own programs, although, as with welfare, they would receive a block grant from the federal government to help them do so. The Medicaid spending reduction for the federal government was estimated at $72 billion over six years—an amount equivalent to the proposed welfare savings.[133]

The three House committees with jurisdiction over the bill—ways and means, economic and educational opportunities, and agriculture—marked it up in June. Some of the more radical GOP proposals were amended, but not those concerning immigrants. In the Senate, meanwhile, two committees held jurisdiction—finance and agriculture, nutrition, and forestry—but neither made any significant amendments to the provisions affecting immigrants. However, at the same time the bill was passing through both chambers' committees many Republicans, especially junior ones, changed their position regarding the efficacy of a joint bill. They believed that a new welfare law would aid their electoral prospects more than a Clinton veto on a combined welfare-Medicaid bill. If he must veto again, he should be made to veto the welfare reform only and not use Medicaid as an excuse, they reasoned. Further, the Republican governors' enthusiasm for reform wavered because the Senate finance committee weakened some of the Medicaid provisions in order to win over a number of key Democrats; the states would have less leeway to design their own programs and determine the level and cost of cover under the revised provisions. Finally, the political drive for a combined bill was also mitigated by Dole's resignation from Congress. Thus, in early July the Republican leadership changed tack and abandoned the Medicaid reforms.[134]

Many congressional Democrats who had previously opposed the joint bill changed their stance. With further amendments in place to smooth the radical edges of the House version, "I suspect we're going to have a good welfare reform bill that we can pass and send on to the president," said Senate minority leader Tom Daschle. White House spokesperson Mike McCurry concurred: "We now stand on the verge of having a welfare reform proposal that can get bipartisan support and the president's signature." Clinton himself said to the NGA on July 16 that "we have now reached a real turning point, a breakthrough for welfare reform. I'm pleased the congressional leadership made several significant improvements that have made this a much better bill."[135] However, another spokesperson for Clinton said that the administration was still uneasy about denying such a large range of benefits to immigrants and about the extent of the cuts in the food stamp program. The White House was moving toward approving the bill, but was not prepared to give its approval too soon. It would first push for further liberalizing amendments.

The House approved the Medicaid-free welfare bill (HR 3734) 256-170 on July 18. Although few amendments were made on the floor, one significantly altered the already precarious position of legal immigrants: the House approved excluding immigrants, even those already resident in the United States, from the Medicaid program. The Senate passed its version (S 1956) 74-24 on July 23. Exactly half of the Senate's forty-six Democrats voted in favor and half against.[136]

The conference committee met in late July. The participants knew that Clinton favored the Senate version, and he again made clear his disapproval of the cuts in aid to immigrants and food stamps. But conservative Republicans did not want to blink first and give Clinton everything he wanted. Clinton, meanwhile, was also coming under considerable pressure from liberal Democrats such as Moynihan and from civil rights and other groups to veto the bill. In the end, Clinton did win some concessions in conference. Cuts in food stamps were scaled back and it would remain a federal program. The House proposal to deny Medicaid to legal immigrants was defeated and replaced by the Senate alternative, which gave the states the power to determine their eligibility. The report also gave the states the power to decide whether low-income undocumented immigrants should be excluded from child nutrition programs, whereas the House bill had mandated they should.[137]

Before Congress voted on the conference report on July 31, Clinton said in a televised announcement that he would sign the bill. "Today, we have a historic opportunity to make welfare what it was meant to be: a second chance, not a way of life. . . . So I will sign this bill—first and foremost because the current system is broken." Gingrich was less generous, arguing Clinton had to sign the bill "because he can't avoid it and get reelected. That is the only reason."[138] After Clinton's announcement the bill passed the House 328-101 on July 31 and the Senate 78-21 on August 1 with little debate. Clinton signed it on August 22.[139]

Of the ninety-eight House Democrats who supported the final bill only two (from thirty-four in the House) were African American, two (of twelve) were Hispanic, and nine (of thirty-one) were women. Conversely, only two House Republicans voted against it, and both were Cuban Americans. Like many of the ethnic-minority Democrats in opposition, they opposed it because it slashed federal aid to legal immigrants.[140]

Knowledgeable scholars have described the welfare act's immigration provisions as "not highly controversial among voters. The public does not approve of natives using welfare benefits, much less newly arrived immigrants. There is also a widespread public perception that government aid should not be redirected from needy citizens to the foreign-born."[141] Despite the "uncontroversial" nature of the provisions, they nevertheless represented a radical change. Nearly half of the welfare act's savings, or $23.7 billion over six years according to the CBO, derived from making most legal aliens ineligible for most federal benefit programs, notably SSI and food stamps, and by allowing states to restrict legal immigrants' access to Temporary Assistance for Needy Families and Medicaid. Although the primary aim of the legislation was to reduce the cost of welfare, not discourage legal entry into the United States, it is unlikely that its provisions would have been so severe absent the anti-immigrant climate in Congress and the country. The antipathy toward immigrants smoothed the path to reform, as did the great number of immigrants claiming benefits, which itself was a product of generous immigration policies over four decades. That history ensured that legal immigrants were at the forefront of the most significant overhaul of the welfare system for sixty years.

Conclusions

During the Democratic-controlled 103rd Congress (1993–1994) some, mainly Republican, members tried to introduce legislation designed to curtail undocumented migration and ameliorate its effects in states with large illegal populations.

Yet radical measures always looked unlikely to pass. The illegal-immigration issue had not yet become a major public concern, and the composition of the legislature suggested that any significant reform to the nation's immigration law would face insurmountable obstacles. However, the prospects for reform improved dramatically in November 1994. Prop. 187's convincing margin of victory provided the impetus for reform and the historic Republican congressional success the opportunity.

The most significant way in which Prop. 187 helped pass federal immigration reform was that it helped set the agenda. Concern over illegal immigration during late 1993 and early 1994 largely centered on California and, to a lesser extent, Florida, Texas, and Arizona. However, as shown above, the high-profile and often vituperative campaign for and against Prop. 187 thrust the issue onto the national agenda as newspapers and television news shows gave the referendum top billing in mid-to-late 1994. Although many of the stories focused on the merits and demerits of Prop. 187 and the racial antagonisms it engendered, others told how the initiative helped its most high-profile supporter, California Governor Pete Wilson, come back from the political dead. Seemingly trailing impossibly in the polls less than a year before polling day, Wilson boarded and rode the illegal-immigration train to an overwhelming victory over Democratic challenger Kathleen Brown. The next day he shared headlines across the United States with Prop. 187 and Newt Gingrich.

The headlines spoke eloquently to politicians across the nation, who heard several interconnected messages. The first was that many Americans were angry about illegal immigration and wanted politicians to act. They were so angry that they were prepared to support an initiative that many respected politicians and commentators labeled nativist, or even racist. And it was not only white conservative Republicans that gave it their support. A quarter of Latinos and nearly half of African Americans and Asians also voted Yes. The second was that there was political capital to be made championing illegal-immigration reform, as evidenced by Governor Wilson's remarkable electoral resurrection. Conversely, opposing reform could have disastrous consequences. Kathleen Brown's career was over and Senator Dianne Feinstein's came very close to being wrecked. The third was that the time was now ripe for pushing immigration reform on the national stage. The momentum provided by Prop. 187 and the new composition of Congress offered an unparalleled opportunity, which both long-term advocates of reform and those new to the cause would have been foolish to ignore. That Prop. 187 had been interred by an "unelected liberal" judge only made the reformers more determined to rewrite federal law.

The new speaker of the House was quick to respond. Newt Gingrich, the unofficial king of the GOP, was an astute, perhaps visionary politician who like his adversary Bill Clinton read the opinion polls and election returns with great care. The evidence suggested to Gingrich that illegal immigration was an issue that could both energize Republican supporters and drive a wedge into the Democratic coalition. It looked like a win-win situation. Consequently, he established the Speaker's Congressional Task Force on Immigration Reform and appointed Representative Elton Gallegly, a Californian Republican, as chair. Its remit was to produce recommendations—some, in the event, inspired by Prop. 187, others building on the Jordan Commission's recommendations, and some new radical ones—that would feed into and help frame the agenda in Representative Lamar Smith's immigration subcommittee. The ultimate aim was radical reform that would further popularize the GOP in the 1996 congressional and presidential elections.

Gingrich also met with Governor Wilson in November 1994 to discuss proposals for immigration reform. At the time only Wilson could challenge Gingrich and Dole as the key player in the Republican Party. As the resurrected second-term governor of the nation's most populous and richest state and a politician who appeared to be in touch with the zeitgeist, Wilson was widely regarded as a potential presidential candidate for 1996, and one that had the ideas and experience to beat Clinton. Clinton was worried, and rightly so. California has one-fifth of the electoral college voters needed to win the presidency, and most analysts and Clinton himself thought that he had to win the Golden State to be sure of reelection. Although Clinton came out against Prop. 187 during the 1994 campaign, he made overtures to Californians by acknowledging that illegal immigration was a serious problem that required federal action. He made frequent trips to the west coast and signed the 1994 crime bill, which allocated $1.8 billion to the states to reimburse them for incarcerating undocumented felons. He also praised the first Jordan Commission report published in September 1994, which proposed establishing a national registry of eligible workers and excluding undocumented residents from public benefits. And, keen not to be let the GOP set the agenda, Clinton introduced his own illegal-immigration proposals into Congress.

Even after Wilson had dropped out of the Republican presidential primary race, immigration remained a prominent, hot-button issue. Perhaps the biggest surprise of the GOP primaries, along with Wilson's early failure, was the success of Patrick Buchanan. After winning the New Hampshire primary, Buchanan stayed in the race with Dole through the California primary in late March. Although he was never likely to win the nomination, Buchanan forced Dole to shore up his right flank. On the immigration issue, this meant extolling his support for Prop. 187 and Gallegly's amendment to exclude undocumented children from public schools. And while Clinton had a free run in the Democratic primaries, Dole, not wanting to be outgunned in the nation's crucial electoral arena, continued to visit California and express his support for tough measures against illegal immigration. Further, as the presidential contenders continued to talk up the immigration issue in the country, it provided additional momentum for those members of Congress seeking to enact radical legislative reform.

In sum, Prop. 187 helped create an environment that was conducive to reform at the national level. Of course, other factors also contributed toward that favorable environment, notably the Republican success in the 1994 congressional elections, which gave control of the key committees to immigration reformers. Also important were the Jordan Commission's reports, which provided options for, and legitimized some of the ideas of, Republican reformers.

The bills signed into law by President Clinton in August and September 1996 were in many respects very similar to Prop. 187. They cut off most public benefits to illegal immigrants, increased the penalties for the use and manufacture of false citizenship documents, and introduced provisions requiring undocumented immigrants to be reported to the INS (although Prop. 187's reporting provisions were much more comprehensive and radical). However, neither the immigration nor welfare act included Prop. 187's most radical provision: the exclusion of undocumented children from public school. Although the House approved the Gallegly amendment and the presidential candidate Dole expressed his support, it was dropped in conference committee because key players thought it too radical and had the power to block it. Moreover, the immigration and welfare acts included many provisions not in the direct democracy initiative. The immigration act tried to craft a more comprehensive solution to the illegal-immigration "problem." The philosophy of Prop. 187 was that illegal immigrants came to the United States generally and California specifically in search of generous public benefits such as welfare, healthcare, and education. The architects of the immigration act also believed that benefits attracted undocumented immigrants, but thought that employment played a major role too. To this end, the act introduced a number of pilot programs to make it more difficult for ineligible labor to find work and, in addition, made a concerted effort to improve detection and deportation procedures. In this sense, the legislators' response was more comprehensive than that offered by the authors of Prop. 187, in part because they wanted to write the most effective law possible, but also because of political considerations. A law that addressed only the work aspect would not likely win support from many Republicans and one that addressed only the benefits aspect would find it difficult to garner Democratic approval. Thus, the need for legislators to build a coalition of interests, as well as to write the best possible law, can help explain the more comprehensive nature of the immigration act. The authors of Prop. 187 were of course were free from such concerns and thus able to write a narrow, radical law without needing to compromise.

Both bills also went beyond Prop. 187 in one further important way. Both tried to address legal immigration. The welfare bill changed fundamentally legal immigrants' access to public benefits, and early incarnations of the immigration bill sought to reduce the level of legal immigration—although Smith and Simpson were ultimately unsuccessful in their efforts. Although Prop. 187 said nothing about these issues, it played an important role in both. Most significantly, Gingrich, Smith, and Simpson recognized that the initiative, despite its focus on undocumented migrants, helped politicize the immigration issue per se and thus opened up an opportunity for legal as well as illegal reform. Their motives differed, however. Smith and Simpson had long wanted to curtail the number of immigrants arriving legally on America's shores, while Gingrich wanted to use the hostility toward immigrants to reduce federal government expenditure and the tax burden.

At first glance it is somewhat surprising that Smith and Simpson failed to enact even a modest reduction in the number of legal immigrants entering each year, while the welfare act changed so radically their eligibility for public benefits. This apparent dissonance was not due to chance or irrational influences, however. The composition of the coalition on each side differed between the bills. Business interests, immigration lawyers, civil rights and pro-immigration groups, many Democrats, and some Republicans opposed reducing immigration levels. Yet business interests and immigration lawyers were less concerned about the efforts to cut benefits. Business was interested in increasing the supply of labor to reduce costs and in filling job vacancies, while immigration lawyers made a living giving advice and litigating on matters of permanent residency and citizenship. Neither had much financial interest in immigrants' public benefits. With only pro-immigration and civil rights groups lobbying hard against benefit cuts, the coalition was not as impressive as that arrayed against reducing immigration levels. Although such groups may have had more leverage in a Democratic Congress, they struggled to gain access to the new Republican majority and especially the radical young Turks in the House. Furthermore, these groups found it difficult to fight on two fronts simultaneously, and directed most of their energies to defeating cuts in immigration levels.

On the other side, few interest groups were lobbying actively in favor of reducing immigration levels; and only FAIR had the resources and organization to make itself heard. However, arrayed against a litany of groups protesting the proposed reductions, FAIR made little headway. Those opposing immigration cuts also enjoyed the support of some smart Republican politicians on the key immigration subcommittees. Senator Abraham, who outmaneuvered Senator Simpson on several key points, was particularly important in this respect. Smith and Simpson also did not have the wholehearted ideological or political support of the Republican leadership. In the House, Gingrich was committed to reducing the welfare burden but cared little for reducing immigration levels; he was instinctively pro-immigrant, and there was too little political capital to be gained from promulgating the restrictionist line. Others, such as the House majority leader Dick Armey (R-TX), were effusive in their praise for legal immigration. "Should we reduce legal immigration? Well, I'm hard-pressed to think of a single problem that would be solved by shutting off the supply of willing and eager new Americans. If anything . . . we should be thinking about increasing legal immigration," he argued.[142] In the more moderate Senate, Dole's position was often difficult to ascertain. He suggested that there was some room to reduce legal immigration—"maybe there are too many . . . legal immigrants coming in"[143]—but would not say by how much, only that there should be a "modest, temporary reduction."[144] And still others, such as Kemp and Bennett, articulated a powerful argument against the GOP pigeonholing itself as the anti-immigrant party. In contrast, the GOP leadership was much more committed to cutting public benefit programs. It recognized the potentially disastrous political consequences of cutting citizens' "entitlements," and that cutting noncitizens' benefits was a less dangerous alternative. Finally, Clinton wanted to make good his promise to end welfare—even if he did not like the specific proposals—although he had made no commitment to reduce immigration levels.

Chapter 8

Immigration Politics at Century's End

The general election of 1994 offered the Republican Party two competing strategies for the future—the Wilson model and the Bush model, in shorthand. Under the Wilson model, the party would shore up its base among conservative white voters and hope to attract more moderate white voters by taking a hard-line on issues such as immigration, welfare, crime, and affirmative action. Doing so, the thinking went, would alienate many nonwhite voters and poor Americans, but not as many as would be attracted by such an uncompromising stance. By driving a wedge into the Democratic coalition, the GOP would splinter off core groups of white voters, appropriate them for itself, and become the majority party in the process. As we saw in the earlier chapters, Wilson used this strategy to good effect in his dramatic come-from-behind gubernatorial victory over Democrat Kathleen Brown in California in 1994. After trailing badly in the opinion polls, and facing the worst recession in the Golden State for sixty years, Wilson's unexpected triumph thrust him onto the national stage. Aided by his close association to Prop. 187, Wilson cultivated his image as a man who knew which way the political wind was blowing and who had the right strategy to win elections, even in the most difficult of circumstances.

Under the Bush model, meanwhile, the Republican Party would not play ethnic hardball, but would instead reach out to ethnic voters by talking the language of ethnic and racial inclusion. George W. Bush and his political svengali Karl Rove argued that Republican philosophy need not be inimical to nonwhite voters. With family values, faith (and antiabortion), economic individualism, and a strong antiwelfare, anticrime stance at the core of its message, the party would be retailed under Bush as the natural political home of instinctively conservative, religious, hardworking Latinos and Asians. To reinforce his inclusive ethnic message, Bush bucked the Republican trend in 1994 and opposed Prop. 187. His reward was a larger than expected Latino vote, which helped him defeat the Democratic incumbent Ann Richards in a close race for Texas governor. Richards, who had previously humiliated George W.'s father at the 1988 Democratic National Convention—"Poor George, he can't help it, he was born with a silver foot in his mouth," she joked of his ineloquence—trailed Bush by 7 percent in the final vote tally.

There is a further reason why Bush opposed Prop. 187. Texas has in recent years enjoyed close political and economic relations with its southern neighbor. Mexico is Texas's largest trading partner, and NAFTA and the growth of maquiladoras, export-oriented assembly plants, on the border have further entwined the two economies. Bush hoped that opposing Prop. 187 would help maintain, even strengthen, his state's friendly relations and economic ties with Mexico at a time of increasing U.S.-Mexican tension. He also hoped that Texas could capitalize on California's close association with the initiative proposition, which resulted in a serious deterioration in its relations with Mexico. Bush figured that a Latino-friendly Texas would encourage Mexican businesses to trade with his state rather than California. He reinforced this message in his inaugural gubernatorial address in 1995 by inviting and praising the governors of the four Mexican states that abut Texas (Chihuahua, Coahuila, Nuevo Leon, and Tamaulipas). Such happy comingling and backslapping were notably absent at Wilson's inaugural.

Bush's pro-immigration, pro-Latino message is sometimes conflated with, or regarded as a central plank of, his "compassionate conservatism" philosophy. Although the two are often regarded as synonymous, compassionate conservatism has its roots in the idea that conservatives should not abandon the poor, the old, the ill, the addicted, and the marginalized. Politicians and society have a duty of care to those in need. Where possible, voluntary and faith-based organizations, not the government, should provide compassion and services to the needy, but government can help facilitate the work of such community organizations through tax credits, vouchers, and, as a last resort, direct grants. Government should only become involved directly in such compassionate work if it cannot facilitate its provision indirectly. In this way, a safety net is provided to those in need (the compassion), but it is done so without recourse to big government (the conservatism).[1] While compassionate conservatism's critics have complained that it lacks ideological coherence, crowds out the voluntary sector, and threatens individual freedom, it nonetheless provided Bush and other Republicans with a useful rhetorical and electoral device to win over moderate voters concerned about the harsh language of conservative Republicans.[2] Similarly, Bush's pro-immigrant, pro-Latino electoral strategy sought to soften the harsh rhetoric of Republicans like Pete Wilson, and thus widen his and the GOP's appeal. It is easy to see how the similarities between the two strands of Bush's electoral strategy have led to their conflation in the minds of observers and in the rhetoric of the president himself, even though each has quite distinct roots, and developed at different times.[3]

Bush continued to articulate his pro-immigration, pro-Latino message and develop his compassionate conservative philosophy after 1994, while the national Republican Party initially walked a different path—one marked by the Wilson model. On the same day that Wilson won reelection as California governor, the Republicans took control of both chambers of Congress for the first time in forty years. Their new standard bearer, Newt Gingrich, rallied his troops with a Contract promising swift and tough congressional action on a range of populist issues. It included plans for longer sentences and more prisons, welfare cuts, lower taxes, stronger armed forces that would refuse to serve under UN command, and term limits to kick out career politicians and replace them with citizen lawmakers.

Although Gingrich did not include an anti-immigrant measure in his Contract, many of the issues—especially crime and welfare—dovetailed neatly with those being pushed by Wilson on the West Coast. It would be wrong to conclude, however, that Wilson's electoral strategy influenced the content of Gingrich's Contract, or vice versa. Each developed independently of the other, although both were developed in a political climate in which people were angry about the recession and with government. Rather, the success of each helped reinforce the pertinence and potency of the other. Both Gingrich and Wilson seemed to be traveling the same political road (although in many ways their background and philosophical instincts were very different), and each seemed to have a touch of the zeitgeist about him.

Wilson did not influence the content of the Contract, yet Gingrich did refocus the congressional agenda in light of Wilson's electoral victory. With Prop. 187 rivaling both Wilson's and Gingrich's victories as the big election story, the immigration issue, although unmentioned in the Contract, was suddenly center stage in Congress. As the previous chapter noted, Gingrich was instinctively pro-immigration, but recognized that he could use the hostility toward immigrants as a way to cut further America's welfare bill. Wilson, meanwhile, despite his pledge to serve a full second term if reelected governor, calculated that his remarkable election victory and close association with Prop. 187 had opened up an opportunity to make an attempt on the biggest prize of all: the presidency of the United States.

The 1996 Republican Presidential Primaries

Early in his second term as governor, Wilson further staked his claim as a populist Republican when he made public his opposition to affirmative action at the February 1995 California Republican Party State Convention in Sacramento. "Let us begin to undo the corrosive unfairness of reverse discrimination. Just as with Proposition 187, let the people of California lead the way in ending unfairness and the increasing festering resentment which it has bred," he said.[4] The Republican audience gave a warm and enthusiastic response to Wilson's new hard-line on welfare, immigration, and affirmative action, while in previous years it had expressed some hostility to his pro-choice policies and first-term tax increase.

Wilson's speech coincided with an effort by two academics, Glynn Custred and Ted Wood, to qualify a California ballot initiative outlawing affirmative action. At the time of Wilson's speech, Custred and Wood had not collected the requisite number of signatures for their "California Civil Rights Initiative" (CCRI), and had previously tried but failed to persuade the Democratic-controlled California legislature to put the CCRI on the ballot in the hope of saving one million dollars in qualification costs and avoiding the initiative becoming a partisan and divisive measure.[5] The campaign had raised little money, and the signature-gathering effort was poorly organized, despite the widespread publicity enjoyed by the prospective initiative and the supposedly hot-button nature of the affirmative action issue. The campaign actually ran out of money in December 1995 and could not pay American Petition Consultants to continue collecting signatures. With the petition drive stalled for three weeks and only

200,000 signatures collected, Wilson stepped in. Recognizing a political opportunity similar to that provided by Prop. 187, Wilson put his own and the California Republican Party's considerable resources at the campaign's disposal. Ward Connerly, an African American businessman and close friend of Wilson, was installed by the governor as campaign chair in mid December. Connerly turned the campaign around by raising $500,000 and delivering 1.1 million signatures to the secretary of state on February 21, 1996.[6]

Wilson and many California Republicans believed that the CCIR would play well for them in the 1996 elections, and Wilson hoped that it might aid him in his quest to become the Republican presidential nominee.[7] In addition, his vast political experience in both national and state politics, an almost unblemished electoral record (he had only ever lost one election), impressive fund-raising credentials, and an apparently skeleton-free private life convinced many political commentators and professional campaign staff that Wilson could win the Republican nomination and pose a serious challenge to President Clinton in 1996. It looked good for Wilson—on paper at least.

Unsurprisingly, immigration and affirmative action formed the core of Wilson's primary campaign. His first campaign ad, launched in August 1995 to coincide with the official announcement of his candidacy, revisited a scene from his 1994 gubernatorial ad in which illegal immigrants are seen running across the border. While the presidential ad did not include the controversial phrase "they keep coming," the voice-over began with Wilson's immigration record:

> The first leader in America to have the courage to stand up against illegal immigration. The nation's first governor to sign both a three-strikes law for career criminals and one strike for rapists and child molesters. The first to outlaw affirmative action quotas in state hiring and end preferences for college admission. And the only governor in America to have the guts to cut spending so much that his state budget was actually less after four years. While others talk about these issues, this determined former Marine has had the courage to do something about them.[8]

The ad was designed to appeal to conservative Republican voters who dominate the party's primary electorate. It said nothing of course about his pro-life stance, his support for guest-worker programs, and his first-term tax increase. Instead the focus was on his hard-line positions on immigration, affirmative action, crime, and spending, reinforced by the mention of his military service and toughness. It also sought to reinforce that Wilson was a doer, not just a talker. He was a man with executive experience who had taken tough and sometimes-controversial decisions.

In part because of Wilson's presence and because of Republican efforts in Congress to curtail both legal and illegal entry to the United States, immigration was a significant issue in the Republican primaries for the first time in several generations. The most radical anti-immigrant candidate was Patrick Buchanan. He proposed a five-year moratorium on legal immigration and stationing military personnel at the U.S.-Mexico border, and had previously called for a trench to be built at the border to keep out illegal immigrants. Buchanan argued that a period of digestion was necessary because,

> If you go back in American history, you have had periods of very high immigration and then lulls, and the lulls have come about because social tensions have increased

and (because of) economic problems. The country has got to regain a measure of social cohesion and assimilation of the 25 million who have come in here in the past 20 years. To do that, people have to be acculturated and assimilated, just as they were when we had a 40-year hiatus from 1924 to 1965.[9]

Both Buchanan and Pete Wilson proposed that children born to undocumented parents should not be automatically granted U.S. citizenship—as the Fourteenth Amendment requires. Phil Gramm, another GOP presidential hopeful, opposed this, but supported a reduction in legal immigration and Gingrich's plan to exclude legal immigrants from welfare programs. Dole, meanwhile, wanted a "modest, temporary reduction" in legal immigration, but refused to state clearly his position on legal immigrants' welfare entitlements, saying only that "we have some obligation" to provide a basic welfare safety net. Hopefuls Lamar Alexander and Steve Forbes both came out against a national version of Prop. 187 and expressed their support for legal immigration. Pete Wilson also expressed his support for legal immigration, and had even begun to lobby on behalf of a new guest-worker program, but remained steadfast in his opposition to illegal immigration. All the Republicans did however agree that the government should do more to secure the country's borders and experiment with ways to make citizenship documents more difficult to counterfeit.[10]

Despite the centrality of the immigration issue to Wilson's campaign specifically and the primary race generally, the California governor never built any momentum. He received just 129 out of 10,598 votes cast in a August 1995 straw poll in Ames, Iowa, coming eighth out of the ten candidates.[11] In other polls of GOP supporters, Wilson was consistently in single figures. He pulled out of the primary race only one month after announcing his candidacy, his campaign chest empty. Wilson's fund-raising team—which had previously raised many millions of dollars under California electoral law, with no limit on the size of political donations in state races—soon discovered the difficulties in raising money for federal contests, where the $1,000 limit on donations required a candidate to have a large pool of medium-size givers to draw on. Even as Wilson was making his candidacy official, the campaign was one million dollars in debt, but Wilson still retained ninety paid employees on his staff. Wilson's team had overestimated their fund-raising prowess, which helped bankrupt the campaign. But Wilson also found it difficult to raise money because he was doing poorly in the polls. Even after running his television ad in New Hampshire for five weeks, polls showed him on just 4 percentage points. Although his hard-line on immigration and affirmative action had helped win over previously skeptical Republican activists in California, it failed outside the Golden State, where his pro-choice stance, liberal views on homosexuality and gun control, and tax-raising past sent all the wrong signals to the Christian right and economic libertarians.

Wilson also found that the style of campaigning in New England differed markedly from California. Television rules in the Golden State, but in the early northeast primaries grassroots organization and pressing the flesh matter more; yet Wilson was a made-for-television candidate, not a natural orator or one-on-one campaigner. There were also internal problems among his campaign team, as often happens when funds and morale are low. Long-term adviser George Gorton resigned after an internecine battle with campaign chair Craig Fuller.[12]

Wilson was further hindered by throat surgery in April 1995 and a campaign hiatus in July while he thrashed out a budget back in Sacramento. Even more damage was done by the revelation that he and his former wife, Betty Hosie, had employed an illegal alien as a housekeeper in the late 1970s when Wilson was mayor of San Diego. While it was not unlawful at that time to (unknowingly) employ undocumented labor, employers had to pay social security taxes, which Wilson and his wife failed to do. Wilson's answer to the embarrassing charge was that he had nothing to do with it: "I can categorically state that I have never knowingly employed an illegal immigrant and never intentionally failed to make payment of the employer's contribution to Social Security for an employee." His ex-wife backed him up: "I employed (her), my husband did not. The house was my responsibility, not his. He rarely even saw (her) before he moved out the house in 1981." The story was an obvious boon to the Democrats, especially as Wilson had chosen to use the illegal-immigration issue as the cornerstone of his presidential campaign.[13] Even Wilson's fellow Republicans sharpened their swords. "Say you made a mistake. . . . Don't say 'She did it! She did it!' This is not what I would call virile Republicanism. It really isn't manly," said old foe William Bennett.[14] Employing undocumented help had already helped cost Michael Huffington a U.S. Senate seat, and Kimba Wood and Zoe Baird the post of U.S. attorney general. As a seasoned campaigner in the toughest electoral arena, who had survived with few stains on his character, keen observers of the political scene were astonished by the revelation that Wilson too had employed illegal help. Why, given that he made illegal immigration the cornerstones of his 1994 gubernatorial and 1996 presidential campaign, did Wilson's people not check out his past to ensure that there were no unpleasant surprises to undermine his credibility or, worse, make him look like a hypocrite? Wilson had apparently had his background checked, but only to 1986 when the IRCA outlawed the employment of illegal workers, unknowingly or not. The governor's aides blamed Kathleen Brown for leaking the story to the *Washington Post*. They said she knew about the undocumented housekeeper during the 1994 gubernatorial contest, but did not publicize it then because she too had employed illegal help. Others suggested that Wilson's Republican presidential rivals, perhaps Bob Dole or Phil Gramm, could have leaked the story to the press. Yet others pointed the finger at Wilson's own aides, arguing that they knew the story would come out sometime soon, and therefore it was best to get it out early.[15] Whoever was behind the story, it hurt Wilson.

Wilson's exit from the primary race did not however lead to significant changes in its tone or content. The candidates continued to appeal to primary voters' concerns on immigration, affirmative action, crime, and welfare. Some critics described the debate and collection of candidates as the most right-wing in U.S. history.[16] Ralph Nader, consumer activist and independent presidential candidate in 1996 and 2000, commented, "These guys give meaning to the word extreme. Even the so-called moderates are pushing agendas that a Gerald Ford or a Richard Nixon would have dismissed as crazy."[17] As the race intensified and with the California primary on March 26 just weeks away, only Dole and Buchanan were left in the field. Buchanan hoped to do well in the Golden State, with his hard-line rhetoric on legal and illegal immigration. Front-runner Dole, keen not to be outgunned, claimed that he had backed Prop. 187 before

Buchanan.[18] Jack Kemp, meanwhile, endorsed Steve Forbes on March 6, which bewildered many Republicans because Forbes was close to leaving the race as Dole had the nomination all but sown up. Buchanan also could not realistically overcome Dole's almost unassailable lead, but thought a victory in California would give him the delegates and momentum at the Republican convention in San Diego to get his policies written into the party platform: "If I could win the California primary, I could get everything. . . . We will get the fence along the border on illegal immigration. We will get our right-to-life plank. We will get everything."[19] Indeed, Buchanan managed to write into the Republican platform a plank proposing to abolish the Fourteenth Amendment and thus deny citizenship to children born in the United States to undocumented parents.

Preelection primary polls in California suggested that Dole would win handsomely there, with 52 percent to Buchanan's 18 percent. Forbes and Alexander trailed with 9 and 4 percent respectively among likely Republican voters. However, in a one-on-one with Clinton, Dole trailed 37 to 58.[20] While in California, Buchanan made immigration the centerpiece of his campaign, visiting the border and repeating his hard-line stance: "[w]hat we have is a lawless situation on the southern border of the United States where this country is literally being overrun by people who are violating our immigration laws and defying the American Constitution. I will stop it cold." Dole also upped his rhetoric on illegal immigration, in part to court California voters but also to court Buchanan, who had made noises about a third party presidential ticket if the Republican Party strayed too far from his hard-line abortion and illegal-immigration positions. Dole visited the border near San Diego where he announced his support for Gallegly's amendment to deny undocumented children schooling, said he would double again (on top of all the recent increases) the Border Patrol to 10,000 agents, and reimburse states' costs regarding illegal immigrants. The effort seemed to work. Buchanan commented that "It appears Senator Dole is making an effort to reach out to our people. . . . [He's] sounding like us. . . . I'm gonna sue that fella for copyright violations."[21] In the event, Dole won the primary by 66 percent to Buchanan's 18.

1996 Presidential Election

Having overcome Buchanan's unorthodox primary challenge, Dole kept in close contact with his former congressional colleagues after his formal resignation from the Senate on June 11, 1996. Dole was keen to ensure that the welfare and immigration reform bills proceeding through Congress would aid his presidential ambitions. In particular, he hoped his support for the immigration bill and especially the Gallegly amendment would enable him to portray Clinton as soft on immigration, although Dole made public his opposition to revoking the Fourteenth Amendment's birthright citizenship provision. Clinton responded by arguing that Dole's congressional voting record showed he was not as tough on immigration as he tried to portray. He noted that Dole had previously voted against reimbursing states for incarcerating illegal immigrants, against removing undocumented children from public schools, and (because he was beholden to business interests) in favor of the IRCA, which amnestied three million undocumented residents.[22]

Dole's eventual defeat at the hands of President Clinton was as unsurprising as it was humiliating, both for Dole and his party. In the postmortem, questions were asked about the efficacy of the Wilson model. In fact, Dole's campaign message was less hard-line than his primary message. Having won the Republican nomination, he began to temper his rhetoric, especially on affirmative action—even though he had come out early in support of the CCRI and had introduced similar legislation into the Senate during the primaries. By mid June, he was rarely raising the issue and when pushed in a television interview on June 10 said, "I've been for affirmative action, [but] I think there are some changes that should be made."[23] Dole also softened his position on abortion and tax cuts, although not on immigration. The CCRI had become particularly troublesome in part because the Democrats were spinning the initiative as an attack not on minorities, but on women. And with half the electorate already feeling indifferent toward him, Dole could not afford to alienate more voters. Ken Khachigian, Dole's California strategist, admitted as much when he said,

> I don't want to indicate any lukewarm attitude toward it [by Dole]—special preferences are outrageous. But if the framing of the debate over CCRI makes it sound negative to support it, then it could affect the manner in which it is embraced or not embraced.[24]

Dole also chose Jack Kemp as his running mate in part in to put a veneer of social inclusivity on his campaign, while appealing to economic conservatives. It did not work, however. The bruising primary battle against Buchanan and the hard-line positions on the "Wilson" issues could not easily be hidden. Moreover, Dole ran a generally poor campaign. The distinguished public servant and war hero failed to capture the imagination of the American public. While Clinton talked about building a bridge to the twenty-first century, Dole was stuck in the past with the Brooklyn Dodgers, who had long since upped sticks for Los Angeles. He flip-flopped on the big issues, failed to carve out a distinct identity for his campaign, fell off podiums, and mangled the English language. Clinton outthought and out-campaigned a man many years his senior, taking 379 electoral college votes to Dole's 159 and 49 percent of the popular vote to Dole's 41.

Dole polled especially badly among nonwhite voters. He won just 22 percent of the Latino vote nationally and 19 percent in California, compared to Bush's 35 percent four years earlier (see tables 8.1 and 8.2). However, the decline in support for Dole among Latinos could be misleading, because a losing candidate would expect to see his support decline across all ethnic groups. One way to control this effect and thus provide a better handle on the changing nature of Latino support is to calculate a ratio statistic, which divides a candidate's share of the white vote by his share of the Latino vote. Tables 8.1 and 8.2 report the ratio statistics for California and the U.S., respectively. With 49 percent of the national white two-party vote and 21.5 percent of the Latino vote, Dole's ratio is 2.3 to 1, or just 2.3 in shorthand. In other words, Dole won 2.3 times as many white votes as Latino votes. Four years earlier, Bush's ratio was much better at 1.4 (where a ratio of exactly 1 shows that the candidate won the same proportions of Latino and white votes).

In California, the drop-off in the Latino vote was even more dramatic. Bush won 44 percent of the white vote and 35 percent of the Latino vote in 1992

Table 8.1 Percentage of Americans Voting Republican in Presidential Contests by Race/Ethnicity, 1980–2000

Year	White (%)	Latino (%)	Ratio (White:Latino)
1980	64.1	43.5	1.5:1
1984	64.6	47.1	1.4:1
1988	61.2	35.2	1.7:1
1992	48.0	35.4	1.4:1
1996	49.2	21.5	2.3:1
2000	52.5	44.2	1.2:1

Source: National Election Studies, Cumulative Data File, 1948–2000.

Table 8.2 Percentage Share of Two-Party Vote in California by Race/Ethnicity, 1990–2002

Year	Candidate-Party	Gubernatorial Elections			Presidential Elections		
		White (%)	Latino (%)	Ratio (White:Latino)	White (%)	Latino (%)	Ratio (White:Latino)
1990	Wilson-R	55	35	1.6:1			
	Feinstein-D	45	65				
1992	Bush-R				44	35	1.2:1
	Clinton-D				57	65	
1994	Wilson-R	62	26	2.4:1			
	Brown-D	38	74				
1996	Dole-R				52	19	2.7:1
	Clinton-D				48	81	
1998	Lungren-R	47	24	2:1			
	Davis-D	53	76				
2000	Bush-R				51	23	2.2:1
	Gore-D				49	77	
2002	Simon-R	52	27	1.9:1			
	Davis-D	48	73				

Notes: Number of California Latinos in 1992 *NES* survey = 20; All other entries >100.
Sources: LA Times Exit Polls 1990, 1994–2002; *NES* 1992.

(a ratio of 1.2), but Dole won 52 percent of the white vote and just 19 percent of the Latino vote (a ratio of 2.7). The California gubernatorial elections tell a similarly sad story for the GOP. Wilson won 35 percent of the Latino vote in 1990, but took just 26 percent four years later when Prop. 187 formed the cornerstone of his reelection campaign. And in 1998, Republican nominee Dan Lungren won just 24 percent. Although Lungren did worse in percentage terms, his ratio of 2 was a small improvement on Wilson's 2.4 in 1994. Still, it was disappointing for Lungren, who had always viewed himself as an inclusive politician with close ties to many Latino groups. This image was damaged while running for reelection as state attorney general when he came out in favor of

Prop. 187 in 1994, a decision for which he was unsurprisingly pilloried during the 1998 gubernatorial election. The 2002 Republican nominee, Bill Simon, did equally badly among nonwhite voters. He took just 27 percent of the Latino vote, yet won a majority of the white vote (52 percent)—a ratio of 1.9. Simon's case is particularly instructive. If he had polled as well among Latino and Asian voters as white voters, he would have beaten Gray Davis. Tony Quinn, political analyst and coeditor of the *California Target Book*, estimated that the minority backlash against the GOP in California is a key reason for the Democrats' recent dominance in the state legislature, and directly responsible for the Republicans losing nine Assembly seats in the 1996 and 1998 elections. Quinn has also estimated that if Latino and Asian support for the GOP was as low as in 1998, Dianne Feinstein would have beaten Pete Wilson in the 1990 governor's race, Tom Bradley would have defeated George Deukmejian in 1982, and Jesse Unruh may have won out against Ronald Reagan in 1970. In each case, the Democratic gubernatorial candidate lost.

In sum, the statistics are stark. Post 1994 Republican support among Latino voters and to a lesser extent Asian voters dropped precipitously. The GOP's close association with Prop. 187 and the wider anti-immigrant movement in the mid 1990s apparently turned off many ethnic voters, especially Latinos. Moreover, while Wilson more than compensated for the Latino drop-off in 1994 by attracting large numbers of white voters, Republican candidates after Wilson did not. Worse still for Republican candidates, ethnic voters seem to have a keen memory. As the immigration issue faded in importance, some white voters drifted back to the Democratic Party but Latino voters who had abandoned the GOP because of its hard-line immigration policies were slower to realign, especially in California. Attempts to court the Latino vote by candidates such as Lungren failed. Indeed, even George W. Bush, highly regarded in contemporary mainstream Republican circles for his supposed ability to connect with Latino voters, did very poorly in California in 2000. He took just 23 percent of the Latino vote, compared to 51 percent of the white vote. Outside of California, Bush did much better, winning similar percentages of Latino and white voters (44 vs. 53%, or a ratio of 1.2). The difference between California and the wider United States is instructive: Latino hostility toward the GOP was most intense where GOP hostility toward Latinos was most intense, and continues to be so. While this is bad news for Republicans seeking statewide office in California, it offers hope to those outside the Golden State. The party's close association with the anti-immigrant movement has not damaged it irrevocably. Inclusive-minded GOP candidates preaching a pro-Latino, pro-immigration message can overcome the 1990s-engendered Latino hostility. Some Republican strategists, especially those working for candidates with national ambitions such as Karl Rove, believe that it is imperative that they do so, for the Republican problem goes much deeper than nonwhite voters switching to the Democratic Party. The GOP faces a further interrelated problem: more Latinos are voting than ever before. The next section shows why.

The Changing Electorate

There are several different ways to think about and measure electoral participation. One is look at the size of a group as a proportion of the total electorate. For example, group A may constitute 15 percent of the electorate while group B constitutes 85 percent. This is often referred to as the *share* of the electorate and is key to judging the relative electoral strength of different groups. However, this statistic does not say anything about how electorally active a group is. For this we need to look at the *rate* of participation, which measures the proportion of a group that is registered to vote or turns out to vote. Group A may constitute only a small *share* of the U.S. electorate, but actually participate at a higher *rate* than group B. In this case, we could say that group A was overrepresented in the voting population even if it actually constituted a smaller share of the electorate.

Another way to think about electoral participation is to examine *changes* over time. Does group A constitute a larger share of the electorate than ten years ago, and if so by how much? Are members of group A participating at higher rates than previously? Such changes can be quantified either as a percentage point difference or a percentage difference. A final measure of electoral participation, and one that is particularly useful here, is *relative change* over time. A law could be said to have a galvanizing or politicizing effect on a group if its turnout rate increases while turnout rates for other groups remain constant. Moving now from the hypothetical to the real, what do the data reveal about the anti-immigrant movement, the backlash to it, and the changing American electorate?

One thing is immediately clear: white voters dominated the U.S. electorate during the 1980s and 1990s, never constituting less than 80 percent of those who turned out on election day—according to Current Population Survey data reported in figure 8.1 and table 8.3.[25] This domination masks some subtle but important changes, however. Although whites remain the key electoral force, their

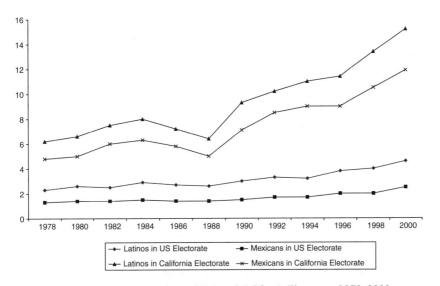

Figure 8.1   Latino and Mexican Share of U.S. and California Electorate, 1978–2000

Source: Bureau of Labor Statistics and Bureau of the Census, November *Current Population Surveys*, 1978–2000.

Table 8.3 Percentage Breakdown of U.S. and California Electorate by Race/Ethnicity, 1978–2000

Year	United States			California		
	Whites	Latinos	Mexicans	Whites	Latinos	Mexicans
1978	89.2	2.3	1.3	84.5	6.2	4.8
1980	87.9	2.6	1.4	82.5	6.6	5.0
1982	87.4	2.5	1.4	81.9	7.5	6.0
1984	86.7	2.9	1.5	79.8	8.0	6.3
1986	86.4	2.7	1.4	81.2	7.2	5.8
1988	87.1	2.6	1.4	81.5	6.4	5.0
1990	86.7	3.0	1.5	79.4	9.3	7.1
1992	85.9	3.3	1.7	76.9	10.2	8.5
1994	86.0	3.2	1.7	76.8	11.0	9.0
1996	84.7	3.8	2.0	73.6	11.4	9.0
1998	84.2	4.0	2.0	71.9	13.4	10.5
2000	82.8	4.6	2.5	68.2	15.2	11.9

Notes: Figures are percentages, representing each race/ethnicities' contribution to the total electorate.
Source: Bureau of Labor Statistics and Bureau of the Census, November *Current Population Surveys*, 1978–2000.

share of the nationwide vote dropped from 89.2 percent in 1978 to 82.8 percent in 2000. Meanwhile, Latino representation doubled from 2.3 to 4.6 percent. The change in California is even starker, where whites constituted 84.5 percent of the electorate in 1978, but only 68.2 percent by 2000—a one-fifth decline in strength in just 22 years—while Latino representation more than doubled from 6.2 to 15.2 percent. It is also notable that while Latino electoral share increased during the 1980s and 1990s in California and the wider United States, it did so more rapidly in the latter decade than the earlier. These trends fit well with the suggestion of social commentators, scholars, and political strategists that Latinos strengthened their electoral base in order to defend themselves against the anti-immigrant movement of the 1990s.[26]

Of course, the difference between the decades may have had nothing to do with the politicized reaction to the anti-immigrant climate. It could instead be simply a matter of demographics. It is possible that Latinos voted and registered to vote in the same proportions they always had, but that more Latinos became eligible to vote because of a relative increase in the size of the Latino population—as a result of continued immigration and high birth rates.[27] Whether the increase in Latino strength is because of demographics or politics is investigated below.

Registration

Table 8.4 and figures 8.2a, 8.2b, 8.2c, and 8.2d show that white citizens registered to vote at considerably higher levels than did Latino citizens between 1978 and 2000 in California and the wider United States, and that registration rates for both groups were higher in presidential election years than in off years as voters responded to the increased salience and perceived importance of presidential elections. The central question, however, is whether Latinos' increased electoral share is a consequence of their registering to vote at higher rates? The answer is not straightforward. While Latino registration rates increased by 4.9 percentage

Table 8.4 Percent U.S. and California Citizens Registered to Vote by Race/Ethnicity, 1978–2000

Year	United States			California		
	Whites	Latinos	Mexicans	Whites	Latinos	Mexicans
1978	71.4	53.6	52.7	71.0	56.1	55.4
1980	76.7	59.5	56.8	77.7	56.2	54.1
1982	74.1	59.9	55.3	75.2	62.5	61.0
1984	77.9	64.5	62.7	80.3	64.5	64.4
1986	73.5	60.8	59.8	76.5	60.6	59.8
1988	76.5	62.2	60.5	79.2	57.5	55.8
1990	73.8	59.2	57.3	77.2	62.9	61.4
1992	80.1	66.4	64.8	83.7	65.4	63.9
1994	74.5	56.9	59.9	79.6	61.2	61.8
1996	78.6	64.9	64.1	81.4	67.2	66.6
1998	76.1	61.3	58.5	76.8	62.4	60.7
2000	80.6	64.4	64.2	81.9	65.9	64.2

Source: Bureau of Labor Statistics and Bureau of the Census, November *Current Population Surveys*, 1978–2000.

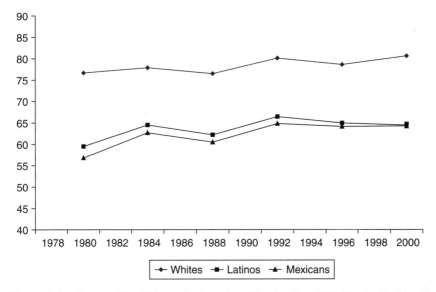

Figure 8.2a Percent U.S. Citizens Registered to Vote by Race/Ethnicity in Presidential Election Years, 1978–2000

Source: Bureau of Labor Statistics and Bureau of the Census, November *Current Population Surveys*, 1978–2000.

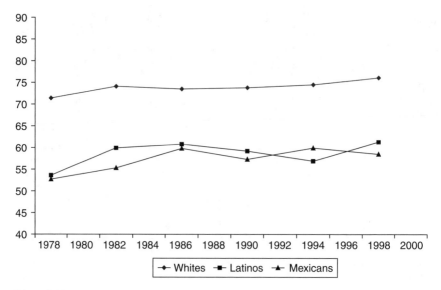

Figure 8.2b Percent U.S. Citizens Registered to Vote by Race/Ethnicity in Non-Presidential Election Years, 1978–2000

Source: Bureau of Labor Statistics and Bureau of the Census, November *Current Population Surveys*, 1978–2000.

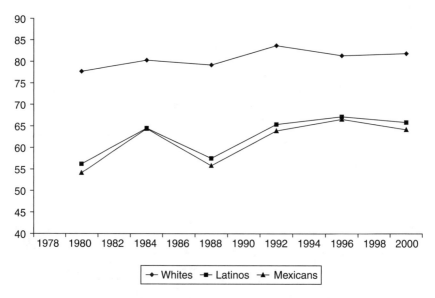

Figure 8.2c Percent California Citizens Registered to Vote by Race/Ethnicity in Presidential Election Years, 1978–2000

Source: Bureau of Labor Statistics and Bureau of the Census, November *Current Population Surveys*, 1978–2000.

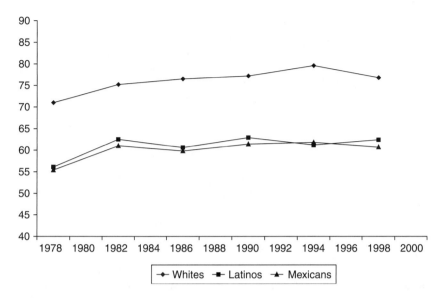

Figure 8.2d Percent California Citizens Registered to Vote by Race/Ethnicity in Non-Presidential Election Years, 1978–2000

Source: Bureau of Labor Statistics and Bureau of the Census, November *Current Population Surveys*, 1978–2000.

points nationally in presidential election ("on") years between 1978 and 2000 and by 7.7 points in non-presidential ("off") years, most of these increases occurred during the late 1970s and early 1980s, not a period especially associated with anti-immigrant sentiment. Furthermore, whites' rate of registration also improved over the same period, suggesting that the Latino increase may have been part of a wider trend, perhaps induced by partisan and nonpartisan registration. There is also no evidence of a mid-1990s surge in Latino registration, in either on or off years, when anti-immigrant sentiment and the backlash to it peaked, confounding the prediction of the central hypothesis.

It is possible, though, that the broad "Latino" tag could be hiding some subtle differences between nationalities. For example, Americans of Mexican descent may have been more likely than those of Cuban descent to respond to the anti-immigrant climate by registering to vote, because Mexican immigrants were the target of many of the anti-immigrant attacks. Indeed, table 8.4 and figure 8.2b shows that while Latino-wide registration fell nationally by 2.3 points between 1990 and 1994, Mexican registration increased by 2.6 points. The same logic suggests that the ethnic differences should be more notable in California than the wider United States, because more Mexican Americans and Mexicans live in California than any other state and because California was the birthplace of Prop 187. The evidence is mixed, however. Table 8.4 and figures 8.2c and 8.2d show, perhaps surprisingly, that there was no surge in the rate of registration among Latinos generally or Mexicans specifically in California in off year elections and in particular between 1990 and 1994, the year of Prop. 187. However, there was a significant improvement in Latino registration in on year elections, while the trend for whites remained flat.

In sum, while the anti-immigrant climate may have had some effect on registration rates in the 1990s in the United States and California, it would be wrong to claim the effect was strong or that there were large differences between whites and Latinos. It would thus be wrong to claim that improved registration rates explain a large portion of the increased electoral presence of Latinos, as measured by their improving vote share. Furthermore, the Prop. 187 effect was minimal at best. It is possible, however, that institutional and structural barriers made it problematic for Latinos to respond quickly to the anti-immigrant climate by registering to vote. The illegal-immigration initiative and the wider anti-immigrant movement may have had a greater impact on the propensity to vote of already registered Latinos.

Registered Voters

The hypothesis is that a greater proportion of already registered Latinos turned out to vote in response to the anti-immigrant climate. Table 8.5 and figures 8.3a and 8.3b report the percentage of registered whites, Latinos, and Mexican Americans who voted in national elections between 1978 and 2000. There is a general downward trend in voting rates by registered citizens in both on and off years across ethnicities. The temporary surge in Latino and specifically Mexican American turnout in the 1992 election is mirrored by an increase in white turnout, indicating ethnicity played no special role in the election. However, the trend lines in figure 8.3b highlight the role that ethnicity, in particular Mexican ethnicity, did play in the 1994 election. While the proportion of white and Latino

Table 8.5 Percent U.S. and California Registered Voters Voting by Race/Ethnicity, 1978–2000

Year	United States			California		
	Whites	Latinos	Mexicans	Whites	Latinos	Mexicans
1978	76.0	73.8	70.6	84.5	78.1	76.0
1980	89.8	83.6	81.9	90.9	85.0	84.8
1982	78.7	74.4	73.1	86.1	78.8	78.5
1984	89.1	83.3	80.8	92.2	85.4	85.4
1986	74.4	69.9	66.8	81.6	74.3	74.2
1988	88.4	82.7	79.0	89.8	78.8	78.4
1990	76.0	67.1	64.0	81.0	70.5	69.0
1992	92.0	84.2	83.1	94.5	84.7	84.2
1994	74.9	66.4	65.9	84.7	83.3	83.4
1996	84.3	77.2	76.4	88.8	81.3	81.8
1998	70.2	62.4	61.0	81.0	77.5	75.3
2000	87.4	79.9	78.7	90.4	85.1	83.9

Source: Bureau of Labor Statistics and Bureau of the Census, November *Current Population Surveys*, 1978–2000.

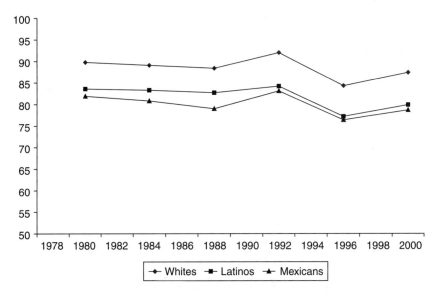

Figure 8.3a Percent U.S. Registered Voters Voting by Race/Ethnicity in Presidential Election Years, 1978–2000

Source: Bureau of Labor Statistics and Bureau of the Census, November *Current Population Surveys*, 1978–2000.

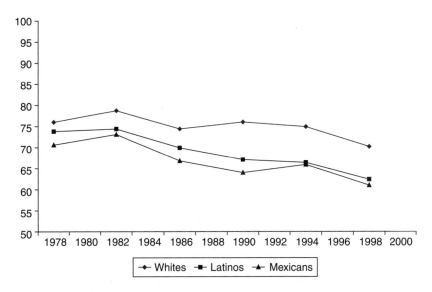

Figure 8.3b Percent U.S. Registered Voters Voting by Race/Ethnicity in Non-Presidential Election Years, 1978–2000

Source: Bureau of Labor Statistics and Bureau of the Census, November *Current Population Surveys*, 1978–2000.

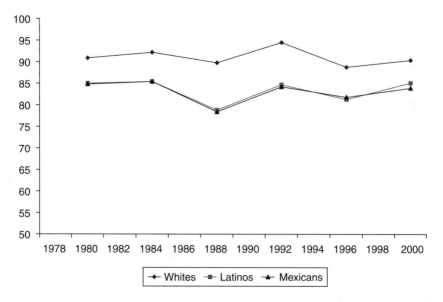

Figure 8.3c Percent California Registered Voters Voting by Race/Ethnicity in Presidential Election Years, 1978–2000

Source: Bureau of Labor Statistics and Bureau of the Census, November *Current Population Surveys*, 1978–2000.

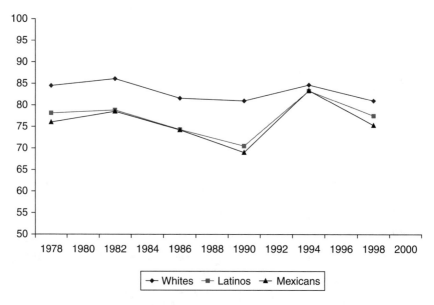

Figure 8.3d Percent California Registered Voters Voting by Race/Ethnicity in Non-Presidential Election Years, 1978–2000

Source: Bureau of Labor Statistics and Bureau of the Census, November *Current Population Surveys*, 1978–2000.

registered citizens who voted fell between 1990 and 1994, the proportion of Mexican Americans increased. The difference is more impressive still in California, where the white vote increased by only 4 percentage points, compared to nearly 13 points for Latinos and over 14 points for Mexican Americans (see figure 8.3d). The difference between whites and Latinos is even more impressive if percentages rather then percentage points are used as the unit of measurement. The percentage increase for whites is just 4.5 percent compared to 18 percent for Latinos and 21 percent for Mexican Americans. However it is measured, the substantial white-Latino difference coincides with the arrival of Prop. 187 on the political agenda and thus signals loudly a role for the initiative proposition and the wider anti-immigrant climate in motivating already registered Latinos to vote.

There is also some evidence to suggest that for Latino voters, at least in California, this "politicization" was more than a temporary phenomenon. Even though the Latino and Mexican American vote dropped off somewhat between 1994 and 1998, it remained at a significantly higher level than in 1990, while white turnout returned to 1990 levels.

Citizenship Applications and Naturalizations

The third way in which Latinos could have improved their electoral position in the 1990s was if a significant number of legal permanent residents (LPRs) applied for and were granted citizenship and thus became eligible to vote. The registration and turnout statistics reported above would hide the impact of such a change because they reveal nothing about the size of the pool of eligible voters.

Prior to the passage of the immigration and welfare reform acts in 1996, citizens enjoyed few advantages over LPRs. Both worked, paid taxes, and were eligible for similar public benefits. One difference was that citizens could vote and LPRs could not, but many viewed this as unimportant. LPR Latinos generally and Mexicans specifically had other reasons for not applying for citizenship. One is the proximity of the United States and Mexico and the relative ease of movement between the two countries. In this thinking, Mexicans migrated to the United States without having to sever their Mexican ties and perhaps even with the intention of returning home at some future date. This psychological connection to the homeland is reinforced by geographic proximity. Another explanation is that the under Mexican law as it then stood, immigrants taking up U.S. citizenship would have lost some Mexican property rights, but LPRs would not. To overcome such barriers, citizenship would have to offer substantial benefits to outweigh the costs. The hypothesis, then, is that the benefits of citizenship increased post-187 while the costs diminished, thus precipitating a rush to citizenship, which in turn increased Latinos' vote share. What is the evidence?

California officials observed that citizenship applications from LPRs increased sharply soon after Prop. 187's electoral victory, causing a severe backlog in unprocessed applications as staff struggled to cope with the surge. For example, in April 1995 INS personnel at the Los Angeles office reported a 500 percent increase in applications on the previous year, which they attributed mostly to Prop. 187. They noted that some applicants wanted to become citizens because they feared that legal residents would lose their benefits in the wake of

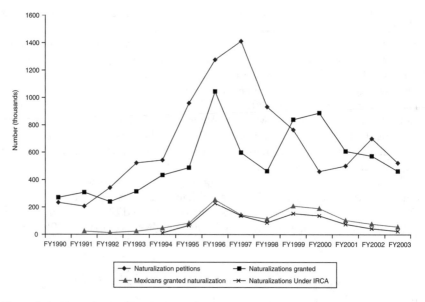

Figure 8.4   Naturalization Trends, 1990–2003

Source: Immigration and Naturalization Service, *Statistical Yearbook of the Immigration and Naturalization Service*, Various Years; Office of Immigration Statistics, *Yearbook of Immigration Statistics*, Various Years.

the illegal-immigration initiative, while others wanted citizenship so that they could exert political power through the ballot box. Other officials noted that citizenship classes had increased in size as Latinos sought to acquire the "skills" necessary to become citizens. "Anti-immigrant attitudes are pushing people to feel their community is being threatened. And they're reacting very rationally by becoming citizens," said one teacher. Another noted that California was "witnessing a clear reaction to recent political events."[28]

National-level data support the local anecdotes, although the increase is less stark. The INS received just over 342,000 applications for citizenship in fiscal year 1992 (October 1, 1991–September 30, 1992), rising to 522,000 in 1993 and 543,000 in 1994. The most dramatic increase, however, came in the wake of Prop. 187's victory in late 1994 (see figure 8.4). In fiscal year 1995, beginning just one month before the vote on Prop. 187, the INS received 960,000 applications, up nearly half a million on the previous year. The numbers continued to rise through 1996 and 1997 to 1,277,000 and 1,413,000 respectively, before dropping back below one million in 1998 through 2000.[29] The timing suggests that Prop. 187 and the anti-immigrant climate caused the initial increase and that the welfare reform and immigration acts contributed toward the record numbers naturalizing in 1996 and 1997. A report by the Office of the Inspector General (OIG) reinforces this interpretation:

INS and CBO [community-based organization] representatives . . . attributed the increase in demand for naturalization to the immigrant community's changing perception of the security of permanent residency status. The 1994 mid-year election campaign saw an increasing linkage between citizenship and benefits. In California, the state with the largest immigrant population, legislation known as Proposition 187 called for termination of various government services and assistance to aliens, including permanent residents. The publicity surrounding this campaign and similar national efforts geared toward welfare reform that would make permanent residents ineligible for benefits were cited to OIG investigators as factors that triggered concern within the immigrant community. According to INS officials and immigrant advocates, the fear of losing benefits (and the desire to safeguard benefits), as well as a general sense of insecurity in their status, provided powerful incentives for permanent residents to naturalize.[30]

However, not all of the increase in applications was because of Prop. 187 and the anti-immigrant laws of 1996. The INS, while recognizing these factors' importance, also pointed to the 1986 Immigration Reform and Control Act and a Green Card renewal program as other causes.[31] The first of the illegal immigrants amnestied under the IRCA provisions became eligible for citizenship in the early 1990s, and many would undoubtedly have taken the opportunity to apply absent the anti-immigrant climate of the mid 1990s. Under the Green Card renewal scheme introduced by the INS in 1992, all cardholders were required to apply for a new card by March 1996. But, as the cost of renewal and the cost of applying for citizenship were comparable, the INS and some advocacy groups encouraged immigrants to apply for citizenship instead.[32] Unfortunately, it is impossible to determine precisely how many applicants were motivated by the renewal scheme, Prop. 187, the federal legislation, and the amnesty. It is likely, however, that each had a significant and independent impact. It is also likely that the conflation of factors would have been a significant motivating force. In a nonhostile climate, many IRCA amnestees may have been content with their legal but noncitizen status, but not when threatened by growing hostility *and* cuts in public benefits. This interaction between variables is, though, also impossible to quantify as the available data do not permit a formal test. Nevertheless, it is probably fair to say that each mattered in isolation and mattered greatly in combination.

To cope with the increase in applications for citizenship, INS commissioner Doris Meissner launched "Citizenship USA" in the summer of 1995. The program aimed to double the number of citizenship applications processed each year and reduce the processing time between application and citizenship oath to six months. This was to be achieved by increasing the number of INS staff processing applications, by further computerization of the process, and by liaising with community-based organizations. Some critics argued that the scheme was nothing more than a plot by the Clinton administration to register more Democrat-friendly voters before the 1996 election.[33] The OIG report cleared the Clinton administration of such machinations, but it criticized the INS for its poor implementation of the scheme and screening of applicants and its inadequate training of staff, which contributed to the naturalization of thousands of immigrants with criminal records. Processing times in some jurisdictions remained poor, and do so to this day. Some immigrants have to wait several years to have their application processed, on top of the five years they have to wait between receiving legal permanent status and applying for citizenship.[34] Even a cursory glance at figure 8.4 demonstrates clearly that the number of LRPs granted citizenship fell dramatically in 1997 and 1998 as the INS struggled to cope with the influx of applications, despite Meissner's reorganization.

While the increase in citizenship applications is a good indicator of the highly charged nature of the immigration issue, it is the number of naturalizations and the percentage of new Latino citizens that matter when seeking to explain the growth in Latino vote share, because only citizens can vote. Figure 8.4 shows that naturalizations tracked applications with a one year lag from 1992 until 1996 when over one million people were granted citizenship. The INS's administrative problems reduced dramatically the number of naturalizations during the next two years, but by 1999 the INS was back on course and naturalizations began to outstrip petitions. In sum, between 1990 and 2000, nearly six million immigrants became U.S. citizens.[35] Assuming that roughly 40 percent of the six million were Latino and assuming that 40 percent of Latinos settled in California, an estimated 2.4 million immigrant Latinos became U.S. citizens and nearly one million chose the Golden State as their home.[36] If we also assume that 80 percent of new citizens were of voting age, and use Citrin and Highton's calculation that 36 percent of recently naturalized Latinos register and vote,[37] the surge in naturalizations between 1990 and 2000 pushed up Latino turnout in the United States by roughly 680,000 and in California by 270,000. In the wider United States, Latino turnout increased over the same period by nearly 2.2 million and in California by 500,000, according to census data and adjusting for differences in turnout between on and off year elections.[38] To calculate the percentage contribution of newly naturalized Latino citizens to increased Latino turnout between 1990 and 2000, the relevant figures are plugged into the following equation:

(Contribution of new Latino citizens to Increase in Latino turnout 1990–2000/Increase in Latino turnout 1990–2000) * 100

Thus for the United States, the increase in Latino turnout attributable to recently naturalized Latino citizens is $.680/2.2 \times 100 = 31$ percent. In California the figure is $.270/.5 \times 100 = 54$ percent. Although the figure for California is larger because it is the most popular state of residence for new citizens and especially new Latino ones, both the California and U.S. cases highlight the impact of naturalization on Latinos' electoral strength, accounting for roughly one half and one third of new Latino votes. Nonetheless, one half of the increase in Latino electoral strength in California and two-thirds in the United States cannot be explained by naturalization.

Some of these residuals can be accounted for by the changes in electoral behavior outlined above, and in particular by improved rates of electoral participation of already registered Latinos. The remaining residual can be attributed to demographic changes, which in turn are in part influenced by immigration levels and the birth/death rates of recent immigrants.

Demographic Trends

Changing demographics matter greatly to politics and politicians. In the case of the GOP and its approach to minority politics in the 1990s, they are supremely important. Figure 8.5 reveals why. Latinos (whether citizens, LPRs, or undocumented) constituted just 6.5 percent of the U.S. population in 1980, but 9 percent

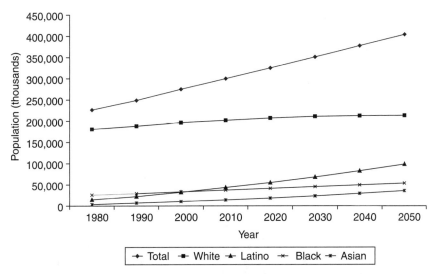

Figure 8.5   U.S. Population and Projections by Race/Ethnicity, 1980–2050
Source: U.S. Census Bureau, *Statistical Abstract of the United States*, 2001, Table 15.

by 1990 and 11.8 percent in 2000. Furthermore, according to U.S. census bureau middle-series projections, these gains are set to continue through 2050 when one in every four Americans will be of Latino descent. Put another way, the Latino population will have grown by over 570 percent between 1980 and 2050, from 15 to nearly 100 million. In contrast, whites have already shrunk as a proportion of the population, and projections suggest they will continue to lose ground. In 1980, 181 million whites constituted 80 percent of all Americans. The white population grew to 197 million in 2000, but fell to just over 70 percent of the whole population as other races and ethnicities grew more quickly. Four decades hence, demographers predict only one in two Americans will be white.

The change in California has been, and will be, more dramatic still. Figure 8.6 plots the data. Nearly one in every five Californians was Latino in 1980, rising to one in four in 1990 and nearly 1 in 3 in 2000. In other words, the California Latino population grew by 132 percent in just two decades, and from an already large base. And U.S. census bureau projections see no end to the rise. The Latino population is predicted to increase by over one quarter each decade until 2040, when it will constitute nearly 50 percent of the total population, or nearly 30 million persons.

As in the wider United States, whites in California will be the main losers in the demographic race. In 1980 two of every three Californians were white. This had fallen to one in two by 2000. And by 2030 it will be nearly one in three, demographers predict. Overall, between 1980 and 2040, the white population is predicted to grow from 16 to 18 million, an increase of just 13 percent, while the Latino population will grow by over 500 percent. More Latino than white babies were born in California in the third quarter of 2001, a trend that will not be

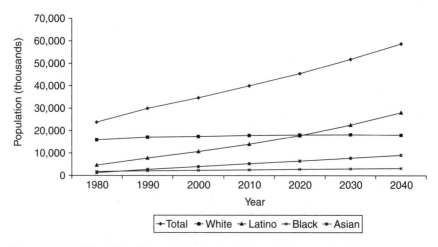

Figure 8.6   California Population and Projections by Race/Ethnicity, 1980–2040

Sources: State of California, Department of Finance, *County Population Projections with Age, Sex and Race/Ethnic Detail; Components of Change for California Counties,* July 1970–July 1990.

reversed for the foreseeable future, if ever. By 2006 the majority of children in kindergarten were Latino. In 2014 they will be in a majority in high schools. In 2017 most new workers will be Latino, and in 2019 so will most new voters. By just 2020 there will be equal numbers of whites and Latinos in California. After 2020 the future is Latino.

In sum, while it is impossible to quantify precisely, the increase in Latino electoral participation is likely the result of the general increase in the size of the Latino population (itself the product of high birth rates and continued immigration) and the large number of Latino immigrants that naturalized during the mid-to-late 1990s. Moreover, while there is little strong evidence to suggest that Latinos responded to the anti-immigrant climate by registering to vote in higher proportions, Latino turnout rates nonetheless increased as already registered Latinos decided to vote.

Whatever the precise reasons for the increase in Latino participation in the late 1990s, many in the Republican Party grew increasingly concerned. More Latinos voted and fewer voted Republican. What's more, demographic projections for the first half of the twenty-first century suggest an even more problematic future for a GOP set on an anti-immigrant and/or anti-Latino course. Whites are predicted to fall to just 53 percent of the U.S. population by 2050, while Latinos are set to rise to 24 percent. If these population estimates prove correct, and if Latinos continue to vote overwhelmingly for Democratic candidates, the GOP faces the possibility of an electoral wipeout in the near future unless it can mitigate Latino opposition with a significantly increased share of the white electorate.

Some in the GOP saw little cause for concern in the mid 1990s. Short-term electoral considerations persuaded politicians such as Pete Wilson, Pat Buchanan, and even Bob Dole of the political efficacy of the anti-immigration, anti-minority strategy. They may have cared little about the consequences of their actions on their party's future, their success trumping the party's. Alternatively, they may have cared deeply about the GOPs future, but convinced themselves that Latinos were natural Republicans who would turn to the party once the ugly dust of the 1990s had settled. If so, such optimism seems misplaced. Even before Pete Wilson and other Republicans set about antagonizing them, Latinos had traditionally voted Democratic because of their socio-economic position and because of the party's New Deal-rooted image as the inclusive, pro-minority party. The GOP's close association with the anti-immigrant movement in the 1990s only reinforced these attachments.

The Response

The 1994 warning of Jack Kemp and William Bennett that the GOP risked turning itself into the minority party if it continued to alienate the growing Latino and Asian populations persuaded few fellow partisans at the time. The Wilson model was firmly in the ascendance. However, increasing publicity about the growth in Latino voters and their increasing hostility to the GOP, Dole's 1996 failure (including losing Florida and Arizona to Clinton), the close loss by 984 votes of incumbent Republican congressman Robert K. Dornan to Democratic challenger Loretta Sanchez in California, the general meltdown of the party in the Prop. 187 state, and the gubernatorial success of the Bush brothers in Texas and Florida persuaded some key strategists began to pursue a different, more Latino- and immigrant-friendly course from that traveled in the mid 1990s. In a first effort to offset some of the damage, the Republican National Committee established the New Majority Council designed to reach out to the Latino community. Representatives from the council were sent out to meet and listen to minority groups, and to portray the Republican Party as a pro-immigrant, pro-Latino party. Speaker Gingrich also hired a Spanish-speaking spokesperson and translated his press releases into Spanish in a further effort to court the Spanish-language media and Latino voters. He and other leaders also encouraged their fellow congressional Republicans to play down their efforts to end affirmative action, bilingual education, and bilingual ballots.[39]

Lamar Smith was reappointed chair of the House immigration subcommittee in the 105th Congress (1997–1998), but was no longer on the offensive. Most of his time was spent fighting off attempts to water down the anti-immigrant reforms of the previous Congress. Moreover, Smith's partner in the 104th Congress, Senator Alan Simpson, was replaced as chair of the Senate immigration committee by Spencer Abraham, the pro-immigration Republican senator who had been instrumental in destabilizing Simpson's and Smith's plans to reduce legal immigration. Abraham—the "poster boy of mass immigration" according to critics[40]—was interested in reforming the Immigration and Naturalization Service (INS) and expanding the number of H-1B visas, not restricting the number of immigrants arriving in the United States.

A key problem for Smith was that what had looked like good politics in the 104th Congress suddenly seemed less efficacious in the 105th. Further, two key pieces of legislation, the 1996 immigration and welfare acts, produced policy outcomes that exacerbated the political problems. The welfare act mandated that SSI payments to about 500,000 poor elderly and disabled legal immigrants would cease on August 22, 1997, one year after Clinton signed the bill, regardless of when they entered the United States. Losing SSI meant claimants would also lose their Medicaid health protection. As the date of the payments' end approached, its salience was heightened by dramatic stories in the nation's newspapers of infirm patriots, such as Vietnamese soldiers who had fought on America's side, about to have their federal safety net swept away by cruel Republicans. Smith, Gingrich, and others always thought that the states would, at least to some extent, step into the void left by the federal government, but the concentration of affected immigrants in a few large states threatened to overwhelm their fiscal capacities as well as upset delicate electoral coalitions, especially as Republicans were increasingly sensitive about appearing anti-immigrant or anti-Latino. In New York, for example, where 80,000 immigrants' SSI was threatened, Mayor Rudolph Gulliani, Governor George Pataki, and Senator Alfonse D'Amato, Republicans all, lobbied furiously for legal immigrants resident in the United States before the passage of the welfare bill to be excluded from the welfare cuts. D'Amato was joined by fellow Republican senators John Chafee of Rhode Island and Mike DeWine of Ohio, to exclude from the cuts legal immigrants already receiving SSI on August 22, 1996.[41] After lobbying by immigrant-rights organizations, the National Governors Association, and the Clinton administration, a majority of both Republican and Democratic lawmakers across both chambers of Congress joined together in August 1997 to pass the Balanced Budget Act (HR 2015, PL 105-33) and restore SSI and associated Medicaid benefits at a cost of $10 billion over five years to 350,000 elderly and/or disabled legal immigrants previously in the country and receiving benefits on August 22, 1996. Those in the country before that date and June 1, 1997, and who later became disabled would also be entitled to SSI and Medicaid.[42] Of course, all legal residents would upon naturalization be entitled to these benefits regardless of their date of entry to the United States—a clear incentive for many to apply for citizenship. In June 1998 a further bipartisan majority passed and President Clinton signed the Agricultural Research, Extension, and Education Reform Act (S 1150, PL 105-185) to restore, at a cost of $818 million over five years, food stamps to 250,000 legal immigrants, also denied them by the 1996 welfare reform.[43]

The 1996 immigration law overturned a 1994 amendment to the Immigration and Nationality Act, known as 245(i), which allowed immigrants illegally in the country to make an application for legal residency status without having to return to their homeland to do so, on payment of a $1,000 fine to the INS. Previous to 245(i), immigrants could only apply for legal residency (absent IRCA-style amnesties) from abroad. The introduction of 245(i) allowed the State Department to relinquish the burden of processing a significant number of visas in its foreign embassies while raising several hundred million dollars annually for the immigration service. Moreover, the logic of 245(i) is that it prevents families being broken up and does not force an immigrant to make a Hobson's choice: obey the law by going home and waiting possibly years to be readmitted, or break the law by staying in the United States. The choice was made more difficult still by the 1996 immigration act because it barred unlawful entrants from reentering the United States for up to ten years. Proponents of the 1996 change argued that allowing undocumented immigrants to apply for lawful residency while illegally in the United States "rewards illegal behavior, provides incentives for continued illegal-immigration, and compromises the integrity of the immigrant admissions process."[44] President Clinton came under considerable pressure from Central American leaders in spring 1997 to restore 245(i), claiming a large, forced influx of returning migrants could destabilize their precarious economies.[45] Clinton subsequently put his weight behind extending 245(i), as did immigrant-rights and religious groups, immigration lawyers, the State Department, and employers. On November 26, 1997, Clinton signed into law a bill (PL 105-119) that revived 245(i) on a temporary basis, allowing otherwise qualified illegal immigrants to submit an application for permanent residency by January 14, 1998. Demonstrating the power of the corporate lobby, the law also included more generous provisions for skilled immigrants and for immigrants sponsored by their employers.

The Republican-dominated Congress also voted to repeal a provision of the 1996 immigration law that would have led to the deportation of more than 300,000 Salvadoran, Guatemalan, and Nicaraguan refugees. The refugees had fled civil wars in the 1980s, but the wars' end led Lamar Smith to include a repatriation provision in the 1996 law. The drive to overturn the provision was led by two Florida Republicans, Representative Lincoln Diaz-Balart and Senator Connie Mack, and on November 19, 1997 Congress passed and President Clinton signed the Nicaraguan and Central American Relief Act (PL105-100) to ease the deportation requirements. It was in effect a mini-amnesty that permitted hundreds of thousands of Latin American refugees and many others from the former Eastern bloc to remain in the United States and gain legal permanent residency status.[46] Similarly, the Haitian Refugee Immigration Fairness Act (PL105-227) signed into law on October 21, 1998 by President Clinton expedited the move toward legal permanent residency for tens of thousands of Haitians.

The immigration act of 1990 set the number of H-1B visas available to skilled workers, most of which went to IT recruits, at 65,000 per year. The visas are for three years and can be renewed once, and they are particularly sought after as the only nonimmigrant visa that permits holders to apply for legal permanent status. The October 1998 American Competitiveness and Workforce Improvement Act (PL 105-277) nearly doubled the limit, albeit temporarily, to 115,000 in fiscal years 1999 and 2000 and 107,500 in 2001, thus providing an additional 142,500 visas over three years. However, under pressure from high-tech industries, the Republican-dominated 106th Congress (1999–2000), with Gingrich replaced as House speaker by Dennis Hastert, continued to build on the work of the 105th Congress and further liberalized U.S. immigration policy. In October 2000 it passed the American Competitiveness in the Twenty-First Century Act (S 2045, PL 106-313) to increase further the number of H-1B visas for skilled workers by an additional 297,500 over three years, raising to 195,000 the number of visas available each year in 2001-03, with researchers and university professors exempt from the total. The legislation was sponsored by Republican Orrin Hatch and won overwhelming bipartisan support in both chambers, as did the 1998 increase. Said House Majority Leader Trent Lott: "We need to recruit as many of the great brains of the world to work and become American as we can."[47] Even the unions were on board in 2000, after opposing the 1998 increase. The only problem faced by proponents of increasing H-1B visas was that almost every advocate of liberal immigration reform wanted to add their pet program to the visa bill, thus threatening to create opposition where none existed previously. Democrats wanted to revive permanently 245(i), allow certain Central Americans to become legal permanent residents, and launch a further amnesty, and some Republicans wanted a new guest-worker program for agriculture. Republican leaders were reluctant to allow votes on such issues, however, for fear that nay votes could be used by opponents to reinforce the party's anti-immigrant persona.[48] As *Congressional Quarterly* noted: "GOP leaders in both chambers, but particularly the Senate, were loath to expose their members to politically sensitive immigration votes during an election year"[49]—in stark contrast to four years earlier. Senator Edward Kennedy nonetheless was still able to turn Republican inaction to the Democrats' advantage: "It is clear that Republican support for the Latino community is all talk and no action. When it's time to pass legislation of real importance to the Latino community, the Republican leadership is nowhere to be found."[50] Speaker Hastert also wanted to avoid debating what were now sensitive political issues for Republicans, and pushed the H-1B bill through quickly on a voice vote at a time when the Democrats were not expecting a vote and were unprepared for debate.

As the 106th Congress drew to a close in late 2000, congressional Democrats with the support of President Clinton continued to push for the liberalization of immigration policy. They pushed the Latino and Immigrant Fairness Act (LIFA) as amendments to an omnibus spending bill for the departments of Commerce, Justice, and State and the federal judiciary. LIFA proposed a new amnesty by moving the "registry" date from 1972 to 1986 to allow around 500,000 undocumented aliens who arrived in the United States between 1972 and 1986 to claim legal status; helping Central Americans and others who had fled communist regimes in the 1980s but were not covered by the 1997 Nicaraguan and Central American Relief Act or 1998 Haitian Refugee Immigration Fairness Act claim legal permanent residency; and reviving 245(i). Clinton threatened to veto the spending bill if LIFA was not attached but did not make good on his promise and instead accepted on December 21, 2000, a Republican alternative known as LIFE, the Legal Immigration Family Equity Act (PL 106-553 and PL 106-554). LIFE again extended temporarily the 245(i) program to April 30, 2001, and created two new visa categories for children and spouses of legal permanent residents (V visas) and U.S. citizens living abroad (K visas) that would allow them to remain in the United States while their claim for legal permanent residency was being processed. More significantly, the act included a provision that would allow around 400,000 undocumented aliens, living in the United States since 1982 who had previously been denied or had not applied for legal status under the INS's narrow interpretation of the amnesty provisions of the 1986 IRCA, to claim legal residency. While not as generous as the Democrats' version in LIFA, and while the Republicans had managed to stall passage until after the 2000 elections, the LIFE immigration reforms included in the omnibus spending bill represented a further expansion of an amnesty program only four years after Republicans had sought to exclude undocumented residents from the American polity. Moreover, congressional Republicans bowed to pressure from organized labor, Latinos, and immigrant-rights groups and dropped plans to include a new agricultural guest-worker program.

In California, meanwhile, another potentially explosive initiative dealing with ethnicity and immigration appeared on the June 1998 primary ballot. Ron Unz's anti-bilingual education measure, Proposition 227, proposed ending the teaching of core subjects to non-English speakers in their native language and replacing it with an intensive one-year immersion program of English-language instruction before moving students into English-only classrooms. While many educational and Latino groups opposed it, the initiative was surprisingly popular with Latino parents who wanted their children to learn English as quickly as possible. Moreover, the initiative did not in the event create as much controversy as Propositions 187 and 209 before it in part because the Republican Party was reluctant to take a definitive position for fear of reinforcing its anti-Latino image and because the front-runners in the gubernatorial primaries, notably Democrat Gray Davis and Republican Dan Lungren, opposed it. Governor Wilson, about to be termed out after his second term, did throw his diminishing weight behind it, much to the chagrin of Unz, who did not want his initiative to become "racialized." In a reaction against Proposition 187 and reflecting the increasing power of the Latino caucus, the Democratic legislature passed a bill restoring undocumented immigrants' access to drivers' licenses, which had been revoked in 1993. Governor Davis vetoed it, however, because he did not want to antagonize white voters still hostile to illegal immigration.

In a stunning volte-face in February 2000, the AFL-CIO, the peak organization representing about seventy trade unions, announced its support for an amnesty program to legalize the status of millions of undocumented residents on the grounds that illegal workers are subject to exploitation by employers. It also called for an end to sanctions for employers who give jobs to illegal aliens, with resources instead retargeted toward prosecuting employers who exploit their workers. Traditionally, American labor unions opposed the entry of new workers because they posed a threat to the job security and wages of their members, that is, existing, native workers. While the AFL-CIO continued to oppose new guest-worker programs, in April, May, and June 2000 it helped organize pro-amnesty rallies around the United States.

In stark contrast to the 1996 primaries, both the two front-runners for the 2000 Republican presidential nomination, George W. Bush and John McCain, ran on pro-legal immigration platforms. Both promised to increase the number of H-1B visas to allow the entry of more highly skilled workers. McCain supported extending legal immigrants' access to welfare benefits, while Bush spoke of his opposition to Proposition 187 and the need for a new guest-worker program with Mexico. While Bush claimed he opposed a "blanket amnesty" for illegal residents, it appeared he was supportive of legalization for some undocumented migrants. The difference between legalization and amnesty was not made clear. What was clear was that the tone of the debate was significantly more liberal than four years earlier. The volume changed, too. None of the mainstream Republican candidates made the immigration issue central to their campaign because the issue was less important to the voters. The 2000 Republican convention and platform, also in a notable reversal from 1996, made significant efforts to reach out to Latino and minority voters—as did the Democrats as they battled the GOP for the ethnic vote. Both Bush and Gore ran Spanish-language campaign commercials in Latino areas and each peppered their speeches with Spanish phrases. Only Pat Buchanan ran on an anti-immigration platform, arguing that "Mexican irredentism is alive and well" and calling for a significant reduction in legal immigration and a steel border wall to halt the "invasion" of illegal immigrants from Mexico. Buchanan, however, was sidelined as the Reform Party's candidate in 2000 and few Americans were listening. A 1995 Gallup poll found that 65 percent of Americans wanted to reduce immigration levels, but its 1999 poll suggested only 44 percent did so. Americans also appeared to be in favor of an amnesty for undocumented residents, although such results were very sensitive to question wording. Moreover, fewer people considered immigration to be one of the most important issues facing the country. Gallup's respondents rated immigration as only the twelfth most important concern.[51] Both the level and intensity of opinion on the issue had declined.

To be sure, some Republicans continued to promulgate an anti-immigrant message, with a few arguing for a reduction in legal immigration, while others opposed plans to offer an amnesty for undocumented immigrants, at least until the border was more secure. But more Republicans, especially those seeking national office, were keen to present a pro-immigration, ethnically inclusive message in the late 1990s than in the middle of the decade. In the first decade of the twenty-first century, the leader of the Republican Party and president of the United States, George W. Bush, would try to push a liberal immigration agenda that included legalizing the status of millions of illegal immigrations, something unthinkable in the anti-immigration atmosphere of the mid 1990s. The next, final chapter tells the story of Bush's attempt to reform immigration policy.

Chapter 9

Immigration Politics in a New Century

The electoral success of Proposition 187 in 1994 and Governor Wilson's astute use of it for his own political ends indicated powerfully the benefits of using immigration and ethnicity to drive a wedge into the Democratic coalition—just as the GOP had used race to help wrench control of the south from the Democrats during the 1970s and 1980s. Ironically, it was the Republican Party's own anti-minority and anti-immigrant machinations in the mid 1990s that helped engender change by the decade's end. Faced with a significant growth in an increasingly Democratic Latino population, and an immigrant population pushing for citizenship and voting rights as its benefits were squeezed and blame for America's ills were heaped upon it, some in the GOP thought they had positioned themselves on the wrong side of history, epitomized by Bob Dole's devastating defeat to Bill Clinton in the 1996 presidential election. As the previous chapters highlighted, the Republican Congress passed two significant laws in the form of the welfare reform and immigration acts only months before Dole's defeat, but less than one year later on August 5, 1997, many Republicans joined with the Democrats to reinstate most legal immigrants' SSI and Medicaid benefits from which they had only just been excluded. The primary reason was a fear of a further political backlash among the fast-growing and increasingly vocal, well-organized, and confident Latino community.[1] The differing fates of George W. Bush in Texas and Dan Lungren in California in the 1998 gubernatorial elections further convinced many in the GOP that the party's future lay in inclusive politics. Bush's convincing reelection victory with 49 percent of the Latino vote contrasted sharply with Lungren's 24 percent, and helped establish him as a serious contender for the 2000 Republican presidential nomination. Of course, Bush's elevation was not due solely to his Latino-friendly persona. His fundraising prowess, name recognition, and folksy image were equally important. However, his inclusive, pro-minority, pro-immigration message dovetailed neatly with the new imperatives of electoral politics in a nation where Latinos were beginning to find their voice.

By the time Pete Wilson was termed out as California governor in 1999, he had become persona non grata among both the Latino community in California and the Republican Party. Bush, as prospective and confirmed 2000 Republican presidential nominee, made several fund-raising and campaign visits to California, but not once did he meet with Wilson in private or appear with him in public. The snub was fully intended. Bush's strategists thought that they did not need Wilson to help their candidate win over wavering Republicans or to get out the vote; they also figured that any association with Wilson would significantly harm Bush's prospects among Latino voters. The situation was very different only four years earlier when the "Wilson issues" continued to dominate the battle for the Republican nomination even after Wilson had withdrawn from the race, and when Dole made Wilson chair of his California campaign.

Bush's elevation to the presidential office appeared to open up an opportunity to press on with and expand significantly the liberalization of immigration policy that had begun toward the end of Clinton's presidency after a short era of restriction and exclusion. The aim of this final chapter is to detail and explain the shifting politics of immigration reform during Bush's tenure in the White House. Bush was ambitious in his immigration goals: he wanted a new guest-worker program and a "path to citizenship" for the millions of illegal immigrants already resident in the United States. At the time of writing, mid 2007, Bush's ambitions have hitherto been thwarted by a combination of events and political factors, most notably 9/11 and the Republican congressional caucus. It is unlikely that the last year-and-a-half of his presidency will produce the necessary and benign combination of politics and context to engender a fundamental liberalization of immigration policy in Bush's image. Perhaps too many congressional Republicans remain un-reconstituted hardliners on illegal immigration and the issue certainly continues to raise the hackles of many conservative activists. However, it is important to recognize how far the Republican Party has moved since the 1990s. It is, of course, not a monolithic beast, but very few in the party, at any level, are calling for a reduction in the level of legal immigration or the benefits of legal immigrants, and, in stark contrast to mid 1990s, a Republican president was prepared to make the legalization of over ten million illegal immigrants the central domestic policy plank of his last years in office.

Bush's First Term

The 107th Congress

Bush made his commitment to liberal immigration reform clear during the 2000 presidential campaign, and many commentators believed that his election at a time of low domestic unemployment and an apparently booming economy opened up a window of opportunity in the 107th Congress (2001–2002). Moreover, the AFL-CIO's declaration of support for amnesty in February 2000 removed one of the key obstacles to liberalization, and Federal Reserve chairman Alan Greenspan's statement that immigration benefited the American economy bolstered the case further. The restrictionist chair of the House immigration sub-committee, Lamar Smith, was replaced in 2001 by Republican George W. Gekas who while no liberal was certainly less conservative than his predecessor. In the Senate the chair was taken by Republican Sam Brownback of Kansas who wanted to introduce a guest-worker program. And across the United States' southern border sat another chief executive who would play an important role in the immigration reform agenda.

The American anti-immigration movement of the mid 1990s helped change the Mexican government's perception of its United States–based expats. By 2002, twenty-two million Mexican citizens were estimated to be living abroad, of whom eighteen million were resident in the United States. Millions more had taken on U.S. citizenship but retained close ties to the homeland. Such large numbers living abroad had significant economic and political implications for Mexico. Most importantly, the remittances sent home each year by Mexicans totaled $9 billion, making them Mexico's most valuable source of income after tourism and oil. Political and economic leaders in Mexico obviously wanted to keep the money pipelines open, because any significant diminution in the flow would have catastrophic economic and thus political consequences. Furthermore, since the passage of Proposition 187, the treatment of Mexicans in the United States had become an important political issue in Mexico. Many Mexicans saw the illegal-immigration initiative as a racist attack on their vulnerable brothers and sisters, who had long provided the backbone to the California economy. They also complained bitterly about the treatment of illegal migrants by "la migra," or U.S. Border Patrol, and citizen vigilante groups. Many believed that they were treated like animals—a perception reinforced by hundreds of border fatalities annually. Some died from exhaustion in the desert heat, others from plunging nighttime temperatures, and still others in car chases with the Border Patrol. Whatever the cause, the deaths caused outrage south of the border and helped reinforce Mexicans' negative perceptions of their northern neighbors.

Responding to such concerns, one of Vicente Fox's central campaign planks when running for the Mexican presidency in 2000 was to establish an office to look after the interests of Mexican migrants, or "paisanos." Fox claimed he would give "primordial importance" to Mexican "heroes" abroad and work with them to formulate policies in their, not the Mexican government's, interest: "I can assure all Mexican migrants that we will not fail you!" he promised.[2] Fox took up office in December 2000 and one month later George W. Bush was sworn in as president. Bush's first foreign visit, reflecting the importance he placed on the relationship, was to Mexico in February 2001. He met Fox at the Mexican president's ranch in Guanajuato and the two leaders made much of their mutual admiration for each other and each other's nations, going well beyond the usual diplomatic niceties—it was genuine and heartfelt. Fox pushed his immigration agenda, arguing that "the United States needs Mexican workers to enable its economy to grow at five percent a year and to keep inflation rates below two percent. . . . Immigration is not bad for the United States. It has given a real stimulus to the American economy."[3] Bush was very sympathetic to Fox's argument. As a first step they established the Mexico-U.S. Migration Working Group. It was a high-powered collaboration with four prominent cochairs: Secretary of State Colin Powell, U.S. attorney general John Ashcroft, Mexico's foreign minister Jorge Castaneda, and Santiago Creel, the interior secretary. The group's mission, which helped set the parameters of the wider immigration reform debate, was to "reach mutually satisfactory results on border safety, a temporary-worker program and the status of undocumented Mexicans in the United States . . . as soon as possible, [and to] create an orderly framework for migration that ensures humane treatment [and] legal security, and dignifies labor conditions."[4] The close working relationship between Fox and Bush also helped move forward the reform process, as did Fox's determination to push the immigration agenda vigorously at every opportunity. The key debate in the working group was whether to propose a guest-worker program, a legalization program with a path to citizenship, or a combination of the two, sometimes referred to as earned legalization. The same options were on the table in Congress, where Republican senator Phil Gramm introduced a guest-worker bill without the prospect of citizenship, Democratic senator Bob Graham a combined guest-worker bill with the prospect of citizenship (S 1814/5), and Democratic representative Luis V. Gutierrez a rolling amnesty that would have allowed nearly all persons illegally in the United States to claim citizenship (HR 500). Generally speaking, but with many exceptions, Democrats were more hostile to the idea of a guest-worker program than amnesty/legalization. However, there were many crosscutting pressures on members of Congress. Fox, many immigration advocates, and Latinos supported a guest-worker program while the AFL-CIO, most industrial unions, and the congressional Hispanic caucus opposed it, because of concern that the transient workers could be poorly treated by employers. On the other hand, Republicans were generally more hostile to amnesty than a guest-worker program. Bush wanted both, but was careful to avoid using the language of amnesty, instead talking about legalization or a path to citizenship.

Pursuant to the bilateral working group's discussions, the Mexican government made public its primary immigration goals: a guest-worker program, more visas for Mexicans wanting to work in the United States or exemption from visa quotas, an end to border violence and deaths, and regularization of the status of the 3.5 million Mexicans illegally resident in the United States. Mexico did not call for an "amnesty" but was careful to use the words "regularization" or "legalization." The differences between them are important, but sometimes obscured by conflicting interpretations. As we shall see later in this chapter, the concept and meaning of "amnesty" is especially contested and politicized and, moreover, appeared to change over time. During his election campaign, Bush had supported a guest-worker program and expressed opposition to a "blanket amnesty" without specifying precisely what either, but especially the latter, meant.

It appears that Bush understood an amnesty to be a program that would allow a group of people to claim legal status and later citizenship in a way that privileged them over other groups seeking the same ends. In this thinking, the 1986 Immigration Reform and Control Act (IRCA) was clearly an amnesty because eligible applicants were awarded legal permanent status automatically and almost immediately. They did not have to leave the country to make the application, or pay a fine, or join the queue with others seeking permanent residency via the family reunification scheme, employer sponsorship, or diversity lottery. Conversely, in Bush's definition, a program would not be considered an amnesty if applicants were penalized for their previously illegal status through payment of a fine and if the "path to citizenship" did not privilege applicants over others seeking the same ends. They would "have to get in line and play by the rules" as Bush was fond of saying. In early 2001 Bush had not yet used the language of "path to citizenship," instead, as noted above, expressing his support for a guest-worker program and opposition to blanket amnesty. The difficulty for observers and participants in the negotiations was whether Bush envisioned that a guest-worker plan should include provisions that allowed participants to earn legal permanent status. This would not, by his definition, amount to an amnesty so long the legal permanent status was not privileged and a penalty was paid. Opponents saw it differently. Critics of Bush's position, which included many in his own party, defined as an amnesty any program that allowed by any means previously illegal residents to get green cards and citizenship. Some of the more radical critics even argued that any guest-worker program that allowed current illegal immigrants to participate was also by definition an amnesty—even if the program did include any form of a path to citizenship—because it "regularized" their status. A further definitional problem was evident in the meaning of "legalization." Many conservatives took legalization to mean amnesty. Others interpreted it to mean the regularization of a person's status without permitting any claim to permanent residency or citizenship, so she or he could, for example, work or get a driver's license. Still others took it to infer a path to citizenship. To confuse matters further, people often changed their definitions or were deliberately opaque when using a particular word for fear of inciting hostility among critics or potential opponents.

The contested nature and politicization of the language of the immigration debate presents problems for an author because there are few value-neutral words available to describe the programs or processes. The problem is exacerbated because the same words can mean different things to different people, and different words for the same thing have different meanings and connotations. In this light, tests of public opinion on immigration issues are extraordinarily sensitive to question wording, ordering, and the alternatives offered. Even when questions and choices are carefully presented to respondents and are consistent over time, ambiguous responses are common. For example, while a majority usually opposes illegal immigration another majority is set against deportation and generally in favor of treating well the illegal immigrants already in country. Americans also seem to be dead set against an amnesty but in favor of legalization. That the difference between amnesty and legalization is essentially semantic but that polls return significantly different responses depending on the word employed by pollsters highlights the problem. Senator Arlen Specter put it well when he said: "Amnesty like beauty is in the eye of the beholder."[5]

In the following discussion I will use whenever possible the language of the active protagonists and attempt to make clear their meaning where it is not. When analyzing the debate, the aim is to steer a middle course. In particular, "regularization" is used to refer to the change of status from illegal to legal worker or resident, usually temporary. It does not permit a change in status to legal permanent resident or citizen. "Legalization" on the other hand is used to describe a change in status from undocumented to legal that includes either legal permanent residency (that is, a green card) or citizenship or a path to them. Many conservatives would argue this is amnesty and they may well be right. However, I also employ President Bush's definition of amnesty, even though it is analytically narrow and logically flawed, because it captures a subtle distinction between getting in line and jumping the queue, which is useful in the present debate.

Whatever the definitional problems, the Mexican government's goals were certainly ambitious and it was confident they were realizable in the short term given the apparently positive climate for reform in the United States. This was reinforced by rumors in July 2001 that the working group was leaning toward recommending both guest-worker and legalization programs. Indeed, the Mexican government was so sure about the likelihood of reform that Foreign Minister Jorge Castaneda boasted that the goal was "the greatest number of rights for the greatest number of Mexicans in the shortest time possible. . . . It's the whole enchilada or nothing."[6] Powell, more circumspect in his choice of words, suggested its findings would not "include just simply a blanket amnesty for everybody. But I'm sure the recommendations will include ways for some of those who are in the country to remain in the country and try to regularize the flow of people back and forth."[7] Despite Powell's cautiousness, the impetus that seemed to be building toward significant reform caused a backlash by conserva-tive House Republicans to the prospect of an amnesty, earned or not, which persuaded Bush to step cautiously. He reiterated his own opposition to a blanket amnesty and emphasized the need for legalization to be earned and gradual. Bush aides also began suggesting that action on liberalization was unlikely before the 2002 midterms and that a guest-worker program, not legalization, was his prior-ity. Democratic leaders issued a statement of principles in August 2001, which included "earned legalization" rather than a blanket amnesty and equal protec-tion of labor law for temporary-workers to protect them against exploitation. Mexican leaders, while still ostensibly bullish, also began to talk of earned legal-ization. It appeared the momentum for reform was slowing slightly, although most observers reckoned the introduction of a guest-worker program was still likely. There was more uncertainty whether it would include any legalization provisions.

The debate over guest-worker and legalization programs overshadowed some-what Bush's actions on resurrecting 245(i) to make it easier for undocumented and "out-of-status" residents to apply for legal permanent residency from within the United States. He hoped that reviving 245(i) would help him and the GOP appeal to immigrants generally and Latinos specifically. In the light of the bilat-eral working group's discussions but lack of actionable proposals and the slowing of the reform process, pushing 245(i) would also help appease Fox. Moreover, there was an administrative reason to extend the program: the INS had been slow to draft rules regarding the previous extension to April 30, 2001, leaving many potential applicants with no time to file.

In a May 1, 2001, letter Bush asked Congress to extend 245(i) for one year. The House was only prepared to allow a four-month extension (HR 1885, passed 336-43 on May 21). The Senate, however, which had reverted to Democratic control after Vermont's Republican senator, Jim Jeffords, left the party to sit as an independent in May 2006, approved a one-year extension on September 6 by voice vote. Congressional action on 245(i) coincided with a visit to the United States by President Fox, who addressed a joint meeting of Congress on September 6. He pushed hard for 245(i) and talked-up the importance and necessity of the guest-worker and legalization programs.[8] Bush, too, said he was committed to reform and claimed that "the United States has no more important relationship in the world than our relationship with Mexico."[9]

However, the 245(i) extension specifically and liberalization generally stalled dramatically on September 11 when terrorists destroyed the world trade center towers in New York City. Immigration suddenly became a security issue, which was reinforced when Americans learned that the pilots had been trained at U.S. aviation schools and, later, that thirteen of the nineteen hijackers had entered the United States legally on student, business, and tourist visas, overstayed and not been removed by the INS. Security was the new mantra and attention turned to immigration controls, including more border agents, careful checks of foreign visitors and visa applicants, additional powers to track, uncover, detain, and remove suspected terrorists, monitor and intercept their funds, and reforming the immigration superstructure. Congress had previously passed in 1996 the Antiterrorism and Effective Death Penalty Act (PL 104-132) in response to the largely failed 1993 attack on the world trade center and the 1995 Oklahoma City bombing. That law plus the 1996 immigration act increased border enforcement and introduced many measures to heighten surveillance of foreign visitors and domestic terror threats, but many in Congress had baulked at the more radical proposals of the Clinton administration. There was little consensus in Congress about the necessary extent and methods of interior enforcement, in part because of concerns about civil liberties and harming cross-border trade. Furthermore, several of the schemes on which Congress and the administration were able to agree and enacted in law were never implemented (such as the entry-exit system to ensure visitors departed in accordance with their visa requirements) or were implemented late with so many modifications as to make the scheme effectively redundant (such as the Student Exchange Visitor Program to monitor foreign students).[10] The response to 9/11 would be more draconian. Three significant security laws were passed. The USA Patriot Act (PL 107-56), signed by the president on October 26, 2001, included many provisions to reinforce the nation's borders, including the northern border, and strengthen law-enforcement agencies' powers to detain and investigate potential alien terrorists. The Enhanced Border Security and Visa Entry Reform Act of 2002 (PL 107-113), signed on May 14, 2002, tightened up the screening and monitoring of aliens, including students. And the Homeland Security Act (PL 107-296), signed on November 22, 2002, disbanded the INS and rolled its and other agencies' functions into the new Department of Homeland Security (DHS), thus structuring immigration agencies and issues more formerly as security ones.[11] The INS's reputation was severely damaged by its failure to deport several of the future terrorists for visa violations before 9/11 became apparent. They were not exceptions. The agency itself estimated that 400,000 foreigners served with deportation orders had not been removed from the United States and some independent estimates put the total nearer one million.[12] A backlog of nearly five million outstanding applications for visas and citizenship further damaged its reputation. Its reputation was ruined utterly when it awarded student visas to two of the deceased 9/11 hijackers, Mohamed Atta and Marwan Al-Shehhi, in March 2002. Today three agencies, located in the DHS, stand in its place: Immigration and Customs Enforcement, Citizenship and Immigration Services, and Customs and Border Protection.

In addition to securitizing immigration issues, September 11 also helped push the United States deeper into recession, thus diminishing further the prospect of liberal immigration reform. Powell offered some limited hope to the Mexican government in January 2002, claiming the U.S. government remained committed to "regularizing the movement of Mexicans back and forth," but offered no promises on specific provisions.[13] Reformers tried to frame liberalization as beneficial to homeland security, arguing every illegal immigrant is an unknown alien while a legal visitor or immigrant is a known alien. James Ziglar, Doris Meissner's replacement as INS commissioner, tried to use the security prism to push a guest-worker program:

> If we could find a way to move a substantial portion of the current illegal flow from Mexico into legal channels via some kind of temporary-worker program and combine that with a new cooperative law enforcement arrangement with Mexico, we could benefit the US economy, we could substantially reduce illegal immigration. And, it could enable the Border Patrol and other law enforcement agencies to focus on the bad guys coming across—not on the flow of people who just want to get into this country to work. . . . The events of September 11 were caused by evil, not immigration. We cannot judge immigrants by the actions of terrorists.[14]

Such arguments carried little weight, however. Bush noted on March 22, 2002, that "I don't think the will of the American people is for blanket amnesty," while reiterating that "the United States has no more important relationship in the world than the one we have with Mexico."[15] The Mexican government was rightly resigned to slow progress, with one Mexican observer noting: "The most important change in Mexico's position is they don't pretend they're going to get the whole enchilada anymore."[16]

Some optimists thought that 2002 would see at best a further temporary extension of 245(i) and perhaps more visas for temporary-workers, but neither was likely. Bush tried again to push the 245(i) provision again in March 2002, but with no success. The House once again gave its approval (275-137) for a further four-month extension, but the Senate refused on national security grounds. A similar push in October met the same fate.[17] While Bush tried and failed to forge a majority coalition on 245(i), the Democrats unveiled their own radical immigration reform proposals, proposing a new amnesty for undocumented residents who had lived in the United States for five or more years and worked for at least two. They stood no chance of success in a post-9/11 Republican Congress, but the aim was not to change the law but to appeal to Latino voters.[18] Even toward the end of 2002, there was little movement on the key issues: "As we get to a more normal life and as we bring our homeland into a firmer basis of security . . . we might be in a better position next year to deal with some of the concerns that Americans have and Congress has had with respect to immigration," said Secretary of State Colin Powell in October 2002.[19] Fox remained determined to push the reform agenda, however. His aides told reporters that he would after the 2002 midterm elections lobby U.S. members of Congress, business, unions, religious groups, and local lawmakers to persuade them of the pro-immigration case.[20] Organized labor and immigrant and religious groups also continued to lobby for a legalization program, joining forces in 2002 to launch the campaigns such as The Reward Work Coalition and Million Voices for Legalization to persuade Americans to send Bush and Congress one million postcards expressing support for a new amnesty.[21] House Democrat Edward Pastor of Arizona introduced a legalization bill (HR 4999) to accompany the campaign, but it quickly stalled, as did the Earned Legalization and Family

Reunification Act (HR 5600) pushed by the House minority leader Richard A. Gephardt.

Despite the new stasis, Bush's efforts on 245(i), the serious high-level discussions on guest-worker and legalization provisions, and the Democrats' radical amnesty plans all highlighted that the nature and tone of the immigration debate changed markedly in a short time. While "immigration reform" during the mid 1990s largely referred to efforts to curtail immigration and immigrants' benefits, by 2000 it meant liberalizing immigration laws. Liberalization remained on the agenda post 9/11, even if concrete successes were unlikely. At the same time, however, 9/11 moved the debate in the conservatives' favor, making it easier for them to defend the status quo on guest-workers and legalization programs and to push for tighter border controls and surveillance of visitors and immigrants. Similarly, 9/11 hardened conservative attitudes, especially on illegal immigration, which was reflected in the growth in Representative Tom Tancredo's immigration reform caucus, the lead group for congressional restrictionists. It reported an increase in membership to sixty-two in March 2002 from sixteen just before the terrorist attacks. The 107th Congress had promised much but delivered little, largely because September 11 stalled progress toward liberal reform.

The 108th Congress

In the 2002 midterm elections the Republicans retained their majority in the House and won back the Senate after Jeffords' defection without much help or hindrance from Latinos. Moreover, immigration issues played little part in the national debate, except in so far as they contributed to the security agenda. There was a small scuffle in California, however, where the legacy of Proposition 187 lingered on. The California Republican Party's 2002 gubernatorial candidate, Bill Simon, was initially keen to disassociate himself from the previous Republican governor, Pete Wilson, to avoid alienating Latino voters still raw over the 1994 illegal-immigration initiative and Wilson's role in it. But as Simon trailed incumbent governor Gray Davis badly in the polls with less than two weeks to election day, he sought Wilson's endorsement in a last-gasp effort to save his faltering campaign. His strategists knew that the Wilson connection would hurt Simon among Latino voters and probably liberal and Democratic ones as well, but they hoped it might on balance do more good than harm than good by getting out to vote conservative Republicans alienated by the poor campaign of the millionaire political neophyte. Democrats were delighted by Wilson's endorsement. Bob Mulholland, a Democratic strategist, claimed "Wilson's anti-Latino tattoo [today] goes on Simon's arm. Big mistake by Simon, to associate himself with the leading immigrant-bashing Republican in the state." Simon himself went out of his way to emphasize that he had opposed Prop. 187 and was a friend of Latinos: "When I talk to members of the Latino community, my message resonates with them," he claimed hopefully.[22] Latinos themselves were less convinced. Simon won just 27 percent of the Latino vote compared to Davis's 73. Ward Connerly acknowledged that its association with Prop. 187 had "made it appear that the Republican Party is anti-Hispanic," even though he claimed Wilson's position on immigration had been willfully misinterpreted and twisted by his opponents.[23]

Simon's defeat may have reinforced Rove and Bush's confidence in their inclusive electoral strategy and encouraged them to push on with immigration reform.

As politicians returned to Washington in January 2003 for the start of the 108th Congress (2003–2004), Mexico's foreign minister, Jorge Castaneda, resigned, citing frustration about lack of progress on migration issues.[24] Castaneda was a genuine admirer of the United States and his departure was a loss to bilateral relations. The U.S.-Mexico relationship also soured after Fox refused to support the invasion of Iraq in 2003. Despite these apparent problems, Fox would be pleased by the momentum for reform built during 2003 that would manifest itself in presidential action in early 2004.

Both Republicans and Democrats introduced significant legislation in Congress. Senator Edward Kennedy sponsored the Agricultural Job Opportunity, Benefits, and Security Act (S 1645), better known as AgJobs, linking business-friendly revisions of the H-2A visa program for temporary farm workers to earned legalization for undocumented agricultural workers. The bill won support from both growers and workers' groups but stalled. President Clinton and House Republicans had previously sunk similar AgJobs legislation in 1998 and 9/11 ended negotiations in late 2001. Other guest-worker bills were also introduced by Republican senators John Cornyn and John McCain, and the Senate judiciary committee approved in October the Development, Relief, and Education for Alien Minors Act (DREAM, S 1545) to provide a path to citizenship for resident undocumented children who graduated from high school and went on to university or military service. It would also allow public universities to charge undocumented students in-state tuition fees rather than higher out-of-state fees. President Bush made appropriate noises of support for various legislative initiatives but did not enter the political fray in favor of any. Some Latino groups criticized his reluctance to become involved specifically and the lack of concrete progress generally on immigration reform in 2003. Bush was accused of playing symbolic politics to attract the Latino vote but failing to deliver promised legislative changes.[25]

On January 7, 2004, the American president finally and firmly put down a marker when he announced his Fair and Secure Immigration Reform plan for a new "temporary-worker program" (TWP) to "match willing foreign workers with willing U.S. employers" but only after employers had made "every reasonable effort" to ensure that no Americans would do the jobs. Initially, matched foreign workers resident abroad or undocumented workers resident in the United States would be given temporary-worker status for three years. Later, to reduce the incentive to enter the United States illegally, only workers resident abroad would be eligible. Employees would be able to work legally in the United States and travel freely back and forth to see family in their homeland. Their temporary legal status could be renewed after three years, but not indefinitely. To provide incentives to return home, workers would be encouraged to set up low-tax savings accounts in the United States that would pay out on their return home, and the U.S. government would also pay credit into their native retirement accounts. While the temporary workers would be able to apply for legal permanent residency in the United States and later citizenship, Bush said they would have to follow the usual process and would receive no special privileges. Finally, to cope with the increased demand for legal permanent residency from

TWP workers, Bush proposed a "reasonable annual increase" in the number of green cards issued to legal immigrants.[26]

While perhaps guilty of overselling his plan, Bush claimed it would encourage economic growth, help secure America's borders and homeland security, be compassionate towards undocumented immigrants, and protect the rights of legal immigrants. Unveiling his proposals at the White House before a carefully selected multicultural audience, Bush argued:

> As a nation that values immigration, and depends on immigration, we should have immigration laws that work and make us proud. Yet today we do not. Instead, we see many employers turning to the illegal labor market. We see millions of hard-working men and women condemned to fear and insecurity in a massive, undocumented economy. Illegal entry across our borders makes more difficult the urgent task of securing the homeland. The system is not working. Our nation needs an immigration system that serves the American economy, and reflects the American Dream.[27]

Bush wanted to court Latino voters in the upcoming presidential election while refuting in the strongest possible terms that the plan was in any way an amnesty for illegal immigrants. The TWP would regularize the status of perhaps 8 million previously illegal residents by turning them into guest-workers. The newly regularized workers would, because of their temporary legal status, be eligible to apply for legal permanent residency and later citizenship. They would have to do so under the same regulations as other temporary legal workers—for example through employer sponsorship or family reunification, or "getting in line and playing by the rules" as Bush preferred to refer to it—with no special privileges or fast-tracking. In Bush's thinking, the TWP was not an amnesty because it offered no automatic path to citizenship. Moreover, given the long wait for green cards, it was likely that most guest-workers would either return home at the end of their contract before a card became available or stay on illegally in the United States. Nonetheless the TWP would open up a path to citizenship that had not previously existed. Prior to legalization, illegal workers would have had no path to legal permanent status unless they could prove residency in United States from at least the "registry" date, 1972.

Despite Bush's grandiose rhetoric, the proposals immediately drew fire. Although he was careful to stress that the plan was a guest-worker program, not an amnesty, opponents on his right argued otherwise: "It's an amnesty, no matter how much they dance around the fact. It's legalizing illegal immigrants" said Mark Krikorian, executive director of the Center for Immigration Studies.[28] Representative Tom Tancredo's increasingly large congressional immigration caucus, constituted largely of conservative Republicans, expressed its opposition, too, arguing it would reward those who broke the law by violating America's borders. Conversely, some liberals pointed out that workers illegally resident in the United States may be reluctant to apply for legal but temporary status absent a guarantee of a green card, because doing so would make them known to the authorities and put them at greater risk of deportation after the program had ended, especially as the 140,000 employment-based green cards currently available each year together with any foreseeable "reasonable" increase would not likely meet demand from potentially millions of temporary workers seeking permanent residency.[29] Other liberals and pro-immigration groups argued that the path to citizenship was overly restrictive and that guest-workers could be exploited by their U.S. employers: "If you are dependent on an employer filing a petition on your behalf, that employer has a tremendous hold over you," said one critic.[30] John Kerry concurred, arguing the plan "rewards business over immigration."[31]

In the face of opposition from both parties but especially conservative Republicans suspicious that the TWP was in effect an amnesty that could weaken national security, Bush did not pursue his plan with any vigor or commitment in Congress during 2004. It was never written up into a formal bill and introduced in the legislature, despite pleas from reform-minded politicians that strong presidential leadership was needed to overcome a Congress divided on the issue. Nor did it figure as a main theme of Bush's reelection campaign, because there was little difference between him and his Democratic challenger, John Kerry, on the key immigration issues, because Bush figured it would not help him win over middle America or energize his political base, and because only one of the five big immigration states was in play (Florida, but not California, Texas, Illinois, or New York). However, Bush cleverly tailored his message to suit his audience. While he mostly avoided the immigration reform issue when speaking to white audiences, it was central to his message to Latino audiences and in many Spanish-language television and newspaper ads run during the campaign. Emphasizing different messages to different audiences proved a shrewd tactic. While his white base turned out to vote in large numbers, driven in part by the prospect of a close contest and by the appeal of his moral values agenda, Latinos appeared to respond to the targeted ads, with support increasing to 44 percent, an impressive 9 percentage points higher than four years earlier.[32] In comparison, Bush's support increased by only 4 points among whites, 3 points among Asians, and 2 points among African Americans.

Bush's Second Term

The 109th Congress

After winning reelection, Bush promised Mexico's President Fox, who was desperate to establish an immigration legacy before leaving office in 2006, that he would once again push for immigration reform in Congress, despite the opposition of some in his own party. "I'm going to find supporters on the Hill and move it . . . [by] working it," Bush suggested,[33] although Secretary of State Colin Powell warned that it would be wrong to "over promise" and that the administration would "make an assessment with the new Congress of the pace at which we can proceed with the temporary-worker programs, how fast and how far we can move and over what period of time."[34] Bush reiterated the need for a guest-worker program in his 2005 State of the Union address, but after the buffeting from conservatives in 2004 over his Fair and Secure Immigration Reform plan he did not mention legalization or a path to citizenship and again rejected "amnesty."

America's immigration system is also outdated—unsuited to the needs of our economy and to the values of our country. We should not be content with laws that punish hardworking people who want only to provide for their families, and deny businesses willing workers, and invite chaos at our border. It is time for an immigration policy that permits temporary guest-workers to fill jobs Americans will not take, that rejects amnesty, that tells us who is entering and leaving our country, and that closes the border to drug dealers and terrorists.[35]

Despite his caution over legalizing the status of undocumented residents, Bush looked in a strong position postelection. He had increased his majority in the electoral college, won a clear majority of the popular vote, and seen his fellow Republicans improve their hold over the House and Senate. Moreover, while not exceptionally popular in the country at large, Bush built himself a considerable reputation among the Washington community during his first term. He pushed through several significant tax cuts, restructured the education system, and reformed Medicare drug prescriptions. He was never defeated in a congressional vote on any issue on which he took a public position and never resorted to his veto power.

Bush faced several problems in his second term, however. He became entangled in social security reform, the third rail of American politics, which cost more political capital than he would have wished to spend, and the post-9/11 security implications of immigration reform continued to undermine his efforts. The cost, both human and financial, of the war in Iraq further drained his resources and credibility. The increase in Republican strength in Congress after the 2004 elections was a double-edged sword; the 109th Congress (2005–2006), and especially the House, was dominated more than ever by conservative Republicans from the south and west, a breed more hostile to undocumented migration than their moderate northeastern colleagues. The chairs of the two key House committees, John Hostettler on immigration and James Sensenbrenner on judiciary, both expressed their opposition to an amnesty program, as did John Cornyn, the chair of the Senate immigration subcommittee. Cornyn, however, was supportive of a guest-worker program, as was the House majority leader Tom Delay. Other Republicans, while sympathetic to guest-workers, would only consider a new TWP alongside or subsequent to a strong enforcement bill. Tancredo and many others in the congressional immigration caucus remained implacably opposed to both amnesty and a TWP, or would accept a TWP only with unrealizable enforcement benchmarks.

The president hoped that he would be able to work with security-minded party colleagues in Congress by offering a quid pro quo: he would support their plans for enhanced border and interior security in exchange for their support for his guest-worker program and perhaps some form of legalization. Bush's House colleagues proved unwilling to deliver on their side of Bush's imagined bargain, however. The first immigration-related legislation of the session, the Real ID act (PL 109-13), signed by the president on May 11, 2005, was an enforcement-only bill. The House had rejected an amendment to add a guest-worker program, but Bush signed the bill because he was keen to signal to House Republicans in particular that he could work with them on enforcement, hoping they would deliver later in the session. Designed to "prevent another 9/11-type terrorist attack by disrupting terrorist travel" according to judiciary chair Sensenbrenner, the Real ID act imposed federal standards on state-issued drivers' licenses and

ID cards used for federal purposes such as air travel, barred states from issuing such documents to undocumented residents, gave the Department of Homeland Security additional powers to build border fences, and further tightened asylum procedures.[36]

The Senate was generally more amenable than the House to what became known as "comprehensive" reform, which referred to bills that tried to address security and border issues as well as guest-workers and legalization, but there was little movement in the upper chamber in 2005. The McCain-Kennedy Secure and Orderly Immigration Act (S 1033/HR 2330), which drew heavily on Bush's January 2004 plan but with slightly more generous legalization opportunities, was introduced into the House and Senate on May 12, 2005 but did not progress beyond the committee stage, despite generating substantial debate within and outside Congress. The Cornyn-Kyl Comprehensive Enforcement and Immigration Reform Act (S 1438), with a TWP but no legalization opportunity, fared no better.

Bush's agenda was not helped by the widespread publicity, domestic and international, given to the April 2005 Minuteman Project. Hundreds of armed American citizens began patrolling the U.S.-Mexico border in Arizona in an effort to repel what they perceived to be an alien invasion. The Minuteman story encouraged the perspective that the border was out of control, which was reinforced by new data estimating the number of illegal immigrants had risen above ten million, and by Janet Napolitano and Bill Richardson, the Democratic governors of Arizona and New Mexico, declaring a state of emergency in their border counties. Bush responded by visiting the border and promising yet more border agents and detention beds. Arizona's voters had approved the Prop. 187-style Proposition 200 in November 2004, excluding illegal immigrants from state benefits and requiring state employees to report undocumented persons claiming or seeking to claim benefits. Unlike California's initiative, Arizona's was upheld by the Ninth Circuit Court of Appeals in August 2005, adding further fuel to the anti-immigration fire burning along the border.[37] Reflecting grassroots concerns on the immigration issue, especially over illegal immigration, the membership of Tancredo's congressional immigration reform caucus grew yet further, from sixty-two in 2002 to about ninety in 2005.

These events gave further impetus to the House's enforcement-first agenda, as Bush's previously loyal lieutenants, having already passed the Real ID act, moved again in December 2005. The Tancredo-inspired and Sensenbrenner-authored Border Protection, Antiterrorism and Illegal Immigration Control Act (HR 4437), was approved by the judiciary committee on December 8, 2005 and the full House on December 16 by 239-182, with 203 Republicans and 36 Democrats in support. The bill included neither a guest-worker program nor path to citizenship, and instead contained several controversial provisions, although Tancredo's plan to end birthright citizenship was not included. Religious groups that had long helped undocumented immigrants worried about the provision criminalizing with up to five years' imprisonment people "assisting" illegal aliens "knowingly or in reckless disregard" of their immigration status. Employers and libertarians worried about the provisions increasing the penalties for hiring undocumented workers and mandating employers to verify employees' social security numbers against a DHS national list. State and local law-enforcement agencies worried about the provision instructing them to enforce federal immigration law or lose federal funds. The bill also eliminated the 50,000 "diversity" visas and abandoned the so-called "catch-and-release" policy. Catch-and-release was employed when the Border Patrol caught a non-Mexican undocumented alien; they would be charged and released to appear before an immigration judge at a later date, but few of the hundreds of thousands booked ever turned up, of course. Most controversially the bill appropriated funds for an extra 700 miles of high-security fencing on the U.S.-Mexico border and made "unlawful presence" in the United States a criminal punishable by a year in prison. Significantly, the length of sentence made the crime a felony rather than the lesser misdemeanor.[38] As well as being symbolically important, it would make it more difficult for current illegal immigrants to become guest-workers or earn legal permanent residency if such programs ever became law. According to some sources, Sensenbrenner included the criminalization provision at the suggestion of the White House, but the administration had not suggested making it a felony—that was the judiciary chair's idea.[39]

Although Bush had severe misgivings about the bill, more because of what it excluded than included, he was again keen to signal his support for border enforcement to win over conservative Republicans: "America is a nation built on the rule of law, and this bill will help us protect our borders and crack down on illegal entry into the United States" he argued.[40] The proposed criminalization of undocumented immigrants and the border fence enraged the Mexican government and acted as lightening rod for immigrants and their advocates in both the Latino and Asian communities. About 300,000 people went onto the streets to protest in Chicago on March 10, and between half and one million people protested in Los Angeles and hundreds of thousands of others elsewhere on March 25. Thousands of students in Los Angeles walked out of school in the following week, reminiscent of the anti-187 protests in 1994, and more protested on April 10 in a National Day of Action for Immigrant Justice, including half a million in Dallas.[41]

Republicans were stunned by the size of the marches and the strong passions exhibited by protestors. Having incensed immigrants and minority voters, House Republicans also worried the bill would lead white voters to view them as mean-spirited and that it could harm their chances in the forthcoming 2006 elections. Sensenbrenner quickly offered an amendment to his own bill to make illegal residency a misdemeanor punishable by six months' prison rather than a felony, but it would remain a criminal offense. The amendment was defeated by an unusual coalition of 191 Democrats and sixty-five Republicans. The Republicans in opposition voted against it because it watered down the bill, while the Democrats in opposition voted against it because they "were not going to do anything to make it easier for Republicans to pass an atrocious bill," said Minority Leader Nancy Pelosi's spokesperson.[42] Some Republicans who supported the amendment rather shamelessly tried to spin the Democrats' opposition as hostility to Latino interests, while playing up their own pro-Latino credentials. A Republican National Committee ad on Spanish-language television argued, "Reid's Democrat allies voted to treat millions of hard-working immigrants as felons, while President Bush and Republican leaders work for legislation that will protect our borders and honor our immigrants." "It takes a pile of cynicism to spin this one as *Democratic* callousness," a Washington Post editorial responded.[43]

HR 4437, with the felony provision, was referred to the Senate on January 27, 2006, but it did not form the basis for the upper chamber's considerations, which began in mid March. Nonetheless, the bill had created considerable controversy and the Republican House had put down a strong marker regarding its immigration agenda. In the Senate, Republican presidential hopeful John McCain supported a guest-worker program and path to citizenship, with enhanced border security, which threatened to alienate conservative primary voters. Another hopeful, Majority Leader Bill Frist, keen to appeal to primary voters, introduced a bill (S 2454) with a provision criminalizing illegal residency but without Bush's guest-worker provision, even though Minority Leader Harry Reid promised to scupper any bill without it. After several weeks of debate and inter- and intraparty conflict, McCain and Senator Edward Kennedy threw their considerable weight behind a compromise bill, the Comprehensive Immigration Reform Act (S 2611), authored by Republican senators Mel Martinez and Chuck Hagel and sponsored by Senator Specter. Hagel-Martinez was essentially an amended version of the previous Congress's McCain-Kennedy bill, retaining both guest-worker and earned legalization provisions but splitting illegal immigrants into three categories. Undocumented residents of five or more years (estimated to number about eight million) would become legal guest-workers but have to pay fines and back taxes and work for a further six years to acquire legal residency. Undocumented immigrants resident between two and five years (estimated at three million) would have to leave the country and apply for guest-worker status at a designated port of entry, and would also be able to work towards legal residency. Those resident less than two years (one million) would not be allowed to stay. The bill would double the number of employment-based visas and make available a further 325,000 nonagricultural guest-worker visas for those applying from outside of the United States. The bill included the now usual provisions for beefing up the border, secure social security cards, and more stringent penalties for employing undocumented workers, but it did not like Frist's and Sensenbrenner's bills make unlawful presence a criminal offense.[44]

Prospects for S 2611, Hagel-Martinez, initially looked good in the Senate, with overwhelming Democratic backing and about half the Republican members on side or leaning towards it. However, Bush was initially hesitant about declaring his outright support because he worried that conservative Republicans would view its legalization provisions as an amnesty. In Sensenbrenner's narrow definition it certainly was—any program that switched an individual's status from illegal to legal, whether temporarily or permanently, was an amnesty. Bush, however, defined an amnesty any program that gave a group of people who broke the rules special advantage over those who didn't. Thus, legalization "would be unfair [if] it . . . allow[ed] people who break the law [by coming into the country illegally] to jump ahead of people . . . who play by the rules."[45] And in this definition Hagel-Martinez was probably not an amnesty. Although it offered a path to citizenship, applicants would have to join the queue. On April 24, Bush decided to publicly endorse the Hagel-Martinez: "A person ought to be allowed to . . . pay a penalty for being here illegally, commit him or herself to learn English . . . and get in the back of the line for citizenship."[46]

Despite Bush's endorsement of "the rational middle ground" and declaration that it was not an amnesty, most conservative Republicans believed firmly that it was. This and partisan conflicts stalled the bill. The Senate minority leader Harry Reid tried to stop Republicans offering amendments. He wanted to guard against conservatives postponing the introduction of the guest-worker and legalization provisions until untenable goals about border security were met. Democratic support also wavered after the AFL-CIO expressed opposition to the guest-worker program. John Sweeney, the union's president, while supportive of amnesty, argued that "guest-workers programs are a bad idea and harm all workers. They cast workers into a perennial second-class status and . . . encourage employers to turn good jobs into temporary jobs at reduced wages and diminished working conditions."[47] Senators from both parties were also unsure about the electoral consequences in November. Opinion polls showed Americans wanted tighter border security, but also indicated, subject to question wording, majority support for guest-worker and legalization provisions.[48] If the latter provisions were stripped out of a final bill leaving enforcement-only measures, most Democrats would have to vote against border security measures that most Americans wanted. On the other hand, many Senate Republicans feared being defined by the radical House bill if comprehensive reform failed in the Senate.[49] Most House Republicans, meanwhile, believed border security and cracking down on illegal immigrants domestically were popular in the nation and especially among core conservatives whose high electoral turnout could be critical.

Representatives with their more homogenous constituencies and two-year electoral cycle are traditionally more sensitive to short-term factors and public opinion than senators with larger, heterogeneous constituencies and six-year terms. The concentration of immigration conservatives in the House is no accident, but it presented Bush with one of his greatest challenges as his political stock fell in value: how to push the liberal immigration reform agenda without alienating House Republicans. While liberal immigration reform had sat on the backburner, pushed there largely by 9/11, Bush enjoyed a good relationship with fellow partisans in the House, but it would be strained as the immigration issue moved front and center. Moreover, while Bush's broad position on immigration reform was generally clear, he tried to avoid supporting specific congressional bills to allow fellow partisans to position-take and vote without undermining party unity. Bush's traditional legislative modus operandi was to set broad goals, let Congress thrash out the specifics, and step in at the end to broker a compromise if necessary, but with immigration reform stalled in the Senate, he came under considerable pressure from key Republicans, especially judiciary chair Arlen Specter, and Democrats to go beyond his endorsement and actually take a lead in breaking the deadlock. As senators ruminated on the immigration issue, a further large pro-immigration demonstration took place on May 1. Over 650,000 attended the Day Without Immigrants boycott in Los Angeles and tens of thousands of others marched around the country. While the first protests in March appeared to turn the tide against the harsh criminalizing provisions of the enforcement-only House bill, the May protest's effects were less clear. Bush opposed the demonstration and Senator Martinez worried that it would make compromise more problematic as passions were inflamed and positions entrenched.[50]

Sensing the prospect for reform and perhaps his legacy slipping away, Bush moved dramatically on May 15 by taking his case directly to the American people in his first televised presidential address on a domestic issue. He set out his support for a guest-worker program and path to citizenship, but focused heavily on enhanced security and enforcement measures to win over House Republicans and movement conservatives. He proposed better border fences, more border guards, more detention beds, biometric ID cards for foreign workers, and, most controversially, deploying the National Guard to help the Border Patrol. And when discussing the path to citizenship, great care was taken to emphasize that it was not an amnesty, because it would not fast-track applicants to the front of the legal residency queue as had the 1986 IRCA, and because applicants would have to meet strict criteria and pay fines and back taxes. Key members of the administration, including the president, Vice President Dick Cheney, and advisor Karl Rove, lobbied Congress and radio talk-show hosts on behalf of the plan in the ensuing days.

The response to Bush's intervention was generally underwhelming. Conservatives bemoaned the amnesty idea, whatever the president may have chosen to call it, and criticism on talk-radio was withering. Some of Bush's most vocal critics were conservative grassroots supporters who had backed him solidly through his presidency and continued to on Iraq and the war on terror. Even William Bennett, one of the few vocal Republican critics of Proposition 187, declared his opposition to the liberal bill—he denied his new job as talk-radio host was in any way responsible for the apparent conversion. Meanwhile, liberals complained vociferously that deploying the National Guard represented a de facto militarization of the border. When the Senate returned to immigration reform and started to debate S 2611 again in mid May, conservatives were in the ascendancy. Several important amendments were accepted to enhance security— including a further 370 miles of border fencing and excluding felons from the guest-worker and legalization programs—and to protect American workers from labor-market competition. The bill won the approval of the full Senate on May 25, 62-36. A majority of Republican senators, 32-23, voted against and the vast majority of Democrats voted for, 39-4. One independent also voted in favor. The amendments were designed in part to make the Senate version of immigration reform more attractive to House Republicans, but key GOP leaders there were unmoved by the Senate action and by the continuing lobbying efforts of Bush and others in his administration. Sensenbrenner said that a guest-worker bill may be acceptable to the House, but it would have to exclude legalization and be strong on enforcement. The irony for Bush is that the Senate bill would probably have won a majority in the House in 2006 based on Democratic support, but Republican Speaker Dennis Hastert would not let it come to a vote because it did not command the support of a majority of Republicans: the majority of the majority principle. Hastert had further bad news for Bush when he announced on June 20 House Republicans' plans to hold public immigration hearings over the summer recess. While ostensibly to tap public opinion, the hearings were used by House Republicans to attack and derail the president's liberal immigration agenda and the Senate's bill and represented a significant breakdown of party cohesion as the November 2006 midterm elections approached. Noted Tom Tancredo: "Odds were long that any so-called 'compromise bill' would get to the president's desk this year . . . The nail was already in the coffin of the Senate's amnesty plan. These hearings probably lowered it into the grave."[51] There was no discussion over summer between House and Senate conferees about ways to reconcile their bills.

The summer immigration hearings, along with the declining popularity of President Bush, projections of 2006 midterm seat losses for Republicans, and several immigrant-rights demonstrations in early September that drew much smaller crowds than those in March, April, and May, encouraged House Republicans to push again their enforcement and security agenda at the expense of comprehensive reform. Sensenbrenner's Border Protection, Antiterrorism and Illegal Immigration Control Act (HR 4437), approved by the House in December 2005, was broken up into a series of mini-bills that were swiftly passed, including on September 14 by 283-138 the Secure Fence Act (HR 6061) to build 700 miles of fencing along the U.S.-Mexico border. The Senate approved the Secure Fence Act on September 29, 80-19, as twenty-six Democrats joined fifty-four Republicans in the majority. Only one Republican, Lincoln Chafee of Rhode Island, voted against. While the SFA did not authorize any funds to build the fence—and a separate DHS spending bill, signed by the president on October 4, allocated just $1.2 billion of the estimated $6 billion needed for its construction— it was symbolically important to immigrant-rights activists, to those seeking to curb illegal entry and residency, and especially to the Mexican government, which formally asked President Bush to veto the legislation. President Vicente Fox called the proposed fence "shameful" and President-elect Felipe Calderon said, "the fence doesn't resolve anything. Humanity committed a grave mistake in building the Berlin Wall. I'm sure that the United States is committing a grave mistake in building this fence."[52] The Senate also approved House measures for yet more border guards and detention beds and to require citizens to use a passport to travel outside the United States, but it rejected the more radical measures to require state and local law-enforcement officials to enforce federal immigration law.

While the package of measures passed by the Senate was relatively moderate and modest, its passage was somewhat surprising given the sense in Washington in late 2006 was that Congress was deadlocked on the immigration issue with the elections approaching. Liberal reformers hoped the Senate action on security and enforcement would open up a future opportunity for guest-worker and legaliza-tion programs in the next Congress. "Many people have told me they will sup-port comprehensive immigration reform if we secure the border first. I hope we can use passage of this bill as a starting point toward long-term, comprehensive immigration reform," noted Republican Senator Sam Brownback.[53] "Yes, I'll sign [the SFA] into law. I would view this as an interim step. I don't view this as the final product," hoped Bush.[54] He did not, however, immediately make good on his promise to sign the bill. While the SFA would probably help motivate the conservative base to vote in the upcoming November elections, Bush worried about how it would play in the longer term among Latino voters, whom he had courted so assiduously throughout his presidency. With victory in the midterms looking less assured with each passing day and desperate to rally an increasingly discontented base, short-term considerations triumphed and Bush staged a public signing of the law on October 26 (PL 109-367). However, in his signing address the president emphasized again that the SFA was only one part of the required comprehensive solution and implied that the forthcoming 110th Congress may offer an opportunity for liberal reform.

> The Secure Fence Act is part of our efforts to reform our immigration system. We have more to do . . . .
> We must reduce pressure on our border by creating a temporary-worker plan. Willing workers ought to be matched with willing employers to do jobs Americans are not doing for a temporary—on a temporary basis.
> We must face the reality that millions of illegal immigrants are already here. They should not be given an automatic path to citizenship; that is amnesty. I oppose amnesty. There is a rational middle ground between granting an automatic pass to citizenship for every illegal immigrant and a program of mass deportation. And I look forward to working with Congress to find that middle ground.[55]

In sum, immigration reform in the 109th Congress proved damaging for the GOP and for President Bush. On one side, seeking to bring Latinos into the Republican coalition, Bush pushed hard for liberal reform. On the other, more concerned with their short-term reelection prospects, conservative House Republicans pursued an enforcement-only approach. Many Republican senators sat somewhere in-between, recognizing the political necessity of tying liberal reform to security in a more comprehensive package and perhaps even prioritizing security in an enforcement-first strategy. While never giving up on his plans for a guest-worker program and legalization, Bush too was forced to emphasize security as he worked with the Senate to reach a compromise. Bush's greatest success on immigration reform in the 109th Congress was the Senate's approval in May 2006 of S 2611, the Comprehensive Immigration Reform Act. His greatest failure was the House's rejection of it. Bush, however, refused to let the issue die, much to the chagrin of many in conservative circles who could not understand why he was prepared to invest so much political capital in an issue which divided the party ideologically and electorally.

The 110th Congress

The politics of immigration reform changed again after the 2006 midterm elections as the Democrats took control of both the Senate and House, ostensibly opening up the opportunity for President Bush to strike a deal on comprehensive immigration reform with the new majority whose median position was closer to his than was his own party's. At his first postelection press conference, Bush highlighted immigration as "a vital issue . . . where I believe we can find some common ground with Democrats," and his appointment of Mel Martinez, a Cuban refugee and coauthor of the Senate's comprehensive immigration legislation (S 2611), reaffirmed the national GOP leadership's determination to push ahead with liberal reform. The defeat of several prominent enforcement-only Republicans in the midterms—including incumbents such as House immigration subcommittee chair John Hostettler in Indiana, J. D. Hayworth in Arizona, and Rick Santorum in Pennsylvania, and challengers such as Minuteman cofounder Randy Graf who failed to win an open seat in Arizona—suggested that comprehensive reform may be a more potent electoral force than enforcement-only. New speaker Nancy Pelosi and new Senate majority leader Harry Reid said they hoped they could work with the president, who with Iraq threatening his ratings, prestige, and legacy, was keener than ever to push comprehensive reform. It would perhaps be his last chance of success before bowing out of politics in 2008.

Even with Senator Edward Kennedy installed as the Senate immigration sub-committee chair, comprehensive reform was far from a done deal, however. The labor unions continued to express doubts about a guest-worker program, although they were generally onside for legalization. It was not a top priority for Democrats in the midterms and did not constitute part of their first "100 Hours" agenda. Pelosi and Reid's primary short-term concern was to ensure the Democrats retained control of Congress in 2008, and it was not clear that comprehensive immigration reform would aid that goal. The uncertain longer-term electoral consequences of Bush signing a comprehensive reform bill—would Democrats share in the credit, or would it hand the Republican Party the keys to the Latino vote for generations to come?—further reduced the incentives for Democrats to push hard for reform. Many of the 2007 Democratic freshmen were so-called "blue-dogs," as conservative on immigration issues as many Republicans. Enough Democrats now opposed a guest-worker and/or legalization program to require Bush and the liberal reformers to rely on Republican votes in both houses. "Just because we have the majority doesn't mean we have enough votes for an immigration reform bill. We're going to have to take the temperature," noted House Democrat Lorreta Sanchez.[56] The forthcoming 2008 presidential primaries and election would further politicize the immigration issue and complicate the electoral calculus on an issue where public opinion was already difficult to read. Moreover, immigration is "a hot-button issue, it's a racism issue, it's a terrorism issue; of course it's scary for Democrats to get in the way of that. [It's] hard to explain in 30 seconds, particularly if the other side is using the word amnesty," reasoned one Latino strategist concerned about conservative attempts to frame the debate in terms Democrats would find difficult to defend.[57] Finally, the bitter interparty conflict on Iraq would tarnish the dealings between parties on all issues and make compromise more difficult to reach on immigration.

Whatever the impediments to reform in the 110th Congress, the prospect looked better than it had done prior to the 2006 November midterms. Even before Congress convened in January, Kennedy was already busy preparing the ground to push a comprehensive reform bill in 2007, working with senators McCain and Specter, representatives Jeff Flake, an Arizona Republican, and Luis Gutierrez, an Illinois Democrat, and some White House staff. As McCain and the representatives began to drift away from the negotiations, Kennedy began to work closely with two cabinet secretaries, Michael Chertoff of homeland security and Carlos Gutierrez of commerce, and around a dozen senators, evenly split between the parties, to thrash out a bipartisan comprehensive reform bill. The lead Republican negotiator was John Kyl of Arizona and he was joined by Saxby Chambliss (Georgia), Lindsey Graham (South Carolina), Johnny Isakson (Georgia), Mel Martinez (Florida), and Arlen Specter (Pennsylvania). The other five Democrats in addition to Kennedy were Richard Durbin (Illinois), Dianne

Feinstein (California), Patrick Leahy (Vermont), Ken Salazar (Colorado), and Charles Schumer (New York). Two senators, Democrat Robert Menendez (New Jersey) and Republican John Cornyn (Texas), dropped out when compromises were struck which they could not support. The group became known as the grand bargainers and would play a crucial role in the progress of immigration reform in the 110th Congress (2007–2008).

Reform-minded Republicans tried to build support by pointing to declining apprehension figures on the border and suggesting that the Republican midterm defeat was in part a consequence of the GOP's hard-line in the House. "I think we have to understand that the election did speak to one issue, and that was that it's not about bashing people, it's about presenting a hopeful face. . . . Border security only, enforcement only, harshness only is not the message that I believe America wants to convey," argued Martinez. "To be the party of the future means that we also have to be a party that opens the door wide so that all Americans feel welcome."[58] Other Republican strategists suggested that the enforcement-only approach pushed Latinos to the polls and toward the Democratic Party—the GOP won only 30 percent of the Latino vote in 2006, while Bush won over 40 percent two years earlier—while failing to motivate moderate and swing voters. Critics of the Martinez-Rove-Bush outreach to Latinos, however, spun defeat as the public's rejection of the president's immigration agenda, comparing the GOP's loss of nearly 12 percent of its congressional seats with Tancredo's immigration caucus's 6 percent. They also found comfort in a January 2007 *LA Times/Bloomberg* poll that showed that while 14 percent of respondents thought the president and Congress should make tighter enforcement of immigration laws their top priority only 2 percent said it should be a guest-worker program.[59] Still others argued that the defeat was a consequence of congressional and White House scandals, Katrina, Iraq, misinformation about weapons of mass destruction (WMD), and negative economic perceptions, not immigration policy.

Early Moves

Bush renewed his determination to push forward with reform in his 2007 State of the Union address, although his language was again cautious given the bruising battles with his own party in the previous Congress. He noted the "need to resolve the status of the illegal immigrants who are already in our country, without animosity and without amnesty," while calling for moderation, because "convictions run deep in this Capitol when it comes to immigration. Let us have a serious, civil, and conclusive debate so that you can pass—and I can sign—comprehensive immigration reform into law." Kennedy complimented the president's commitment, but Tancredo promised to fight him while admitting he was now on the defensive, seeking to preserve the enforcement-only triumphs of the 109th Congress. Others complained that Bush was tearing the party apart. "You can hear the hammer drive the wedge right into the Republican Party," declared Republican representative Steve King of Iowa.[60] In the mid 1990s, in contrast, the party had tried to drive the immigration wedge into the Democratic coalition.

Democratic strategists initially estimated that comprehensive reform required the support of about twenty Senate and forty House Republicans to provide cover for Democrats opposed to the proposals. Twenty-one of the twenty-three

Republican senators who voted for S 2611, Hagel-Martinez, in May 2006 retained their seats in the midterms, suggesting comprehensive reform stood a good chance in the upper chamber in 2007. In the House, however, no vote had been taken on comprehensive reform so it was more difficult to calculate with any certainty the likelihood of success. The forty GOP votes was a very rough estimate. Most observers thought the best chance of success would be realized by moving the bill slightly to the right to win over some conservative Democrats, moderate Republicans, and the more moderate of the conservative Republicans— the staunchly conservative Republicans would never vote for it. In practice this would require a bill heavy on interior and border enforcement and light on amnesty. Legal permanent residency would have to be hard-earned by previously illegal immigrants with large fines and fees, many years of guest-work, and the possibility of leaving the United States to make an application. In this light, the Hagel-Martinez path to citizenship was perhaps too generous and, anyway, its three-tier approach looked overly complex and had been criticized by the Bush administration as potentially difficult for the immigration bureaucracy to implement. Pushing the bill too far to the right was not a problem-free solution, however, because it risked alienating liberal Democrats.[61] Any vote would likely be precariously balanced.

According to Kennedy, he met with Bush on January 8 and was assured by his commitment to comprehensive reform. The administration worked hard behind the scenes in January and February 2007 to allay the fears of key lawmakers, with Secretary Chertoff playing the point role. He held one-to-one briefings with enforcement-first members of Congress to detail recent successes in strengthening the border and deterring illegal immigration, evening taking some skeptics and members of the immigration and judiciary committees from both chambers on a helicopter tour of the U.S.-Mexico border to witness the extra security, including the construction of new sections of fence and expanded detention facilities. Chertoff hoped that the expansion of border security and interior enforcement, including stepped-up work-site raids on large employers of illegal labor (farms and meat-packing plants, for example) and a drop in the number of border interceptions, would persuade them to throw their weight behind comprehensive reform.[62] Meanwhile, Bush met with Democrats at their annual retreat in early February, the first time since 2001, and joked that he had been "shot in the back" by House Republicans on immigration. Both he and new House speaker Nancy Pelosi suggested they could work together to find common ground on the controversial issue.[63]

Hearings on immigration reform began in the Senate on February 28, 2007, in Patrick Leahy's judiciary committee but Kennedy continued to work outside the committee system to construct his grand bargain. Despite clear evidence of behind-the-scenes engagement by the White House in thrashing out a compromise bill, some Democrats still worried about the extent to which the administration, and Bush in particular, would engage with congressional Republicans to persuade or pressure them to support liberal reform, especially given the extent to which the issue was dividing the party in Washington and at the grassroots. Secretaries Chertoff and Gutierrez both emphasized Bush's support. "We believe that with some hard work a solution can be found, and we pledge to roll up our sleeves and work with you on a bipartisan basis," promised Gutierrez.[64]

However, neither official specified Bush's preferred solution to the question of legalizing illegal immigrants already in the United States, which many Republicans would regard as an amnesty even if they paid a fine and were not allowed to jump the citizenship queue. It was also not clear how much influence they and Bush would have on recalcitrant Republicans given the president's declining authority and political leverage largely but not entirely as a result of the Iraqi quagmire. As noted above, Bush liked to set broad goals, let members of Congress hammer out the details, and come in at the end to deliver the make-or-break votes, but both Democrats and Republicans now called for his decisive and early intervention. Bush, in turn, expressed concern about the absence of "a coherent Republican position in the Senate" while admitting that Republican support for a bill was critical to any deal.[65]

As the congressional debate dragged on, the immigration issue raised its head in the presidential contest. Many commentators suggested that Congress would have to strike a deal before August 2007, after which presidential politics would further politicize the issue, making compromise on comprehensive reform more problematic. However, the particularly open nature of both parties' primaries and a primary season pushed forward by states eager to influence the outcome in 2008 made the initial assessment of August look optimistic. The issue began to impinge as early as February 2007 when presidential hopeful and former liberal Republican governor of Massachusetts, Mitt Romney, criticized John McCain's position on immigration reform, categorizing it as support for amnesty and linking him closely with liberal icon, Senator Kennedy. Romney's attack was not without risk given that he had already been embarrassed by revelations that he employed undocumented gardeners, by evidence that he had previously called McCain's immigration position "reasonable," and by allegations that his new anti-immigration, anti–gay marriage, pro-life, and pro-gun positions were little more than political expediency born of desperation to appeal to the conservative Republican primary electorate.[66]

To add to Bush's problems, the bipartisan negotiators struggled to agree the details of a new comprehensive reform package through March. McCain was particularly concerned about increased labor protections demanded by unions for guest- and native workers and the extent of the legalization program. His commitment to reform, or at least leading the reform effort, waned further as the Republican primary contest intensified more than nine months before the first formal vote. During a March trip to Iowa, he was pilloried for his pro-immigration position and shocked by the vehemence of citizens' attitudes. Immigration never previously figured as a particularly salient issue in the early primary states of Iowa, New Hampshire, and South Carolina, but as more illegal immigrants migrated north from the border states to find jobs in meatpacking factories, the issue grew in importance.[67] Matters worsened for McCain and other liberal reformers when Tancredo entered the presidential race on April 2. Tancredo, who resigned as chair of the congressional immigration caucus to concentrate on his presidential bid and who claimed that Karl Rove told him "never to darken the doorstep of the White House" because of his anti-immigration views, made his announcement on talk-radio, a medium where illegal immigration was a prominent talking point, and suggested that it would form the centerpiece of his campaign. He followed it up with around twenty more calls to radio stations around the United States rather than holding the traditional public rally. Unlike most elite Republicans, Tancredo had little sympathy for big business's appetite for cheap, plentiful migrant labor and was more in touch with Republican rank-and-file attitudes. His presence in the race not only made the immigration issue more salient but helped pull the locus of debate to the right. In response, McCain tried to distance himself from Kennedy and legislation he helped write less than a year ago and intimated that he was increasingly attracted by the idea that illegal residents would have to leave the United States to apply for legal residency status.

The focus on immigration also proved problematic for another leading contender for the Republican nomination, Rudy Giuliani, former Mayor of New York City. During the 1990s Mayor Giuliani was a prominent Republican defender of legal immigration. He even led efforts to encourage illegal immigrants to become citizens, instructed his city's employees not to enquire about a person's immigration status, and equated the anti-immigrant climate of the 1990s to the nativist movement of the late nineteenth and early twentieth centuries. Given his past and the climate among Republican primary voters, Giuliani rarely raised the immigration issue voluntarily during his quest for the presidency in 2007. When he was forced to address it by the press or public, he emphasized the importance of enforcement and security and learning English and tried to underplay his earlier support for a Bush-McCain-Kennedy-style legalization program, referring instead to his opposition to amnesty.[68] Tancredo noted skeptically, "It's certainly the case that the rhetoric is beginning to shift. I don't believe for a second that anybody's heart is shifting with it."[69]

The machinations surrounding the presidential contest exacerbated Kennedy's and other negotiators' difficulties in constructing a new Senate bill, but the White House tried to talk up the likelihood of a breakthrough, putting the word around that there was enough Republican support in Congress for comprehensive reform to win a vote. Democratic leaders were less sure. They now estimated that twenty-five Republican votes would be needed in the Senate and perhaps as many as seventy in the House, compared to original estimates of twenty and forty respectively. Support against comprehensive reform appeared to be hardening on both sides of the partisan divide. In mid April the Senate still had no bill to consider, yet Reid had set aside the second half of May to discuss it.

Frustrated by the lack of progress in the Senate, Gutierrez and Flake introduced their own comprehensive reform bill in the House on March 22, called the Security Through Regularized Immigration and a Vibrant Economy Act (STRIVE, HR 1645). The bill drew on the negotiations between them, Kennedy, and McCain, but was designed to appeal to conservatives wary of amnesty by requiring illegal immigrants to leave the United States, albeit briefly, and reenter legally to be eligible for the path to citizenship. As well as numerous security and enforcement provisions, the bill also included DREAM and AgJobs, but made no progress in the chamber. The White House also tried to kick-start the process by presenting its own comprehensive reforms in early April. However, in contrast to the very public presentation and subsequent failure of the president's last plan in January 2004, the current presentation was in private to Republican members of Congress only. The proposals included indefinitely renewable three-year guest-worker visas costing $3,500 each time, and a path to citizenship requiring the guest-workers to return home to make an application for legal residency accompanied by payment of a $10,000 fine. When news of the plan became public, immigrant-rights advocates reacted angrily to the size of the fees and fines and the impediments put in the path toward citizenship. Reaction from conservative Republicans was also critical, describing the legalization provision as an amnesty. The White House responded by suggesting that the plans were not concrete, just ideas for discussion.

Debate but No Bill

By late April, with two weeks' floor debate scheduled to begin May 14, a bipartisan bill remained elusive. Republicans were looking to move any nascent bill to the right, arguing that the political environment had shifted in favor of security and enforcement. While some Republican senators were prepared to support a relatively liberal bill in May 2006 in the knowledge that the more conservative House would strip out objectionable provisions, they were determined to take a harsher stance in 2007 out of fear that a liberal bill could be liberalized further by the now Democratic House. Liberal Democrats, on the other hand, thought the negotiations had already pushed the prospective bill too far to the right, and immigrant-rights advocates were whispering that it was too conservative to support. Polls showed the public wanted action. In Gallup's May 21–24 poll 24 percent of respondents placed immigration as the "top priority for the president and Congress to deal with at this time," surpassed only by the Iraq war; and its April 13–15 poll showed that only 12 percent thought "the US had made progress in dealing with illegal immigration in the past year," compared to 43 percent who thought ground had been lost and 42 percent who saw no change.[70] All sides exhorted Bush to step up to the mark: "The president has got to be personally involved. He cannot just send up Cabinet members and ask them to speak with a few members of the president's party and [expect] that that's going to get you through," said Senate judiciary chair Patrick Leahy.[71]

Popular outrage among the Latino and immigrant communities was muted, however, compared with one year earlier. A repeat of the May 1 demonstration drew much smaller crowds in 2007 across the nation. The demonstration in Los Angeles proved an exception to the generally low-key protests, not because of its size but because it ended in violence. Protestors threw missiles at police officers, who responded with baton charges and foam bullets. The heavy-handed tactics were captured by television cameras, and two senior officers were reassigned to lower grade posts by LAPD police chief Willie Bratton in response.[72] Conservatives also tried to put pressure on Congress and the White House to reconsider comprehensive reform. Numbers USA organized an impressive grass-roots campaign, sending hundreds of thousands of letters, faxes, and emails to members of Congress expressing outrage at the prospect of an amnesty and overwhelming their phones with angry calls. In one innovative event, coorganized by the Federation for American Immigration Reform, more than thirty radio talk-show hosts and some of their listeners gathered in Washington in late April to broadcast and lobby. Tancredo was their hero and Bush, McCain, and Kennedy their enemies.[73]

While Congress continued to struggle to find a solution to the immigration problems, states and cities offered their own solutions. Many cities, such as Farmers Branch outside Dallas, Texas, and Hazelton, Pennsylvania, outlawed renting apartments to undocumented residents. Hazelton also required its residents to prove their citizenship by registering with city authorities and threatened to close down businesses that employed illegal workers. Many bills filed in state legislatures threatened to cut illegal immigrants' access to state healthcare and welfare benefits, tax the remittances wired by U.S.-based workers to their families back home, and bar illegals from obtaining drivers' licenses and in-state tuition fees. Colorado passed some of the nation's harshest anti-illegal-immigrant laws, which, according to farmers, resulted in severe labor shortages. In response, farmers tried to strike a deal to use convicts in the state prisons to harvest the crops. It became a crime to use fake citizenship documents in Wyoming and for state agencies to do business with firms employing undocumented labor in Arkansas. The National Conference of State Legislatures estimated that over 1,000 bills dealing with immigration were introduced in state capitols in the 2007 legislative session, double the previous year's, which itself represented a significant increase on earlier years. Not all were restrictive initiatives, however. Some sought to protect undocumented children, others to improve the quality of noncitizens' legal representation. Some cities declared themselves havens for undocumented residents and instructed law-enforcement personnel not to query people's immigration status. On an individual level, some businesses, especially close to the border, began to accept payment for goods and services in pesos as well as dollars.[74]

The negotiators missed Reid's deadline of May 14, but managed to produce a bipartisan bill on May 17. It was very long at 760 pages, complicated, unwieldy, full of inelegant compromises and caveats, and delicately held together in places, but it was a bill as promised. Its path to citizenship was surprisingly generous in scope, with nearly all the estimated twelve million illegal immigrants in the United States before January 2007 eligible for legal status. Having won a permit to remain, previously illegal workers could on passing a criminal background check and paying a $6,500 fee/fine apply for new Z visas of four years' duration, renewable indefinitely. The visas would allow holders to live and work legally in the United States. After eight years they would be able to apply for legal permanent residency and five years later citizenship, but neither would be automatic. There would be no privileges over others seeking green cards; they would have to get in line. They would not have to leave the United States to apply for Z visas, but would have to "touch back" home to make the permanent residency application.

Its guest-worker program, which was decoupled from the legalization provisions, would provide about 400,000 workers resident outside the United States with two-year visas, renewable three times, after which they must return home with no prospect of permanent residency. Workers would have to leave the United States for one year between each work period. Unions argued the TWP would push down wages of American workers.

Significantly for conservatives, the introduction of the legalization and guest-worker programs would be triggered only after a massive build up of border and workplace security, including nearly 600 miles of real and virtual fences, seventy camera towers, more detention facilities, and an expansion of Basic Pilot to meet the requirement that employers check the legal status of all new hires within eighteen months and all current employees within three years. Chertoff optimistically estimated that the enforcement provisions could be in place in eighteen months, which was the nonbinding deadline set by the bill for the authorities to achieve "operational control" of the border. A new points system would be established to allow in highly skilled and educated workers, with extra points available for English speakers, family ties, and work experience with U.S. firms in tight labor markets. The new points-based visas would be at the expense of some visas for parents, adult children and siblings set aside under the old family reunification rules, which alarmed many Asian and some Latino advocacy groups, and thus many members of Congress.[75]

Response

Immediate prospects for the bipartisan deal did not look good, with nearly all sides finding some things objectionable. While acknowledging the bill was far from perfect, supporters pleaded with colleagues to recognize that it probably represented the only opportunity to reform what they and the public considered a broken system. "The world is watching to see how we respond to the current crisis. Let's not disappoint them," said Kennedy.[76] Many in opposition were more than happy to disappoint the world and Kennedy. The bipartisan negotiators, or grand bargainers, were shocked by the vehemence of Tancredo's and other conservatives' reaction to the legalization provisions, but also by the negative reactions of most interested parties. Even high-tech firms, widely regarded as a big winner in the bill, and business groups objected that the TWP was impractical and the points-based visas inflexible; they complained too about having to verify workers' status. Very liberal senators, such as Vermont independent Bernard Sanders and California Democrat Barbara Boxer, also opposed the TWP and expressed grave concern about the loss of family reunification visas. The League of United Latin American Citizens and other Latino advocacy groups also came out against the bill. Even with opinion polls suggesting widespread support among Americans for the bill's key measures and the Senate voting 69-23 to continue debate on the issues, the prospect of progressing to a final vote looked poor as dozens of wrecking amendments were tabled and conservatives promised a filibuster.[77]

To protect the bill from attacks the bipartisan grand bargainers promised to hold firm against amendments that threatened its philosophical underpinnings: enhanced border and interior security including effective employer monitoring of employees' status, the legalization of undocumented persons already in the United States, a TWP for future workers, and a points-based system to reward skills and education over family ties. While they were largely successful, at least initially, the grand bargainers were unable to force a vote on the bill before Congress recessed for a week-long Memorial Day break at the end of May and feared that critics would use it rally opposition and that supporters would begin to waver under the pressure. Some did. The opposition of several prominent Latino groups made some liberal Democrats, such as senators Hillary Clinton and Robert Menendez, question the efficacy of downgrading family reunification. Under pressure from industrial unions, other Democrats worried about the effects of the TWP on American workers, although countervailing pressure from service unions helped reinforce support for legalization. Republican senators and grand bargainers Saxby Chambliss and Lindsey Graham felt the heat from Republican constituents in Georgia and South Carolina who booed and heckled them for their support for the bipartisan bill. Rush Limbaugh took to calling it the Destroy the Republican Party Act and conservative bloggers attacked it unremittingly. Grassroots conservatives continued to make a lot of noise against the bill; few liberals made much noise in support.

Republicans traded psephological wisdoms and insults as immigration conservatives made the case for restriction and immigration liberals for inclusion. Limbaugh said legalization not only alienated core Republican voters and potential swing voters but would deliver the Democrats "a brand new electorate . . . to win election after election after election." Martinez countered that

> to not play this card would be the destruction of our party. Hispanics make up about 13% of our country and by 2020 will be closer to 20%. It is a demographic trend that one cannot overlook. He [Limbaugh] has emotion on his side, but I think I have logic on mine.[78]

In a debate between ten Republican presidential candidates in New Hampshire on June 5, immigration vied with Iraq as the most prominent and contentious issue, but only McCain offered his support for the bipartisan bill. It was described as "a typical Washington mess" by Giuliani and "disastrous" by Representative Duncan Hunter. Hunter also reminded the audience of McCain's current and Giuliani and Romney's previously liberal positions on immigration: "I think the guy who's got the most influence right here with these three gentlemen is Ted Kennedy." Tancredo complained that the United States was "becoming a bilingual nation" and all candidates expressed support for making English America's official language. However, the other candidates chided Tancredo when he suggested legal immigration should be suspended. There was considerable hostility to illegal immigration within the GOP, but Tancredo's position on legal immigration, regarded as mainstream in Republican circles a decade ago, was now viewed as extreme.[79]

In a moment of rare candor and a sign of Bush's frustration, the intra-party conflict reached a new low on May 29 when the president turned on conservative critics of the bill in a ferocious attack that could well help define his legacy and relationship with his base. In a speech at the Federal Law Enforcement Training Center in Georgia where, among others, border guards are trained, he accused conservatives of not having read the bill and using "empty political rhetoric" to "rile up people's emotions" and undermine the "last, best chance" to reform a broken system. "The bill is not an amnesty bill. If you want to scare the American people, what you say is 'the bill's an amnesty bill.' It's not an amnesty bill. That's empty political rhetoric trying to frighten our fellow citizens."[80] Conservative sensibilities were especially offended by Bush's apparent impugning of their patriotism when he said, in an alleged ad-libbed addition to the speech, that those who opposed the bill "don't want to do what's right for America."[81] Establishment conservatives expressed disappointment and hurt at Bush's attack, but internet message boards and bloggers were much less restrained, with some writers mentioning impeachment.

As senators returned to work on June 4 after the Memorial Day recess, the grand bargainers were confident they could hold together the tentative majority coalition, despite the furor caused by Bush's attack on his own party. They had hitherto rebuffed several killer amendments to remove the legalization and TWP provisions, two of the bill's core tenets, and believed that they had won the argument that a broken immigration system needed fixing in the current and perhaps only window of opportunity. However, opponents continued to table amendments designed to undermine the solidarity of the grand bargainers by trying to offer provisions that would be irresistible to some but anathema to others. Several were accepted that undermined but didn't destroy the delicate compromise. A successful Democratic proposal to scrap the TWP after five years lost the bill the support of several Republicans. In a Machiavellian twist, four conservative Republicans supported the amendment only two weeks after opposing it, enabling it to win a narrow one vote victory. "I've been trying to kill [the bill] since the beginning," noted a satisfied Jim Bunning, one of the Republican senators who switched their vote.[82] Conversely, a successful Republican proposal to deny legalizing immigrants' access to earned-income tax credit lost the bill the support of several Democrats, who argued it was becoming overly punitive.

More significantly for the bill's progress, Majority Leader Reid became increasingly frustrated with what he perceived to be a conservative filibuster to prevent a final vote. His personal support for the bill was never more than tepid. He had severe reservations about the grand bargain, the compromise at its core, with liberals getting legalization and conservatives border and interior security, a TWP, and a points-based visa system, and he had long viewed the bill as the president's, not the Democratic Party's. Reid decided to try to invoke cloture on June 7 to stop debate and force a final vote. A first attempt in the morning garnered only thirty-three votes, well short of the sixty necessary to end debate. Every Republican and fifteen Democrats voted against it. Knowing that Reid was planning a further cloture vote and would probably pull the bill from the floor if it were not successful, GOP leaders including Minority Leader Mitch McConnell and Minority Whip Trent Lott worked hard the rest of the day to tie down conservatives to a finite list of amendments, but could not reach an agreement. Various pressure groups did not help the cloture case, either, urging friendly senators to hold out against ending debate in order to win changes for the groups' various and often incommensurate causes. The United States Conference of Catholic Bishops, for example, and several immigrant-rights advocacy groups suggested they were prepared to see the bill die rather than allow a cut in family reunification visas, and business groups who wanted changes to the TWP threatened to withdraw their support if they didn't get them. The collective pressure exerted by special interests was significant and detrimental to helping end debate, but it appeared that they had not considered the consequences of their actions. They were shocked at what happened next, but they should not have been.

Two Failures

At around 7 pm on June 7 Kennedy met with Reid to plead for more debate time to mollify Republican senators. The majority leader refused and pushed a second attempt at cloture at about 9 pm, knowing it was unlikely to receive the necessary sixty votes. It failed as expected. Thirty-seven Democrats, seven Republicans, and one independent, a total of forty-five, supported cloture while eleven Democrats, thirty-eight Republicans and one independent, a total of fifty, voted to continue debate. Reid pulled the bill from the floor. It appeared dead. The majority leader squarely blamed Republicans for filibustering the bill with an interminable series of amendments and blamed Bush for being unable to deliver the Republican votes necessary for passage—with thirty-eight of forty-eight Republicans voting against cloture on the president's primary domestic policy initiative, it was an argument not without basis, although Bush was in Europe during the debate making personal intervention problematic. Chertoff and Gutierrez had remained in Washington to lobby Republican senators directly, but had little effect. Republicans in turn blamed Reid for unnecessarily and presumptively trying to end debate on key issues of concern. Specter, a participant in immigration reform for many years, blamed both sides, but apportioned greater fault to his own party: "The Democrats were wrong" to stifle debate, "but Republicans were wronger [sic]" for not striking a deal among themselves to end it.[83] Martinez said it was a terrible indictment of the Senate, which "today bipartisanly failed the American people. That's plain and simple."[84]

Several of the grand bargainers claimed that the bill was not dead. Arlen Specter said it was only on life support and Kennedy made clear his intent to try again. Many pressure groups switched position, suddenly realizing that a flawed bill was better than no bill—as a grand bargain, it offered something for all sides, but it required compromises on all sides—and began to lobby for its revival. Reid said immediately after pulling the bill that he would not try again, but soon recanted under pressure, suggesting he may bring it back to the floor with some preconditions: "The White House has so far failed the rally Senate Republicans behind tough, fair and practical immigration reform. I will bring the immigration bill back to the Senate floor as soon as enough Republicans are ready to join us in moving forward on a bill to fix our broken immigration system."[85] Reid was looking for the Republicans to commit to a limited number of amendments in exchange for extra debate time possibly in late June, a proposal the lead Republican grand bargainer Senator Jon Kyl endorsed, even though he originally voted against cloture. Martinez announced that the president would fight on after his return from Europe and planned to lobby personally for it on Capitol Hill at the Republican senators' weekly policy luncheon on June 12.[86]

Motivated by Bush's personal intervention and inspired by Reid's conditional promise to bring the bill back, the grand bargainers set to work again to find a compromise on a limited package of amendments, eventually settling on about a dozen each from Republican and Democratic senators. The Bush administration also worked to win back the support of business groups, especially high-tech firms, and Republican whip Trent Lott claimed he could deliver enough GOP votes for cloture.[87]

Reid agreed to bring the bill back to floor, but its progress remained uncertain in the face of a difficult series of procedural hurdles and the renewed commitment of conservative Republicans to kill it. "The process has been rigged from the beginning," said South Carolina Senator Jim DeMint, referring to the small, closed group of grand bargainers who wrote the law and Reid's controversial bypass of the usual committee process, "which we think gives us justification to use every measure possible to slow this thing down and stop it."[88] President Bush did not escape DeMint's ire, either: "The White House has climbed way out on a limb, and we're going to cut it off," he promised.[89] Procedurally, the bill had to win a cloture motion before debate could begin and another before a final vote could take place. Thus, sixty senators' approval was required for the bill to go to the floor for consideration of the new amendments. Most observers were confident there was enough support, because wavering senators were keen to see if the bill could be changed to their liking. Observers were much less sanguine about the success of the second cloture motion to close debate and permit a final vote. Supporters of the bill had managed to rally only forty-five votes to end debate on June 7, and several Democrats and Republicans had since defected to the opposition, including two Republican grand bargainers, Georgia senators Isakson and Chambliss. Moreover, the Republican minority leader Mitch McConnell was increasingly ambivalent about the bill. He had been throughout his term a White House loyalist and he wanted to help the president achieve his domestic policy goals, but he did not want to use his leadership position to bully Republican senators into supporting a bill a majority of them opposed. Moreover, he personally thought it a poor piece of legislation and was uneasy with the compromise. He continued to work to facilitate debate without taking a definitive stand on it.[90] Trent Lott, his deputy and minority whip, did put his head above the parapet, intimating his support for the bill and criticizing talk-radio hosts for whipping up hysteria. He stock among conservatives, previously high, sunk rapidly. Bloggers called him a traitor, his offices received thousands of angry letters, and anti-immigration activists jammed his phone lines to protest his support for the bill. Lott later appeared to backtrack, claiming, "I'm not committed to voting for the final produce. The wheels may come off. But I'm committed to trying."[91] The cacophony of grassroots voices looked like it may tip a few other senators into opposition, too.

Negotiators continued to fine-tune the various amendment as supporters won the first cloture vote, as expected, 64-35 on June 26. Thirty-nine Democrats, twenty-four Republicans, and one independent voted to restart debate on the bill; nine Democrats, twenty-five Republicans, and one independent voted against. However, worryingly for supporters, the vote indicated that Democratic support was waning—five switched their June 7 vote from support to opposition. Meanwhile, a further blow was struck in the House where the Republicans passed a nonbinding resolution expressing disapproval of the Senate immigration bill, 114-23. The twenty-three in support was well short of the seventy Republican votes Speaker Pelosi estimated she needed to shepherd a liberal, comprehensive immigration reform bill though the lower chamber.[92]

The Senate negotiators were in very difficult position. Most of the significant prospective amendments they had crafted were aimed at accommodating conservative Republicans' concerns about "amnesty" and border security, but as the bill moved to the right it looked likely to alienate enough Democrats to seriously jeopardize success in the second cloture motion. During debate on June 27 supporters managed to defeat most amendments that challenged the bill's core, such as a conservative one to prevent holders of Z visas applying for legal permanent residency and a liberal one to tilt the points system in favor of family ties. However, they were unable to defeat an amendment undermining the requirement for employers to check their employees' legal status. Moreover, conservative Republicans led by DeMint used parliamentary maneuvers to stifle debate on amendments designed to appeal to fellow conservatives. Specter described it as "trench warfare" and the congressional switchboard and servers collapsed under the weight of calls and emails from citizens.[93] With the Senate unable to fully consider several amendments that the grand bargainers had designed to move the bill subtly to the right to win over wavering Republicans, Reid invoked another cloture motion on June 28 to try to end debate and force a final up-down vote. It lost, and by a considerable margin. Supporters were only able to garner forty-six votes in favor of cloture from thirty-three Democrats, twelve Republicans, and one independent, fourteen short; opponents won fifty-three votes from fifteen Democrats, thirty-seven Republicans, and one independent. The bill was dead and President Bush defeated.

Conclusions

Emotions after the vote were mixed. Many of the bill's opponents, especially conservative Republicans, were jubilant. Bush was downcast, depressed even, an emotion rarely exhibited by the preternaturally positive president. Kennedy was furious, calling opponents "voices of fear."[94] Specter turned on Republican colleagues who had supported and even helped write the bill, implying but not naming senators Chambliss and Isakson, both grand bargainers, but who abdicated when grassroots pressure built. Specter called them cynical and contrasted them with the principled and courageous Senator McCain.[95] Mexican president Felipe Calderon called the defeat a "grave error."

For Bush the defeat represented the end of his immigration reform agenda and his grand second-term ambitions. He had planned to spend his political capital reforming social security and the tax code, limiting medical malpractice suits and creating an ownership society, as well as leaving a significant electoral and policy legacy with immigration reform.[96] There was little return on his considerable investment. All the lobbying, all the effort, came to nought. Worse still for Bush, defeat on immigration reform came in the same week that Richard Lugar, the highly respected ranking Republican on, and former chair of, the Senate armed services committee, argued that Bush's strategy in Iraq had failed and that the United States must withdraw. His presidency was unraveling at a remarkable speed.

During Bush's tenure, Congress spent nearly seven years on and off examining immigration problems and potential solutions. Several times the president's favored comprehensive reform came back from the political dead; it is unlikely to from the June 28 defeat, however. Bush himself offered little hope: "A lot of us worked hard to see if we couldn't find a common ground. It didn't work." Martinez was equally pessimistic: "It's time to get real. I don't see where the will is there for this issue to be resolved."[97] Two of the Senate's oldest heads, while disappointed, took a longer-term view. "We will be back. This issue is not going away. And we will ultimately be successful . . . You cannot stop the march for progress in the United States," observed Kennedy, drawing on the example of the civil rights movements and its defeats over the years.[98] Specter, Kennedy's bipartisan colleague, noted sanguinely, "some legislation takes many years . . . this is just a bump in the road."[99]

The reasons for the defeat of Bush's comprehensive immigration reform are many. Most notably, Bush was undone by events, first 9/11 and later Iraq. After 9/11 immigration became a security issue and liberalization slipped from the political agenda. Harsh critics may charge that Bush had a window of opportunity before the terrorists struck, but it is highly unlikely that the president, any president, would have been able to put together a comprehensive reform package, which included amnesty/legalization, and pushed it through Congress during his first eight months in office. During his second term, Bush's public prestige and professional reputation were a casualty of the descent toward anarchy and civil war in Iraq. But Iraq was different from 9/11, because Bush chose to go to war and his choice shaped the political environment. War was not inevitable. History may very well judge it wrong. It certainly undermined his efforts on immigration.[100] He had little influence on even his own party's senators. In May 2006 twenty-three Republican senators voted for S 2611, Hagel-Martinez. After more than a year's campaigning, arm twisting, cajoling, persuading, promising, and bargaining, Bush and his allies could muster only twelve Republican votes for cloture on June 28 out of a possible forty-nine. The statistics are even more compelling for those senators facing reelection in 2008. Of the twenty-one Republicans seeking another term, eighteen voted against cloture. The electoral lifeboats were full of Republicans fleeing Bush's sinking ship of state. Bush could not even rely on the GOP leadership for support. Jon Kyl (Republican Conference chair and grand bargainer) and Trent Lott stayed on board, but Mitch McConnell and Kay Bailey Hutchison (Republican Policy Committee chair) jumped.

The race for the Republican presidential nomination also played its part in undermining the prospects for immigration reform in several ways. Most candidates judged that liberal positions on social and cultural issues would reduce their appeal to a conservative primary electorate. Following Richard Nixon's advice to Bob Dole, then, they tacked to the right on immigration, but also on other social and cultural issues such as abortion, gay marriage, and stem-cell research. Mitt Romney was the most obvious example, desperate to shed his image as a "liberal" Republican governor, but Rudi Giuliani's change of direction was significant, too, as he hardened his positions. John McCain refused to buckle but it looked very much like his "courage" would spell the end of his presidential ambitions. The imperative to reposition was reinforced by the entry of Tom Tancredo into the race, whose campaign was built almost wholly around the totems of resisting amnesty and constructing an impregnable border.

It was not only Bush's unpopularity that persuaded many senate Republicans to vote against him. Grassroots conservatives had a significant impact, too. They were vocal, much more so than the bill's supporters, and very well-organized and active, in part motivated by incessant discussion on talk-radio. California senator Dianne Feinstein observed that "about 20 percent of the population came alive very strongly against the bill."[101] Senators sympathetic to liberalization were bombarded with letters, faxes, emails, phone calls, and in some cases threats. Several senators noted that it was the most impressive mobilization effort they had ever witnessed, and some whispered to reporters that they would not speak out against talk-radio hosts having witnessed the vitriolic reaction that greeted Lott's criticism of the paranoia engendered by the medium. The response of senators to the grassroots mobilization reinforces V. O. Key's famous and astute observation that American politics rewards intense minorities over passive majorities.

The opposition was also advantaged by the design of the American political system. The founding fathers, worried about minority and majority tyranny, deliberately fractured the policymaking process and put many obstacles in the way of change. The system privileges the status quo and tempers innovation. When combined with entrenched interests and pressure group politics, the barriers to change can be insurmountable. Nearly everyone agreed that America's immigration system was hopelessly inadequate, but too many individuals and groups had an interest in maintaining it, fighting for their little corner of the bigger broken puzzle, and too few had an interest in changing it. The opposition was further advantaged by its ability to frame the terms of debate. It had one particular advantage in doing so, or rather one particular word: amnesty. The charge that the bipartisan bill was an amnesty was critical. Polls showed a majority approved of most of its provisions, including the legalization provision so long as pollsters did not use the word amnesty to describe it. But opponents succeeded in branding the bill as an amnesty and thus supporters struggled to win public support. The president tied himself in linguistic knots trying to explain how legalization or a path to citizenship was not an amnesty, so that his speeches were often complex but ambiguous, detailed but somehow vague. Bush suffered much populist criticism, ridicule even, throughout his presidency over his use of language, but could be at his best a savy and effective communicator—witness how the "war on terror" and "axis of evil" were used as powerful political tools. The language of immigration reform offered him no such opportunities; the opposition had all the best lines.

It is also difficult to sell a compromise, and at the heart of comprehensive immigration reform was a grand bargain. It was not one that enough in the Senate were willing to buy. The bill made enemies on all sides and engendered an unholy but effective opposition alliance with conservatives and liberals arrayed against moderates, but it also pitted liberals against liberals and conservatives against conservatives: Limbaugh and the American Civil Liberties Union united against Bush and Kennedy; the National Council of La Raza and the Mexican American Legal Defense and Educational Fund fighting the League of United Latin American Citizens; and service sector unions pitted against industrial unions. Observers' initial sense about the bill's defeat was that the right and left overcame the center, but the right and left were themselves split and the center was almost impossible to identify. Whatever it was, it could not hold.

There are two possible further reasons for the failure of Bush's reform agenda: racism and distrust of government. Kennedy hinted that the "angry voices" had whipped up unpleasant sentiments. Republican senator Lindsey Graham went further. "There's racism in this debate," he said. "Nobody likes to talk about it, but a very small percentage of people involved in this debate have [made] racial and bigoted remarks."[102] It is undoubtedly true that some of the cultural arguments articulated by grassroots activists in particular were reminiscent of the unpleasant nativist rhetoric of the early twentieth century and drew on the same themes as the more conservative supporters of Proposition 187 in the late twentieth century. But at the elite level, politicians were generally more restrained in their use of racially and ethnically specific language and imagery. There was no repeat, for example, of Governor Pete Wilson's infamous "they keep coming" ad, which featured shadowy Latino figures darting through the traffic on a border highway. Moreover, while racist attitudes probably did influence some people's opposition to the bipartisan bill, the desire to appear antiracist or at least inclusionary possibly persuaded others to support it for symbolic reasons, even though they may have been unsure about its efficacy. Finally, Senator Jim DeMint tried to spin the bill's defeat as a triumph of the people against an overweening government that is simply not trusted to make and enforce the laws. While there is no direct evidence to support DeMint's contention, research on trust in government demonstrates that innovative and grand public policy solutions to entrenched social problems are more likely to pass when trust is high than low. It is ironic that trust in government was at its highest since the 1960s in the immediate aftermath of 9/11, but that 9/11 itself closed off the opportunity for immigration reform. As trust fell, in part due the dissipation of the rally-round-the-flag effect and but also in part due to the imbroglio in Iraq, so did Bush's leeway for action.

The consequences of the immigration reform debate generally and the failure of the bipartisan bill specifically are more difficult to pin down than the causes of defeat. At the time of writing, it is simply too early to tell with any surety, but it is possible to make some tentative inferences. In terms of reform itself, is possible that the Democratic Congress may try to break up the comprehensive reform bill and pass certain parts of it as stand-alone bills, but it is perhaps more likely, given the energy expended and divisions caused, that the issue will be legislatively dormant until a new president takes office.

More certain is that Karl Rove's strategy to bring Latinos into the Republican fold has hitherto failed—Gallup's Minority Rights and Relations survey, which polled interviewees between June 4 and 24, 2007, when the Senate action on immigration reform was most salient, revealed a four to one Latino advantage for the Democratic Party over the GOP in party identification[103]—but it is of course possible that the strategy may reap its rewards in the longer run. Rove's first assault on the Latino vote may have failed, but he may have paved the way for more successful attempts in the future. However, the electoral benefits from any current or future Republican success on immigration reform would always likely be shared with a Democratic Party equally if not more supportive of minority and immigrant rights. The challenge for the GOP, though, is not to become the Latino party par excellence, although that is some strategists' goal, but to not slip too far behind the Democratic Party at a time when the Latino electorate is growing in size and voice. The machinations of Republican senators in 2006–2007 and, more importantly, House representatives in 2005 may have set back that cause, but it has not damaged the party irrevocably. It is also important to remember that many Latinos worry about illegal immigration and are supportive of tough border controls, which are not inimical to conservative Republican thought. What matters as much to Latinos as the specific policy is the tone of the debate. While still harsh at times in the first decade of the twenty-first century, it was much improved on the last decade of the twentieth century. In the 1990s it was common for Republicans, including those with national ambitions, to portray themselves as anti-immigrant, in favor of closing the door on both illegal and legal immigrants. Legal immigrants' benefits were targeted, too, with nearly half the savings in the 1996 welfare reform accruing from cuts to their welfare payments. The GOP has since helped restore most of the cuts, and legalizing the status of perhaps twelve million illegal immigrants and a new guest-worker program are on the political agenda, put there by a Republican president. The locus of debate, both within the country and the GOP has moved to the left, the rhetoric is less shrill, the tone less harsh. Bush and others may still think there is a way to go, but Kennedy thinks it inevitable.

The immigration debate damaged both the Republican Party and the presidency of George W. Bush. It split the party between conservatives and liberals, restrictionists and inclusionists, but it also divided the president from grassroots and congressional Republicans. The key to the party's strength and success during Bush's first term was its unity, and in particular Bush's loyal support among rank-and-file Republicans and his lieutenants in the House, but it and his presidency unraveled as he pursued immigration reform with increasing tenacity. The immigration issue, however, is unlikely to be divisive enough to cause any significant long-term damage or split in the GOP. Indeed, the growing strength of the Latino electorate should help convince many more Republican members of Congress that their future electoral survival is best served by a liberal immigration reform. The irony is that Latinos' electoral importance is in part a product of the Republican Party's own machinations over the past two decades.

Appendix A

Opinion Poll Details

(Note: Aggregate data for all *Los Angeles Times Polls* are available online at http://www.latimes.com/news/custom/timespoll/la-statsheetindex.htmlstory.)

Field (California) Poll, #94-03, Sample population: California, *April 1–9, 1994.* Telephone poll. Sample size 1,010.

———, #94-05, Sample population: California, *July 12–17, 1994.* Telephone poll. Sample size 847.

———, #94-07, Sample population, California, *October 21–30, 1994.* Telephone poll. Sample size 1,404.

Los Angeles Times Poll, #278, Sample population: California, *April 23–26, 1992.* Telephone poll. Sample size 1,395; registered voters 1,395; margin or error +/−3%.

———, #282, Sample population: California, *May 16–19, 1992.* Telephone poll. Sample size 1,469; registered voters 1,469, likely voters 795; margin or error +/−3%.

———, #297, Sample population: Orange County, *August 22–23, 1992.* Telephone poll. Sample size 1,359; registered voters 1,067; margin or error +/−3%.

———, #298, Sample population: California, *September 10–13, 1992.* Telephone poll. Sample size 1,695; registered voters 1,330; margin or error +/−3%.

———, #300, Sample population: LA city, *October 9–14, 1992.* Telephone poll. Sample size 1,383; margin or error +/−3%.

———, #301, Sample population: California, *October 20–23, 1992.* Telephone poll. Sample size 1,354; registered voters 1,110; likely voters 833; margin or error +/−3%.

———, #306, Sample population: LA city, *January 28–February 2, 1993.* Telephone poll. Sample size 1,618; registered voters 1,149; margin or error +/−3%.

Los Angeles Times Poll, #310, Sample population: California, *March 20–22, 1993.* Telephone poll. Sample size 1,294; registered voters 1,032; margin or error +/−3%.

———, #314, Sample population: LA city, *May 8–10, 1993.* Telephone poll. Sample size 1,503; registered voters 1,048; margin or error +/−3%.

———, #315, Sample population: LA city, *May 27–30, 1993.* Telephone poll. Sample size 1,506; registered voters 1,091; margin or error +/−3%.

———, #318, Sample population: southern California, *August 7–10, 1993.* Telephone poll. Sample size 1,232; margin or error +/−3%.

———, #319, Sample population: Orange County, *August 12–15, 1993.* Telephone poll. Sample size 943; margin or error +/−4%.

———, Sample population: California, *September 10–13, 1993.* Telephone poll. Sample size 1,162; margin of error +/−3%.

———, #324, Sample population: California, *October 16–19, 1993.* Telephone poll. Sample size 1,718; registered voters 1,301; margin or error +/−3%.

———, #325, Sample population: LA city, *October 22–24, 1993.* Telephone poll. Sample size 1,279; margin or error +/−3%.

———, #333, Sample population: California, *March 26–29, 1994.* Telephone poll. Sample size 1,608; registered voters 1,211; margin or error +/−3%.

———, #335, Sample population: California, *May 21–25, 1994.* Telephone poll. Sample size 1,984; registered voters 1,471; margin or error +/−3%.

———, #338, Sample population: LA county, *June 17–20, 1994.* Telephone poll. Sample size 1,239; margin or error +/−3%.

———, #340, Sample population: San Fernando Valley, *July 9–10, 1994.* Telephone poll. Sample size 1,094; margin or error +/−4%.

———, #343, Sample population: California, *September 8–11, 1994.* Telephone poll. Sample size 1,503; registered voters 1,165; likely voters 721; margin or error +/−3%.

———, #344, Sample population: LA county, *September 17–23, 1994.* Telephone poll. Sample size 1,703; margin or error +/−3%.

———, #346, Sample population: California, *October 8–11, 1994.* Telephone poll. Sample size 1,641; registered voters 1,232; likely voters 821; margin or error +/−3%.

———, #348, Sample population: California, *October 22–25, 1994.* Telephone poll. Sample size 1,659; registered voters 1,253; likely voters 762; margin or error +/−3%.

———, #350/exit poll, Sample population: California, *November 8, 1994.* Sample size 5,336; margin or error +/−3%.

———, #355, Sample population: California, *March 4–9, 1995.* Telephone poll. Sample size 1,390; registered voters 1,011; margin or error +/−3%.

————, #365, Sample population: California, *September 7–10, 1995*. Telephone poll. Sample size 1,343; registered voters 1,065; margin or error +/−3%.

————, #383, Sample population: California, *September 14–17, 1996*. Telephone poll. Sample size 1,333; registered voters 1,059; margin or error +/−3%.

————, #400, Sample population: California, *October 4–7, 1997*. Telephone poll. Sample size 1,396; registered voters 1,092; margin or error +/−3%.

————, #403, Sample population: California, *November 18–December 12, 1997*. Telephone poll. Sample size 2,804; margin or error +/−3%.

————, #410, Sample population: California, *April 4–9, 1998*. Telephone poll. Sample size 1,409; registered voters 1,105; likely voters 566; margin or error +/−3%.

————, #416, Sample population: California, *September 12–17, 1998*. Telephone poll. Sample size 1,651; registered voters 1,270; likely voters 684; margin or error +/−3%.

————, #420/exit poll, Sample population: California, *November 3, 1998*. Sample size 3,693; margin or error +/−3%.

————, #428, Sample population: California, *June 10–14, 1999*. Telephone poll. Sample size 1,602; registered voters 1,179; margin or error +/−3%.

————, #451, Sample population: California, *January 4–5, 2001*. Telephone poll. Sample size 575; margin or error +/−4%.

————, #453, Sample population: California, *February 14–15, 2001*. Telephone poll. Sample size 579; margin or error +/−4%.

————, #461, Sample population: California, *June 23–26, 2001*. Telephone poll. Sample size 1,541; registered voters 1,216; margin or error +/−3%.

————, #464, Sample population: California, *January 23–27, 2002*. Telephone poll. Sample size 1,294; registered voters 1,294; likely voters 563; margin or error +/−3%.

Appendix B

Proposition 187: Text of Proposed Law

This initiative measure is submitted to the people in accordance with the provisions of Article II, Section 8 of the Constitution.

This initiative measure adds sections to various codes; therefore, new provisions proposed to be added are printed in *italic type* to indicate they are new.

Proposed Law

SECTION 1. Findings and Declaration.

The People of California declare as follows:

That they have suffered and are suffering economic hardship caused by the presence of illegal aliens in this state.

That they have suffered and are suffering personal injury and damage caused by the criminal conduct of illegal aliens in this state.

That they have a right to the protection of their government from any person or persons entering this country unlawfully.

Therefore, the People of California declare their intention to provide for cooperation between their agencies of state and local government with the federal government, and to establish a system of required notification by and between such agencies to prevent illegal aliens in the United States from receiving benefits or public services in the State of California.

SECTION 2. Manufacture, Distribution or Sale of False Citizenship or Resident Alien Documents: Crime and Punishment.

Section 113 is added to the Penal Code, to read:

113. Any person who manufactures, distributes or sells false documents to corneal the true citizenship or resident alien status of another person is guilty of a felony, and *shall be punished by imprisonment in the state prison for five years or by a fine of seventy-five thousand dollars ($75,000).*

SECTION 3. Use of False Citizenship or Resident Alien Documents: Crime and Punishment.

Section 114 is added to the Penal Code, to read:

114. Any person who uses false documents to conceal his or her true citizenship or resident alien status is guilty of a felony, and shall be punished by imprisonment in the state prison for five years or by a fine of twenty-five thousand dollars ($25,000).

SECTION 4. Law Enforcement Cooperation with INS.

Section 834b is added to the Penal Code, to read:

834b. (a) Every law enforcement agency in California shall fully cooperate with the United States Immigration and Naturalization Service regarding any person who is arrested if he or she is suspected of being present in the United States in violation of federal immigration laws.

(b) With respect to any such person who is arrested, and suspected of being present in the United States in violation of federal immigration laws, every law enforcement agency shall do the following:

(1) Attempt to verify the legal status of such person as a citizen of the United States, an alien lawfully admitted as a permanent resident, an alien lawfully admitted for a temporary period of time or as an alien who is present in the United States in violation of immigration laws. The verification process may include, but shall not be limited to, questioning the person regarding his or her date and place of birth, and entry into the United States, and demanding documentation to indicate his or her legal status.

(2) Notify the person of his or her apparent status as an alien who is present in the United States in violation of federal immigration laws and inform him or her that, apart from any criminal justice proceedings, he or she must either obtain legal status or leave the United States.

(3) Notify the Attorney General of California and the United States Immigration and Naturalization Service of the apparent illegal status and provide any additional information that may be requested by any other public entity.

(c) Any legislative, administrative, or other action by a city, county, or other legally authorized local governmental entity with jurisdictional boundaries, or by a law enforcement agency, to prevent or limit the cooperation required by subdivision (a) is expressly prohibited.

SECTION 5. Exclusion of Illegal Aliens from Public Social Services

Section 10001.5 is added to the Welfare and Institutions Code, to read:

10001.5. (a) In order to carry out the intention of the People of California that only citizens of the United States and aliens lawfully admitted to the United States may

receive the benefits of public social services and to ensure that all persons employed in the providing of those services shall diligently protect public funds from misuse, the provisions of this section are adopted.

(b) A person shall not receive any public social services to which he or she may be otherwise entitled until the legal status of that person has been verified as one of the following:

(1) A citizen of the United States.

(2) An alien lawfully admitted as a permanent resident.

(3) An alien lawfully admitted for a temporary period of time.

(c) If any public entity in this state to whom a person has applied for public social services determines or reasonably suspects, based upon the information provide to it, that the person is an alien in the United States in violation of federal law, the following procedures shall be followed by the public entity:

(1) The entity shall not provide the person with benefits or services.

(2) The entity shall, in writing, notify the person of his or her apparent illegal immigration status, andt hat the person must either obtain legal status or leave the United States.

(3) The entity shall also notify the State Director of Social Services, the Attorney General of California, and the United States Immigration and Naturalization Service of the apparent illegal status, and shall provide any additional information that may be requested by any other public entity.

SECTION 6. Exclusion of Illegal Aliens from Publicly Funded Health Care.

Chapter 1.3 (commencing with Section 130) is added to Part 1 of Division 1 of the Health and Safety Code, to read:

CHAPTER 1.2. PUBLICLY-FUNDED HEALTH CARE SERVICES

130. (a) In order to carry out the intention of the People of California that, excepting emergency medical care as required by federal law, only citizens of the United States and aliens lawfully admitted to the United States may receive benefits of publicly-funded health care, and to ensure that all persons employed in the providing of these services shall diligently protect public funds from misuse, the provisions of this section are adopted.

(b) A person shall not receive any health care services from a publicly-funded health care facility, to which he or she is otherwise entitled until the legal status of that person has been verified as one of the following:

(1) A citizen of the United States.

(2) An alien lawfully admitted as a permanent resident.

(3) An alien lawfully admitted for a temporary period of time.

(c) If any publicly-funded health care facility in this state from whom a person seeks health care services, other than emergency medical care as required by federal law, determines or reasonably suspects, based upon the information provided to it, that the

person is an alien in the United States in violation of federal law, the following procedures shall be followed by the facility:

(1) The facility shall not provide the person with services.

(2) The facility shall, in writing, notify the person of his or her apparent illegal immigration status, and that the person must either obtain legal status or leave the United States.

(3) The facility shall also notify the State Director of Health Services, the Attorney General of California, and the United States Immigration and Naturalization Service of the apparent illegal status, and shall provide any additional that may be requested by any other public entity.

(d) For purposed of this section "publicly-funded health care facility" shall be defined as specified in Section 1200 and 1250 of this code as of January 1, 1993.

SECTION 7. Exclusion of Illegal Aliens from Public Elementary and Secondary Schools.

Section 48215 is added to the Education Code, to read:

48215. (a) No public elementary or secondary school shall admit, or permit the attendance of, any child who is not a citizen of the United States, an alien lawfully admitted as a permanent resident, or a person who is otherwise authorized under federal law to be present in the United States.

(b) Commencing January 1, 1995, each school district shall verify the legal status of each child enrolling in the school district for the first time in order to ensure the enrollment or attendance only of citizens, aliens lawfully admitted as permanent residents, or persons who are otherwise authorized to be present in the United States.

(c) By January 1, 1996, each school district shall have verified the legal status of each child already enrolled and in attendance in the school district in order to ensure the enrollment or attendance only of citizens, aliens lawfully admitted as permanent residents, or persons who are otherwise authorized under federal law to be present in the Untied States.

(d) By January 1, 1996, each school district shall also have verified the legal status of each parent or guardian of each child referred to in subdivisions (b) and (c), to determine whether such parent or guardian is one of the following:

(1) A citizen of the United States.

(2) An alien lawfully admitted as a permanent resident.

(3) An alien admitted lawfully for a temporary period of time.

(e) Each school district shall provide information to the State Superintendent of Public Instruction, the Attorney General of California, and the United States Immigration and Naturalization Service regarding any enrollee or pupil, or parent or guardian, attending a public elementary or secondary school in the school district determined or reasonably suspected to be in violation of federal immigration laws within forty-five days after becoming aware of apparent violation. The notice shall also be provided to the parent or legal guardian of the enrollee or pupil, and shall state that an existing pupil may not continue to attend the school after ninety calendar days from the date of the notice, unless legal status is established.

(f) For each child who cannot establish legal status in the United States, each school district shall continue to provide education for a period of ninety days from the date of the notice. Such ninety day period shall be utilized to accomplish an orderly transition to a school in the child's country of origin. Each school district shall fully cooperate in this transition effort to ensure that the educational needs of the child are best served for that period of time.

SECTION 8. Exclusion of Illegal Aliens from Public Postsecondary Educational Institutions.

Section 66010.8 is added to the Education Code, to read:

66010.8. (a) No public institution of postsecondary education shall admit, enroll, or permit the attendance of any person who is not a citizen of the United States, an alien lawfully admitted as a permanent resident in the United States, or a person who is otherwise authorized under federal law to be present in the United States.
(b) Commencing with the first term of semester that begins after January 1, 1995, and at the commencement of each term or semester thereafter, each public postsecondary educational institution shall verify the staus of each person enrolled or in attendance at that institution in order to ensure that enrollment or attendance only of United States citizens, aliens lawfully admitted as permanent residents in the United States, and persons who are otherwise authorized under federal law to be present in the United States.
(c) No later than 45 days after the admissions officer of a public postsecondary educational institution becomes aware of the application, enrollment, or attendance of a person determined to be, or who is under reasonable suspicion of being, in the United States in violation of federal immigration laws, that officer shall provide that information to the State Superintendent of Public Instruction, the Attorney General of California, and the United States Immigration and Naturalization Service. The information shall also be provided to the applicant, enrollee, or person admitted.

SECTION 9. Attorney General Cooperation with the INS.

Section 53069.65 is added to the Government Code, to read:

53069.65. Whenever the state or a city, or a county, or any other legally authorized local governmental entity with jurisdictional boundaries reports the presence of a person who is suspected of being present in the United States in violation of federal immigration laws to the Attorney General of California, that report shall be transmitted to the United States Immigration and Naturalization Service. The Attorney General shall be responsible for maintaining on-going and accurate records of such reports, and shall provide any additional information that may be requested by any other government entity.

SECTION 10. Amendment and Severability.

The statutory provisions contained in this measure may not be amended by the Legislature except to further its purposes by statute passed in each house by rollcall vote entered in the journal, two-thirds of the membership concurring, or by a statute that becomes effective only when approved by voters.

In the event that any portion of this act or the application thereof to any person or circumstance is held invalid, that invalidity shall not affect any other provision or application of the act, which can be given effect without the invalid provision or application, and to that end the provisions of this act are severable.

Appendix C

Additional Tables

Table 1 Feinstein/Huffington Ratings

	October 22–25, 1994		October 8–11, 1994		September 8–11, 1994	
	Registered Voters	Likely Voters	Registered Voters	Likely Voters	Registered Voters	Likely Voters
Feinstein	46	48	49	49	49	49
Huffington	42	45	40	42	40	43
Other	2	1	1	1	1	—
Don't Know	10	6	10	8	10	8

Source: September 8–October 25, 1994 *LA Times* Polls.

Table 2 Translating Change in Electoral Behavior into Change in Electoral Share

	E.g. 1	E.g. 2	E.g. 3	E.g. 4	E.g. 5
Old Proportion of Eligible Population that Votes[1]	.660	.660	.660	.660	.660
Old Proportion of Eligible Latino Population that Votes[1]	.562	.562	.562	.562	.562
New Proportion of Eligible Latino Population that Votes[1]	.659	.659	.659	.659	.659
Latino Share of Eligible Vote[1]	*.100*	*.300*	*.500*	*.700*	*.900*
Extra Proportion of Eligible Population that Votes[2]	.0097	.029	.049	.068	.087
New Proportion of Eligible Population that Votes[3]	.670	.689	.709	.728	.747
Old Latino Share of Actual Vote[4]	.085	.255	.426	.596	.766
New Latino Share of Actual Vote[5]	.098	.287	.465	.634	.791
Proportion Increase in Latino Share of Vote[6]	*.013*	*.032*	*.039*	*.038*	*.025*

Notes:

1 = The entries in Row 1 are real data from 1980. The entries in Rows 2 and 3 are real data based on Latino political participation in 1980 and 2000 respectively. And the entries in Row 4 are hypothetical and designed to illustrate how the impact of changes in voting rates on the increase in vote share are conditional on an ethnicity's original share of the vote. All other cell entries are calculations based on the original entries on Rows 1–4, holding everything else constant (e.g., changes in proportions or numbers of whites that vote).

2 = (New Proportion of Eligible Latino Population that Votes − Old Proportion of Eligible Latino Population that Votes) × Latino Share of Eligible Vote.

3 = Old Proportion of Eligible Population that Votes + Extra Proportion of Eligible Population that Votes.

4 = (Old Proportion of Eligible Latino Population that Votes * Latino Share of Eligible Vote) / New Proportion of Eligible Population that Votes.

5 = (New Proportion of Eligible Latino Population that Votes * Latino Share of Eligible Vote) / New Proportion of Eligible Population that Votes.

6 = New Latino Share of Actual Vote − Old Latino Share of Actual Vote.

Source: Bureau of Labor Statistics and Bureau of the Census, November *Current Population Surveys*, 1978–2000.

Notes

1 Introduction

1. The Pew Research Center for the People and the Press and the Pew Hispanic Center, "America's Immigration Quandary: No Consensus on Immigration Problem or Proposed Fixes," March 30, 2006.
2. Two essential works on the immigration and eugenics of this period are Higham, *Strangers in the Land* and King, *Making Americans.*
3. I have chosen to use the word "Latino" rather than "Hispanic" to describe Latin Americans living in the United States, apart from when quoting others or when employing federal government agencies' categorizations, which continue to use the term Hispanic. In terms of meaning, oftentimes the terms are interchangeable but they are not identical. Hispanics' key reference point is Spain, especially Spanish language and culture. Latinos' reference is Latin America. Of course, there is considerable overlap but they are not the same. A Hispanic should, tightly defined, descend from Spain; a Spanish person living in the United States is not a Latino. Latinos can have European descendants but need not. An indigenous person from Latin America should not be referred to as Hispanic. Latino is therefore the best geographic descriptor, but it also more culturally or sociopolitically appropriate. For some Latin Americans in the United States, Hispanic has offensive connotations because it draws on concepts of whiteness and Europe's imperial legacy and is still used by the U.S. government, for example the Census Bureau, to describe Latin Americans. For these reasons, some, but by no means all or even a majority, prefer Latino. Fewer insist on Hispanic. Most are ambivalent, however. See *The American Heritage Dictionary of the English Language* (Boston, MA: Houghton Miffin Co., 2003).
4. The "suspected" phrase has no weight or meaning in federal immigration law. The authors of Proposition 187 were widely criticized for employing it because, opponents argued, it was potentially discriminatory. It would be Latinos or Asians, not whites, who were predominantly suspected of illegal residence based on their race and/or ethnicity. This point is developed further in later chapters.
5. Most published work on Proposition 187 seeks to either (1) explain Californians' vote choices on Proposition 187 (see Alvarez and Butterfield, "The Resurgence of Nativism in California?"; Burns and Gimpel, "Economic Insecurity, Prejudicial Stereotypes, and Public Opinion on Immigration Policy"; Fetzer, "Economic Self-interest or Cultural Marginality?"; Hood and Morris, "Brother, Can You Spare a Dime?"; Mac Donald and Cain, "Nativism, Partisanship, and Immigration"; Morris, "African American Voting on Proposition 187"; Newton, "Why Some Latinos Supported Proposition 187"; Schockman, "California's Ethnic Experiment and the Unsolvable Immigration Issue"; Tolbert and Hero, "Race/Ethnicity and Direct

Democracy"), or (2) discuss the constitutionality of the initiative (see, inter alia, Biegel "The Wisdom of *Plyler v. Doe*"; Cervantes, Khokha, and Murray, "Hate Unleashed"; Garcia, "Critical Race Theory and Proposition 187"; Knight, "Proposition 187 and International Human Rights Law"; Mitchell Kurfis, "The Constitutionality of California's Proposition 187"; Schuck, "The Message of Proposition 187"; Sklanksy, "Proposition 187 and the Ghost of James Bradley Thayer"; Wagley, "Newly Ratified International Rights Treaties").

6. See, for example, Allswang, *The Initiative and Referendum in California*; Bowler, Donovan, and Tolbert, *Citizens as Legislators*; Broder, *Democracy Derailed*; Butler and Ranney, *Referendums Around the World*; Cronin, *Direct Democracy*; Ellis, *Democratic Delusions*; Magleby, *Direct Legislation*.

7. Notable exceptions include Sears and Citrin's examination of California's Tax Revolt initiatives of the late 1970s, *Tax Revolt*; Daniel A. Smith's analysis of anti-tax initiatives in California, Massachusetts, and Colorado, *Tax Crusaders and the Politics of Direct Democracy*; and Lydia Chavez's examination of the California Civil Rights Initiative of 1996—also known as Proposition 209, the anti-affirmative action initiative—*The Color Bind*.

8. See, for example, Hajnal, Gerber, and Louch, "Minorities and Direct Legislation." They argue that

    Almost immediately after [the property-tax reducing initiative] Prop. 13 passed in California, 37 other states reduced property taxes, 28 cut income taxes, and 13 restricted sales tax collections (Magleby 1994). In the 8 months after California's [anti-affirmative action initiative] Prop. 209 was passed, 20 states moved on bills or resolutions to limit affirmative action, with 15 of them copying California's Civil Rights Initiative word for word (Maharidge). (p. 158)

    See also Gandara, "Learning English in California."

9. For instance, one well-respected researcher notes that

    [T]he reader will find no mention of differences among immigrants by race or country of origin. That is because such information does not bear upon the most important question for immigration policy: the overall number of immigrants that are admitted to the country. (See Simon, *Immigration*)

10. Johnson, "An Essay on Immigration Politics."

11. Ibid. pp. 648–649.

12. Ibid., p. 634. "Suspect classifications" apply different rules/laws to different groups of people. In U.S. constitutional law, the Supreme Court applies a strict scrutiny standard to laws that it perceives discriminate on the basis of race or national origin, because such laws are based on potentially suspect classifications. However, because Proposition 187 applied to all illegal immigrants, not those of a specific country, ethnicity, or race, Johnson argues it was unlikely to be regarded as suspect and therefore would not be subjected to the higher level of scrutiny.

13. For a review of the evidence, see Schuman, Steeh, and Bobo, *Racial Attitudes in America*; Carmines and Champagne, "The Changing Content of American Racial Attitudes."

14. Bobo, "'Whites' Opposition to Busing"; Citrin, Reingold, and Green, "American Identity and the Politics of Ethnic Change"; McConahay, "Self-interest versus Racial Attitudes"; Sears, Hensler, and Speer, "'Whites' Opposition to Busing"; Sears and Citrin, *Tax Revolt;* Sears and Funk, "Self-interest in Americans' Political Opinions." Critics, however, have argued that such symbolic measures confuse cause and effect and thus stifle debate. See Sniderman and Tetlock quoted in Carr, *"Color-Blind" Racism*, p. 172; Kuklinski et al., "Racial Prejudice and Attitudes toward Affirmative Action," p. 404.

15. Citrin, Reingold, and Green, "American Identity and the Politics of Ethnic Change," pp. 1137, 1140–1142.
16. Johnson, "Public Benefits and Immigration"; Johnson, "An Essay on Immigration Politics"; Richard Walker, "California Rages against the Dying of the Light."
17. Guerin-Gonzales, *Mexican Workers and American Dreams.*
18. Schuck and Smith, *Citizenship Without Consent.*
19. Schuman, Steeh, and Bobo, *Racial Attitudes in America*, pp. 176–185.
20. Daniels and Kitano, *American Racism*, pp. 35–40.
21. Olzak, *The Dynamics of Ethnic Competition and Conflict.*
22. Tolbert and Hero, "Race/Ethnicity and Direct Democracy," p. 808.
23. For an examination of Latino support on Proposition 187, see Newton, "Why Some Latinos Supported Proposition 187." Newton shows that Latinos who speak English and are U.S. citizens were more likely to support Proposition 187 than Spanish-speaking noncitizens. She argues that the former group supported Proposition 187 because they perceived little personal threat from it, and the latter group opposed it because they perceived a signficant threat.

2 Learning from History

1. There was some limited taxation of immigration by local and state governments, but this was designed primarily to raise revenues, not curtail entry. See DeSipio and de la Garza, *Making Americans, Remaking America*, p. 15.
2. Indeed, this disconnection between public and elite opinion on immigration is a notable feature of U.S. history. As this and later chapters show, the American public has consistently opposed the further opening of the country's doors, while politicians' default position is to roll out the welcome mat.
3. The Declaration of Independence, July 4, 1776. The full clause states: "He has endeavored to prevent the population of these States; for that purpose obstructing the Laws of Naturalization of Foreigners; refusing to pass others to encourage their migrations hither, and raising the conditions of new Appropriations of Lands."
4. Quoted in Reimers, *Unwelcome Strangers*, pp. 8–9.
5. Daniels, *Coming to America*, pp. 112–118; DeSipio and de la Garza, *Making Americans, Remaking America*, pp. 25–29.
6. For example, Daniels points out that wealthy steamship passengers were not counted, while those in steerage were (*Coming to America*, pp. 123–124). A detailed breakdown of immigration statistics can be found in the Office of Immigration Statistics' annual *Yearbook of Immigration Statistics.*
7. DeSipio and de la Garza, *Making Americans, Remaking America*, Table 2.2, pp. 19–21.
8. Quoted in Reimers, *Unwelcome Strangers*, p. 12.
9. Asians born in the United States were citizens automatically under the birthright provisions of the Fourteenth Amendment.
10. Non-Asian Californians believed that the coolie immigrants, contracted to the already immigrated Chinese, were "a new form of slavery that enriched other Chinese" (DeSipio and de la Garza, *Making Americans, Remaking America*, p. 37).
11. Daniels, *Coming to America*, p. 255.
12. For an excellent review of the work of the eugenicists and their influence on U.S. immigration policy, see King, *In the Name of Liberalism*, Chapter 4; and King, *Making Americans.* See also the classic work by John Higham, *Strangers in the Land.*

13. Quoted in Reimers, *Unwelcome Strangers*, p. 16.
14. Ibid.
15. Quoted in Higham, *Strangers in the Land*, p. 276.
16. King, *In the Name of Liberalism*, p. 99.
17. Reimers, *Unwelcome Strangers*, p. 17.
18. Quoted in King, *In the Name of Liberalism*, p. 104.
19. Ibid., p. 105.
20. Higham, *Strangers in the Land*, pp. 301–302.
21. Ibid., pp. 266–267. Higham reports that 5,000 immigrants per day were arriving at Ellis Island in September 1920 (p. 267).
22. Johnson became chair in 1919, and would remain so until 1933 (King, *In the Name of Liberalism*, p. 107).
23. Each country's quota was 3 percent of its U.S. census total. The Act also imposed an annual ceiling of 357,000 for all countries combined. See King, *In the Name of Liberalism*, p. 107, and also Higham, *Strangers in the Land*, pp. 308–311.
24. Quoted in Reimers, *Unwelcome Strangers*, p. 22. See also Higham, *Strangers in the Land*, pp. 318–319.
25. Now each country's quota was set at 2 percent, and the annual combined ceiling was reduced to 150,000 (King, *In the Name of Liberalism*, p. 102).
26. Ibid., p. 111.
27. Reimers, *Unwelcome Strangers*, p. 22.
28. See King, *In the Name of Liberalism*, Chapter. 4, and Higham, *Strangers in the Land*, Chapters 10 and 11.
29. For a brief but excellent account of Mexican immigration to the United States, see Durand, Massey, and Charvet, "The Changing Geography of Mexican Immigration to the United States: 1910–1996." See also Cornelius and Bustamante, *Mexican Migration to the United States*; Guerin-Gonzales, *Mexican Workers and American Dreams*; Gutierrez, *Walls and Mirrors*; Lowenthal and Burgess, *The California-Mexico Connection*.
30. Cervantes, Khokha, and Murray, "Hate Unleashed," p. 2.
31. The California supreme court immediately repealed the tax, however.
32. California voters approved another ostensibly nonracial initiative in 1986 when 73 percent voted Yes on Proposition 63 to make English the official language of the state. The anti-alien land law of 1920 is the third most popular initiative (when measured by percent voting Yes) in California's history and the English-only law is the seventh most popular. See California Secretary of State, *A History of the California Initiative Process*, p. 9. For details of California's anti-immigrant legislation, see, inter alia, the above publication, LaVally, *Addressing Immigration Issues in California*, pp. 6–12; Mu and Barnhart, *Summary Report for Assembly Select Committee*, pp. 17–18; Garcia y Griego, "History of U.S. Immigration Policy," pp. 3–8.
33. Other sources used in this review of U.S. and California immigration policy include LaVally, *Addressing Immigration Issues in California*, pp. 6–12; Mu and Barnhart, *Summary Report for Assembly Select Committee*, pp. 17–18; Garcia y Griego, "History of U.S. Immigration Policy," pp. 3–8.
34. King, *Making Americans*, Chapter 8.
35. A comprehensive account of the congressional debates and machinations on the 1965 law (and post-1965 laws, too) can be found in Gimpel and Edwards, *The Congressional Politics of Immigration Reform*. See also, King, *Making Americans*, Chapter 8.
36. Again, the cap was permeable because immediate family members were excluded from the totals.
37. Daniels, *Coming to America*, p. 338.

38. For analyses of the IRCA, see Daniels, *Coming to America*, pp. 391–397; LaVally, *Addressing Immigration Issues in California*, pp. 6–8; Mu and Barnhart, *Summary Report for Assembly Select Committee*, pp. 12–18; Garcia y Griego, "History of U.S. Immigration Policy," pp. 3–8.

39. Durand, Massey, and Charvet, "The Changing Geography of Mexican Immigration," pp. 9–10; Martin, "Good Intentions Gone Awry."

40. Quoted in *New York Times*, October 15, 1994, p. A-1.

41. The Supplemental Security Income Program was restored for permanent resident aliens in 1997, however (DeSipio and de la Garza, *Making America, Remaking Americans*, Chapter 2), in part because of a Latino backlash that threatened Republican electoral prospects. This important development is discussed in more detail in the later chapters.

42. Several scholars have analyzed the "agenda-setting process" in order to explain why certain problems/questions become issues and why others do not. Among the most notable are Cobb and Elder, *Participation in American Politics*; Kingdon, *Agendas, Alternatives, and Public Policies*; Schattschneider, *The Semisovereign People*. Although all three works provide valuable insights into the agenda-setting process, it is not my intention in this study to examine which if any of these "explain" the genesis of the illegal-immigration issue. In the first instance, this study of Proposition 187 has not been designed to "test" competing theories such as those offered by the above scholars. In the second, these works focus on the process by which an issue arrives on the governmental agenda. Clearly, direct democracy procedures allow issues to be debated and solutions offered without the participation of governmental institutions. Thus, the relevance of the "orthodox" agenda-setting literature must be questioned.

43. George Borjas has made this point in multiple publications.

44. Daniels, *Coming to America*, p. 339.

45. Gimpel and Edwards, *The Congressional Politics of Immigration Reform*, esp. p. 4 for "fiercely partisan" quote.

3   The Early Politicization of the Illegal-Immigration Issue

1. Starr, *Coast of Dreams*, pp. 142–143.

2. Ibid., p. 182.

3. U.S. Bureau of the Census, *Statistical Abstract of the United States: 1994*, pp. xii–xxi; *New York Times*, August 24, 1993, p. 12.

4. Starr, *Coast of Dreams*, p. 233.

5. See ibid., Part II, and Davis, *City of Quartz*.

6. Hunter, *Culture Wars*.

7. Republican Party convention, Houston, Texas, August 17, 1992.

8. Fiorina, Abrams, and Pope, *Culture War?*

9. See Nivola and Brady, *Red and Blue Nation?* Vol. 1.

10. King, "The Polarization of American Political Parties."

11. Simon and Alexander, *The Ambivalent Welcome*, p. 244.

12. Sigler, *Civil Rights in America*, p. 189.

13. *LA Times*, San Diego edition, May 24, 1992, p. A-1.

14. Ibid.

15. *LA Times*, Home edition, January 8, 1993, p. B-3.

16. Clearly 16 percent overestimates the "politicization" of the immigration issue compared with the 2 percent who rated it the most important problem in the previous *LA Times* poll in March 1993. Unfortunately, however, the *LA Times* poll

did not solicit two replies prior to the September 1993 poll, and thus the time series must be treated cautiously. Hence, I have reported in the main text the increase of 350 percent rather than 700 percent, which represents the increase from 2 to 16 percent but masks the change from accepting one–two replies. All *LA Times* polls after September 1993 record Californians' top two concerns.

17. The Orange County Annual Survey conducted by the University of California at Irvine (August 20–29, 1993 [*LA Times*, Orange County edition, September 7, 1994, p. A-1]). Orange County residents were asked: Considering all the public policy issues in Orange County, which of these do you think is the most serious problem: Population growth and development; transportation and traffic congestion; housing and availability; crime and public safety; quality of public schools; foreign immigration; jobs and the economy; or something else? (Only one reply accepted). The results of this survey are not easily comparable with those of the *LA Times* polls. First, the question is different. Second, the UCI poll offers several prompts/alternatives; it is not a truly open-ended question. Third, it allows only one response. However, it does give an indication of the trend, particularly when compared to the results of the previous UCI Orange County poll (August 26–September 2, 1992) in which 10 percent said immigration. This represents an increase of 90 percent over the year.

18. For a discussion on this point see, Key, Jr., *Public Opinion and American Democracy*, Chapter 9.

19. The responsibilities of the INS were split between three new agencies in the aftermath of 9/11, and folded into the new Department of Homeland Security. The INS had been part of the Department of Justice.

20. Before the 2000 Census, California's representation in the House was fifty-two seats, thus giving it fifty-four electoral college votes.

21. See Higham, *Strangers in the Land*; King, *Making Americans*.

22. For a critique of these figures and a wider debate on calculating them and some alternatives, see Conference Proceedings, "California Immigration: 1994," pp. 11–23.

23. 1986: $2,374,000/27,102,000 \times 100 = 8.76\%$; 1994: $1,600,000/31,431,000 \times 100 = 5.09\%$.

24. The legal immigration numbers are: 1989: 1,090,924; 1990: 1,536,483; 1991: 1,827,167; 1992: 973,997; 1993: 904,292; 1994: 804,416; 1995: 720,461.

25. Exactly what constitutes self-interest is contested. However, Sears and Funk provide a relatively uncontroversial and sensible "middle-level" definition of self-interest: "the (1) short-to-medium impact of an issue (or candidacy) on the (2) material well-being of the (3) individual's own personal life (or that of his family)" ("Self-interest in Americans' Political Opinions," p. 148). Importantly, this definition permits the existence of other motives. In particular, it allows symbolic predispositions to be defined in opposition to self-interest, where "political symbols [such as party identification, liberal/conservatism, racial tolerance, etc.] evoke longstanding affective responses rather than rational and self-interested calculations" (ibid., p. 149).

26. Ibid., pp. 147–148.

27. See Citrin and Green, "The Self-interest Motive," pp. 10; Sears and Citrin, *Tax Revolt*; Sears and Funk, "Self-interest in Americans' Political Opinions," pp. 154–158.

28. Green and Cowden, "Who Protests"; Citrin and Green, "The Self-interest Motive"; Schuman, Steeh, and Bobo, *Racial Attitudes in America*.

29. Walker, "California Rages against the Dying of the Light," p. 63; Johnson, "Public Benefits and Immigration"; Johnson, "As Essay on Immigration Politics," p. 633.

30. Harwood, "Alienation."

31. Citrin et al., "Public Opinion toward Immigration Reform," pp. 7–8, 14–15, and Tables 2 and 4b.

32. See Olzak, *Dynamics of Ethnic Competition and Conflict*; Daniels and Kitano, *American Racism*.

33. Higham, *Stranger in the Land*.

34. Guerin-Gonzales, *Mexican Workers and American Dreams*.

35. Citrin et al., "Public Opinion toward Immigration Reform," pp. 15–19; Espenshade and Calhoun, "An Analysis of Public Opinion toward Undocumented Immigration," p. 207.

36. Citrin et al., "Public Opinion toward Immigration Reform," p. 12.

37. Espenshade and Calhoun, "An Analysis of Public Opinion toward Undocumented Immigration," p. 209.

38. There are a few studies, however, that show that increased nativist sentiment occurred at times of relative prosperity. For example, the rise of progressivism, which was a movement touched by nativism, occurred during a time when the economy was relatively buoyant. See Brogan, *The Penguin History of the United States of America*; Hofstadter, *The Age of Reform*.

39. Citrin and Green, "Self-interest Motive," pp. 21–22; Sears and Funk, "Self-interest in Americans' Political Opinions," pp. 159–160.

40. Sears and Funk, "Self-interest in Americans' Political Opinions," pp. 160–161.

41. Citrin et al., "Public Opinion toward Immigration Reform," pp. 8–10; Sears and Funk, "Self-interest in Americans' Political Opinions," p. 161.

42. Citrin and Green, "Self-interest Motive," pp. 17–20; Citrin et al., "Public Opinion toward Immigration Reform," pp. 8–10.

43. Green and Cowden, "Who Protests." They argue that self-interest influences behavior (but not opinions) because behavior involves greater costs than opinions/sentiments, and therefore people will examine their personal interest more closely when deciding whether to act or not.

44. *LA Times*, Southland edition, February 10, 1993, p. B-3.

45. *LA Times*, Home edition, September 19, 1993, p. A-1.

46. See, for example, Mayhew, *Congress*; and King, *Running Scared*.

47. Riker, *The Theory of Political Coalitions*, pp. 208–210.

48. Cain, "Lessons from the Inside Revisited," pp. 241–262.

49. *LA Times*, Home edition, July 12, 1992, p. A-1; Home edition, November 10, 1992, p. B-1; Home edition, September 3, 1992, p. B-1.

50. *LA Times*, Home edition, May 16, 1992, p. A-20.

51. *Washington Post*, February 29, 1992.

52. *LA Times*, Orange County edition, May 24, 1992, p. A-1; Home edition, June 3, 1992, A-2; Home edition, November 10, 1992, p. B-1; Home edition, January 8, 1993, p. B-3.

53. *LA Times* poll, #306, January 28–February, 1993. See appendix A for details.

54. Ibid., #318, August 7–10, 1993. See appendix A for details.

55. *LA Times*, Home edition, July 21, 1994, p. A-1.

56. Johnson, "An Essay on Immigration Politics," p. 636.

57. LaVally, *Addressing Immigration Issues in California*, p. 24.

58. *LA Times*, Orange County edition, August 22, 1993, p. A-1.

59. *LA Times*, Orange County edition, August 22, 1993, p. A-1; Home edition, September 19, 1993, p. A-1.

60. Although Feinstein had never balked at discussing illegal immigration, she was wary about making it an election issue. Democrats could not out-anti-immigrant Republicans on this issue in the 1990s; nor would most want to. Given the Republican position and the position of the median voter on illegal immigration,

it made great sense for the Republicans to use it for electoral purposes—so long as they could avoid accusations of extremism and/or racism. See, inter alia, Ansolabehere and Iyengar, "Riding the Wave and Claiming Ownership Over Issue"; Rabinowitz and Macdonald, "A Directional Theory of Issue Voting"; and Iyengar and Simon, "New Perspectives and Evidence on Political Communication and Campaign Effects."

61. *LA Times*, Home edition, September 19, 1993, p. A-1.

62. The *LA Times* did test opinion between March and September, but only at the local-level, not statewide. For example, 4 percent of southern Californians placed immigration as one of their top two concerns in early August 1993 (*LA Times* poll #318, August 7–10, 1993). Although this is instructive, the differing level of analysis precludes a direct comparison.

63. LaVally, *Addressing Immigration Issues in California*, pp. 32–37.

64. *LA Times*, Home edition, January 13, 1994, p. B-6. The *Times* later came out against Proposition 187, although it endorsed Wilson. The paper editorialized that it recognized illegal immigration was a legitimate concern, but argued that immigration policy was a federal responsibility. Its decision to support or oppose an illegal-immigration proposal was determined by this premise. Thus, if the federal government proposed an initiative to address the problem—for example, by increasing the funding of the Border Patrol—the paper would generally lend its support (see, for example, *LA Times*, Home edition, April 18, 1994, p. B-6).

65. Felix de la Torre (state policy analyst for the Mexican American Legal Defense and Education Fund), Interview, September 7, 1995.

66. In 1993, Wilson worked with the Democrat-controlled legislature to produce the first budget on time for seven years. He also encouraged legislators to enact tax breaks and incentives for business in order to create jobs, and he signed legislation that substantially amended the workers' compensation program. In April 1993, 44 percent of respondents in a *Times* poll thought the Democrats were best able to handle California's problems, but by September this had dropped to 32 percent. Republican support on this question increased from 20 to 28 percent over the same period (*LA Times*, Home edition, September 17, 1993, p. A-1).

67. Of those who approved of Wilson's performance in the October 1993 *LA Times* poll (#324, see appendix A), 23 percent did so because of his views on illegal immigration—the most frequent response. A further 18 percent approved of Wilson because he was doing the best he could, 16 percent because they liked him for no particular reason, 13 percent because they thought he was improving the economy or they liked his economic policies and 9 percent because he managed the budget well. See also *LA Times*, Home edition, October 22, 1993, p. A-1.

68. *LA Times*, Home edition, September 17, 1993, p. A-1.

69. *New York Times*, July 2, 1994, pp. A-1 and A-8.

70. *LA Times*, Home edition, April 30, 1994, p. A-24.

71. *LA Times*, Home edition, May 14, 1994, p. A-22.

72. John Marelius, *San Diego Tribune*, October 25, 1994, p. A-1. Quoted in Johnson, "An Essay on Immigration Politics," p. 653, fn. 109.

73. *LA Times*, Home edition, May 14, 1994, p. A-22.

74. Ibid.

75. *New York Times*, October 15, 1994, pp. A-1, A-10; *New York Times*, October 24, 1994.

76. *LA Times*, Home edition, April 26, 1994, p. A-3; Home edition, April 22, 1994, p. B-6; Home edition, April 30, 1994, p. A-24. Wilson filed suit even though the U.S. House of Representatives had already voted on April 20 to reimburse the states for imprisoning undocumented persons. Moreover, the House voted

417-12 on April 21 to more than double the Border Patrol's existing 4,100 agents by adding a further 6,000 new recruits and to increase spending to $900 million over the next five years.

77. *LA Times*, Home edition, June 1, 1994, p. B-8.

78. *LA Times*, Home edition, March 19, 1994, p. A-28.

79. The state's Health and Welfare Agency estimated that nearly 300,000 illegal immigrants gave birth each year in California, of which 40 percent were paid for by the Medi-Cal program. The agency could provide no figures on how many of these women received prenatal care (see *LA Times*, Home edition, July 7, 1994, p. A-3).

80. *LA Times*, Home edition, July 7, 1994, p. A-3.

81. *LA Times*, Home edition, July 7, 1994, p. A-3; Home edition, July 8, 1994, p. A-16. Wilson argued that money spent on prenatal care saves money in the long run because it helped prevent premature births and infant illnesses and therefore saved money that would have been spent on treatment. This argument formed the basis of Wilson's health policy agenda (Healthy Start) and specifically Access for Infants and Mothers (AIM), which provided well-baby and prenatal care for uninsured Californians (*LA Times*, Home edition, January 8, 1994, p. A-1).

82. *LA Times*, Home edition, June 8, 1994, p. A-1; Home edition, June 9, 1994, p. A-1. People living in gated communities or security buildings were more likely than others to express a fear of crime (*LA Times*, Metro edition, May 16, 1993, p. B-1).

83. Espenshade and Calhoun, "An Analysis of Public Opinion toward Undocumented Immigration," pp. 209–210. Other research has shown that the people most likely to fear crime—the white middle class—are the least likely to suffer its effects (see Walker, "California Rages against the Dying of the Light," pp. 59–62).

84. Citrin and Green, "Self-interest Motive," p. 16; Sears and Funk, "Self-interest in Americans' Political Opinions," p. 156. For an analysis of why people use racial stereotypes, how these stereotypes are operationalized, and the effects they have on questions of crime, see Peffley, Hurwitz, and Sniderman, "Racial Stereotypes and Whites' Political Views of Blacks in the Context of Welfare and Crime"; Hurwitz and Peffley, "Public Perceptions of Race and Crime."

85. *New York Times*, October 24, 1994, p. A-1.

86. *New York Times*, August 8, 1993, p. 16.

87. *New York Times*, January 14, 1994, p. 29.

88. *New York Times*, August 11, 1993, p. 10.

89. *LA Times*, Home edition, April 26, 1994, p. A-3.

90. *LA Times*, Orange County edition, June 19, 1994, p. B-3.

91. *New York Times*, August 23, 1993, p. 15.

92. Of the 1,200,000 deportable aliens located by the INS in 1993, 1,169,000 or 97.4 percent were of Mexican origin (U.S. Bureau of the Census, *Statistical Abstract of the United States: 1994*, p. 208).

93. *New York Times*, October 15, 1994, p. A-18. Quoted in Johnson, "An Essay on Immigration Politics," p. 654.

94. *LA Times*, Home edition, September 19, 1993, p. A-1.

95. Less than a year earlier, only 39 percent of Republicans thought he should stand for reelection while 32 percent wanted to see a primary challenge to him (*LA Times* poll, September 1993. See *LA Times*, Home edition, September 17, 1993, p. A-1).

96. The *LA Times* October 1993 poll may be a rogue survey. The results of the poll are contrary to trends established in previous polls and continued in later ones.

97. *LA Times*, Home edition, June 8, 1994, p. A-1; Valley edition, June 9, 1994, p. B-1; Home edition, June 9, 1994, p. A-1.

98. *LA Times*, Home edition, May 29, 1994, p. A-1.

4 The Increasing Salience of Illegal Immigration and the Qualification of Proposition 187

1. Quoted in California Commission on Campaign Financing, *Democracy by Initiative*, p. 37.
2. For analyses of the philosophy of the Progressives and the implementation and operation of their reforms, with specific reference to initiatives, see, Brogan, *The Penguin History of the United States of America*, pp. 385–480; California Commission on Campaign Financing, *Democracy by Initiative*, pp. 1–78; Cronin, *Direct Democracy*; Dubois and Feeney, *Improving the California Initiative Process: Options for Change*; Ellis, *Democratic Delusions*; Hofstadter, *The Age of Reform*; Goodwyn, *The Populist Movement*; Magleby, *Direct Legislation*; George E. Mowry, *The California Progressives*.
3. Ellis, *Democratic Delusions*.
4. Magleby, "Direct Legislation in the American States," Figure 7.3, p. 233.
5. For a statute initiative, California requires signatures equivalent to 5 percent of the total voting in the previous gubernatorial election; for a constitutional initiative, 8 percent.
6. Some states, for example California, also place initiatives on primary ballots, too.
7. Brown speaking to California Assembly hearings held in the 1970s on the initiative process (quoted in McCuan, Donovan, and Bowler, "Grassroots Democracy and California's Political Warriors," p. 4).
8. Broder, *Democracy Derailed*, pp. 17, 141, 163–164.
9. See Banducci, "Direct Legislation," pp. 126–128; and Magleby, "Direct Legislation in the American States," p. 250.
10. Banducci, "Direct Legislation," pp. 127–128; Cronin, *Direct Democracy*, p. 109; and Donovan et al., "Contending Players and Strategies: Opposition Advantages in Initiative Campaigns."
11. See Garrett, "Money, Agenda Setting, and Direct Democracy."
12. Karen Kapler and Jackie Steinman (campaign managers for Taxpayers Against 187), Interview, April 14, 1998; Scott Macdonald (press officer for Taxpayers Against 187), Interview, April 8, 1998; de la Torre, Interview.
13. Ellis, *Democratic Delusions*, pp. 79–81.
14. Alan Nelson (former INS commissioner and coauthor of 187), Interview, September 11, 1995; Ron Prince (chair of 187 campaign), Interview, April 4, 1998. See also, Lubenow, *California Votes*.
15. Bell, "The Referendum: Democracy's Barrier to Racial Equality"; Gamble, "Putting Civil Rights to a Popular Vote."
16. Gamble, "Putting Civil Rights to a Popular Vote," pp. 246–247.
17. Eule, "Checking California's Plebiscite"; and Linde, "When Is Initiative Lawmaking Not 'Republican Government'?"
18. Cronin, *Direct Democracy*, p. 92; Hajnal, Gerber, and Louch, "Minorities and Direct Legislation," p. 157.
19. Todd Donovan and Shaun Bowler, "Responsive or Responsible Government?" in Bowler, Donovan, and Tolbert (eds.), *Citizens as Legislators*; Donovan and Bowler, "Direct Democracy and Minority Rights." See also (for evidence from Switzerland) Frey and Goette, "Does the Popular Vote Destroy Civil Liberties?"
20. Hajnal, Gerber, and Louch, "Minorities and Direct Legislation."
21. Barbara Coe, an anti-immigrant activist on the 187 committee, commented: "Ron set everything up. It was all his idea." Quoted in *LA Times*, Orange County edition, September 4, 1994, p. A-1.
22. Prince was, before his involvement in 187, an accountant working for the family firm in Downey, Orange County. At the time he resided in Tustin, in the same county.

23. *LA Times*, Orange County edition, September 4, 1994, p. A-1.

24. Ibid.

25. Prince, Interview.

26. Ibid.

27. Ibid. Kiley also commented that "We realized right from the very beginning that this issue belonged in [the U.S.] Congress; it was a federal issue, not a state issue. But the problem was that they refused to even discuss it. [Moreover,] the twenty-nine bills that [Assemblyman] Dick Mountjoy authored up in Sacramento never came out of [the] hearing[s]. They were killed before they go to the floor of the Assembly" (Robert Kiley, Interview, April 10, 1988). Mountjoy also argued that 187 was a reaction to the inaction of the state legislature to address the issue (*LA Times*, Orange County edition, May 17, 1994, p. A-3).

28. Robert Kiley said that he and Prince had "been friends for many years through the political structure here in Orange County, California" (Interview).

29. Kiley said that he had worked as "A public political consultant for twenty-six years and [had been] involved in politics from City Council right the way up to the presidency, working for Ronald Reagan for six years" (Interview).

30. *LA Times*, Orange County edition, September 4, 1994, p. A-1. However, Ezell contradicted Kiley's claim that it was not about the money. Ezell commented that the Kiley "knew very little about illegal immigration at the time. It was a business consideration for them at the time. That's their business—campaigns." (*LA Times*, Home edition, December 14, 1994, p. A-3).

31. Kiley, Interview.

32. Quoted in Johnson, "An Essay on Immigration Politics," p. 655.

33. Nelson, Interview.

34. Kiley, Interview.

35. There is some confusion among the participants about exactly who contacted whom. Bill King said that Ezell had contacted him, and he in turn contacted Coe. Robert Kiley said that Ezell contacted Coe. And Coe was very vague about the dynamics (Barbara Coe, Interview, April 9, 1998; Kiley, Interview; William King, Interview, April 9, 1998).

36. Coe, Interview.

37. Ibid.

38. King soon left the CCIR and joined Nelson and Ezell in their new group, Americans Against Illegal Immigration (Ibid.).

39. Ibid.

40. Nelson, Interview. Nelson resigned his post—as do all top bureaucratic appointees—when George H. W. Bush became president. Bush accepted Nelson's resignation. There had been increasing embarrassment over Nelson's controversial tenure as head of the INS. Nelson reportedly spent $1,500 of his agency's budget on a portrait of himself, and he commissioned a video tribute entitled "The Nelson Years" to record and publicize his achievements. He also had a conflictual relationship with the attorney general and, after a Justice Department audit of the INS, was accused of inefficiency and poor leadership (see *LA Times*, Orange County edition, September 4, 1994, p. A-1; Johnson, "An Essay on Immigration Politics" p. 656).

41. Ron Prince refused to release the minutes of the meeting. He argued that this would be unfair as one of the participants had died—referring to the death of Alan Nelson (Prince, Interview).

42. Ibid. The participants also discussed the text of another anti-illegal-immigration initiative that was at that time trying to qualify for the ballot. The proposed initiative was written by former Los Angeles supervisor Pete Schabarum—who had also been involved with the earlier Proposition 140 term-limits initiative. Schabarum's

measure proposed the introduction of an identity-card system. However, the 187 people elected not to get involved with his measure. Prince suggested that the main reason for Schabarum's involvement was to update his mailing list (Prince, Interview). Schabarum's measure faltered at the signature-gathering phase. Nelson referred to it as "a still birth" (Nelson, Interview). Schabarum said that his proposal had received "only tepid support [and] questionable enthusiasm." By January 11, 1994, he had raised only $50,000 of the estimated $500,000 necessary to qualify an initiative proposition and had still not received approval from the California secretary of state to circulate the petition (*LA Times*, Home edition, January 12, 1994, p. B-2).

43. Nelson, Interview.
44. Both Prince and Kiley later said that Nelson's "legislative successes" were exactly that: legislative successes that would have little real impact on the problem (Prince, Interview; Kiley, Interview).
45. Nelson, Interview.
46. *Plyler v. Doe*, 472, U.S. 202 (1982). They did not establish a "fundamental right" to education, however.
47. It was a 5–4 decision, with Brennan, Marshall, Blackmun, Stevens and Powell on the majority and Burger, Rehnquist, O'Connor, and White in the minority.
48. Nelson, Interview; *LA Times*, Orange County edition, September 4, 1994, p. A-1; Home edition, December 14, 1994, p. A-3.
49. Kiley, Interview; Prince, Interview.
50. Prince, Interview.
51. Nelson, Interview.
52. *LA Times*, Home edition, December 14, 1994, p. A-3.
53. Prince, Interview.
54. For example, Robert Valdez of the RAND Corporation commented that "what people have not recognized is that this is part of a concerted effort in California. California is the battleground of the nation, and FAIR has laid out a strategic plan to make [illegal immigration] a major issue" (*LA Times*, September 19, 1993, p. A-1). Felix de la Torre, MALDEF's California analyst, similarly argued that after Wilson politicized the illegal-immigration issue, "Nelson, FAIR, and these other groups, who have for twenty-five years been trying to find a way to curb immigration, saw the opportunity, drafted the initiative and jumped on it" (de la Torre, Interview).
55. Kiley, Interview. Nelson died shortly after the end of campaign.
56. Another of member of the Coe's California Coalition for Immigration Reform (CCIR), Amanda Tilson, also attended the October 5 meeting. However, Tilson did not play as important role as Coe in the genesis of Prop. 187.
57. On this point, Kiley noted that

> I don't believe in trying to create a new wheel out there every time you do a new campaign. If this issue has been around for as long as it has been around, there will be other organizations out there that have been trying to do something. We wanted to find what areas they were hitting on and see if we could meet with them to find out their take on this whole thing. (Kiley, Interview)

58. Nelson, Interview.
59. The campaign-finance statements are filed in the Political Division of the Secretary of State's Building in Sacramento. The relevant statements are made on California Form 419, Schedule A, Monetary Contributions Received; California Form 419, Schedule B-Part 1, Loans Received; California Form 419, Ballot Measure Committee Summary Page. The 187/SOS committee's identification number is

931819. The campaign-finance statements filed with the secretary of state show that in the year before signature gathering began, the 187 committee received just over $11,000 in monetary and nonmonetary contributions. Prince therefore donated nearly one quarter of the money the committee received during this period.

60. In sum, then, during the first three months of qualification, the Proposition 187 committee received $175,500.

61. Secretary of State, *Financing the Qualification of Statewide Initiatives*, p. 4.

62. For example, during the January–March period, the committee failed to pay Alan Nelson the $26,500 he was owed for his professional services. Prince commented that

> the deal with Ezell and Nelson was that they could bill the committee for their advice, but they would only be paid if there was enough money in the pot—and there wasn't. In fact, Mr Ezell never returned his contract with us when it was clear that we were not raising money. (Prince, Interview)

With a professional signature-gathering firm charging between $1 and $2 per signature and about 500,000 signatures required for qualification, the donations, loans, and in-kind contributions received by the committee did not constitute a significant sum when compared to the potential cost of employing a professional firm to collect all the necessary signatures.

63. Prince, Interview.

64. Nelson, Interview.

65. King, Interview. Although King and Coe establish Citizens for Action Now (CAN) and later the CCIR, King left soon to set up Americans Against Illegal Immigration with Alan Nelson and Harold Ezell. Consequently, he refers to the CCIR as Coe's rather than his and Coe's organization.

66. Coe said the *911* newsletter was

> the primary vehicle for getting information out to the grassroots groups throughout the state . . . [A]nd we would prepare fax messages; fax bulletins; alerts about who needed to be where and when; what the latest situation was on the situation [*sic*]; places that had been found to be very viable locations [for signature gathering] such as major shopping malls; those who were amenable to our efforts; those who were in opposition to our efforts; places that people could go and collect signatures from the greatest number of people. (Coe, Interview)

67. Coe, Interview.

68. Ibid.

69. King, Interview.

70. Prince, Interview.

71. *LA Times*, Orange County edition, April 14, 1994, p. B-7.

72. Prince's evidence was that the campaign had received calls from supporters enquiring why their checks had not been cashed and why their requests for more petition forms had not been fulfilled; he thus concluded that the Santa Ana post office must have been responsible. The city of Santa Ana is 65 percent Latino (*LA Times*, Home edition, October 22, 1993, p. A-1).

73. The Prop. 187 committee set its own deadline of April 1. This was not met. The deadline released to press was April 22 (*LA Times*, Orange County edition, April 14, 1994, p. B-7). This was not met. The real deadline was late May, which was met.

74. Kiley, Interview.

75. Secretary of State, *Financing the Qualification of Statewide Initiatives*, p. 4.

76. Nelson, Interview.

77. For example, in the April–June period eleven politicians—the vast majority Republicans—gave $1,000 or more to the committee, with one notable sum of

$10,000 given by Jim Brulte on April 19. The committee also received two notable loans in this period. Republican politician Rogers loaned $25,000 on April 19 and Ron Prince loaned $20,000 on May 6. Furthermore, a nonmonetary contribution of $10,000 was received from the California Republican Party to pay for an absentee-ballot mailing. Despite these large donations, however, the committee was still heavily in debt at the end of June owing nearly $200,000. Notably, Robert Kiley was owed over $50,000 for his consultancy services and American Petition Consultants was owed nearly $40,000 for its efforts.

78. Rohrabacher introduced two amendments to a U.S. Congress education bill in March 1994. One sought to stop federal funding of undocumented schoolchildren. The other mandated schools to keep a record of how many of pupils were undocumented and how many legal resident children had one or more undocumented parents (*LA Times*, Home edition, March 3, 1994, p. B-2; Orange County edition, March 4, 1994, p. A-34).

79. *LA Times*, Orange County edition, February 16, 1994, p. B-4. Rohrabacher was correct in part and wrong in part. When he spoke, a majority of Mexican Americans did indeed support the initiative. By election day, however, a majority opposed it.

80. *LA Times*, Orange County edition, May 17, 1994, p. A-3; Orange County edition, June 19, 1994, p. B-3.

81. *LA Times*, Home edition, May 27, 1994, p. A-3 (emphasis added).

82. *LA Times*, Home edition, June 16, 1994, p. A-3.

83. For example, Ted Moreno, Democrat Santa Ana councilman, during the Democratic primary campaign for the Sixty-ninth Assembly District (Garden Grove) in Orange County, endorsed the measure during the taping of a television debate between the Democratic candidates on May 20. Several hours after the debate, Moreno issued a statement saying that he had reversed his endorsement after fully considering the text of the proposed initiative. He said, "I cannot in good conscience support such a mean-spirited, wrongheaded proposal that does nothing to resolve the real problems associated with illegal immigration." Moreno reversed his position after realizing that he had antagonized potential Latino donors including Latino Assembly members who had earmarked $20,000 for his campaign. Moreover, the sixty-ninth district in Santa Ana was two-thirds Latino. Although whites accounted for 70 percent of the district's voters because of low Latino registration, Moreno would have required a good proportion of the Latino vote to win the seat (then held by Tom Umberg who was retiring to run for state attorney general). The Latino caucus in the Assembly had not at this point made its position clear, but its leader, Richard Polanco, seemed to be moving toward opposition as the campaign progressed and the issue bifurcated along racial lines (*LA Times*, Orange County edition, May 21, 1994, p. B-1; Orange County edition, May 29, 1994, p. B-3).

84. *LA Time*, Home, March 12, 1994, p. A-29.

85. In an op-ed piece in the *LA Times*, Ruben Navarrette Jr. suggested that the Latino caucus would only have an impact when it entered and learnt the new language of the debate over border control and realized that a majority of Latinos in America are seriously concerned about illegal immigration (*LA Times*, Home edition, March 20, 1994, p. M-2 [opinion]).

86. *LA Times*, Home edition, January 7, 1994, p. B-1.

87. *LA Times*, Home edition, January 8, 1994, p. B-3.

88. The One Stop Immigration and Educational Center, a private, non-profitmaking organization that provided English and naturalization classes and advice, was one of the key organizers of the coalition. Juan Jose Gutierrez was the director of the

center and would later play an important role in the campaign against 187 (*LA Times*, Home edition, February 20, 1994, p. *City Times*-6).

89. *LA Times*, Southland edition, February 27, 1994, p. A-30.
90. Organizers hoped to attract between 3,000 and 5,000 people to defend themselves and fight those mobilizing against them (*LA Times*, Home edition, February 20, 1994, p. *City Times*-6).
91. Nelson, Interview.
92. Prince, Interview.
93. Ibid.
94. This is Robert Kiley's own phrase (Interview).
95. About professionalization, see Magleby, *Direct Legislation*, pp. 62, 67; McCuan, Donovan, and Bowler, "Grassroots Democracy and California's Political Warriors," pp. 10–15.
96. *LA Times*, Home edition, June 23, 1994, p. A-3.
97. Kiley, Interview; Nelson, Interview; Prince, Interview.
98. Nelson, Interview.
99. Prince, Interview.
100. However, the May poll must be treated cautiously; the *LA Times* polls immediately before and after the May poll show majority Latino support for Prop. 187, suggesting that it may have been a rogue poll.
101. *LA Times*, Home edition, May 29, 1994, p. A-1.
102. Gorton quoted in Lubenow, *California Votes—the 1994 Governor's Race*, p. 47.
103. Dresner quoted in ibid., p. 138.
104. Prince, Interview. Prince was wrong about the governor being 20 points behind in September 1994, as the next chapter will show.
105. Kiley, Interview.
106. Prince, Interview.
107. Nelson, Interview. Prince believed that Wilson voted against Prop. 187; that Wilson's anti-immigrant television ads harmed Prop. 187; and that *Field* polls were fixed to show low support for his initiative (Prince, Interview).
108. Nelson, Interview (emphasis added).

5   The Campaign

1. Macdonald, Interview. Although Macdonald, Kapler, and Steinman were all campaign professionals and employees of Woodward and McDowell, they all felt that they became personally and emotionally involved in the No campaign. Macdonald commented that, for example, "This really meant something. We worked our asses off" (Macdonald, Interview; see, also, Kapler and Steinman, Interview).
2. Kaper and Steinman, Interview.
3. *LA Times*, Home edition, November 4, 1994, p. B-1.
4. *LA Times*, Home edition, October 11, 1994, p. B-1; Orange County edition, October 2, 1994, p. B-2; see also Home edition, October 3, 1994, p. B-7. Unz also sponsored the anti-bilingual initiative, Proposition 227, which was passed by California voters in June 1998 by 61–39 percent.
5. *LA Times*, Home edition, October 19, 1994, p. B-1.
6. *LA Times*, Home edition, November 4, 1994, p. B-7. Hicks was the executive director of the Southern Christian Leadership Conference of Greater Los Angeles. Rice was the Western Regional counsel for the National Association for the Advancement of Colored People.
7. *LA Times*, Home edition, July 24, 1994, p. B-1.

8. *LA Times*, Home edition, October 9, 1994, p. B-1; Home edition, October 25, 1994, p. B-7.

9. The California Business Roundtable and the Los Angeles Chamber of Commerce decided to take no position on the initiative, however (*LA Times*, Valley edition, October 28, 1994, p. B-4). As with some farm associations, business benefits from the cheap labor illegal immigrants provide. But some of their organizations decided to stay neutral because of the controversy surrounding and high support for the measure. Not all businesspeople and business associations spoke out against 187 or remained neutral, however. The San Fernando Valley United Chambers of Commerce voted to support it, for example. See *LA Times*, Home edition, October 21, 1994, p. A-3; Valley edition, October 28, 1994, p. B-4.

10. *LA Times*, Home edition, November 4, 1994, p. A-3.

11. *LA Times*, Home edition, August 17, 1994, p. B-2; Home edition, September 29, 1994, p. A-21; Orange County edition, October 18, 1994, p. B-6; Home edition, October 19, 1994, p. B-1; Orange County edition, November 3, 1994, p. B-1.

12. Macdonald, Interview. The message was developed in response to and tested on focus groups (Kapler and Steinman, Interview). For the political theory behind such empirical reasoning, see Riker, *The Theory of Political Coalitions*. See also Cain, "Lessons from the Inside Revisited."

13. Macdonald, Interview.

14. Taxpayers Against 187, "Key Points," October 3, 1994 (original emphasis). Macdonald commented that people were

> just pissed off . . . 187 won because illegal immigration was a problem. If you lived in southern California at that time, and even to a certain extent today, you drive down the street and see Latino men looking for work. This is not a bad thing . . . but people drive by there and think all these people are illegal immigrants, which is wrong, but that's what they think. They go to a McDonald's restaurant and they can't order a hamburger because the person taking their order can't speak English—it makes them crazy. None of these things make any logical sense when you think of 187, but this is the atmosphere that it was presented in. It passed because there was this atmosphere. (Macdonald, Interview)

15. Macdonald, Interview; Kapler and Steinman, Interview.

16. Block said he was "as concerned about illegal immigration and its impact on this state as anyone else. But Proposition 187 does not address the problem in any fashion and, in fact, to my mind, actually exacerbates the problem." He suggested that a more effective response to the illegal-immigration problem would be enhanced border enforcement (*LA Times*, Home edition, August 19, 1994, p. A-3).

17. Macdonald, Interview.

18. Kapler and Steinman, Interview.

19. Macdonald, Interview.

20. *LA Times*, Home edition, September 26, 1994, p. A-1.

21. Macdonald, Interview. Macdonald also noted that the grassroots No campaign spent thousands of dollars to bring Jesse Jackson to Los Angeles to speak against Prop. 187. Yet "people who are Jesse Jackson's fans are No on 187. We don't need to spend thousands of dollars to bring him out here." He said that the money would have been better spent on an early buy of radio ads for example (Macdonald, Interview).

22. *New York Times*, October 27, 1994, p. A-29.

23. Kapler and Steinman, Interview.

24. Woodward and McDowell had a year to get its message across in the successful defeat of Big Green in 1990 (*LA Times*, Home edition, September 26, 1994, p. A-1).

25. *LA Times*, Home edition, September 26, 1994, p. A-1.

26. Ibid.

27. *LA Times*, Home edition, September 25, 1994, p. A-1.

28. In its successful 1990 campaign against Big Green, Woodward and McDowell spent over $12 million, raised mainly from business interests, nearly three times more than its opponents' $4.5 million (John Tweedy Jr., "Coalition Building and the Defeat of California's Proposition 128," p. 131).

29. A representative of the Nisei Farmers League, an organization representing over 1,000 fruit growers in California, said, "Lets face it, fifty percent, if not more, of the agricultural work force in this [San Joaquin] valley is illegal. We'd sink economically without them" (*LA Times*, Home edition, September 27, 1994, p. A-3; see also *LA Times*, Home edition, October 2, 1994, p. A-3).

30. *LA Times*, Home edition, September 27, 1994, p. A-3.

31. *LA Times*, Home edition, September 26, 1994, p. A-1.

32. Ibid.

33. *LA Times*, Home edition, October 7, 1994, p. B-1.

34. Ibid., p. A-34.

35. *LA Times*, Home edition, August 27, 1994, p. B-7.

36. *LA Times*, Home edition, September 14, 1994, p. A-3.

37. *LA Times*, Home edition, September 16, 1994, p. A-1. On September 15, Wilson also signed two pieces of legislation into law. The first prohibited state contracts to be given to employers who had been convicted of employing undocumented workers. The second made it easier for illegal-immigrant felons to be transferred from state to federal prisons.

38. *LA Times*, Home edition, September 18, 1994, p. A-3.

39. July 12–17 Field (California) Poll.

40. University of California-Irvine, Poll, August 19–29.

41. *LA Times Poll*, September 8–11 (*LA Times*, Home edition, September 13, 1994, p. A-1).

42. Ibid.

43. *LA Times*, Home edition, September 10, 1994, p. B-3. For an excellent analysis of the politics and research of Shockley, see William H. Tucker, *The Science and Politics of Racial Research*. The president of the Pioneer Fund, Harry Weyher, responded to the Taxpayers claims by pointing out that the word "white" was removed from the organization's charter in 1985 (*LA Times*, Home edition, September 10, 1994, p. B-3).

44. *LA Times*, Home edition, September 10, 1994, p. B-3.

45. Ibid.

46. The ad intoned that Prop. 187 would kick "300,000 kids out of school . . . and onto our streets, and that means more crime" (*LA Times*, Home edition, October 12, 1994, p. A-3).

47. *LA Times*, Home edition, October 12, 1994, p. A-3.

48. Ibid.; and Nelson, Interview.

49. *LA Times*, Home edition, October 12, 1994, p. A-3.

50. *LA Times*, Home edition, September 14, 1994, p. A-3.

51. *LA Times*, Home edition, September 16, 1994, p. A-1.

52. *New York Times*, September 18, 1994, p. A-1; December 13, 1994, p. A-1.

53. *LA Times*, Home edition, September 21, 1994, p. B-1.

54. Ibid.

55. *LA Times*, Home edition, October 19, 1994, p. A-1.

56. *LA Times*, Home edition, October 22, 1994, p. A-1; see also *New York Times*, October 22, 1994, pp. A-1, A-9. Kapler and Steinman later suggested that Clinton's

"unconstitutional" argument may not have helped the No campaign because some people may have felt that they could vote Yes without risking the consequences of the proposed law (Interview).

57. *New York Times*, October 22, 1994, pp. A-1, A-9; *LA Times*, Home edition, October 22, 1994, p. A-1.

58. *LA Times*, Home edition, October 22, 1994, p. A-1. In an attempt to mitigate the electoral effect of her opposition to Prop. 187, Feinstein again visited the California-Mexico border at the end of October. At Imperial Beach, California, one of the most porous parts of the border, she watched the Border Patrol use their new night-vision scopes to identify and apprehend illegal border crossers. This was her fourth visit to the border during her first six years as senator. Feinstein emphasized that she had voted in favor of increased funding for the Border Patrol and INS (*LA Times*, Home edition, October 24, 1994, p. A-3). Huffington had closed the gap considerably on Feinstein during September and October (See table 1 in appendix C).

The Feinstein-Huffington illegal-immigration battle continued through October and early November. Toward the end of October, it was revealed that Huffington had employed an undocumented nanny for nearly five years—thus violating the IRCA's provisions that required employers to check and verify their employees had valid papers—and failed to pay the required taxes for the first two years of her appointment. Huffington admitted that he had done so (*LA Times*, Home edition, October 28, 1994, p. A-1). On November 2, with just one week to go before election day, Huffington accused Feinstein of also employing an illegal immigrant as a domestic help (*LA Times*, Home edition, November 3, 1994, p. A-3). He also accused Feinstein of bribery and forgery. However, he offered no proof to substantiate his allegations. Huffington initially said on November 2 that he would provide proof for his allegation that Feinstein had employed an undocumented nanny on November 3 or 4. However, later that day, he said he may not provide proof until November 6, telling reporters, "you'll have to wait" (*LA Times*, Home edition, November 3, 1994, p. A-3). Clearly irritated and exasperated by her opponent's tactics, Feinstein said,

> [w]hat can I do? . . . I have said it is false. You know this is someone who doesn't tell the truth. I mean, we have been through it over and over and over again . . . And now, when his hand is caught in the cookie jar, he says, "Oh well, she has done it too." And yet he has not submitted one iota of proof. (Ibid.)

It appears that Huffington was waiting for the INS to check his claims. On November 3, the INS admitted that it had made a mistake—it had been looking at the records of another immigrant—but not before Huffington ran a television ad branding Feinstein a liar. Subsequent investigation by the INS revealed that Feinstein's housekeeper had been working without the necessary papers, but six years before the passage of the IRCA in 1986. Feinstein claimed that she checked her employee's papers and found they were in order. The employee, Ms. Realegeno, also claimed that she had the correct papers and that she had shown them to Feinstein (who was then mayor of San Francisco), who in turn verified them (*New York Times*, November 5, 1994, p. 1–11).

59. *LA Times*, Home edition, October 12, 1994, p. A-3.

60. *LA Times*, Home edition, October 21, 1994, p. A-1.

61. Ibid.

62. *LA Times*, Home edition, October 19, 1994, p. A-1. Governor Wilson accused Kemp and Bennett of being Washington insiders who were not in touch with public opinion (*New York Times*, October 24, 1994, p. A-1).

63. *LA Times*, Home edition, October 19, 1994, p. A-1.
64. Ibid.
65. *LA Times*, Home edition, November 22, 1994, p. A-1.
66. *LA Times*, Home edition, November 4, 1994, p. A-3. This coalition of conservative organizations was put together by Cesar V. Conda, executive director of the Alexis de Tocqueville Institution. At a press conference, Conda reiterated the appeal to conservative values: "basically, in our view, [Prop. 187 is] a Big Brother, big government scheme that will do little to deter illegal immigration" (ibid.).
67. William F. Buckley, Jr., "It's all right, Jack," *National Review*, September 16, 1996.
68. Nelson, Interview.
69. Robert Kiley quoted in *LA Times*, Home edition, October 22, 1994, p. A-1.
70. *LA Times*, Home edition, October 25, 1994, p. A-1 (emphasis added).
71. *New York Times*, October 27, 1994, pp. A-1, A-27.
72. *LA Times*, Home edition, October 25, 1994, p. A-1.
73. *LA Times*, Home edition, October 27, 1994, p. A-1.
74. October 21–30 *Field* Poll; *LA Times*, Home edition, October 25, 1994, p. A-1. Woodward and McDowell's tracking polls in the last few days of October showed support for Prop. 187 at 46 percent and opposition at 42 percent (*LA Times*, Home edition, October 25, 1994, p. A-1). When Prince was asked to account for Prop. 187's decline in the polls, he suggested that both the *LA Times* and *Field* polls were unreliable. He said that the people behind the polls wanted to show that Prop. 187 was losing support, so this is what the polls showed. He said, for example, that one of the *LA Times* polls was conducted in the Pico-Union district of Los Angeles, which is "heavily illegal," and this skewed the result against Prop. 187— "It was an effort to manufacture a response to a poll. I don't think it was legitimate." Prince's position is that support for his initiative never really dropped (Prince, Interview).
75. *LA Times*, Home edition, October 18, 1994, p. B-1. The march was organized by the National Coordinating Committee for Citizenship and Civic Participation (NCCCCP)—another coalition of grassroots activists.
76. The march's organizers estimated that 100,000 people took part (*LA Times*, Home edition, October 21, 1994, p. B-7).
77. Their plan to create a new civil rights movement faced many structural obstacles. California Latinos were and are a heterogeneous population, split across nationalities. Some were citizens, others legal residents, and still others illegal immigrants. There were also class and wealth divisions, as well as psychological differences between those loyal to their homelands and those who had been acculturated. Some of the march's organizers compared the events of October 16 with the Chicano movement of the 1960s and 1970s. The Chicano movement, however, did not have to face many of the divisions noted above. The political environment of the 1960s and 1970s was in many ways much less complex than it was in the 1990s. For example, the Chicano movement consisted largely of U.S. citizens of Mexican descent, whereas the 1990s California Latino population was deeply divided on grounds of citizenship and nationality (*LA Times*, Home edition, October 18, 1994, p. B-1). Although creating an effective opposition to Prop. 187 within the Latino community was difficult, the creation of an interethnic opposition coalition was even harder. The problem of creating an anti-187 coalition across ethnic boundaries can be highlighted by the conflict between the Latino and African American populations. Many black leaders came out against 187 while recognizing that many African Americans would vote for the initiative. With 40 percent of black youths unemployed, it is easy to see why some may have been

sympathetic to the message that illegal immigrants took jobs. Moreover, the Latino and black populations in California have never really worked together despite their attachments to the Democratic Party. It is interesting to speculate that perhaps the most effective type of race card in constituencies with large minority populations is one that splits the nonwhite vote.

78. *LA Times*, Orange County edition, October 17, 1994, p. A-1; Home edition, September 26, 1994, p. A-16.

79. Macdonald, Interview.

80. *LA Times*, Home edition, October 25, 1994, p. B-6.

81. *LA Times*, Home edition, October 18, 1994, p. B-1.

82. For example, one student leader, Angel Cervantes, a graduate student at Claremont College, had formed the "October Student Movement" as an anti-Wilson vehicle. But after attending CUAP 187's summer conference, he was recruited into the coalition and his own group became an anti-187 mobilizing force. Cervantes said that he

> had been trying to organize students for years, but this [Prop. 187] is the one issue I've been waiting for. We want to have statewide, organized student mobilizations—hopefully in the form of sit-ins and forums . . . and precinct walking. And our goals are 100% after the election to continue this movement. (*LA Times*, Home edition, November 4, 1994, p. B-1)

On October 14, around 1,500 students from several Los Angeles schools staged a walkout. On October 21, 200 students from Estancia High School in Costa Mesa, Orange County, held an unruly but peaceful march against 187 and Governor Wilson, shouting slogans such as "viva la raza" and "Mexico, Mexico, Mexico" (*LA Times*, Orange County edition, October 22, 1994, p. B-1; Home edition, October 22, 1994, p. B-1). Another five largely peaceful walkouts and marches took place in Los Angeles on October 21. However, in one of these marches in Paramount, Los Angeles, police fired two rubber "stingball" grenades (nonlethal devices that explode emitting rubber pellets) to dispel 500 high school protestors (*LA Times*, Home edition, October 22, 1994, p. B-1; Valley edition, October 25, 1994, p. B-1). Although most of the protests took place in the Los Angeles School District, other districts also experienced walkouts and sit-ins. For instance, 1,500 mainly Latino students from Oxnard staged a weekend rally at the end of October and the protests continued in the district through to polling day. Although most teachers and school administrators did not condone the direct-action protests, punishments varied across school districts and individual schools. Some schools suspended the organizers of the walkouts, while the majority just issued warnings. The Los Angeles Unified School District's policy was, initially, not to punish students as long as there was no trouble and they returned to school after the demonstration. In fact, administrators and teachers generally worked to draw attention to what they saw as the damaging consequences of 187 (*LA Times*, Valley edition, October 22, 1994, p. B-1; Valley edition, October 25, 1994, p. B-1; Home edition, November 5, 1994, p. A-24).

83. *LA Times*, Home edition, October 26, 1994, p. B-3; Home edition, November 2, 1994, p. B-1; Home edition, November 4, 1994, p. B-1. Latino students already enjoyed an effective communication within and between high schools and colleges—the Movimiento Estudiantil Chicano de Aztlan (MEChA)—that could have only exacerbated the snowballing effect (*LA Times*, Home edition, November 4, 1994, p. B-1).

84. Macdonald, Interview.

85. *LA Times*, Home edition, November 4, 1994, p. A-3.

86. The California Teachers Association, which was already the largest donor having given $433,000 previously, contributed another $100,000. Univision, also having

already contributed substantial amounts, gave a further $200,000. David Gelbaum of the Newport Beach firm, Sierra Partners contributed $180,000, and $100,000 was donated by John Moores, the Texas businessman, who was one of Kathleen Brown's main financial backers (*LA Times*, Home edition, November 8, 1994, p. A-3).

87. *LA Times*, Home edition, November 8, 1994, p. A-3.

88. Macdonald, Interview.

89. *LA Times*, Home edition, November 8, 1994, p. A-3.

90. Ibid.; *LA Times*, Home edition, October 13, 1994, p. B-1; Orange County edition, September 4, 1994, p. A-1.

91. *LA Times*, Home edition, November 3, 1994, p. A-25.

92. Campaign-finance Statements.

93. One protest became violent as black and Latino students from two different Los Angeles schools fought each other. See *LA Times*, Home edition, November 4, 1994, p. B-1; Home edition, November 5, 1994, p. A-24.

94. *LA Times*, Home edition, November 8, 1994, p. A-3.

95. Prince, Interview. It seems, however, that this is part of Prince's paranoia about Pete Wilson and the Republican Party. For other examples see chapter 4.

96. *LA Times*, Home edition, October 26, 1994, p. B-3; Home edition, November 2, 1994, p. B-1; Home edition, November 4, 1994, p. A-3; Home edition, November 5, 1994, p. A-24.

97. For example, a statement issued on election day by the Latino advocacy group, El Concilio del Condado de Ventura, said, "students are particularly urged not to walk out of school on the days immediately following the election" (*LA Times*, Ventura West edition, November 8, 1994, p. B-1).

98. *New York Times*, November 3, 1994, p. A-29. The previous year, the Mexican Foreign Ministry had criticized Wilson's focus on illegal immigration (*LA Times*, Home edition, August 15, 1994, p. A-3; Home edition, August 16, 1994, p. B-6). The Mexican government contacted Latino groups in California. It offered advice on tactics and arguments and promised money to help fight the initiative in the U.S. courts. However, on the advice of California strategists, the Mexican government's actions mostly consisted of rhetorical language for fear of promoting a backlash in California (*New York Times*, November 3, 1994, p. A-29).

99. *New York Times*, September 14, 1994, pp. A-1, A-14; October 27, 1994, p. A-27; November 3, 1994, p. A-29; November 9, 1994, p. A-1. A boycott of U.S. businesses on the American side of the border on November 20–21 produced a 7 percent drop in legal border crossings into the United States from Mexico. Millions of dollars of business was lost in San Diego and other border cities (*New York Times*, October 27, 1994, p. A-27; November 9, 1994, p. A-1).

100. October 22–25 *LA Times Poll. LA Times*, Home edition, October 27, 1994, p. A-1.

101. *New York Times*, October 27, 1994, p. A-29.

102. The exact percentages are 58.93 percent Yes (5,063,537 votes), 41.07 percent No (3,529,432 votes). Bill Jones, Secretary of State, *Statement of Vote: November 8, 1994, General Election*, p. xxv.

103. October 8–11, 1994, *LA Times Poll* #346. See appendix A for details.

6 The Judicial Death of Proposition 187

1. See, for example, *Fresno Bee*, November 9, 1994, p. B-1; November 10, 1994, p. A-1; *Christian Science Monitor*, November 10, 1994, p. A-1; *Houston Chronicle*, November 11, 1994, p. A-1; *LA Times*, November 9, 1994, p. A-1; *Orange County Register*, November 9, 1994, p. E-2; *San Francisco Chronicle*, November 10,

1994, p. A-1; *San Francisco Examiner*, November 9, 1994, p. A-1; *USA Today*, November 9, 1994, p. A-2; *Washington Post*, November 9, 1994, p. A-25; *Washington Times*, November 11, p. A-15.

2. *Fresno Bee*, November 9, 1994, p. B-1; *LA Times*, Ventura West edition, November 9, 1994, p. B-1; *LA Times*, Home edition, November 11, 1994, p. A-1; Home edition, November 24, 1994, p. J-11; Home edition, February 12, 1995, *City Times*-3; Home edition, February 17, 1995, p. B-3; Home edition, February 26, 1995, *City Times*-9; *Orange Country Register*, November 10, 1994, p. E-12; *The Recorder*, November 11, 1994, p. 3; *San Francisco Chronicle*, November 10, 1994, p. A-1.

3. *LA Times*, Orange County edition, November 24, 1994, p. B-1; Home edition, December 17, 1994, p. A-27; Ventura West edition, December 18, 1994, p. B-1; Orange County edition, December 31, 1994, p. A-1; Home edition, January 28, 1995, p. B-2; Home edition, March 1, 1995, p. E-3; *USA Today*, November 21, 1994, p. A-1.

4. *Associated Press*, November 9, 1994; *LA Times*, Home edition, November 11, 1994, p. A-1; Home edition, November 12, 1994, p. B-1; Ventura West edition, November 20, 1994, p. B-1; Orange County edition, November 26, 1994, p. A-1; *Plain Dealer*, November 19, 1994, P. A-10; *San Francisco Chronicle*, November 26, p. A-14.

5. *San Francisco Chronicle*, November 29, A-18.

6. *Associated Press*, November 23, 1994; *LA Times*, Orange County edition, November 23, 1994, p. A-1; Orange County edition, December 4, 1994, p. B-13; *Orange County Register*, November 24, 1994, p. B-8; *San Francisco Chronicle*, November 24, 1994, p. A-1.

7. *LA Times*, Orange County edition, November 26, 1994, p. A-1; Home edition, November 29, 1994, p. B-1. The autopsy revealed Julio had acute leukemia.

8. *LA Times*, Home edition, November 23, 1994, p. B-1.

9. *LA Times*, Home edition, November 11, 1994, p. A-1.

10. *LA Times*, Home edition, December 10, 1994, p. A-38.

11. Ultimately, the civil rights lawyers billed the state for their legal work against Prop. 187. Mark Rosenbaum of the ACLU billed California for $464,621 or 1,304 hours at $375 per hour. Peter Schey of Center for Human Rights and Constitutional Law billed for $1,053,500 or 3,010 hours at $350 per hour. The total bill for all lawyers in the class action reached over $3 million. A federal law permits lawyers on the winning side in civil rights cases to recover their costs from the state. The law was designed to enable nonprofit firms to mount costly legal challenges to civil rights abuses (see *Associated Press*, September 6, 1998; *LA Times*, September 6, 1998, p. A-1).

12. *LA Times*, Home edition, March 14, 1995, p. A-1.

13. The best-organized recall effort was directed against Mark Slavkin, president of the Los Angeles Unified School District Board. The petition drive—which needed to collect 53,000 signatures in 120 days to place the recall measure on the ballot— was organized by Glenn Spencer and his Voices of Citizens Together anti-immigrant pressure group. By the deadline for collecting signatures, April 14, 1995, Spencer and his fellow campaigners had collected about 30,000 signatures, well short of the required number (*LA Times*, Home edition, April 15, 1995, p. B-1).

14. *LA Times*, Home edition, November 10, 1994, p. A-1.

15. Ibid.

16. *LA Times*, Home edition, November 16, 1994, p. A-1.

17. *LA Times*, Home edition, November 17, 1994, p. A-1. Of course, he meant Frankenstein's monster, not the scientist himself.

18. *LA Times*, Home edition, November 16, 1994, p. A-1; Home edition, January 27, 1995, p. A-3; Home edition, January 28, 1995, p. A-18.
19. Spaeth and Smith, *The Constitution of the United States*, p. 148.
20. *Plyler v. Doe*, 457.
21. *LA Times*, Home edition, December 15, 1994, p. A-1
22. Following Pfaelzer's lead, Judge Pollak then issued a preliminary injunction against the education provisions on February 8, 1995 (*LA Times*, Home edition, February 9, 1995, p. A-3).
23. *LA Times*, Home edition, April 25, 1995, p. B-14.
24. *LA Times*, Home edition, January 5, 1995, p. B-1.
25. It is worth repeating here an observation from an earlier chapter: Ron Prince believed that Wilson did not even vote for Prop. 187. Prince thought that Wilson hijacked the campaign for his own political ends, and only harmed the anti-immigrant cause. In this light, it is easy to see why he would think Wilson et al. were not fully committed to defending the initiative in court.
26. *LA Times*, Home edition, January 28, 1995, p. A-18.
27. *Orange County Register*, January 28, 1995, p. A-22.
28. Ibid.
29. *LA Times*, Home edition, January 31, 1995, p. A-18.
30. *LA Times*, Home edition, July 15, 1995, p. A-21.
31. *LA Times*, Home edition, February 4, 1995, p. A-22.
32. *LA Times*, Home edition, March 17, 1995, p. B-2.
33. *LA Times*, Home edition, March 14, 1995, p. A-1.
34. *LA Times*, Home edition, April 1, 1995, p. B-2.
35. *LA Times*, Home edition, February 14, 1995, p. A-3. Wilson appealed Keep's ruling, but the US Supreme Court refused to hear the case, and it died in October 1997. See *United Press International*, October 7, 1997.
36. *LA Times*, Home edition, February 14, 1995, p. A-3.
37. *LA Times*, Home edition, February 16, 1995, p. A-3.
38. *LA Times*, Home edition, February 21, 1995, p. A-3.
39. Ibid.
40. *LA Times*, Home edition, February 25, 1995, p. A-21.
41. *LA Times*, Home edition, May 2, 1995, p. A-3; Home edition, April 18, 1995, p. A-21.
42. Kristine Berman, a Wilson spokesperson in *LA Times*, Home edition, May 2, 1995, p. A-3.
43. Ibid.
44. UCLA law professor Erwin Chemerinsky in *LA Times*, Home edition, May 2, 1995, p. A-3.
45. Mark D. Rosenbaum, ACLU legal director, ibid.
46. *LA Times*, Home edition, July 27, 1995, p. A-3.
47. *LA Times*, Home edition, September 8, 1995, p. A-3.
48. *LA Times*, Home edition, November 21, 1995, p. A-1; *San Francisco Examiner*, November 21, 1995, p. A-1.
49. Ibid; *San Francisco Chronicle*, November 21, 1995, p. A-1.
50. *San Francisco Chronicle*, November 21, 1995, p. A-1.
51. *The Recorder*, November 22, 1995, p. 1.
52. *LA Times*, Home edition, November 21, 1995, p. A-1; Home edition, November 22, 1995, p. A-3.
53. *LA Times*, Home edition, November 21, 1995, p. A-1.
54. Ibid.

55. Although they later changed their argument arguing instead that the single final judgment rule did not permit appeals on partial judgments.

56. *LA Times*, Home edition, December 13, 1995, p. A-3; Home edition, February 1, 1996, p. A-3.

57. *The Recorder*, November 27, 1996, p. 1.

58. *LA Times*, Home edition, November 2, 1996, p. A-1.

59. *The Recorder*, November 27, 1996, p. 1.

60. *LA Times*, Home Edition, November 2, 1996, p. A-1.

61. *The Recorder*, November 27, 1996, p. 1.

62. *Copley News Service*, November 21, 1996; *Business Wire*, February 4, 1997; *LA Times*, Home Edition, February 5, 1997, p. A-1; *United Press International*, February 21, 1997.

63. *LA Times*, Home Edition, December 27, 1996, p. B-9.

64. *United Press International*, March 4, 1997; *LA Times*, Home Edition, March 4, 1997, p. A-1. In effect, however, the state and federal regulations were not alike. Under the federal scheme, illegal aliens are reported. Under the state one, however, those "suspected" of being illegal aliens would be reported. Moreover, while the federal regulations established closer links between the INS and other government agencies, they did not require individual teachers, doctors, and so on to report "suspected" unauthorized persons direct to the INS.

65. Quoted in Starr, *Coast of Dreams*, pp. 212–213.

66. *Metropolitan News-Enterprise*, November 10, 1997; *LA Times*, November 8, 1997, p. A-1.

67. Ibid.

68. *LA Times*, Home Edition, November 8, 1997, p. A-1.

69. See *Copley News* Service, November 15, 1997; *LA Times*, Home Edition, November 15, 1997, p. A-1; *Migration News*, December 1997, Vol. 4, No. 12; *New York* Times, Late Edition, November 15, 1997, p. A-8; *Siskind's Immigration Bulletin*, December 1997, online at http://www.visalaw.com/97dec/14dec97.html, accessed November 12, 2007; *Washington Post*, Final Edition, November 15, 1997, p. A-3.

70. *Migration News*, December 1997, Vol. 4, No. 12; *LA Times*, Home Edition, November 15, 1997, p. A-1; *Washington Post*, Final Edition, November 15, 1997, p. A-3; *New York Times*, Late Edition, November 15, 1997, p. A-8.

71. *LA Times*, Home Edition, November 15, 1997, p. A-1.

72. Mark Rosenbaum of the ACLU, in *LA Times*, Home Edition, November 15, 1997, p. A-1.

73. Peter Schey of the Center for Human Rights and Constitutional Law, in *LA Times*, Home Edition, November 15, 1997, p. A-1.

74. It also superseded and thus ended the court case in Judge Pollak's San Francisco Superior Court, which had challenged Prop. 187's exclusion of undocumented students from the state's public colleges and universities.

75. Dan Stein, Federation for American Immigration Reform Press Release, PR Newswire, March 18, 1998.

76. *Copley News Service*, May 23, 1998.

77. *LA Times Exit Poll #413*, California Primary Election, June 2, 1998.

78. In the open primary, all candidates appear on the same ballot paper. Thus, Republican hopeful Lungren appeared alongside Democratic hopefuls Gray Davis, Jane Harman, and Al Checchi. The open primary has since been declared unconstitutional.

79. *LA Times Exit Poll #413*, California Primary Election, June 2, 1998. Gray Davis won 35 percent of the overall vote, but took 36 percent of the Latino vote, more than double that won by Lungren.

80. *Copley News Service*, July 19, 1998.
81. Ibid.
82. *Associated Press*, October 13, 1998.
83. Ibid.
84. *LA Times Exit Poll, #420*, California General Election, November 3, 1998.
85. *LA Times*, November 4, 1998, p. A-1.
86. Gray Davis, First Inaugural Address, January 4, 1999.
87. *Christian Science Monitor*, April 1, 1999, p. 1; *LA Times*, March 25, 1999, p. A-3.
88. *LA Times*, March 26, 1999, p. B-6; March 26, 1999, p. A-3.
89. *LA Times*, April 14, 1999, p. A-1.
90. See, inter alia, *Associated Press*, April 15, 1999; *City New Service*, April 15, 1999; *Copley New Service*, April 16, 1999; *LA Times*, April 16, 1999, p. A-1; April 19, 1999, p. A-3; *New York Times*, April 16, 1999, p. A-14; *San Francisco Chronicle*, April 15, 1999, p. A-17; April 16, 1999, p. A-21; April 17, 1999, p. A-13; *Washington Times*, April 16, 1999, p. A-3;
91. *San Francisco Chronicle*, April 22, 1999, p. A-23; *LA Times*, April 22, 1999, p. A-3.
92. One coalition of minority leaders—including the National Black Chamber of Commerce, the California Hispanic Chamber of Commerce, the California Council for Equal Opportunity, and the Mexican American Political Association—wrote an open letter to Bustamante, praising him for "standing tall for the rights of all Californians. . . . Had the lieutenant governor and governor of California spoken out in a similar fashion in 1941–42, our nation might have avoided the incarceration of hundreds of thousands of loyal Japanese American citizens" (*San Francisco Chronicle*, April 29, 1999, p. A-17).
93. *Associated Press*, April 26, 1999; *San Francisco Chronicle*, April 27, 1999, p. A-15; April 29, 1999, p. A-17. Legislative insiders said Davis had assumed that Democratic Latino leaders would back his mediation decision, and that he did not consult Bustamante and other key leaders before announcing his plan (*LA Times*, May 11, 1999, p A-1).
94. *New York Times*, April 16, 1999, p. A-14.
95. The Howard Jarvis Taxpayers Association, veterans of several initiative battles including Prop. 13 of 1978, sued Davis in the state supreme court in June 1999, arguing that sending initiatives to mediation "will establish a precedent that will undermine the people's sacred right of initiative" (*LA Times*, June 2, 1999, p. A-16).
96. Professor Erwin Chemerinsky, USC Law School, quoted in *San Francisco Chronicle*, April 17, 1999, p. A-13.
97. Mediators for the court regularly scan the court's docket for cases amenable to mediation. Interestingly, they rejected mediation for Prop. 187 in May 1998. Governor Davis, however, would probably not have announced his decision to go to mediation unless he had received informal assurances from the court that it could accept the case.
98. *LA Times*, April 19, 1999, p. A-3.
99. Ibid.
100. As expected, Pfaelzer accepted the settlement on September 13, 1999 (*Associated Press*, September 13, 1999).
101. *United Press*, July 29, 1999.
102. *Washington Post*, July 30, 1999, p. A-3.
103. *United Press*, July 29, 1999.
104. *LA Times*, August 4, 1999, p. A-1.
105. *LA Times*, July 29, 1999, p. A-1.
106. Ibid.
107. *LA Times*, July 30, 1999, p. A-1.

108. Ibid.

109. *Copley News Service*, April 16, 1999.

110. *Associated Press*, August 5, 1999. See also *Associated Press*, August 4, 1999.

111. *Associated Press*, October 22, 1999.

112. *Associated Press*, August 4, 1999.

113. All California governors since Edmund G. Brown have faced a recall attempt (*LA Times*, February 18, 2003).

114. *LA Times*, April 8, 2000, p. A-10.

115. *Fresno Bee*, August 15, 2000, p. A-1.

116. *Copley News Service*, March 18, 2000; *San Diego Union-Tribune*, March 19, 2000, p. A-3.

117. *Orange County Register*, April 21, 2000, p. A-11.

118. *LA Times*, August 13, 2000, p. A-33.

119. Evelyn Miller of the California Coalition for Immigration Reform, quoted in *Orange County Register*, April 21, 2000, p. A-11.

120. *PR Newswire*, April 10, 2000.

121. Ibid.

122. The bills would, for example, have removed the legal residency requirement for acquiring a driving license and made discrimination against immigrants illegal.

123. *Copley News Service*, November 21, 1999; *San Francisco Chronicle*, May 6, 1999.

124. *San Francisco Chronicle*, August 19, 1999, p. A-17.

125. Beth Parker, Equal Rights Advocates program director, in *San Francisco Chronicle*, August 19, 1999, p. A-17.

126. *LA Times*, November 14, 1999, p. M-6.

7 The Legislative Revival of Proposition 187

1. *LA Times*, Home edition, November 14, 1994, p. A-1.

2. The Heritage Foundation opposed Prop. 187 in the 1994 election.

3. *LA Times*, Home edition, November 19, 1994, p. A-1.

4. *LA Times*, Home edition, December 5, 1994, p. A-1.

5. Barbara Sinclair, a respected congressional scholar, argued that subcommittee chairs are greatly coveted by members "because most are now personal vehicles for the chair who can use them for agenda setting, for attempting to shape debate on an ongoing issue, for garnering personal publicity, [and] for catering to specialized constituencies." Quoted in Davidson and Oleszek, *Congress and Its Members*, p. 211.

6. *USA Today*, November 15, 1994, p. A-2.

7. *LA Times*, Home edition, November 19, 1994, p. A-1.

8. Ibid.

9. *LA Times*, Home edition, December 8, 1994, p. A-32.

10. U.S. Commission on Immigration Reform, *U.S. Immigration Policy: Restoring Credibility*, September 1994, Executive Summary, pp. ii–iii.

11. Ibid.

12. Ibid., p. vi.

13. Ibid., p. xii.

14. Ibid., p. xix.

15. *Orange Country Register*, October 1, 1994, p. B-9.

16. *LA Times*, Home edition, October 1, 1994, p. A-1.

17. Ibid.

18. *San Francisco Chronicle*, October 1, 1994, p. A-2.

19. *Orange Country Register*, October 1, 1994, p. B-9. See also, *Chicago Sun-Times*, October 2, 1994, p. 38; *LA Times*, Home edition, October 1, 1994, p. A-1.

20. The president of the ABA, George E. Bushell, said he was

    deeply disturbed [by the registry proposal because it] would require every employer to obtain federal government approval before job applicants could be hired. The registry would involve the development of national data files on every citizen and legal resident. . . . These issues threaten the basic privacy rights of citizens. (*Chicago Sun-Times*, October 2, 1994, p. 38)

21. *Orange Country Register*, October 1, 1994, p. B-9.
22. *LA Times*, Valley edition, December 17, 1994, p. B-5.
23. Congressional Task Force on Immigration Reform, *Report to the Speaker*, June 29, 1995, p. 1.
24. Rep. Solomon Ortiz (D-TX) later made the same allegation about the absence of Latinos and that only two Texans were on the commission (*States News Service*, June 30, 1995). However, few voices were raised at the time.
25. Congressional Task Force on Immigration Reform, *Report to the Speaker.*
26. *LA Times*, Ventura West edition, April 4, 1995, p. B-1.
27. Op-ed piece in *LA Times*, Home edition, April 4, 1995, p. B-7. The bill was cosponsored by thirty Republicans and Democrats.
28. *San Francisco Examiner*, January 31, 1995, p. A-11.
29. *LA Times*, Ventura West edition, March 16, 1995, p. B-6.
30. *LA Times*, Orange County edition, 1995, p. A-32.
31. *LA Times*, Home edition, January 19, 1995, p. A-3.
32. *LA Times*, Home edition, January 28, 1995, p. A-16.
33. *LA Times*, Home edition, February 9, 1995, p. A-1.
34. *LA Times*, Home edition, March 9, 1995, p. A-3.
35. Congressional Task Force on Immigration Reform, *Report*, pp. 3–6.
36. *LA Times*, Home edition, June 29, 1995, p. A-1.
37. *Washington Times*, June 9, 1995, p. A-11.
38. Ibid.
39. *LA Times*, Home edition, June 29, 1995, p. A-1; Ventura West edition, June 30, 1995, p. B-1; Home edition, June 30, 1995, p. A-3; *Washington Times*, June 9, 1995, p. A-11; June 29, 1995, p. A-3
40. *LA Times*, Home edition, November 22, 1994, p. A-1.
41. In the Contract, Gingrich promised only that there would be "no troops under UN command." Nothing else was said about free trade or foreign policy.
42. In the Contract with America, Gingrich promised to cut welfare to child mothers and to not increase AFDC payments to welfare mothers who had additional children. He also promised to place a limit of two years on the time that individuals could claim welfare, and to make them work for their welfare.
43. *LA Times*, Home edition, March 22, 1995, p. A-5. Included within these figures were 230,000 children who would become ineligible for AFDC and Medicaid.
44. *LA Times*, Home edition, January 10, p. A-1.
45. State of the Union Address, January 24, 1995 (delivered version).
46. For details, see *Congressional Quarterly Weekly Report*, February 11, 1995, Vol. 53, No. 6.
47. *LA Times*, Home edition, February 8, 1995, p. A-3.
48. *LA Times*, Home edition, February 5, 1995, p. A-1.
49. Ibid.
50. *LA Times*, Home edition, February 8, 1995, p. A-3.
51. See Gimpel and Edwards, *The Congressional Politics of Immigration Reform.*
52. *LA Times*, Home edition, May 7, 1995, p. A-1.
53. Ibid.

54. *LA Times*, Home edition, February 21, 1995, p. A-3; Home edition, October 11, 1995, p. A-11; Home edition, October 14, 1995, p. A-1.

55. *LA Times*, Home edition, October 25, 1995, p. A-6.

56. *LA Times*, Home edition, January 13, 1996, p. A-18; Home edition, January 22, 1996, p. B-5; Home edition, February 9, 1996, p. A-1.

57. *LA Times*, Valley edition, July 15, 1995, p. B-4.

58. HR 1915 was introduced on June 22, 1995, and HR 2202 on August 4, 1995. *Congressional Quarterly Almanac 1995*, Vol. 2001, p. 6.9.

59. Immigration data available from U.S. Census Bureau, *Statistical Abstract of the United States: 1999*, pp. 10–14.

60. *CQ Almanac 1995*, p. 6.10.

61. Ibid., pp. 6.9–6.18; *San Francisco Examiner*, January 31, 1995, p. A-11.

62. *CQ Almanac 1995*, p. 6.9.

63. U.S. Commission on Immigration Reform, *Legal Immigration: Setting Priorities*, June 1995, Executive Summary, p. i.

64. Ibid.

65. Family visas had not been subject to strict numerical limits, and thus the family reunification scheme produced an oversupply of immigrants above and beyond that prescribed in earlier legislation.

66. U.S. Commission on Immigration Reform, *Legal Immigration*.

67. Ibid., p. xxx.

68. Ibid.

69. *New York Times*, June 8, 1995, p. B-10; *San Francisco Examiner*, June 8, 1995, p. A-2. Clinton and Smith made their remarks before the official publication of the report. Jordan had released a draft of the report in early June so key players could comment on its recommendations. Her plan was to rework the draft before presenting it to Congress in late June.

70. She appeared before Smith's committee to give evidence on February 24 and March 30, 1995.

71. Gimpel and Edwards, *The Congressional Politics of Immigration Reform*, pp. 220–221. One significant difference, however, between Smith's and Simpson's bills and the commission's report was that the latter did not recommend excluding legal immigrants from receipt of welfare and other federal benefits.

72. *The San Francisco Examiner*, June 8, 1995, p. A-2.

73. Ibid.

74. Gimpel and Edwards, *The Congressional Politics of Immigration Reform*, p. 225.

75. Ibid., pp. 243–244.

76. *Austin American-Statesman*, June 25, 1995, p. 1.

77. *CQ Almanac 1996*, p. 5.16; Gimpel and Edwards, *The Congressional Politics of Immigration Reform*, pp. 243–244.

78. *CQ Almanac 1996*, p. 5.5.

79. *CQ Almanac 1996*, p. 5.6; Gimpel and Edwards, *The Congressional Politics of Immigration Reform*, pp. 247–248.

80. *CQ Almanac 1996*, p. 5.6.

81. Ibid., p. 5.10.

82. Ibid.

83. Gimpel and Edwards, *The Congressional Politics of Immigration Reform*, pp. 254–255

84. *CQ Almanac 1996*, p. 5.15.

85. Gimpel and Edwards, *The Congressional Politics of Immigration Reform*, pp. 257–259.

86. *LA Times*, Home edition, March 21, 1996, p. A-1.

87. Gimpel and Edwards, *The Congressional Politics of Immigration Reform*, p. 263.

88. *CQ Almanac 1996*, p. 5.14; Gimpel and Edwards, *The Congressional Politics of Immigration Reform*, pp. 261–262.
89. *LA Times*, Valley edition, April 12, 1996, p. B-5.
90. *LA Times*, Home edition, May 26, 1996, p. A-18.
91. Ibid.
92. Clinton tried to turn the vote to his advantage by congratulating the Senate on the "important legislation which ratifies *my* administration's comprehensive immigration strategy" (*CQ Almanac 1996*, p. 5.11, emphasis added).
93. *LA Times*, Orange County edition, May 3, 1996, p. A-1.
94. Ibid.
95. Ibid.
96. *LA Times*, Home edition, May 26, 1996, p. A-18.
97. Simpson noted after the bruising debate, "My fingers have been shorn off. I've messed with [the legal immigration bill] all I care to" (*CQ Almanac 1996*, p. 5.11).
98. *LA Times*, Home edition, June 11, 1996, p. A-16.
99. *LA Times*, Home edition, June 20, 1996, p. A-1.
100. Ibid.
101. Ibid.
102. *LA Times*, Home edition, June 23, 1996, p. M-5.
103. Scott Reed, Dole's campaign manager, went to Washington to lobby Smith and Simpson on the importance of retaining the Gallegly amendment. Some members of Congress argued in turn that a weakened bill was better than no bill and that it would be better for Dole to run for office on the strength of real immigration reform rather than a presidential veto (*CQ Almanac 1996*, p. 5.16).
104. Gimpel and Edwards, *The Congressional Politics of Immigration Reform*, pp. 272–273.
105. *LA Times*, Home edition, July 10, 1996, p. B-9.
106. *LA Times*, Home edition, July 9, 1996, p. A-3.
107. Ibid.
108. *CQ Almanac 1996*, p. 5.16.
109. Gimpel and Edwards, *The Congressional Politics of Immigration Reform*, pp. 272–282. In an election-year ploy, the House also voted separately on the Gallegly amendment, approving it 254-175, although it was obvious the amendment would not survive the Senate and White House.
110. Gimpel and Edwards, *The Congressional Politics of Immigration Reform*, pp. 282–283.
111. *Congressional Quarterly Weekly Report*, June 18, 1994, Vol. 52, No. 24, p. 1622.
112. The $4 billion in savings included $3.7 billion from restricting access to AFDC, SSI, and food stamps, and $300 million from denying nonresident aliens the earned-income tax credit.
113. *Congressional Quarterly Weekly Report*, June 18, 1994, Vol. 52, No. 24, pp. 1622–1624, and November 5, 1994, Vol. 52, No. 43, p. 3182.
114. Ibid., p. 1622.
115. *Congressional Quarterly Weekly Report*, November 19, 1994, Vol. 52, No. 45, pp. 3335, 3372; January 14, 1995, Vol. 53, No. 2, pp. 159–162; CQ *Almanac 1995*, p. 7.36.
116. *Congressional Quarterly Weekly Report*, January 14, 1995, Vol. 53, No. 2, pp. 159–162; January 28, 1995, Vol. 53, No. 4, pp. 280–283; *CQ Almanac 1995*, pp. 7.35–7.36.
117. *CQ Almanac 1995*, p. 7.36.
118. Ibid., pp. 7.37–7.43.
119. Ibid., pp. 7.43–7.44.

120. Rep. George Miller (D-CA), in *CQ Almanac 1995*, p. 7.41.
121. *CQ Almanac 1995*, p. 7.43.
122. Ibid., p. 7.44.
123. Ibid., p. 7.50.
124. Ibid., pp. 7.44–7.48.
125. Ibid., pp. 7.49–7.50.
126. Ibid., p. 7.48.
127. Ibid., pp. 7.44–7.48.
128. Ibid., pp. 7.50–7.51.
129. *CQ Almanac 1996*, p. 6.4.
130. State of the Union Address, January 23, 1996. Delivered version, available at http:// clinton2.nara.gov/WH/New/other/sotu.html, accessed November 12, 2007.
131. *CQ Almanac 1996*, p. 6.40.
132. Ibid.
133. Ibid., p. 6.6.
134. Ibid., pp. 6.7–6.11.
135. All three quotes from ibid., pp. 6.11–6.12.
136. Ibid., pp. 6.12 and 6.21.
137. Ibid., pp. 6.23–6.24.
138. Quotes from Ibid., p. 6.24.
139. Ibid.
140. Ibid.
141. Gimpel and Edwards, *The Congressional Politics of Immigration Reform*, p. 284.
142. *LA Times*, Orange County edition, May 14, 1995, p. A-1.
143. *LA Times*, Orange County edition, May 14, 1995, p. A-1.
144. *LA Times*, Home edition, March 2, 1996, p. A-10.

8   Immigration Politics at Century's End

1. Ashbee, "The US Republicans: Lessons for the Conservatives?"
2. For a right-leaning critique of compassionate conservatism, see, for example, Andrew Bernstein, "Bush's Compassionate Conservatism Will Undermine the Republicans and Capitalism," in *Capitalism Magazine*, July 15, 1999, available online at http://www.capmag.com/article.asp?ID=127, accessed November 12, 2007, or Crane, "The Dangers of Compassionate Conservatism."
3. Some conservatives, including Bush, argue that the 1996 welfare act is an example of a compassionately conservative law, because it encourages people to move off welfare and into work. However, at the time of its passage, no one described it as such. The term compassionate conservatism was not in general use, and had no ideological meaning. Although Bush promoted compassionate conservative-style programs in Texas in 1996 (the Charitable Choice program that sought to encourage churches to increase their commitment to the poor by helping those on welfare is one example), he also did not use the term. Only later in 1997 did he meet and was reportedly influenced by Myron Magnet, who, together with Marvin Olasky, is considered one of the founders of compassionate conservatism. While Magnet wrote a key compassionate conservatism text called *The Dream and the Nightmare* in 1993, there is no record of Bush using the term compassionate conservatism before 1998. The term became widely known and commented on only in July 1999, after Bush outlined his compassionate conservative philosophy in

a speech in Indianapolis—the centerpiece of which was $8 billion worth of tax incentives to help voluntary and faith-based organizations help the poor.

4. *LA Times*, Home edition, February 27, 1995, p. A-3.

5. Ibid. Political consultant for the initiative, Arnold Steinberg, confirmed this: "I'm trying to do coalition-building with the Democrats."

6. As a constitutional initiative, 690,000 verified signatures were required. Paid signature gatherers collected about 800,000, a direct mailing yielded 145,000, and volunteers provided just 147,000. The total cost of the petition drive was $1.3 million, with Wilson raising $300,000 and the state Republican Party contributing $250,000. Unlike Prop. 187, the petition stage was far from a grassroots effort.

7. On Prop. 209, see Chavez, *The Color Bind*; and Ron Unz, "California and the End of White America," *Commentary*, November 1999.

8. *New York* Times, August 25, 1995, p. A-22; *LA Times*, Home edition, August 9, 1995, p. A-16. His announcement speech before the Statue of Liberty in New York, which coincided with the launch of the television ad, echoed the text of another 1994 ad:

> Millions of newcomers from every corner of the globe came to America through this harbor. They did it the right way. They played the rules, waited their turn and obeyed the law. Let's get it straight. There's a right way to come to America and a wrong way. Illegal immigration is not the American way.

9. *LA Times*, Orange County edition, May 14, 1995, p. A-1.

10. Ibid. For a comprehensive report of Wilson's positions on immigration across time, see *LA Times*, Home edition, May 15, 1995, p. A-1.

11. *New York Times*, August 25, 1995, p. A-22; August 28, 1995, p. B-8; Washington *Times*, August 28, 1995, p. A-3.

12. *LA Times*, Home edition, September 30, 1995, p. A-1.

13. Bill Press of the California Democratic Party argued the incident "proves he's the biggest hypocrite in the history of California politics. He's obviously a man with no principles, no shame and no memory" (*LA Times*, Home edition, May 4, 1995, p. A-1).

14. *LA Times*, Home edition, May 10, 1995, p. E-1.

15. *LA Times*, Home edition, May 5, 1995, p. A-1; Home edition, May 7, 1995, p. M-6.

16. Craig Butler, executive director of Fund for New Priorities in America, quoted in John Nicols, "Righter than Thou: In the Republican Presidential Race, Extremism is the Norm," *The Progressive*, June 1995.

17. Quoted in Nicols, "Righter than Thou."

18. *LA Times*, Home edition, March 2, 1996, p. A-10.

19. *LA Times*, Home edition, March 10, 1996, p. A-3.

20. *LA Times*, Home edition, March 19, 1996, p. A-1. Poll taken March 13–17, 1996.

21. *LA Times*, Home edition, March 23, 1996, p. A-1. In spite of Buchanan's fiery rhetoric on immigration, he, like many other Republican politicians was a relatively recent convert. Throughout the 1980s, he lauded undocumented workers as a driving force of the U.S. economy (see Unz, "California and the End of White America").

22. *LA Times*, Home edition, June 11, 1996, p. A-16.

23. *LA Times*, Home edition, June 13, 1996, p. A-1.

24. Ibid.

25. All data on registration and voting are from the Bureau of Labor Statistics and Bureau of the Census November, *Current Population Surveys*, 1978–2000, available online from Unicon Research at http://www.unicon.com. Respondents' race/

ethnicity is self-ascribed. Similarly, respondents are asked whether they are registered to vote, whether they voted in the previous election, and how they voted; no external check is made to validate these responses. Of course, respondents tend to overstate their civic responsibility and thus the data overestimates the proportions registering and voting. However, so long as respondents consistently overstate their registration and voting habits, over time the trends will be accurate.

26. See, for example, Citrin and Highton, *How Race, Ethnicity, and Immigration Shape the California Electorate*, p. 23, and Unz who argued that "political movements targeting immigrants have the unintended consequence of generating an unprecedented wave of . . . voter registration among Latinos and Asians" ("California and the End of White America").

27. The impact of changes in voting rates is not linear. They are conditional on an ethnicity's share of the vote. See table 2 in appendix C.

28. *LA Times*, Home edition, December 11, 1994, City Times-3. See also, *LA Times*, Home edition, December 4, 1994, p. A-1; Ventura West edition, March 12, 1995, p. B-4; Home edition, April 10, 1995, p. A-1; Home edition, April 30, 1995, p. M-6.

29. U.S. Immigration and Naturalization Service, *Statistical Yearbook of the Immigration and Naturalization Service* Various Years; Office of Immigration Statistics, *Yearbook of Immigration Statistics*, Various Years. The *Statistical Yearbook* changed its name to the *Yearbook of Immigration Statistics* in 2002 after the reorganization of the immigration services into the Department of Homeland Security.

30. OIG report, pp. 2–7, available online at www.usdoj.gov/oig/cusarpt/cusaimp. pdf, accessed November 2002.

31. See INS, *Statistical Yearbook of the Immigration and Naturalization Service, 2000*, pp. 198–201, available online at http://www.ins.usdoj.gov/graphics/aboutins/ statistics/ybpage.htm, accessed November 2002.

32. OIG report, pp. 2–7.

33. Meissner had originally envisaged that Citizenship USA would encourage LPRs to apply for citizenship. However, when she realized the extent of the backlog of applications and the record numbers who were applying for citizenship without official encouragement, Meissner backtracked. The program's focus changed to processing. Thus, counter to what some have argued, Citizenship USA should not be regarded a *major* factor in the increase in citizenship applications. However, it is probably correct to say that it may have had a minor effect on the number of applications, because some local INS's branches continued to encourage LPRs to apply for citizenship despite Meissner refocusing the program's objectives.

34. www.usdoj.gov/oig/cusarpt/cusaimp.pdf, accessed November 2002; http:// www.murthy.com/UDoigini.html; and *LA Times*, Home edition, February 28, 1996, p. B-3.

35. INS, *Statistical Yearbook of the Immigration and Naturalization Service*, Various Years, and Office of Immigration Statistics, *Yearbook of Immigration Statistics*, Various Years.

36. INS and CPS data do not provide precise calculations. These statistics are inferred from various publications, including *Statistical Yearbook of the Immigration and Naturalization Service*, Various Years; *Yearbook of Immigration Statistics*, Various Years; U.S. Census Bureau, Table 4, "Reported Voting and Registration, by Sex, Race, and Hispanic Origin, for States: November 1990" available online at http://www.census.gov/population/www/socdemo/voting/p20-453.html, accessed November 2002; U.S. Census Bureau, Table 4a, "Reported Voting and Registration of the Total Voting-Age Population, by Sex, Race, and Hispanic Origin, for States: November 2000" available online at http://www.census.gov/ population/www/ socdemo/voting/p20-542.html, accessed November 2002.

37. Citrin and Highton, *How Race, Ethnicity, and Immigration Shape the California Electorate*, Table 4.2, calculate that turnout is 36 percent for first generation California-resident Latino immigrants who naturalized between 1980 and 2000. However, Adrian D. Pantoja, Ricardo Ramirez, and Gary M. Segura, "Citizens by Choice, Voters by Necessity: Pattens in Political Mobilization by Naturalized Latinos," demonstrate that turnout is 75 percent among the same population naturalized between 1992 and 1996, and 56 percent for those naturalized before 1992. They also point out that turnout is much lower for Florida and Texas residents, however, at 25 and 32 percent respectively for the 1992–1996ers and 38 and 37 percent respectively for the pre-1992ers (Table 2 on p. 61), because residents of these two states were unpoliticized especially compared with California's.

38. See *Yearbook of Immigration Statistics*, Various Years; U.S. Census Bureau, Table 4, "Reported Voting and Registration, by Sex, Race, and Hispanic Origin, for States: November 1990;", Table 4a, "Reported Voting and Registration of the Total Voting-Age Population, by Sex, Race, and Hispanic Origin, for States: November 2000." In the 1990 U.S. elections 2.9 million Latinos voted, when the Latino turnout rate (as a percentage of the whole Latino population) was 21 percent, compared with 5.9 million and a rate of 27.5 percent in 2000. In California 884,000 Latinos voted in 1990 at a rate of 24.5 percent. In order to adjust the 1990 figure to take account of low turnout during off year elections in the United States, simply assume turnout was 27.5 percent in 1990. Thus adjusted turnout = $(.275 \times 2.9$ million$)$ +2.9 million = 3.7 million. The difference between 2000 and 1990 = 5.9 million -3.7 million = 2.2 million. For California, adjusted turnout = $(.245 \times .884)$+.884 = 1.1 million. And the difference between 2000 and 1990 = $1.6-1.1$ = .5 million.

39. Lindsay Sobel, *The Hill*, October 8, 1997.

40. "Congress: No Major Legislation Expected in 1997," *Migration News*, Vol. 4. No. 2, February 1997.

41. "Republicans Feeling the Heat over Immigration Policy," *Congressional Quarterly Weekly Report*, May 17, 1997, in *CQ Guide to Current American Government*, Fall 1997.

42. *CQ Almanac 1997*, pp. 6.31–6.36.

43. *CQ Almanac 1998*, pp. 4.3–4.9, 17.3–17.4.

44. Lamar Smith quoted in *CQ Almanac 1997*, p. 5.12.

45. Ibid., pp. 5.12–5.13.

46. Ibid.; "245(i) and Central Americans," *Migration News*, Vol. 4, No. 11, November 1997; "Congress: Central Americans, 245(i)," *Migration News*, Vol. 4, No. 12, December 1997.

47. *CQ Almanac 2000*, p. 15.4.

48. "Juggling Business' Agenda and Immigrants' Interests," *Congressional Quarterly Weekly Report*, September 23, 2000, in *CQ Guide to Current American Government*, Spring 2001.

49. *CQ Almanac 2000*, p. 15.3.

50. Ibid., p. 15.11.

51. "Polls and Politics," *Migration News*, Vol. 7, No. 5, May 2000; "Elections 2000," *Migration News*, Vol. 7, No. 12, December 2000.

9 Immigration Politics in a New Century

1. See *CQ Almanac 1997*, p. 5.11.

2. *LA Times*, Home edition, August 7, 2002, p. A-3. See also, *Fort Worth Star-Telegram*, August 7, 2002, p. 1; and *The Arizona Republic*, August 7, 2002, p. A-4.

3. "Guest Workers: Mexico-US Negotiations," *Rural Migration News*, Vol. 8, No. 2, April 2001.

4. Congressional Research Service, "Mexico–United States Dialogue on Migration and Border Issues, 2001–2005," June 2, 2005; "Guest Workers, Legalization," *Migration News*, Vol. 8, No. 4, August 2001.

5. "Grass-roots Lobby says it won't Stop with Vote," *Orange County Register*, June 29, 2007.

6. "Guest Workers, Legalization," *Migration News*, Vol. 8, No. 8, August 2001.

7. Ibid.

8. *CQ Almanac 2001*, pp. 14.13–14.15.

9. "Mexico: Bush-Fox, Economy," *Migration News*, Vol. 9, No. 11, November 2002.

10. See, for example, "Terrorism: September 11, 2001," *Migration News*, Vol. 8, No. 10, October 2001.

11. *CQ Almanac 2001*, pp. 2.9–2.12, 14.3–14.13. The Patriot Act did offer help to aliens seeking legal permanent residency who had lost jobs or family in the attacks.

12. "INS: Reorganize, Police, Sanctions," *Migration News*, Vol. 9, No. 4, April 2002.

13. "Mexico: Legalization, Returns, Economy," *Migration News*, Vol. 9, No. 2, February 2002.

14. "Enhanced Border Security," *Migration News*, Vol. 9, No. 3, March 2002; "Mexico: US, Migrants, Politics," *Migration News*, Vol. 9, No. 3, March 2002.

15. "Bush-Fox, Border, 245(i)," *Migration News*, Vol. 9, No. 4, April 2002.

16. "Mexico: Legalization, Returns, Economy," *Migration News*, Vol. 9, No. 2, February 2002.

17. *LA Times*, Home edition, October 15, 2002, p. A-19.

18. As a safeguard to keep out undesirables and especially potential terrorists, the Democrats also proposed that immigrants pass a background security check.

19. *LA Times*, Home edition, October 27, 2002, p. A-3.

20. Ibid.

21. "Welfare, Labor, H-1B," *Migration News*, Vol. 9, No. 7, July 2002; "Congress, Integration," *Migration News*, Vol. 9, No. 11, November 2002.

22. *LA Times*, Home edition, October 24, 2002, p. B-1. Protestors outside the fundraiser where Wilson endorsed Simon held placards proclaiming "Simon-Wilson, Prop. 187's Team."

23. Ward Connerly had previously chaired the anti-affirmative action Proposition 209 in 1996. *LA Times*, Home edition, October 24, 2002, p. B-1.

24. Congressional Research Service, "Mexico-United States Dialogue on Migration and Border Issues, 2001–2005," June 2, 2005.

25. "Congress: AgJOBs, Guest Workers," *Migration News*, Vol. 10, No. 4, October 2003.

26. Office of the Press Secretary, White House Press Release, "Fact Sheet: Fair and Secure Immigration Reform," January 7, 2004.

27. Office of the Press Secretary, White House Press Release, "President Bush Proposes New Temporary Worker Program," January 7, 2004.

28. "Bush Would Give Illegal Workers Broad New Rights," *New York Times*, January 7, 2004.

29. Only 10,000 of the 140,000 employment-based green cards are reserved for low-skilled workers.

30. "Bush Would Give Illegal Workers Broad New Rights," *New York Times*.

31. "Incumbent Reaches Beyond His Base," *Washington Post*, January 8, 2004, p. A-1.

32. *National Election Pool* poll conducted by Edison/Mitofsky for Associated Press, ABC, CBS, CNN, Fox and NBC. The *LATimes* national exit poll put Latino support for Bush at 45 percent, 1 point higher than the NEP poll.

33. "Bush Renews Migrant Pledge," *LA Times*, November 22, 2004.

34. "Mexico: Legalization, Labor," *Migration News*, Vol. 12, No. 1, January 2005.
35. Available at http://www.whitehouse.gov/news/releases/2005/02/20050202-11. html. Accessed October 23, 2007.
36. *CQ Almanac Plus 2005*, p. 13.3; *Congressional Research Service*, "Immigration Legislation and Issues in the 109th Congress," May 12, 2006, pp. 2–5.
37. "Congress: Bills, Emergencies," *Migration News*, Vol. 12, No. 4, October 2005.
38. *CQ Almanac Plus 2005*, pp. 13.8–13.9.
39. "Senate Approves CIRA," *Migration News*, Vol. 13, No. 3, July 2006.
40. "Bush and Congress: Action?" *Migration News*, Vol. 13, No. 1, January 2006.
41. "Senate: No Agreement, Polls," *LA Times*,; March 26, 2006; *Migration News*, Vol. 13, No. 2, April 2006.
42. "Immigrant Bill Fallout May Hurt House GOP," *Washington Post*, April 12, 2006, p. A-1.
43. "Few Protections for Migrants to Mexico," *Washington Post*, April 19, 2006, p. A-16.
44. Congressional Research Service, "Immigration Legislation and Issues in the 109th Congress," May 12, 2006, pp. 15–16; "Senate Pact Offers Permits to Most Illegal Immigrants," *Washington Post*, April 7, 2006, p. A-1.
45. "Senate: No Agreement, Poll," *Migration News*, Vol. 13, No. 2, April 2006.
46. "Senate Approves CIRA," *Migration News*, Vol. 13, No. 3, July 2006.
47. "12 Million Unauthorized, Jobs," *Migration News*, Vol. 13, No. 2, April 2006.
48. *LA Times/Bloomberg* National Poll, #527, April 21–27, 2006; May 5–7, 2006, *Gallup* poll.
49. "Senate Deal on Immigration Falters," *New York Times*, April 7, 2006; "Immigrant Bill Snared by Web of Suspicion," *LA Times*, April 8, 2006; "Immigrant Bill Fallout May Hurt House GOP," *Washington Post*, April 12, 2006, p. A-1.
50. "Immigrants Demonstrate Peaceful Power," *LA Times*, May 2, 2006.
51. "GOP Plans Hearings on Issue of Immigrants," *Washington Post*, June 21, 2006, p. A-1.
52. "Mexican Anger over U.S. Border Fence," *BBC*, October 27, 2006, at http://news.bbc.co.uk/1/hi/world/americas/6090060.stm, accessed November 12, 2007.
53. "Border Barrier Approved," *LA Times*, September 30, 2006.
54. "Congress Resumes Immigration Efforts," *Washington Post*, September 21, 2006, p. A-3.
55. http://www.whitehouse.gov/news/releases/2006/10/20061026.html. Accessed November 11, 2007.
56. "Still No Slam Dunk on Immigration Bill," *LA Times*, November 23, 2006.
57. Ibid.
58. "Martinez Urges GOP to Reach Out," *Miami Herald*, January 20, 2007, and *Human Events Online*, November 20, 2006.
59. Two replies accepted. Poll #524, January 22–25, 2007.
60. "President Renews Push for Bill on Immigration," *Washington Times*, January 24, 2007.
61. "Fresh Potential on Immigration," *LA Times*, January 29, 2007.
62. "White House Pushes Immigration Overhaul," *LA Times*, February 28, 2007.
63. "Bush Builds Bonds with House Democrats at Retreat," *Washington Times*, February 4, 2007.
64. "Democrats Seek Bush Help on Immigration," *Washington Post*, February 28, 2007.
65. "Bush Promises a Compromise on Immigration," *LA Times*, March 13, 2007; March 15, 2007.
66. "GOP Candidates Confront Immigration Politics," *New York Times*, March 20, 2007.
67. Ibid.

68. "Giuliani Shifts His Tone on Immigration," *New York Times*, April 16, 2007.
69. "Immigration Issues Nag at GOP Candidates," *Washington Post*, April 24, 2007.
70. A similar percentage identified immigration as a top priority a year earlier when the Senate voted on S 2611; in the intervening year between 10 and 15 percent did so.
71. "Reid Forces New Senate Debate on Immigration," *Washington Post*, May 10, 2007.
72. "Small Turnout, Big Questions," *LA Times*, May 2, 2007 and May 8, 2007.
73. "Talk-radio Crowd Pumps up the Volume on Immigration," *LA Times*, April 28, 2007.
74. "State Lawmakers Ramp Up Immigration Efforts," *Stateline.org*, April 20, 2007; "Colorado to Use Inmates to Fill Migrant Shortage," *LA Times*, March 1, 2007; "City's Illegal Immigration Laws go on Trial," March 13, 2007; "As Texas Governor, Bush Defended Immigrants," *Dallas Morning News*, January 28, 2007; "Pizza Chain Takes Pesos, and Complaints," *New York Times*, January 15, 2007.
75. "Deal on Immigration Reached," *Washington Post*, May 18, 2007.
76. "Immigration Compromise Faces New Opposition," *Washington Post*, May 22, 2007.
77. Ibid. See May 18–23 *New York Times/CBS News* Poll for data on support for bill's provisions.
78. "Immigration Debate Puts up a Wall in the GOP," *LA Times*, May 27, 2007.
79. "Immigration, Bush in Crossfire," *LA Times*, June 6, 2007; "McCain Sets Self Apart in Debate," *Washington Post*, June 6, 2007, p. A-1.
80. "Bush Chides GOP Critics of Immigration Plan," *Washington Post*, May 30, 2007.
81. "President's Push on Immigration Tests GOP Base," *New York Times*, June 3, 2007.
82. "Immigration Overhaul Bill Stalls in Senate," *Washington Post*, June 8, 2007, p. A-1.
83. Ibid. For discussions of the debates and machinations on the bill, see also "Immigrant Bill, Short 15 Votes, Stalls in Senate," *New York Times*, June 8, 2007; "Kennedy Plea was Last Gasp for Immigration Bill," June 9, 2007; and "Broad Effort to Resurrect Immigration Bill," June 16, 2007.
84. "A Failure of Leadership in a Flawed Political Culture," *Washington Post*, June 8, 2007, p. A-4.
85. "Kennedy Plea was Last Gasp for Immigration Bill," *New York Times*.
86. Ibid.
87. "Immigration Bill has New Life in Senate," *Washington Post*, June 15, 2007, p. A-1.
88. "Opponents Vow to Try to Block Immigration Bill," *New York Times*, June 21, 2007.
89. "Bush Counting on Tougher Enforcement to Carry Revised Bill," *Wall Street Journal*, June 26, 2007, p. A-6.
90. "Border Bill Backers Seek Boost in Enforcement Provisions," *The Congress Daily*, June 21, 2007; "McConnell Wavering on Immigration Bill," *Washington Post*, June 21, 2007.
91. "Senators Push for Support on Immigration," *Associated Press*, June 25, 2007.
92. "Immigration Bill's Support Slipping," *LA Times*, June 27, 2007.
93. "Senate Faces Showdown on Immigration," *LA Times*, June 28, 2007.
94. "McConnell Avoids Immigration Bill Deliberations," *Washington Times*, June 28, 2007
95. "Bingaman, Domenici Say Immigration Bill Unworkable," *Associated Press*, June 28, 2007.
96. "Immigration Bill Dies in Senate," *Washington Post*, June 29, 2007.
97. "Senators Looking to Pick Up Pieces," *Houston Chronicle*, June 29, 2007.
98. Ibid.

99. "GOP Inflicts Bush's Latest Wounds," *LA Times*, June 29, 2007.

100. See Neustadt, *Presidential Power and the Modern Presidents.*

101. "Senators Looking to Pick Up Pieces," *Houston Chronicle.*

102. "Senate Blocks Efforts to Revive Immigration Overhaul," *New York Times*, June 28, 2007.

103. Democratic Party id, 42 percent; Republican Party id, 11 percent; Independent, 39 percent.

Bibliography

Allswang, John M., *The Initiative and Referendum in California, 1898–1998* (Stanford, CA: Stanford University Press, 2000).

Almaguer, Tomas, *Racial Fault Lines: The Historical Origins of White Supremacy in California* (Berkeley and Los Angeles, CA: University of California Press, 1994).

Alvarez, Michael R., and John Brehm, "Are Americans Ambivalent towards Racial Policies?" *American Journal of Political Science*, 1997, Vol. 41, pp. 345–374.

Alvarez, Michael R., and Tara L. Butterfield, "The Resurgence of Nativism in California? The Case of Proposition 187 and Illegal Immigration," *Working Paper* 1041 (Pasadena, CA: California Institute of Technology, Division of the Humanities and Social Sciences, 1997).

———, "The Resurgence of Nativism in California? The Case of Proposition 187 and Illegal Immigration," *Social Science Quarterly*, 2000, Vol. 81, pp. 167–179.

Ansolabehere, Stephen, and Shanto Iyengar, "Riding the Wave and Claiming Ownership Over Issues: The Joint Effects of Advertising and News Coverage in Campaigns," *Public Opinion Quarterly*, 1994, Vol. 58, pp. 335–357.

Ashbee, Edward, "The U.S. Republicans: Lessons for the Conservatives?" in Mark Garnett and Philip Lynch (eds.), *The Conservatives in Crisis* (Manchester, UK: Manchester University Press, 2003).

Banducci, Susan A., "Direct Legislation: When Is It Used and When Does It Pass?" in Bowler, Donovan, and Tolbert (eds.), *Citizens as Legislators*.

Bell, Derrick A., "The Referendum: Democracy's Barrier to Racial Equality," *Washington Law Review*, 1978, Vol. 54, pp. 1–29.

Bernstein, Andrew, "Bush's Compassionate Conservatism Will Undermine the Republicans and Capitalism," *Capitalism Magazine*, July 15, 1999.

Biegel, Stuart, "The Wisdom of *Plyler v. Doe*," *Chicano-Latino Law Review*, 1995, Vol. 17, pp. 46–63.

Bobo, Lawrence, "'Whites' Opposition to Busing: Symbolic Racism or Realistic Group Conflict?" *Journal of Personality and Social Psychology*, 1983, Vol. 45, pp. 1196–1210.

Bosniak, Linda S., "'Nativism' the Concept: Some Reflections," in Perea (ed.), *Immigrants Out!*

Bowler, Shaun, Todd Donovan, and Caroline J. Tolbert (eds.), *Citizens as Legislators: Direct Democracy in the United States* (Columbus, OH: Ohio State University Press, 1998).

Broder, David S., *Democracy Derailed: Initiative Campaigns and the Power of Money* (New York: Harcourt, 2000).

Brogan, Hugh, *The Penguin History of the United States of America* (London: Penguin Books, 1990).

Bureau of Labor Statistics and Bureau of the Census, November *Current Population Surveys*, 1978–2000, available online from Unicon Research at http://www.unicon.com. Accessed November 12, 2007.

Burns, Peter, and James G. Gimpel, "Economic Insecurity, Prejudicial Stereotypes, and Public Opinion on Immigration Policy," *Political Science Quarterly*, 2000, Vol. 115, pp. 201–225.

Butler, David and Austin Ranney, *Referendums Around the World: The Growing Use of Direct Democracy* (Washington, DC: AEI Press, 1994).

Cain, Bruce E., "Lessons from the Inside Revisited," in Lubenow (ed.), *California Votes—the 1994 Governor's Race*.

California Commission on Campaign Financing, *Democracy by Initiative: Shaping California's Fourth Branch of Government* (Los Angeles, CA: Center for Responsive Government, 1992).

California Secretary of State, *A History of the California Initiative Process* (Sacramento, CA: Secretary of State's Office, August 1993).

Cantril, Henry, "The Intensity of an Attitude," *Journal of Abnormal and Social Psychology*, 1946, Vol. 41, pp. 129–135.

Carmines, Edward G., and Richard A. Champagne, "The Changing Content of American Racial Attitudes: A Fifty Year Portrait," in Long (ed.), *Research in Micropolitics*, Vol. 3.

Carr, Leslie G, *"Color-Blind" Racism* (Thousand Oaks, CA: Sage Publications, 1997).

Cervantes, Nancy, Sasha Khokha, and Bobbie Murray, "Hate Unleashed: Los Angeles in the Aftermath of Proposition 187," *Chicano-Latino Law Review*, 1995, Vol. 17, pp. 1–24.

Chavez, Lydia, *The Color Bind: California's Battle to End Affirmative Action* (Berkeley, CA: University of California Press, 1998).

Citrin, Jack, and Benjamin Highton, *How Race, Ethnicity, and Immigration Shape the California Electorate* (San Francisco, CA: Public Policy Institute of California, 2002).

Citrin, Jack, and Donald P. Green, "The Self-interest Motive in American Public Opinion," in Long (ed.), *Research in Micropolitics*, Vol. 3.

Citrin, Jack, Beth Reingold, and Donald P. Green, "American Identity and the Politics of Ethnic Change," *Journal of Politics*, 1990, Vol. 52, pp. 1124–1154.

Citrin, Jack, Donald P. Green, Christopher Muste, and Carla Wong, "Public Opinion toward Immigration Reform: The Role of Economic Motivation," *Journal of Politics*, 1995, Vol. 59, pp. 858–881.

Cobb, Roger W., and Charles D. Elder, *Participation in American Politics: The Dynamics of Agenda Building* (Boston, MA: Allyn and Bacon, 1972).

Conference Proceedings, *California Immigration, 1994* (Sacramento, CA: California State Capitol, April 29, 1994).

Congressional Quarterly Almanac (Washington, DC: Congressional Quarterly, Inc., Various Years).

Congressional Quarterly Weekly Report (Washington, DC: Congressional Quarterly, Inc., Various Issues).

Congressional Task Force on Immigration Reform, *Report to the Speaker*, June 29, 1995 (Washington, DC: U.S. Congress, 1995).

Cornelius, Wayne A., and Jorge A. Bustamante (eds.), *Mexican Migration to the United States: Origins, Consequences, and Policy Options* (San Diego, CA: Center for U.S.-Mexico Studies, University of California, 1989).

CQ Guide to Current American Government (Washington, DC: Congressional Quarterly, Inc., Various Issues).

Crane, Edward H., "The Dangers of Compassionate Conservatism," *Cato Policy Report*, May/June 2001.

Cronin, Thomas E., *Direct Democracy: The Politics of Initiative, Referendum, and Recall* (Cambridge, MA: Harvard University Press, 1989).

Daniels, Roger, *Coming to America: A History of Immigration and Ethnicity in American Life*, 2nd edition (New York: HarperCollins, 2002).

Daniels, Roger, and Harry H. L. Kitano, *American Racism: Exploration of the Nature of Prejudice* (Upper Saddle River, NJ: Prentice Hall, 1970).

Davidson, Roger H., and Walter J. Oleszek, *Congress and Its Members*, 4th edition (Washington, DC: CQ Press, 1994).

Davis, Mike, *City of Quartz: Excavating the Future in Los Angeles* (London: Vintage, 1992).

DeSipio, Louis, and Rodolfo de la Garza, *Making Americans, Remaking America: Immigration and Immigrant Policy* (Boulder, CO: Westview Press, 1988).

Donovan, Todd, and Shaun Bowler, "Direct Democracy and Minority Rights: An Extension," *American Journal of Political Science*, 1998, Vol. 42, pp. 1020–1024.

Donovan, Todd, Shaun Bowler, David McCuan, and Ken Fernandez, "Contending Players and Strategies: Opposition Advantages in Initiative Campaigns," in Bowler, Donovan, and Tolbert, *Direct Legislation*.

Dubois, Philip L., and Floyd F. Feeney, *Improving the California Initiative Process: Options for Change* (Berkeley, CA: California Policy Seminar, University of California, 1992).

Durand, Jorge, Douglas S. Massey, and Fernando Charvet, "The Changing Geography of Mexican Immigration to the United States: 1910–1996," *Social Science Quarterly*, 2000, Vol. 81, pp. 1–15.

Ellis, Richard J., *Democratic Delusions: The Initiative Process in America* (Lawrence, KS: University Press of Kansas, 2002).

Espenshade, Thomas J., and Charles A. Calhoun, "An Analysis of Public Opinion toward Undocumented Immigration," *Population Research and Policy Review*, 1983, Vol. 12, pp. 189–224.

Eule, Julian N., "Checking California's Plebiscite," *Hastings Constitutional Law Quarterly*, 1989, Vol. 17, pp. 151–158.

Fetzer, Joel S., "Economic Self-interest or Cultural Marginality? Anti-immigrant Sentiment and Nativist Political Movements in France, Germany and the USA," *Journal of Ethnic and Migration Studies*, 2000, Vol. 26, pp. 5–23.

———, *Public Attitudes toward Immigration in the United States, France, and Germany* (Cambridge: Cambridge University Press, 2000).

Field Institute, *Field (California) Poll, April 1994*, [Machine-Readable Data File] (San Francisco, CA: The Field Institute, 1994, Field [California] Poll 94-03).

———, *Field (California) Poll, July 1994* [Machine-Readable Data File] (San Francisco, CA: The Field Institute, 1994, Field [California] Poll 94-05).

———, *Field (California) Poll, October 1994* [Machine-Readable Data File] (San Francisco, CA: The Field Institute, 1994, Field [California] Poll, 94-07).

Fiorina, Morris P., Samuel J. Abrams, and Jeremy C. Pope, *Culture War? The Myth of Polarized America* (New York: Pearson, 2005).

Frey, Bruno S., and Lorenz Goette, "Does the Popular Vote Destroy Civil Liberties?" *American Journal of Political Science*, 1998, Vol. 42, pp. 1343–1348.

Gamble, Barbara S., "Putting Civil Rights to a Popular Vote," *American Journal of Political Science*, 1997, Vol. 41, pp. 245–269.

Gandara, Patricia, "Learning English in California: Guideposts for the Nation," in Suarez-Orozco, Suarez-Orozco, and Qin (eds.), *The New Immigration.*

Garcia, Ruben J., "Critical Race Theory and Proposition 187: The Racial Politics of Immigration Law," *Chicano-Latino Law Review,* 1995, Vol. 17, pp. 118–148.

Garcia y Griego, Manuel, "History of U.S. Immigration Policy," in Conference Proceedings, *Californian Immigration, 1994.*

Garrett, Elizabeth, "Money, Agenda Setting, and Direct Democracy," *Texas Law Review,* 1999, Vol. 77, pp. 1845–1890.

Gilens, Martin, "'Race Coding' and White Opposition to Welfare," *American Political Science Review,* 1996, Vol. 90, pp. 593–604.

Gilljam, Mikael, and Donald Granberg, "Intense Minorities and the Pattern of Public Opinion," *International Journal of Public Opinion Research,* 1995, Vol. 7, pp. 199–210.

Gimpel, James G., and James R. Edwards, *The Congressional Politics of Immigration Reform* (Boston, MA: Allyn and Bacon, 1999).

Goodwyn, Lawrence, *The Populist Moment: A Short History of the Agrarian Revolt in America* (New York: Oxford University Press, 1978).

Green, Donald P., and Jonathan A. Cowden, "Who Protests: Self-Interest and White Opposition to Busing," *Journal of Politics,* 1992, Vol. 54, pp. 471–499.

Guerin-Gonzales, Camille, *Mexican Workers and American Dreams: Immigration, Repatriation, and California Farm Labor, 1900–1939* (New Brunswick, NJ: Rutgers University Press, 1994).

Gutierrez, David G., *Walls and Mirrors: Mexican Americans, Mexican Immigrants, and the Politics of Ethnicity* (Berkeley and Los Angeles, CA: University of California Press, 1995).

Hajnal, Zoltan L., Elisabeth R. Gerber, and Hugh Louch, "Minorities and Direct Legislation: Evidence from California Ballot Proposition Elections," *The Journal of Politics,* 2002, Vol. 64, pp. 154–177.

Harwood, Edwin, "Alienation: American Attitudes toward Immigration," *Public Opinion,* 1983, Vol. 6, pp. 49–51.

Hero, Rodney E., and Caroline J. Tolbert, "A Racial/Ethnic Diversity Interpretation of Politics and Policy in the States of the U.S.," *American Journal of Political Science,* 1996, Vol. 40, pp. 851–871.

Higham, John, *Strangers in the Land: Patterns of American Nativism, 1860–1925* (New York: Atheneum, 1965).

Hofstadter, Richard, *The Age of Reform: From Bryan to F. D. R* (New York: Alfred A. Knopf, 1961).

Hood III and Irwin L. Morris, "Brother, Can You Spare a Dime? Racial/Ethnic Context and the Anglo Vote on Proposition 187," *Social Science Quarterly,* 2000, Vol. 81, pp. 194–206.

Hunter, James Davison, *Culture Wars: The Struggle to Define America* (New York: Basic Books, 1991).

Hurley, Norman L., "Do People Really Feel What They Tell Us in Surverys? Toward Unobtrusive Measures of Racial Attitudes," Paper Presented at the Annual Meeting of the American Political Science Association (Washington Sheraton Hotel, Washington, DC, August 28–31, 1997).

Hurwitz, Jon, and Mark Peffley, "Public Perceptions of Race and Crime: The Role of Racial Stereotypes," *American Journal of Political Science,* 1997, Vol. 41, pp. 375–401.

Iyengar, Shanto, and Adam F. Simon, "New Perspectives and Evidence on Political Communication and Campaign Effects," *Annual Review of Psychology*, 2000, Vol. 51, pp. 149–169.

Jackman, Mary R., and Michael J. Muha, "Education and Intergroup Attitudes: Moral Englightenment, Superficial Democratic Commitment, or Ideological Refinement?" *American Sociological Review*, 1984, Vol. 49, pp. 751–769.

Johnson, Hans, *Immigrants in California: Findings from the 1990 Census* (Sacramento, CA: California Research Bureau, September 1993).

Johnson, Kevin R., "An Essay on Immigration Politics, Popular Democracy, and California's Proposition 187: The Political Relevance and Legal Irrelevance of Race," *Washington Law Review*, 1995, Vol. 70, pp. 629–675.

———, "Public Benefits and Immigration: The Interaction of Immigration Status, Ethnicity, Gender, and Class," *University of California Law Review*, 1995, Vol. 42, pp. 1–65.

Jones, Bill, *California Ballot Initiative Process* (Sacramento, CA: Secretary of State's Office, 1997).

———, *Statement of Vote: November 8, 1994, General Election* (Sacramento, CA: Secretary of State's Office, 1994).

Key, Jr., V. O., *Public Opinion and American Democracy* (New York: Alfred A. Knopf, 1965).

Kinder, Donald R., and D. Roderick Kiewiet, "Economic Discontent and Political Behavior: The Role of Personal Grievances and Collective Economic Judgments in Congressional Voting," *American Journal of Political Science*, 1979, Vol. 23, pp. 495–527.

King, Anthony, *Running Scared: Why America's Politicians Campaign Too Much and Govern Too Little* (New York: Free Press, 1997).

King, David C., "The Polarization of American Political Parties and the Mistrust of Government," in Nye, Jr., Zelikow, and King (eds.), *Why People Don't Trust Government*.

King, Desmond, *In the Name of Liberalism: Illiberal Social Policy in the United States and Britain* (Oxford: Oxford University Press, 1999).

———, *Making Americans: Immigration, Race, and the Origins of the Diverse Democracy* (Cambridge, MA: Harvard University Press, 2000).

Kingdon, John W., *Agendas, Alternatives, and Public Policies* (Boston, MA: Little, Brown and Company, 1984).

Knight, Stephen, "Proposition 187 and International Human Rights Law: Illegal Discrimination in the Right to Education," *Hastings International and Comparative Law Review*, 1995, Vol. 19, pp. 183–220.

Krosnick, Jon A., David S. Boninger, Yao C. Chuang, Matthew K. Berent, and Catherine G. Carnot, "Attitude Strength: One Construct of Many Related Constructs?" *Journal of Personality and Social Psychology*, 1995, Vol. 65, pp. 1132–1151.

Kuklinski, James H., and Darrell M. West, "Economic Expectations and Voting Behavior in United States House and Senate Elections," *American Political Science Review*, 1981, Vol. 75, pp. 436–447.

Kuklinski, James H., Michael D. Cobb, and Martin Gilens, "Racial Attitudes and the 'New South,'" *Journal of Politics*, 1997, Vol. 59, pp. 323–349.

Kuklinski, James H., Paul Sniderman, Kathleen Knight, Thomas Piazza, Philip E. Tetlock, Gordon R. Lawrence, and Barbara Mellers, "Racial Prejudice and

Attitudes toward Affirmative Action," *American Journal of Political Science*, 1997, Vol. 41, pp. 402–419.

Kurfis, Mitchell, "The Constitutionality of California's Proposition 187: An Equal Protection Analysis," *California Western Law Review*, 1995, Vol. 32, pp. 129–166.

LaVally, Rebecca, *Addressing Immigration Issues in California*, Briefing Paper Prepared for Senator Bill Lockyer (Sacramento, CA: California Senate Office of Research, March 1994).

Lewis-Beck, Michael, "Pocketbook Voting in U.S. National Election Studies: Fact or Artifact?" *American Journal of Political Science*, 1985, Vol. 29, pp. 348–357.

Linde, Hans A., "When Is Initiative Lawmaking Not 'Republican Government'?" *Hastings Constitutional Law Quarterly*, 1989, Vol. 17, pp. 159–173.

Long, Samuel (ed.), *Research in Micropolitics* (Greenwich, CT: JAI Press, 1990).

Los Angeles Times, *Los Angeles Times Poll: California General Election Exit Poll, November 8, 1994* (Archived at Roper Center, CT).

Lowenthal, Abraham F., and Katrina Burgess (eds.), *The California-Mexico Connection* (Stanford, CA: Stanford University Press, 1993).

Lubenow, Gerald C. (ed.), *California Votes—the 1994 Governor's Race: An Inside Look at the Candidates and Their Campaigns by the People Who Managed Them* (Berkeley, CA: Institute of Governmental Studies Press, University of California, 1995).

Mac Donald, Karin, and Bruce E. Cain, "Nativism, Partisanship, and Immigration: An Analysis of Prop. 187," in Michael B. Preston, Bruce E. Cain, and Sandra Bass (eds.), *Racial and Ethnic Politics in California*, Vol. 2 (Berkeley, CA: Institute of Governmental Studies Press, 1998).

MacKuen, Michael B., Robert S. Erikson, and James A. Stimson, "Peasants or Bankers? The American Electorate and the U.S. Economy," *American Political Science Review*, 1992, Vol. 86, pp. 597–611.

Magleby, David B., *Direct Legislation: Voting on Ballot Propositions in the United States* (Baltimore, MD: John Hopkins University Press, 1984).

———, "Direct Legislation in the American States," in Butler and Ranney (eds.), *Referendums Around the World*.

Mansbridge, Jane J. (ed.), *Beyond Self-Interest* (Chicago, IL: University of Chicago Press, 1990).

Martin, Philip L., "Good Intentions Gone Awry: IRCA and U.S. Agriculture," *The Annals of the Academy of Political and Social Sciences*, 1994, Vol. 534, pp. 44–57.

Mayhew, David R., *Congress: The Electoral Connection* (New Haven, CT: Yale University Press, 1974).

McConahay, John B., "Self-Interest versus Racial Attitudes as Correlates of Anti-busing Attitudes in Louisville: Is It the Buses or the Blacks?" *Journal of Politics*, 1982, Vol. 44, pp. 692–720.

McCuan, Dave, Todd Donovan, and Shaun Bowler, "Grassroots Democracy and California's Political Warriors: Campaign Professionals and the Initiative Process," Paper Presented at the Annual Meeting of American Political Science Association (Washington Sheraton Hotel, Washington, DC, August 28–31, 1997).

Miller, Tony, Acting Secretary of State, *California Ballot Pamphlet: General Election, November 8, 1994* (Sacramento, CA: Secretary of State's Office, 1994).

Miller, Warren E., and J. Merrill Shanks, *The New American Voter* (Cambridge, MA: Harvard University Press, 1996).

Morris, Irwin L., "African American Voting on Proposition 187: Rethinking the Prevalence of Interminority Conflict," *Political Research Quarterly*, 2000, Vol. 53, pp. 77–98.

Mowry, George E., *The California Progressives* (Berkeley, CA: University of California Press, 1951).

Mu, Jennifer, and Brent Barnhart, *Summary Report for Assembly Select Committee on Statewide Immigration Impact* (Sacramento, CA: Assembly Office of Research, May 1994).

National Election Studies, *Cumulative Data File, 1948–2000*.

Neustadt, Richard E., *Presidential Power and the Modern Presidents: The Politics of Leadership from Roosevelt to Reagan* (New York: Free Press, 1990).

Newton, Lina Y., "Why Some Latinos Supported Proposition 187: Testing Economic Threat and Cultural Identity Hypotheses," *Social Science Quarterly*, 2000, Vol. 81, pp. 180–193.

Nivola, Pietro S., and David W. Brady (eds.), *Red and Blue Nation? Characteristics and Causes of America's Polarized Parties*, Vol. 1 (Washington, DC: Brookings Institution, 2006).

Nye, Joseph S., Philip D. Zelikow, and David C. King (eds.), *Why People Don't Trust Government* (Cambridge, MA: Harvard University Press, 1997).

Office of Immigration Statistics, *Yearbook of Immigration Statistics* (Washington, DC: Department of Homeland Security/U.S. Government Printing Office, Various Years). NB. Pre-2002 known as the Immigration and Naturalization Service's *Statistical Yearbook of the Immigration and Naturalization Service.*

Olzak, Susan, *The Dynamics of Ethnic Competition and Conflict* (Stanford, CA: Stanford University Press, 1992).

Omi, Michael, and Howard Winant, *Racial Formation in the United States: From the 1960s to the 1990s* (New York: Routledge, 1994).

Ono, Kent A., and John M. Sloop, *Shifting Borders: Rhetoric, Immigration, and California's Proposition 187* (Philadelphia, PA: Temple University Press, 2002).

Pantoja, Adrian D., Ricardo Ramirez, and Gary M. Segura, "Citizens by Choice, Voters by Necessity: Pattens in Political Mobilization by Naturalized Latinos," *Political Research Quarterly*, 2001, Vol. 54, pp. 729–750.

Peffley, Mark, Jon Hurwitz, and Paul M. Sniderman, "Racial Sterotypes and Whites' Political Views of Blacks in the Context of Welfare and Crime," *American Journal of Political Science*, 1997, Vol. 41, pp. 30–60.

Perea, Juan F. (ed.), *Immigrants Out! The New Nativism and the Anti-immigrant Impulse in the United States* (New York: New York University Press, 1997).

Price, Charles M., "The Initiative: A Comparative State Analysis and Reassessment of a Western Phenomenon," *Western Political Quarterly*, 1975, Vol. 28, pp. 243–262.

Rabinowitz, George, and Stuart Elaine Macdonald, "A Directional Theory of Issue Voting," *American Political Science Review*, 1989, Vol. 83, pp. 93–121.

Reimers, David M., *Unwelcome Strangers: American Identity and the Turn against Immigration* (New York: Columbia University Press, 1998).

Riker, William H., *The Theory of Political Coalitions* (New Haven, CT: Yale University Press, 1962).

Schattschneider, E. E., *The Semi-sovereign People: A Realist's View of Democracy in America* (New York: Holt, Rinehart and Winston, 1960).

Schlesinger, Arthur, *The Disuniting of America: Reflections on a Multicultural Society* (New York: W.W. Norton and Co., 1992).

Schockman, H. Eric, "California's Ethnic Experiment and the Unsolvable Immigration Issue: Proposition 187 and Beyond" in Michael B. Preston, Bruce E. Cain, and Sandra Bass (eds.), *Racial and Ethnic Politics in California*, Vol. 2 (Berkeley, CA: Institute of Governmental Studies Press, 1998).

Schuck, Peter H., "The Message of Proposition 187," *Pacific Law Journal*, 1995, Vol. 26, pp. 989–1000.

Schuck, Peter H., and Roger M. Smith, *Citizenship Without Consent: Illegal Aliens in the American Polity* (New Haven, CT: Yale University Press, 1985).

Schuman, Howard, and Stanley Presser, *Questions and Answers in Attitude Surveys: Experiments on Question Form, Wording, and Context* (Thousand Oaks, CA: Sage Publications Inc., 1996).

Schuman, Howard, Charlotte Steeh, and Lawerence Bobo, *Racial Attitudes in America: Trends and Interpretations* (Cambridge, MA: Harvard University Press, 1985).

Scott, Jacqueline, and Howard Schuman, "Attitude Strength and Social Action in the Abortion Dispute," *American Sociological Review*, 1988, Vol. 53, pp. 785–793.

Sears, David O., and Carolyn L. Funk, "Self-interest in Americans' Political Opinions," in Mansbridge (ed.), *Beyond Self-Interest*.

Sears, David O., and Jack Citrin, *Tax Revolt: Something for Nothing in California* (Cambridge, MA: Harvard University Press, 1985).

Sears, David O., Carl P. Hensler, and Leslie K. Speer, "Whites' Opposition to Busing: Self-Interest or Symbolic Politics?" *American Political Science Review*, 1979, Vol. 73, pp. 369–384.

Secretary of State, *Financing the Qualification of Statewide Initiatives: California's 1994 General Election* (Sacramento, CA: Secretary of State's Office, October 1994).

Shanks, J. Merrill, "Political Agendas," in John P. Robinson, Phillip R. Shaver, and Lawrence S. Wrightsman (eds.), *Measures of Political Attitudes* (San Diego, CA: Academic Press, 1998).

Sigler, Jay A., *Civil Rights in America: 1500 to the Present* (New York: Gale, 1998).

Simon, Julian L., *Immigration: The Demographic and Economic Facts* (Washington, DC: Cato Institute and National Immigration Forum, 1985).

Simon, Rita J., and Susan H. Alexander, *The Ambivalent Welcome: Print Media, Public Opinion and Immigration* (Westport, CT: Praeger, 1993).

Skerry, Peter, *Mexican Americans: The Ambivalent Minority* (Cambridge, MA: Harvard University Press, 1993).

Sklansky, David A., "Proposition 187 and the Ghost of James Bradley Thayer," *Chicano-Latino Law Review*, 1995, Vol. 17, pp. 24–45.

Smith, Daniel A., *Tax Crusaders and the Politics of Direct Democracy* (New York: Routledge, 1998).

Smith, Rogers M., "Beyond Tocqueville, Myrdal, and Hartz: The Multiple Traditions in America," *American Political Science Review*, 1993, Vol. 87, pp. 549–566.

Sniderman, Paul M., and Thomas Piazza, *The Scar of Race* (Cambridge, MA: Belknap Press, 1993).

Spaeth, Harold J., and Edward Conrad Smith, *The Constitution of the United States* (New York: HarperCollins, 1991).

Starr, Kevin, *Coast of Dreams: A History of Contemporary California* (New York: Penguin Books, 2006).

State of California, Department of Finance, *Components of Change for California Counties, July 1970–July 1990* (Sacramento, CA: July 1999).

———, *County Population Projections with Age, Sex and Race/Ethnic Detail* (Sacramento, CA: December 1998).

Steinberg, Stephen (ed.), *Race and Ethnicity in the United States: Issues and Debates* (Oxford: Blackwell, 2000).

Suarez-Orozco, Marcelo M., Carola Suarez-Orozco, and Desiree Baolian Qin (eds.), *The New Immigration: An Interdisciplinary Reader* (New York: Routledge, 2005).

Tolbert, Caroline J., and Rodney E. Hero, "Race/Ethnicity and Direct Democracy: An Analysis of California's Illegal Immigration Initiative," *Journal of Politics*, 1996, Vol. 58, pp. 806–818.

Tucker, William H., *The Science and Politics of Racial Research* (Chicago, IL: University of Illinois Press, 1994).

Tweedy, John Jr., "Coalition Building and the Defeat of California's Proposition 128," *Stanford Environmental Law Journal*, 1992, Vol. 11, pp. 114–148.

U.S. Bureau of the Census, *Statistical Abstract of the United States* (Washington, DC: U.S. Bureau of the Census, Various Years).

U.S. Commission on Immigration Reform, *Legal Immigration: Setting Priorities* (Washington, DC: U.S. Government Printing Office, 1995.

———, *U.S. Immigration Policy: Restoring Credibility* (Washington, DC: U.S. Government Printing Office, 1994).

U.S. Immigration and Naturalization Service, *Statistical Yearbook of the Immigration and Naturalization Service* (Washington, DC: U.S. Government Printing Office, Various Years). NB. The *Statistical Yearbook* changed its name to the *Yearbook of Immigration Statistics* in 2002 after the reorganization of the immigration services into the Department of Homeland Security.

Wagley, Anne Paxton, "Newly Ratified International Human Rights Treaties and the Fight against Proposition 187," *Chicano-Latino Law Review*, 1995, Vol. 17, pp. 88–117.

Walker, Richard, "California Rages against the Dying of the Light," *New Left Review*, 1995, Vol. 209, pp. 42–72.

Warren, Robert, "Undocumented Immigrants in California: How Many?" in Conference Proceedings, *California Immigration, 1994.*

Index